THE PUBLIC FINANCES
An introductory textbook

The Irwin Series in Economics
Consulting Editor   Lloyd G. Reynolds   *Yale University*

The public finances

An introductory textbook

JAMES M. BUCHANAN
*Virginia Polytechnic Institute
and State University*

MARILYN R. FLOWERS
University of Oklahoma

FIFTH EDITION 1980

RICHARD D. IRWIN, INC.
Homewood, Illinois 60430

*Irwin-Dorsey Limited
Georgetown, Ontario L7G 4B3*

ISBN 0-256-02333-6

Library of Congress Catalog Card No. 79–90537

Printed in the United States of America

1 2 3 4 5 6 7 8 9 0 MP 7 6 5 4 3 2 1 0

Preface

Two problems—inflation and growth of government—dominated the changes made in the fourth edition of this text which was published in 1975. In this, the fifth edition, published in 1980, discussion of these two topics has been further expanded. Inflation remains an important topic to a student of contemporary public finance because of its persistence. The price level in the United States almost doubled between 1968 and 1978, and by 1979 the economy appeared to be headed for another bout with double-digit inflation. Discussion of inflation as a tax and of its impact on real rates of personal income taxation has been retained from previous editions along with a rather detailed discussion of the possibility of indexing the personal income tax as a means of neutralizing the latter effect. In addition, some evidence suggests that the corporate income tax is also very sensitive to inflation. This effect is examined in some detail here along with an expanded discussion of the general effects of inflation on resource allocation.

The expanded discussion of government growth contained in this new edition deals not with continued growth, but rather with curtailment. The late 1960s were characterized by a veritable explosion in public spending. The shifting in American fiscal institutions which accompanied this expansion was discussed in the third edition of this text, and additional material was added to the fourth edition in an attempt to offer some explanatory basis for understanding government growth. The late 1970s, on the other hand, were marked by an apparent dramatic shift of public attitudes in opposition to continued growth in government. The apparently burgeoning "taxpayers' revolt" was manifest in numerous attempts at both state and federal levels to impose consitutional constraints on government size. Material on government growth has been retained and provides a context for the new material dealing with constitutional limits on taxing and spending which has been included in this new edition.

The social security program now ranks second to national defense in terms of total federal government outlays. Long a program of almost unchallenged political popularity, certain aspects of social security began to become topics of controversy and concern during the 1970s. A separate chapter on social security has been a part of this textbook since the third edition. It has been expanded considerably in this fifth edition to deal with these issues, including the future financing problems confronting social security, the effect of the program on capital formation and economic growth, and equity issues arising from the current structure of spouse benefits.

Other changes have been made in this edition. A new chapter has been added dealing with the effects of capital taxation and deficit finance on economic growth. New theoretical work on the effects of certain taxes has been included and, in the public choice unit, a section has been added dealing with agenda control as a means of manipulating voting outcomes. Significant insitutional changes have also been noted, including such things as changes in capital gains taxation and changes in the rate structure of the corporate income tax. The earned income credit introduced a limited version of a negative income tax in 1975 and became a permanent feature of the personal income tax structure in 1978. Federal estate and gift taxes also underwent significant legislative changes in 1976.

We have attempted, in this fifth edition, to eliminate both institutional and analytical material that is not essential. Our objective has been to keep the size of the textbook within manageable limits, suitable to a one-term introductory course in public finance. Even more than in earlier editions, we have shunned the temptations to convert an introductory textbook into a treatise.

We can claim that the original methodology of this textbook retains its advantages—indeed, that its comparative relevance should have increased substantially over its potential competitors. Earlier editions were often criticized for the positivist stance that was assumed, for an unwillingness to adopt explicitly normative judgments about prevailing or proposed fiscal patterns. A text that makes some attempt to remain value-free surely carries more relevance to the world in which basic values are being transformed. This suggests that sticking to the positivist methodology is the best course to follow here, while trying to reexamine the institutions that emerge and the pressures for changes that are present.

A century ago people studied "political economy." Today they study "economics" and "politics." The additional specialization that this change has produced is, in certain respects, advantageous. But when we come to study the public finances of a nation, the change has been retrogressive in effect. For "public finance" as a field of study is, by definition, the study of the political economy. The student of economics can examine the working of a market system within a specified set of constraints; the student of politics can examine the organization and the processes through which social decisions are made. But the two must join in studying the effects of political or collective decisions on the economy. The study of public finance, both at its simplest and at its most complex levels, must involve two stages. Some attention must be given to the aims and the objectives that motivate individuals to behave as they do in the political process. In other words, what does "government" try to accomplish, and how efficient are its efforts in attaining its objectives? Second, how do the institutions organized to carry out collective objectives affect the behavior and the conditions of individuals in the private or market economy? These questions have always been important, but they assume added significance in this age of big government.

This book is designed to provide students with an introduction to American fiscal institutions as these exist, and by way of this introduction, to provide them with some elementary steps in any answer to the basic questions just posed. No attempt is made to trace carefully the historical development of these institutions, and exhaustive factual detail is avoided whenever this is possible.

A positive approach is taken in describing and analyzing the fiscal system. No attempt is made to judge the "goodness" or the "badness" of the separate aspects of the fiscal system from some presumed criterion of "general interest" or "general welfare." Where possible, the alleged advantages and disadvantages of certain fiscal practices are indicated and arrayed against each other. Traditional "principles" of public finance are discussed, but only along with other principles for fiscal organization based on the acceptance of wholly different objectives.

This introductory textbook does not contain sufficient historical, institutional, or analytical detail to provide the student with the full understanding of the fiscal system that is required for competent evaluation. Such is not its purpose. We hope that the book will serve to introduce students to the wide range of issues that the fiscal system represents, to show them some of the complexities that are necessarily involved, and, most of all, to stimulate them to further study and effort in what must become an increasingly important field of social science, the public finances.

Acknowledgments

We should like to acknowledge the comments made by various users of earlier editions of this text. We have tried to take account of all of these, and, especially, to respond to what seemed to us to be the major reactions.

Anyone who has ever had to prepare a lengthy manuscript knows the value of able secretarial assistance. We have been especially fortunate in this regard and would like to take this opportunity to acknowledge our debt to Gena Mattox at the University of Oklahoma and Betty Tillman Ross at Virginia Polytechnic Institute and State University. Without their hard work, preparation of this fifth edition would not have been possible.

February 1980   *James M. Buchanan*
                                                Marilyn R. Flowers

Contents

part III
THE FISCAL DECISION PROCESS:
THE THEORY OF PUBLIC CHOICE   **115**

and spending. Simultaneous consideration of spending and taxation. Earmarked taxes—sectoral budgeting. Budget balance. Separation of tax bases or sources and of governmental functions among levels of government. Quantitative constitutional constraints: Outlays or revenues as a designated share of GNP or GSP. Tax base constraints. Direct constitutional constraints on specified rates of taxation.

Federal grants-in-aid to state and local governments: *Conditional grants-in-aid.* Unconditional grants — revenue-sharing.

part I

The public economy

1

The no-government economy

Democracy's early philosophers suggested that the government is best which governs least, and communism's sacred books promise a withering away of the state. Considered as hypotheses, both norms have been effectively refuted. The position of government, both relatively and absolutely, has continually grown more important in the Western democracies, and the monolithic state of communism has withered little, if at all. "Government" is, therefore, worthy of considerable attention, no matter what our purpose. The old adage about the certainty of "death and taxes" is surely relevant and true.

Political theorists have long adopted the device of explaining the origin of government by assuming conjecturally that it does not exist. This has proved to be a useful expository device, and it will provide a helpful starting point. Despite the fact that this book is to be devoted, almost exclusively, to the government, or the public economy, we shall find it useful to begin by discussing the hypothetical situation or model in which such an economy is absent.

THE ORDERLY ANARCHY

It requires considerable abstraction even to think of a situation in which there is no government at all. One description of such a social order, and probably a highly realistic one, would be summarized by the word "chaos." This will not suit our purposes here, however, and we are interested in the model for its expository usefulness, not for its descriptive accuracy. In order that we may derive the logical origins of the public or collective economy, we need to assume the existence of an orderly and ideally working anarchy. Let us heroically assume that all individuals are ethically reasonable, and that they each respect the equal freedoms of their fellowmen. Assume also that there exists a well-defined structure of property rights. How would the economy of such a society work? You will note that this is similar to the model of government that is implicitly assumed to be in existence when elementary economics is presented to the college sophomore. This chapter may be taken as a very elementary review of the principles of economic organization.

THE ECONOMIC ORGANIZATION

Individuals in such a hypothetical society would find it advantageous to conduct their economic affairs through markets, and such institutions would emerge to facilitate the many exchanges that persons might want to make, one with another. Resources, human and nonhuman, would become specialized to particular employments, and business enterprises, business firms, would arise to organize production aimed at meeting consumer needs. This simple and familiar model of the no-government economy is shown in the "wheel of income" diagram, Figure 1-1.

The economic units are of two kinds: individuals or families on the one hand, and business units, or firms, on the other. Trade takes place among these units in two broadly defined markets. These are the markets for consumer or final goods and services and the market for productive services. The bottom half of Figure 1–1 indicates the consumer goods market; the top half shows the productive services market. In the consumer goods market, private individuals or families receive consumer goods and services from business firms. In the other market, the suppliers and demanders are reversed. Private people supply productive services (labor, land, capital) to firms. In a broad sense, therefore, looking at the whole wheel, private people "trade" productive services for final products. Firms buy productive services and transform them into final products.

Direct barter would be grossly inefficient, however, and some particular commodity would be agreed upon as an appropriate mone-

FIGURE 1-1
The wheel of income

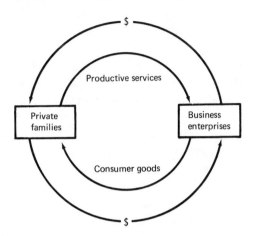

tary commodity. Once selected, this "money" commodity would be used in the direct discharge of all obligations. The "money" would allow the structure of interlocking markets to be completed. Individuals would sell productive services to business firms for money, and, in turn, they would take this money and purchase from business firms final goods and services. The circular flow would be closed, and the economic activity of the community would be a continuous process.

Business firms exist with a view toward making profits. For this reason the firms will be guided in their decisions concerning the organization of production by the desires of consumers. The tastes and wants of individuals as consumers are the basic determinants of what the economy shall produce and how its resources shall be allocated among the many possible employments. The operation of the economy in this way is said to follow the principle of *consumer sovereignty*.

PRINCIPLE OF CONSUMER SOVEREIGNTY

As are all such principles, that of consumer sovereignty is an oversimplification in application to the way in which the no-government economy would really operate. Any complete description would require a careful enumeration of several qualifying factors, such as inconstancy in consumer wants, persuasion by business firms, and the existence of uncertainty. This sort of discussion is not, however, needed at this point. The principle is useful as a starting point of discussion because it does provide an indication of the fundamental organizing influence in the no-government economy. Despite imperfections, the resources of the economy would, by and large, be directed toward the production of goods and services which individuals, expressing their desires as consumers, indicate a willingness and an ability to purchase.

The consumers' ability to purchase goods and services, and in this way their ability to direct the organization of economic production, is limited by the number of monetary units which they can command. And this, their "income," is in turn determined by their ability to sell their productive services to firms or to other individuals. Individuals who are unable to earn income in the marketplace for productive services, and who have no accumulated wealth, cannot influence the organization of production at all. The economy organized purely on the basis of consumer sovereignty has, for these reasons, been called the "one dollar-one vote" system in contrast to the system of political democracy which presumably makes decisions at least ideally, on the basis of "one man-one vote." The pure market economy, which is a shorthand name for an economy organized solely on the basis of consumer sovereignty, does not, therefore, respond to other than the pecuniary needs of individuals. This economy does not necessarily utilize its resources where they are most "needed" on some undefined nonmarket criterion of "need."

THE VOLUNTARY ECONOMY

What can be said in favor of and against an economy organized in this way? In the first place, individuals are free within the limits of their economic power. No individual coerces any other individual; a market transaction represents a wholly voluntary exchange from which both parties expect to receive benefits. The market economy is an organized method of securing voluntary cooperation among individuals. It is essentially a system of spontaneous order which arises out of individual participation of numerous buyers and sellers. Resources are allocated to the many possible employments and apportioned within the separate individual employments; goods and services are produced and distributed without a direct central plan ever having been discussed, approved, formulated, or even contemplated. The first main advantage of this sort of economy is, therefore, that it is "free" or "voluntary." Individuals need not conform; each person may "do his own thing" in a market economy. There is no prohibition against "opting out" if the one who does so is prepared to accept the consequences.

The second main advantage is that the market economy incorporates a high degree of "efficiency." This means quite simply that the individually inspired motivations of consumers, workers, property owners, and business enterprises combine to secure an overall economic organization which is not grossly extravagant in its usage of scarce resources available for disposition. Decisions are decentralized private decisions, and therefore, mistakes are individualized private mistakes.

SOCIAL JUSTICE, MONOPOLY, INSTABILITY, GROWTH, AND THE QUALITY OF LIFE

What are the disadvantages of this pure market organization, even in this hypothetically reasonable world? First of all, individuals would surely differ in their capacities to earn income and hence to share in the social product of the economy. Capacities to earn income depend on the initial distribution of property rights and on the distribution of skills. There is no assurance that the working of the market process could offset or correct for these initial differences in capacities sufficiently to generate a regime meeting standards for "social justice." Ethical norms may conflict sharply with observed economic results, and many persons may be unwilling to accept these results. We shall not try to define "social justice," but Chapter 8 will be devoted to an examination of some of the problems that arise in distributional policy, an area that now commands widespread attention among economists. Here we need only note that if the market economy does not distribute its product in such a manner as to be acceptable to a majority of individuals, some attempts will be made to implement changes. Such attempts imply political action. But a word of caution even at this early stage. Acceptability to academic intellectuals is not equivalent to acceptability to a dominant political coalition in a democracy.

A second major difficulty with the pure market economy arises when it is acknowledged that individuals and groups may prevent the orderly functioning of the economic process by securing excessive power over particular submarkets. Monopoly power may emerge in the no-government economy, and insofar as this is the case, the operation of the principle of consumer sovereignty is distorted. Monopoly presents the consumer with false alternatives from which to choose, and it may prevent the entry of prospective suppliers into various occupational and productive categories. Market values may come to reflect artificial values, not based on resource costs, as these are derived from consumer choices. Overall efficiency in the economy is reduced.

A third major problem with this highly simplified no-government economy is introduced when we recognize that the tastes of individuals are highly changeable and that this shifting of tastes applies to the monetary commodity as well as to everything else. A sudden shift in favor of holding larger amounts of money inactive will reduce the total money demand for goods and services. This reduction in aggregate demand may cause prices to fall, but prices are likely to be relatively rigid. If this is the case, unemployment may arise and remain for more or less prolonged periods of time. Or, conversely, a sudden shift toward holding smaller amounts of money inactive may set off inflation in the level of prices. Attempts to stabilize the level of aggregate monetary demand become a function of government.

Tied to both of the above problems is a further problem, that of generating long-term economic growth. Insofar as monopoly prevents full efficiency in resource use, and insofar as fluctuations in demand generate unemployment and inflation, the growth potential of the economy may not be realized, suggesting an appropriate area of governmental action.

Finally, and almost by definition, the no-government economy may not be successful in resolving problems raised by complex economic interdependencies. When the economic behavior of a person affects the utility or costs of many other persons, marketlike exchanges may not arise spontaneously. This is the domain of "public" or "collective" goods and services, and under sufficiently broad and inclusive definitions we can categorize all "market failures" in these terms, including those mentioned above. Modern concern about the "quality of life," and specifically about the effects of individual and business behavior on the physical environment may be discussed in these terms, along with the more familiar public goods issues. Chapter 4 will treat this set of problems in some detail.

A BASIS FOR FURTHER DISCUSSION

The hypothetical and unrealistic model of the no-government economy was introduced in this initial chapter only to provide a basis for subsequent discussion. A rudimentary understanding of the way that the market economy functions is essential for an understanding of the effects generated by the introduction of a public or governmental sector. This does not imply that, necessarily and always, governmental economic activity constitutes an "interference" with the working of the actual market or private economy. Government activity can make the market work better or worse, or it may be neutral in its impact. And, of course, the results here depend strictly on the criteria for "better" and "worse" that are selected.

2

The all-government economy

$\mathbf{I}$n the previous chapter we made the heroic assumption that government did not exist in order to discuss a pure market economy and to show how an economic origin of government can be traced to difficulties in this economy. In this chapter we shall go to the other extreme of the private-public spectrum. We shall assume that *all* economic activity is governmental. This assumption may seem even more heroic than its opposite, but it will be helpful in providing the framework for an analysis of the mixed economy that exists.

THE COLLECTIVITY OF CHOICE

The distinguishing feature of governmental or public organization that we want to emphasize here is the collectivity of choice. In a market economy, individuals (families) make *private* decisions; the individual alone chooses to buy potatoes rather than turnips and also chooses how many pounds of potatoes to buy. Such market decisions may affect the choice alternatives that other buyers and sellers confront, but this is done indirectly. By sharp contrast, in a governmental or collective economic setting, it becomes impossible for the individual (the family) to choose *privately*. The choice must be collective, in that the same result may be applicable to all participants, and this result must be directly selected. If garbage collection is governmentally organized, the individual family cannot decide independently or privately that its own refuse shall be collected twice weekly without regard to the rate of collection to be provided other families in the community. When choosing among differing rates of collection, the individual or family is choosing a result that will, once chosen, be made applicable to *all* other individuals or families in the community. Under certain conditions, publicly provided goods and services may be made differentially available to different groups in the community; some "privileged" families may have twice-weekly garbage pickups while others have fortnightly service. These conditions would, however, be exceptional. As a general principal, the "one man-one vote" basis of the democratic decision process along with generally accepted respect for standards of equality ensures that publicly provided services shall be made *equally available* to all members of the community.

As the discussion in Chapter 4 will emphasize, the technological characteristics of certain goods and services make them amenable to collectivization. With such goods and services, the most efficient means of provision may require that all members of the group be allowed equal access. The modern theory of public goods represents an extension of the orthodox efficiency norms to such goods and services, often called collective consumption or public goods. We shall defer specific discussion of such goods and services until Chapter 4. In this chapter, by contrast, discussion is concentrated on the central features that emerge from governmental or collective provision, or supply of goods and services, regardless of the technological characteristics. Let us assume, for this chapter's discussion, that some goods and services provided collectively are divisible among persons in final consumption, while some are indivisible in a technological sense.

We propose to examine in somewhat further detail the economy in which all goods and services are provided collectively, through some political decision process in contrast with a market process. Further, let us assume that the political decision structure is effectively democratic. (The precise implications of this assumption will be discussed in some detail in Part III.) As we have noted above, the primary difference between the result emerging in this all-government economy and that which emerges in the no-government market economy will be that, in the latter, individuals can adjust *privately* with each person making his or her own consumption decisions whereas, in the former, individuals must adjust to commonly available, and collectively determined, rates of consumption for all goods and services. Private expressions of preference exhibited through differential purchase patterns could not be observed. The all-government economy would, therefore, be described by a uniformity of consumption patterns among all members of the political community.

THE POTENTIAL FOR TRADE IN PRESENCE OF A NUMERAIRE

If individuals' preferences for final goods and services differ, one from the other, and if all individuals are provided with uniform quantities for consumption, uniform quantities for all goods, some of which are technologically divisible, gains from trade must exist. Those persons who like oranges more than apples can secure mutual advantages in trades with those who have the opposing preferences. This suggests that the all-government economy, the all-collectivized world, will tend to depart from its pattern of conformity in consumption *if trade can take place*. The necessary condition for trade to take place is the existence of some one commodity that can be utilized as a numeraire or money unit. So long as one such commodity exists, the emergent trading process will tend to reproduce the results of the market economy, regardless of the initial collectivization of supply. This allows us to state an important principle. So long as the goods involved are technologically such that divisibility in consumption among separate persons is efficient, attempts to enforce conformity in consumption of such goods through collective provision must fail provided only that a single divisible or numeraire commodity exists. Socialist governments have learned this principle by experience. Attempts to provide all families with "free" milk, "free" housing, "free" bread result in retrading of allotted quantities of these goods for other goods and services that are, to some persons, privately, more desirable.

The pressures toward the elimination of the gains from trade involved in uniform or in arbitrarily selected consumption patterns, and the emergence of trade unless prohibited, suggest the major difficulty that would emerge in an all-government economy. Such an organization of the economic structure fails to accommodate the differential preferences of individuals. As suggested in Chapter 1, the major advantage of a market economy is that individuals are free to express their own preferences; the converse of this is the major disadvantage of the government or controlled economy; individual preferences cannot readily be satisfied, regardless of the way in which collective decisions are made. This conclusion remains valid in a pure democracy as well as in other political structures.

COLLECTIVE ORGANIZATION AND ECONOMIC EFFICIENCY

A second advantage that has been claimed for the market organization of economic activity is its efficiency in the utilization of resources. Despite many imperfections, a market economy tends to channel resources into those uses that are most valued in pecuniary terms, as indicated by the "votes" of consumers. An overall directing influence comparable to "consumers' sovereignty" does not exist in collective organization. Even in the ideal or "pure" democracy, where all individuals have equal political power vested in their vote, varying intensities of preference cannot be normally expressed. The failure of collective organization to allow for adequate expressions of individual preferences, therefore, produces the corollary failure of such an organization to meet standard efficiency norms. If we define economic efficiency in terms of the degree to which individual preferences are satisfied, that is, if values relevant to the measurement of efficiency are derived from individuals' utility functions, collective organization and/or control of an economy must be given low marks on this count. If, of course, we choose to define efficiency on the basis of some other set of values which is not based on individuals' utilities as expressed in their behavior we can get almost any result we seek.

COLLECTIVE ORGANIZATION AND DISTRIBUTION

The all-government economy ranks poorly in terms of individual freedom and economic efficiency. It ranks highly in terms of equality in distribution of goods and services, at least insofar as the political reality matches the ideal model of equal power democracy. As we noted in Chapter 1, one of the difficulties in the pure market economy is its tendency to satisfy pecuniary demands, demands that are related strictly to the dollar votes of individuals. Insofar as different individuals enter the market with widely different monetary endowments, the results must embody widely different levels of consumption. Inequality in consumption, not only of particular goods and services, but of all goods and services, tends to be characteristic of the pure market economy. The central socialist critique of the market economy is based on a recognition of this characteristic feature. The more extreme advocates of extensive socialist or collectivist organization of the economy are willing to sacrifice the advantages of individual freedom and economic efficiency in order to secure what they consider a more important objective, equality among persons in consumption standards.

The inequality in distribution produced in the pure market economy, along with the suppression of individual expressions of preference and the inefficiency of resource use in the pure collectivist economy, has led many economists and social philosophers to support a "compromise" attempt to secure the best of both worlds. Market economists, who are at the same time egalitarians, and socialist economists, who at the same time value individual freedom and economic efficiency (and there is little fundamental difference between these two groups despite differing labels) have often proposed that, as regards the divisible goods sector of an economy, collective action be limited to the redistribution of income and wealth among persons and that, once the desired redistribution of income and wealth takes place, individuals be allowed to express their preferences through the workings of a market economic order. In one sense, the mixed economy of the United States finds its intellectual origins in this combination.

The implied isolation or separation of the distributional function of government from the actual provision of goods and services has, however, rarely been observed in political reality. Governments provide goods and services; insofar as they do so, equality tends to characterize the distributional pattern among persons, not equality in overall incomes or purchasing power but equality in the particular consumption availability of the specific goods and services that are collectively supplied. It is perhaps misleading to discuss income-wealth redistribution as an independent and separate function of government. Income-wealth redistribution is accomplished through governmental political action, but, as a general rule, the redistribution per se is not the primary objective. Instead, the objective is the provision of specific goods and services to all qualified recipients on a nondiscriminatory basis. And this is the characteristic feature of collectivist organization that is emphasized in this chapter.

THE WORLD OF EQUALS

It is a useful exercise to construct a model in which the no-government economy (in which economic resources are allocated by a perfectly functioning market) and the all-government economy (in which economic resources are allocated exclusively by the political decision structure, assumed here to be democratically organized), generate roughly equivalent results. This would be the case if all persons should be identical, both with respect to initial endowments or capacities (human and nonhuman) and to preferences or utility functions. Since their initial endowments are identical, final consumption patterns could not diverge due to income-wealth differentials. There should arise little or no objection to market allocation of resources on the grounds of distributional results. On the other hand, because preferences are identical, there would be little or no objection if the whole economy were to be collectively organized either. Since all preferences are the same by definition, almost any political decision rule would produce results that would satisfy all preferences. In such an extreme model, there would be little or no difference in the workings of an economy organized on purely market lines and one organized on purely collectivist lines.

EQUAL ENDOWMENTS AND
DIFFERENTIAL PREFERENCES

Individuals are not, of course, identical, one with another, either in initial endowments or capacities or in their preferences. It will be useful, however, to relax these two assumptions separately. In so doing, the implied assumptions about human nature in both capitalist and in socialist organization are revealed. For now, let us assume only that individuals differ in their preferences; that utility functions differ, while they remain identical in their initial resource endowments (human and nonhuman). In this case, the relative advantages of market over collectivist economic organization become apparent. Since, by definition, individuals do not differ in their basic or inherent capacities, there can be little or no legitimate objection to the market-determined allocation of resources on distributional grounds. By contrast, because they do differ in preference patterns, the collectivist organization of the economy would generate strong objections. Conformity would be introduced, along with the corollary inefficiency, without compensating distributional advantages.

DIFFERENTIAL ENDOWMENTS AND
EQUAL PREFERENCES

Let us now reverse the model and assume that all persons possess identical utility functions but that they differ in basic or inherent resource endowments or capacities (both human and nonhuman). This model provides the strongest support for the collectivist organization of the economy. Because individuals are, by assumption, equal in preferences, any differentials in consumption patterns that result from the market allocation of resources can be traced directly to initial differences in endowments or capacities. All inequality in the final consumption of goods and services is due to distributional differences among persons. The imposition of uniform consumption patterns under collectivist organization of the economy in this model only seems to thwart the expression of individual preferences. The latter differ one from another only because of initial inequalities in endowments or capacities. Market allocation, by contrast, would, in this model, allow for the satisfaction of the apparent but not real differentials in preferences while doing nothing toward achieving distributional objectives.

DIFFERENTIAL ENDOWMENTS AND
DIFFERENTIAL PREFERENCES

We know, of course, that individuals differ in both their basic endowments and their preferences. Essentially, the long and continuing debate between the advocate of the market economy and the collectivist reduces to their contrasting assumptions about human nature. Advocates of the market order assume with Adam Smith, that the differences between the philosopher and the street porter are not large, that observed inequalities in consumption patterns largely reflect differences in taste. At the least, they assume that, with appropriate arrangements collectively made to ensure that each person has an opportunity to utilize his or her inherent capacities to the fullest extent desired, distributional results will not be wholly objectionable. Advocates of collectivist order assume, with Plato, that there are fundamental and basic differences in the capacities of human beings to produce economic values. Even with the widest practicable opening of the opportunities for individuals to utilize these capacities to the fullest, the collectivist predicts that distributional inequalities will persist and on such a scale as to be unacceptable. Such differences in preferences as are acknowledged to exist are assumed to be less relevant for social policy than the differences in capacities that generate the distributional inequalities.

THE UNITED STATES IN 1980

The mixed market-collectivized economies of the United States and other Western countries reflect a continuing and shifting compromise between these two essentially opposing views of human nature and their divergent implications for socioeconomic and political arrangements. Especially in the United States in the late 1970s, this compromise seemed to be becoming an increasingly uneasy one. There was, on the one hand, evidence of rather widespread dissatisfaction with the performance of the public sector reflecting, perhaps, not so much a shift in fundamental assumptions about human nature as a changed perception of the ability of government to accomplish avowed objectives. This increasingly negative view of the performance of collective institutions was reflected most vividly in widespread interest in attempts to impose constitutional limits on public taxing and spending.

It was unclear whether this loss of faith in government institutions was being translated into renewed faith in the ability of markets to organize the economy effectively. There was some evidence that this was happening as, for example, in the political support for deregulation of industries such as transportation. At the same time, however, there appeared to be considerable reluctance to lessen government intervention in other industries, most notably energy and health services.

3

Government as an economic unit

T he mixed economy that we observe includes both market and collective provisions of goods and services, both a private and a public sector. Having introduced the model of the hypothetical market economy in Chapter 1, we shall now discard this for other than reference purposes. This textbook is concerned with the *economics of the public sector*, with *the public economy*, with respect both to the principles of its operation and to the institutional realities that we confront.

THE SUBJECT OF PUBLIC FINANCE

The government, considered as a unit, may be defined as the subject of the study of public finance. More specifically, public finance studies the economic activity of government as a unit. In this respect, as well as in many others, we consider "government" to be an independent entity, a unit, analogous to a person.

In order to illustrate this analogy, let us look at the economic activity of an individual that we might choose to study. There are several stages in our inquiry. First of all, we should want to find out how our person, say, E. J. Jones, earns an income and how much it is. For example, Jones may be paid by the hour, or on salary, or may not work at all but instead, receive an income by clipping coupons for bond interest or by qualifying for some governmental welfare program. Second, how is the income spent? Jones may be a gourmet and delight in fancy foods, or a gold enthusiast, or a connoisseur of pop art, or maybe a genuine miser who spends almost nothing and saves most of these earnings. All of such information might be gathered in the first stage of inquiry into Jones' economic activity.

But we should want to know more than this. We should try to learn something about how Jones makes *decisions* or *choices* among the possible alternatives. Why work at one job instead of another? What criteria determine purchases? These and many more questions arise at a second stage of the investigation. Because we can never expect to read Jones' mind accurately, the answers to some of these questions may never be revealed, but we should try, by studying our subject's behavior as well as by asking direct questions to learn as much as we can. Beyond this we should try to construct models of behavior that will yield certain predictions which might be tested against our observations.

This analogy with the study of Jones' economic activity can be both helpful and misleading when we come to consider the activity of the government. The first stage is very similar. We need to gather the "facts" about the public finances, about the public economy. We shall need to know just how the government secures its revenues (its income) and how these revenues are spent. This involves us with both sides of the government's budget account.

When we come to the second stage, however, some important differences appear. Just as with Jones, we want to know something about the way that the relevant decisions or choice are made. We want to know why the government chooses to collect the major share of its revenues through the personal income tax rather than through, say, a turnover tax. And we want to know why the government spends $80 billion on defense rather than on rebuilding the cities. And why is the total level of spending what it is? To get the answers, or even approximate ones, to such questions as these, we need to examine the way in which governmental decisions are made. But here our analogy with the study of E. J. Jones breaks down. With Jones, we try to understand, as best we can, how a single mind can reach decisions. But we know that governmental decisions are finally reached as a result of the interaction of many individuals participating in some sort of political process. Therefore, any approach to answering the questions here must involve some consideration of the political or collective choice process.

There is another, and third, stage of inquiry where our analogy with the study of private economic activity breaks down. If we study the behavior of *one* individual or one firm *among many*, we need pay little attention to the effect of decisions made upon the remaining members of the group. A change in the behavior of Jones will exert so small an impact on the alternatives open to others that we may neglect these spillover elements in our initial inquiry. (We may, of course, want to take these into account in a more sophisticated analysis.)

Not so when we come to consider government's decisions. The government is important enough in relation to the whole economy that it becomes necessary for us to analyze the impact of its behavior on individuals and firms. As a matter of fact, the questions raised in this third stage of inquiry have traditionally been central to the study of public finance. There are two parts or subdivisions here. First of all, governmental activity will exert some aggregative effects on the workings of the economy. By changing the conditions under which individuals work, consume, and invest, government can influence the size of the national income, the level of employment, and the purchasing power of money. This part, or subdivision, which would be central to a more comprehensive study of public finance, is not included in this textbook. Undergraduate courses in macroeconomic policy are largely devoted to questions that emerge in this subdivision; reasons of space dictate that we concentrate on the second part, or subdivision, here. This involves a study of the manner through which governmental activity influences the purely private behavior of individuals, firms, and families. What are the effects of the personal income tax on incentives to work and to save? How will the increased rates of social security tax and the level of social security benefits modify the long-run rate of saving? These questions arise during the third stage of inquiry. In one sense, the whole approach is shifted in this third stage. For no longer is the government the *subject* of study. Rather, the individual components in the private economy become the subject, with governmental decisions assumed as data.

A final stage of our inquiry into government activity is that of evaluation. Here, also, there is a less than perfect analogy with our study of the economic activity of a single person. In most circumstances, individuals can reasonably be presumed to be the best judges of their welfare. Except in those cases in which the individuals' actions have a significant impact on the well-being of their neighbors, there is little need for any external evaluation of those actions as good or bad. In contrast, because government activity necessarily affects all of the individuals in a society, evaluation of that impact becomes a topic of concern. However, as we shall see, the choice of an appropriate criterion against which to evaluate government action is difficult and controversial. We have moved into the realm of normative rather than positive analysis and as a result, conflicting opinions cannot be resolved by any appeal to the facts.

WHAT IS GOVERNMENT?

It is clear that the conception of government will influence the approach to the questions suggested above, particularly those relating to examination of the decision-making process and the evaluation of government activity. What is the state? This fundamental issue in political theory cannot be treated exhaustively in this textbook. However, some answer must be provided, explicitly or implicitly, before the field of public finance is to be properly outlined.

There are essentially two ways of looking at government. The state can, quite literally, be considered as a unitary being. In other terms, the government can be considered as a legal person quite similar to the manner in which a business corporation is treated for many purposes. Its decision process can be considered to be similar to that of a private person, and the same sort of reasoning may be employed in describing its behavior.

Private persons are presumed to direct their activity toward satisfying certain goals that may be summarized under "utility." It is, of course, impossible to state that individuals do, in fact, try to maximize some such thing as "utility." But by making such an assumption about their motivation, economists have been able to make certain predictions about behavior that seem to be corroborated by observations.

The difficulty in applying this method to governmental actions is evident. How can "social utility" or "general welfare" be defined? Any definition must be arbitrary. And this makes it extremely difficult, if not impossible, to evaluate collective choices on the basis of some "social utility" criterion. Does a projected outlay of $10 billion on urban reconstruction, financed by federal tax monies, represent an increase in "social utility" or a decrease? In the case of single persons making their own choices we can think of their preferences as being in some way integrated so that they choose consistently among alternatives. But when we consider the government, the existence of some "fiscal brain" possessing an integrated preference system seems wholly unrealistic and indeed fanciful.

Despite this, we may proceed, for some purposes to discuss the public finances by using some such "fiscal brain" assumption. If the government is not democratic and if society is ruled by a despot, we may reduce public finance to a study closely paralleling private finance. If the E. J. Jones of our example should be the absolute dictator of the country, then the examination of Jones' own decisions would be one of the domains of public finance. The dictator's income would then be the government's; the dictator's spending would be equivalent to the government's. Here it would not be especially difficult to think of Jones trying to make all decisions in accordance with some rationally integrated plan. Even in this extreme model, however, we should have to reckon with the reactions that Jones, the dictator, might face from the suffering flock. The behavior of the ordinary little people will impose severe constraints on the freedom of Jones, the dictator, to act without regard for their opinions. This unitary model of government may have been descriptive of the kingships that characterized the emerging nation-states of Europe in the premodern epoch.

In the modern world, however, a more realistic model of government, applicable to many countries of the world, emerges when we allow governmental decisions to be made by a small ruling group, or clique. Here the theory of committees and small groups can be helpful in analyzing behavior of the "rulers," who must, as in the single-person dictatorship, reckon with the reactions of those outside the ruling group. Although group decision processes enter into this model, the government remains as an entity that is divorced from the people.

For our purposes in this textbook, we are relatively uninterested in despotic government, regardless of how it might be organized. We are primarily concerned here with the public finances of democratically organized governments. Here the unitary or organic conception of the state does not readily apply, although, even here, it may be helpful to look at certain fiscal problems in this framework. We shall see this when we come to discuss budgeting.

Many approaches to the evaluation of government action are based, at least implicitly, on a unitary conception of government. The issue here is not whether government does, in fact, act as to maximize some measure of social utility, but rather whether there exists some such measure which government *should* maximize. Attempts to evaluate government activity in this framework are generally hampered by the inherent arbitrariness of any definition of social welfare. For example, early scholars in public finance assumed that the utility of separate persons could be added up to produce some "social utility." If this were possible, the obvious goal of taxation would be to reduce this as little as possible. On the basis of reasoning such as this, the so-called principles of taxation were constructed which remain influential in providing popular support for tax structures. It is now accepted that the presumed measurability and comparability of utilities implicit in the utilitarian approach was an illusion. It is impossible to compare the utilities of Jones and Brown or, indeed, to measure externally the utility of either.

Despite these difficulties, if we make some specific, though admittedly arbitrary, assumptions about utility, it may be possible to derive certain guidelines for tax and expenditure decisions which are widely accepted by individuals in society. We may simply assume that Jones and Brown, and everyone else, are identical in their capacities as pleasure machines. We may know that this assumption violates reality and that it is not scientifically supportable. But it may remain useful as a starting point for discussion. Second, we may assume that additions to total utility caused by the addition of incremental units of income diminish as more income is added. In technical terms, we may assume a diminishing marginal utility of income for each individual recipient. This means, quite plausibly, that Jones, who has $10,000 already, will not get so much enjoyment from an additional $100 as Brown, who only has $1,000 from which to start.

On the basis of such specific assumptions, certain principles of public finance may be derived which enjoy widespread popular support. For example, it may be generally accepted that wealthier individuals should bear a greater tax burden because the utility loss associated with a somewhat greater tax does not exceed the utility loss experienced by a poor person paying a smaller tax. Although the assumptions upon which this norm is based are quite arbitrary, individuals act *as if* they are a true representative of reality.

A second approach, which still utilizes the organic or unitary conception of the state, makes no attempt to add up individual utilities to get "social utility." This approach essentially assumes that something defined as the "public interest" does exist quite apart from the interests of individual citizens. This approach is often observed in discussion of particular budgetary decisions. It is often argued that the "national interest" demands a particular outlay on defense and a given level of expenditure on domestic programs. The overall efficiency of the federal budget is judged somehow on the basis of whether or not this rather vague conception of "national interest" is followed.

A third approach, still within the unitary conception of the state, has the advantage of being unambiguous. Students, teachers, or textbook writers simply define "social interest" or "social welfare" in terms of their own explicitly stated preference scheme. They introduce their own preferences deliberately into the picture at the outset, and then judge revenue and expenditure decisions on their own estimates of "national advantage" or "national interest." This approach is useful only insofar as students can get other persons to agree with them. As one such student, you may feel that the public interest would be served by some reduction in federal highway expenditures coupled with an increase in educational expenditures. But as long as other persons are free to think differently, your own estimation will be of little explanatory value. The point to be made here is that all such evaluations are inherently personal, not scientifically objective. Therefore, little can be done in the way of establishing universally valid criteria for judging governmental actions. "Principles" of public finance, in any normative sense, cannot be derived in this manner.

THE GOVERNMENT AS A MEANS OF INDIVIDUAL ACTION

We approach government differently when we begin to consider it not as some organic or unitary being which acts independently from its citizens but as a means through which private citizens make decisions collectively. Here we must immediately discard as irrelevant all attempts at defining "social utility" or "social welfare" independently of individuals' own preferences. We try instead to understand more fully and adequately the actual processes through which persons make decisions relating to collective activities. We try to examine and to analyze the conditions under which individuals will choose to sacrifice privately enjoyed goods and services in return for publicly provided goods and services.

This conception or model of the political structure, the state, seems clearly to be the more appropriate one when we are studying the public finances of democratic countries. Despite the fact that democracy in its ideal form is rarely, if ever, present, the processes through which collective decisions are made bears a closer resemblance to this ideal than to the opposing one implicit in the unitary being assumption. Ideally, democracy implies that each citizen participates in the decision-making processes of government and, further, that each citizen has an equal power to influence final collective outcomes. The New England town meeting provides perhaps our closest real-world example. But the governmental entities with which we are primarily interested are not New England townships. They are the larger units which utilize the much larger share of economic resources in carrying out their economic functions. Here we immediately recognize that democracy in decision making means something far removed from universal participation and/or equal power. Individuals participate only insofar as they choose among candidates for public office and exert pressure upon these candidates to adopt particular policies. Representative government becomes the ideal type in large governmental units. And even this must seem an ideal that is rarely realized. Actual decisions concerning the collective usage of resources are made by the legislature, the executive, the bureaucracy, and the public, with each group participating continuously and both directly and indirectly in the final outcomes.

As it works in practice, government may seem to possess a momentum, a choosing capacity, of its own that is quite independent of the citizenry. And governmental outcomes may, in fact, seem to be connected only remotely with the desires of the public. Even in communities that are nominally democratic, elements of the authoritarian model may remain, and this model may be of considerable explanatory value. The discipline of political science is primarily concerned with studying the whole process through which decisions finally emerge. This involves the study of voting by individuals, the behavior of political parties, the structure and behavior of the bureaucracy, the organization and functioning of administrative structures, the role of leadership, the impact of public opinion, and many other aspects of collective choice mechanisms.

The study of the public finances, which this book proposes to outline in an elementary fashion, is not the study of political science. We cannot discuss here all of the aspects of decision making in democratic societies. These processes are extremely complex, and this complexity must be recognized by any student of public finance. There are few norms which allow results to be unambiguously judged, and it becomes almost impossible to derive "principles of public finance" in the traditional normative sense. Only if there is consensus or general agreement is it possible to evaluate government action. When consensus is absent, which is often the case, we cannot evaluate separate configurations of the fiscal structure on the basis of "better" or "worse" criteria. At best, we can develop some understanding of how and why certain outcomes emerge from democratic decision making.

4

Collective goods and services

Recall now the no-government economy that was introduced in Chapter 1. Assume that this economy is working perfectly in respect to the basic problems mentioned; there is full and free competition; there is stability in employment; there is a satisfactory growth rate; and there is widespread acceptance of the distributive results. In this chapter we shall examine the basis for the rise of government even under such restricted and idealistic conditions. We shall discuss the concept of *collective* as contrasted with *private* goods and services.

Let us assume that our hypothetical society consists of fishermen living on an isolated island. After the experience of having several boats run aground on surrounding rocks and shoals, the need for a lighthouse becomes clear. Actually, the existence of such a lighthouse will be of benefit to each fisherman. But the private market economy, in its simplest form of operation, might not get the lighthouse built. One enterprising individual might consider building the lighthouse and then licensing rights to use the beams to the several fishermen. But since the boats can secure guidance from the lighthouse whether their owners pay for the privilege or not, the owner of the lighthouse has no way of restricting the usage of his product. He could not really sell individual shares of the benefits to the separate fishermen.

COLLECTIVE GOODS

A lighthouse of this nature is the classic example of a *collective good.* Once it is built, each fisherman can benefit from its services; and this is true whether it is built by one fisherman for his own use or whether all fishermen join in its construction. The distinguishing characteristic of the collective or public good is the *indivisibility* of the services among separate persons. In the example here, if one boat gets the light beams, all boats may do likewise. There is no easy manner in which the services of the lighthouse may be directed toward particular boats. Particular individuals may not be *excluded* from the benefits without undue costs. It is relatively expensive and inefficient to exclude potential users of the service under the existing definition of property rights.

A slightly different manner of defining collective goods is to say that these are characterized by significant *external economies in consumption.* The activity of one person in providing a good or service for his own usage, his own consumption, generates external or spillover benefits for other persons for which he cannot readily exact specific charges. In the extreme case, when precisely the same quantity of the service is made available to each and every person in the group, the external economies in consumption may be said to be complete. Although this extreme case is rarely, if ever, encountered in real-world applications, the model is nonetheless useful in analyzing the collective goods provision when the external economies are less than complete.

The sensible manner for the community of fishermen to secure the lighthouse is for them to organize *collectively.* The organization may be voluntary. The fishermen may join together and work out a plan whereby each one of them contributes an agreed amount to the construction and operation of the lighthouse. Each fisherman will benefit from this plan, and the whole community will clearly be better off. The precise sharing of the costs may be a matter for bargaining and much discussion, but as long as the lighthouse is genuinely beneficial, some plan acceptable to all parties should be finally implemented.

In order for the organization to be wholly voluntary, however, one of two things must be present. Either the fishermen must have the right to force an unreasonable man to move off the island, or there must be no really unreasonable men present. If neither of these conditions is met, the voluntary arrangement may break down. This is easy to demonstrate: Suppose that one unscrupulous fisherman says to himself: "The others are going to organize and build the lighthouse; once it is built I can secure the benefits as well as they. Hence, why should I contribute anything at all? I can simply wait and get the benefits free of charge." It is the likelihood that such *free riders* will be present that makes political, or governmental, action necessary in many cases. If the first alternative mentioned, that of being able to exclude noncooperative persons, were realized, political organization need not arise. Individuals could simply throw out such attempted free riders. This is, for example, the way a private golf club operates. Once constructed, the benefits are available to all members alike. But any member who does not carry the assigned share of the cost is dropped from the club. This alternative may not be open to organizations that provide services over spatially defined areas, however. *Political* organization, which necessarily embodies potential coercion, may be required.

The great advantage of political or governmental organization in this respect is that it does have available to it power of compelling all members of the group to contribute toward the costs of the collective goods. Individual beneficiaries from the lighthouse may agree to contribute toward the project only insofar as they are assured that all individuals in the group will be forced to bear some share of the common burden of payment. In a sense, all members of the group agree to allow themselves to be coerced in order to ensure an acceptable sharing of the common burden.

With the aid of this very simple lighthouse example, we have been able to demonstrate how individuals may join together to do things *collectively* rather than privately, and we have also shown why their organization tends to become coercive. The organization takes on the essential characteristics of government. We have shown, therefore, how government might arise for purely economic reasons. In one sense, the theory of collective goods is an "economic theory of government."

THE RANGE OF COLLECTIVE GOODS

When we drop our assumption about the group being composed of island fishermen and instead introduce a bit more reality into our model, we can see that the idea of collective goods may be extended. Many of the traditionally accepted functions of government in the Western world may be explained, in whole or in part, through this distinction between *collective* and *private* goods. We may now try to examine these functions more carefully.

THE COMMON DEFENSE

Defense against external enemies seems to fall squarely within the collective goods category. The early settlers soon found that collective efforts were required to build forts. A fortress strong enough to withstand attack was beneficial to all members of the group. Its services were *indivisible*.

Quite similarly, the services which we now receive from the national defense establishment are indivisible. The addition of a Minuteman missile or a Polaris submarine adds to the overall deterrent threat. It is impossible that I could have available to me the services of the Polaris patrol without my neighbor, at the same time, having similar services available to him.

The common availability of collective goods or services does not, of course, imply that similar evaluations are placed on these by different persons. The presence of American troops in Western Europe demonstrates this point. The protection offered by these troops is equally available to all U.S. citizens. But the value placed on this protection may range from significantly positive levels for those who are most concerned about the Soviet threat to significantly negative levels for those who feel that unilateral disarmament is desirable.

LAW AND ORDER

The provision of internal defense, or defense of individuals against the predatory behavior of others of their own group, belongs in a category of collective goods similar to external defense. The system of law enforcement, of the courts, and of judicial processes is beneficial to all individuals in the group. The ordinary and accepted pattern of social life takes these common benefits more or less for granted. And social intercourse of various sorts can proceed in accordance with reasonable expectations of stability because this inherently indivisible service is provided by government.

In the political structure of the United States, this function is shared between the central and the subordinate units of government. And, in any case, this function is rather unimportant in terms of the economic resources which it absorbs. Therefore, in the study of public finance, which concentrates attention on the economic aspects of government, the attention given to this particular collective service will be much less than would be deserved in any more comprehensive consideration of government and its functions. As an illustration of this, the U.S. Supreme Court, as a vital part of the whole system of law and order, is far more important than might be indicated by the relatively small proportion of the federal budget allocated to its maintenance.

Just as with external defense, different persons and groups may place different valuations on specific elements of "law and order." The differences here, however, are mainly concerned with the appropriate methods of organization and control of the actual enforcement agencies, with the "mix" among components of the public good. Few persons or groups place negative values on internal order as such.

ENVIRONMENTAL CONTROL

Closely related to internal defense is some measure of governmental action to prevent the creation of "public bads" by individuals and groups. The last third of the 20th century finds this role of government becoming increasingly important. If confined within appropriate limits, collective goods and services are produced when government takes action to reduce air and water pollution, to reduce noise in all its forms, to conserve dwindling natural resouces, to prevent undue concentrations of population in space, or, generally, to reduce congestion. This essentially preventive action by government is possibly more important than action designed to supply or finance specific provision of goods and services, as such. The dangers of overzealous or excessive governmental action in these respects should be noted, especially in the light of the experience of the early 1970s.

MONETARY STABILITY

Although it is not so generally recognized because governments have rarely fulfilled their role appropriately in this connection, the provision of monetary "order" is an important collective service. Each member of the society must accept the common monetary system, and this system should, so far as is possible, be arranged so as to ensure against unpredictable changes in the value of the monetary unit. Experience suggests, however, that governments, as they actually perform, probably create the "public bad" of inflation more often than the "public good" of maintaining monetary stability.

REGULATORY MEASURES

Many specific regulatory measures provide genuinely collective services. For example, governmental requirements that a certain air traffic pattern be followed by all users of the air lanes are beneficial to the whole population. The pure food and drug laws allow all individuals to carry on the process of food consumption without great fear or poison, although, once again, too much regulation can result in keeping helpful new drugs out of use. Traffic regulations on our nation's highways and streets provide an additional example. The enforcement of the rule that automobiles shall be driven on the right side of the road is an indivisible service beneficial to all road users. Many other types of regulatory activity fit this pattern.

As the case with law and order, the provision of regulatory services may not be significant in terms of budgetary allocation. The enforcement of traffic regulation is a relatively small proportion of the nation's total outlay on roads.

POLITICAL BOUNDARIES AND INDIVISIBILITY

The boundaries of the political units may not, of course, coincide with the range of indivisibility characterizing a genuinely collective good or service. For example, the provision of a lighthouse at St. Marks, Florida, may be a collective service under any rigorous and careful definition of this term. But the mere fact that this is accepted does nothing to suggest that all citizens of the United States, or even of the state of Florida, benefit from the services of this lighthouse. The range of indivisibility may be considerably more limited than that indicated by the boundaries of the political unit. And it may be appropriate for the financing scheme to reflect this fact.

In other words, even though a good is collective in the sense that its services are commonly available or indivisible among all persons, public or governmental action may not be required to provide it unless it is also the case that exclusion is costly and inefficient. The fact of indivisibility does not, in itself, imply that all citizens of the political unit in being need be called on to support the service. The range of the collective consumption interaction provides the basis for an economic theory of the division of governmental functions in a multigovernmental economy, often referred to as the theory of fiscal federalism.

PUBLIC FINANCING AND PUBLIC OPERATION

It is useful to distinguish between public or governmental support or financing of a particular service and the actual governmental operation or provision of a service. This distinction has seldom been made sufficiently clear in discussion of public finance.

By showing that a particular service is indivisible among separate users and that exclusion is costly, we may explain collective *financing* of the service. The actual operation may be carried out directly by governmental agencies or by private firms hired through governmental funds. This latter decision should rest solely on efficiency grounds. If a task can be done more efficiently by direct governmental action, obviously this should be the means adopted. On the other hand, if the task can be more economically performed through contracting out to private firms, this arrangement should be implemented.

Examples to illustrate the point are not hard to find. The Defense Department procures most of its weapons and equipment by contracting with private firms. No serious consideration is given to development and construction of nationalized aircraft factories or rifle manufacturing plants. Presumably, the bulk of defense "hardware" can be supplied more efficiently through the contracting out of orders with private suppliers. There is no inherent reason why other public services cannot be handled similarly. The public *operation* of a school system, for example, has no economic justification except insofar as such a system can be shown to be more efficient than some alternative arrangement.

The distinction emphasized here provides the basis for an economic theory of the *organization* of publicly financed services and will be examined in somewhat greater detail in Chapter 14.

QUASI-COLLECTIVE OR IMPURELY PUBLIC GOODS AND SERVICES

The earlier listing has clearly not exhausted the categories of goods and services which are, in fact, provided publicly through government. Governments do many other things, but as we move beyond those goods and services which are *collective* in a relatively pure sense, a different classification is suggested. For this reason we have chosen to set up a category of quasi-collective goods and services.

These take on collective characteristics in that some of the benefits provided are indivisible, but they assume also characteristics of private goods and services in that a portion of the benefits are divisible.

Many examples come to mind immediately in this category. Public expenditure for education is obviously of this sort. The whole community benefits from the advantages of having a well-educated citizenry. To this extent, the services provided by public expenditure on education are indivisible. But private families also benefit directly when their children's education is publicly financed. This part of the service provided by public expenditure on education is divisible.

National, state, and municipal parks provide another example. Citizens of the western states benefit generally from Yosemite, just as citizens of eastern states benefit generally from the Smoky Mountains National Park. But those particular citizens who visit the parks surely secure private and divisible benefits that nonvisitors do not enjoy.

The continuing debate concerning the appropriate extent of governmental activity is centered around functions falling within this quasi-collective category. The relative importance given to the *collective* and to the *private* aspects of the particular services will determine an individual's attitude on the appropriate role of government with respect to financing. If direct charges levied on users and related to their private consumption of the services produce sufficient revenues to finance the total operation of an activity, and if, at the margin of provision, no collective elements remain, then the private market organization of the activity is indicated, even when the quasi-collective nature of the total benefits is fully acknowledged. Or should the activity be organized through a public agency, direct charges levied on users should be sufficient to finance the whole operation, and no general taxes need be employed to supplement these. When collective elements of benefit remain at the margin of provision, some mixed financing is indicated in any efficient organization; that is to say, direct user charges supplemented by general taxes, and combined in various ways, would be the financing scheme for such activities.

The relative importance or even the presence of private and collective benefits in the performance of an activity cannot, however, be measured scientifically or objectively. Individuals must make their own subjective estimates, and individuals may differ on their evaluations. Thus, we find that different governments do different things with respect to both the organization and the financing of quasi-collective goods and services. Contrast the American and the British attitude on medical care. The National Health Service in Great Britain is publicly financed, in large part from general taxes levied on the whole population, and the persons who receive benefits get these free or at very low cost to themselves individually. The British people have apparently decided that the indivisible benefits to the community at large outweigh the disadvantages which arise due to the absence of direct user prices. On the other hand, medical care in the United States was, up until the mid-1960s, financed and provided largely through privare market processes, supplemented in important ways by both government and charitable organizations. With the advent of Medicare and Medicaid, the collective properties of medical services, at least for the aged and poor, were emphasized relative to the privately divisible components. The manner in which this collective interest in medical care has been implemented has created some major problems in the 1970s. The imposition of collectively-financed demands for services over and above privately-financed demands has placed severe price pressures on artificially-restricted supplies. Despite these problems, political pressure for further collectivization of medical care through some sort of national health insurance scheme remains. Presumably a decision will be made during the early 1980s as to whether or not to extend collectivization in this area.

PRIVATE SERVICES PUBLICLY PROVIDED

From the previous discussion, it is clear that there is no sharp dividing line that may be drawn between goods and services that fall properly within the provision or financing of government and those that are within the province of the private market economy. As we shall discuss more fully in the next section, almost any good or service has both collective and private attributes. But a third category may be introduced: relatively private goods and services that are sometimes provided or financed by governmental units, for various reasons. These are private in that the benefits are largely *divisible* among separate personal users.

Any examination of the activities that governments actually do perform will suggest that several fall within this category. The interesting point to be noted is, however, that such services are normally *financed* as if they were wholly private. Examples are numerous. Government provision of postal services is perhaps the best. The beneficiaries of the service are the direct users of the system, and these benefits are almost wholly divisible. Governments operate postal systems as if they were private in that the major financial support is based on revenues out of direct user charges. This is as it should be. Some governmental regulation of postal activity is, of course, in the collective interest. All potential users must be granted access to the facilities; users must be guaranteed against fraud. But these involve the regulation of the way in which the service is operated, not the support of the service itself. The almost universal provision of postal service by governments can best be explained as an historical accident. Increasing recognition of the privately divisible nature of postal services along with the glaringly obvious bureaucratic inefficiency of the U.S. system by comparison with private enterprise led to mounting demands that basic structural modifications be introduced. The postal service was reorganized as a quasi-independent public corporation in 1970. But services continue to deteriorate, and demands mount for a change in the arbitrary monopoly position of the government postal authority.

The second service which is primarily private but which is provided by government is that of highway facilities and services. Here the benefits are clearly divisible, and the actual operation and construction of the facilities is financed by various charges levied on users. As with the postal services, there are collective aspects of the road system, but again, universal public operation seems to stem from historical developments rather than from any distinctly collective attributes of the services provided.

Postal and highway services are essentially *public utilities.* This amounts to saying that the benefits from such services are divisible among separate users, but, for some reason or another, there are legitimate reasons for collective or governmental interest in the regulation or operation of the industry. Postal and highway systems are almost universally operated by governments. Other public utilities are handled differently in different countries. In European countries both the railroad system and the telephone and telegraph system are normally government operated, while in the United States these are privately operated but publicly regulated. Radio and television systems are publicly operated in most European countries. In the United States, we witness a peculiar structure of the radio-television industry in which the organization is nominally private, but users are not allowed to purchase services directly with user charges.

COLLECTIVE INTEREST AND MARKET ACTIVITY

We have classified the goods and services that are normally financed or provided by governments in three groups: genuinely collective services, quasi-collective services, and publicly provided private services or public utilities. These are useful categories, but the dividing lines among them and those services that are organized primarily through private markets should not be over emphasized. In particular, the existence of some collective characteristics is not sufficient to assure that government provision will always be superior to market provision.

Efficient provision of a collective good requires that the summed marginal evaluations of consumers equal the marginal cost of production. Market provision will generally fail to achieve this result because the market process cannot generate an accurate revelation of consumer demand for a collective consumption good. However, it is important to realize that there is nothing inherent in democratic political process which insures a correction of the market's failure in this regard. The choice of the appropriate institutional setting within which to provide a good or service with collective consumption characteristics is thus made between two inefficient alternatives and must rest on a presumption that one arrangement will provide a better allocative result than the other. In some cases government provision seems quite clearly more desirable than market provision. Few would argue that market provision of national defense, for example, would ever approach satisfactory levels. On the other hand, there may be some indivisible or collective benefits in the maintenance and development of the cultural tradition inherent in the fine arts. There is, however, little political pressure for widespread government support here, reflecting a belief that the market is performing satisfactorily.

In summary, the existence of some collective interest should not be taken to suggest that some governmental interference with or encouragement of market activity is justified. As long as the market itself functions so as to ensure a satisfactorily large production of goods and services in which there is a collective interest, the indivisible benefits are secured along with the divisible ones, and society secures a net gain at no additional cost. In the final determination of the appropriate role for governmental financing, one must always recall that here, as elsewhere, decision should be made at the appropriate margins.

MISCELLANEOUS GOVERNMENT SERVICES

We have tried to discuss briefly some of the economic reasons for the provision of public services. We have made no attempt to exhaust the range of expenditures that governments actually undertake. Many of these arise for no apparent economic reason. Governments may subsidize particular groups; for example, veterans. Or a particular industry may secure public funds for any of several reasons. Other government spending may arise because of earlier spending beyond revenues; the interest on the national debt has become a major item in the federal budget. In another important role not explicitly treated in this summary, the government may act as an insurance agency. The social security system may be partially explained on these grounds.

At appropriate places later in this book, many of the specific services performed by governments at all levels will be discussed in some detail. This chapter has not been intended to catalog all publicly provided services; instead it has been intended to give an elementary understanding of the economic reasons for public activity.

SUPPLEMENTARY READING

For a more sophisticated discussion of the economic basis for governmental activity, the student should consult R. A. Musgrave, *The Theory of Public Finance* (New York: McGraw-Hill Book Co., 1959), chap. 1. And, for a discussion relating the public sector to welfare economics, the work of Baumol is recommended. See William J. Baumol, *Welfare Economics and the Theory of the State*, rev. 2d ed. (Cambridge, Mass.; Harvard University Press, 1952; 1965).

Two articles by Paul A. Samuelson are widely regarded as the standard works on the modern theory of purely collective goods. See "The Pure Theory of Public Expenditure," *The Review of Economics and Statistics*, vol. 36 (November 1954), pp. 387–89; "Diagrammatic Exposition of a Theory of

Public Expenditure," *Review of Economics and Statistics,* vol. 37 (November 1955), pp. 350–56.

For a monograph-length discussion of collective or public goods, the student should see James M. Buchanan, *Demand and Supply of Public Goods* (Chicago: Rand McNally & Co., 1968).

5

The development of the public sector

Government, as such, exists, and its activities, whether subject to reasonable explanation or not, are extremely important in shaping the environment in which we live. It is time to take explicit account of this fact and attempt to place some quantitative significance on it.

A historical approach seems to be suggested here. We shall trace the growth of the collective or public sector of the economy in order to be able better to understand the current quantitative significance of this sector.

In the rather abstract discussion of preceding chapters, we have referred to "government" as if there were only one unit affecting each citizen. The political structure of the United States is a federal one. Not one but two or more units of government affect individual citizens simultaneously. They possess dual citizenship and hold dual loyalties. The federal, or central, government must be distinguished from the state governments, which, in their turn, must be distinguished from the various local units: counties, townships, cities, school districts, and so on. In studying the growth of the public sector, we shall be interested in seeing how governmental activity has developed at all levels, but we shall also want to see how this activity has been distributed among the separate units.

THE CONSTITUTIONAL SETTING: GOVERNMENT AS REFEREE

That which we call "government" serves two conceptually distinct roles in society, and it is useful that these two roles be carefully separated. Orderly society requires the establishment and maintenance of a legal framework in which the rights of separate individuals and groups are defined, including the rights and limits of government itself. These rights must be enforced; those who violate the "rules of the game" must be identified and penalized. This suggests that an umpire, or referee, must be assigned the task of ensuring that these rules are maintained and honored; that individuals and groups are protected in their rights. Government, in one of its two roles, serves in this protective, or referee, role. In this capacity, government does not "produce" anything; it enforces the rules. The judicial branch of government clearly falls within this protective role, or capacity, as does a major part of the executive branch. The function of government in this capacity is that of providing the framework of "law and order" within which social interaction may take place. In this capacity, there is no place for legislation, for positive promotion of "social good."

GOVERNMENT AS PRODUCER-SUPPLIER
OF "PUBLIC GOODS"

Confusion arises, however, because government simultaneously fulfills a second major role in society. Government is the means or process through which individuals provide for themselves certain goods and services that, for any reason, they decide to secure collectively rather than privately and independently. It is this function of government which involves the most direct economic impact on individuals. Legislation, through representative assemblies, becomes the process through which individuals find themselves subjected to taxes in order to secure the benefits from the goods and services that are produced or purchased by government and made available for use. It is government in this role that will be our primary concern in this textbook. This is the government that spends billions and taxes us to finance those expenditures.

This should not, however, suggest that government in its referee or protective role does not exert major economic impact. To the extent that the rights of individuals and groups are protected and maintained, economic exchange is facilitated, and vice versa. And, more importantly, if the government in its presumed role as referee takes upon itself the highly questionable function of changing the assignment of rights, of changing the rules of the game, or of modifying the legal framework, the whole setting within which both private economic interaction and governmental public goods provision take place, the effective "constitution" may be arbitrarily shifted, with major economic consequences. This fact must be recognized, despite the emphasis in this book on the more measurable impact of government in its producer-supplier role.

WHAT SHOULD WE TRY TO MEASURE?

Before plunging carelessly into the many possible statistical series that might be introduced, it will be useful to state specifically what we should try to measure. Four separate variables may be suggested as possible indicators of the direct economic importance of governmental activity: (1) the values of governmental goods and services, (2) the real cost of governmental services, (3) the extent to which collectively made decisions replace private or individual decisions, and (4) the extent to which resources are organized by the market economy or by the governmental bureaucracy.

The search for any completely suitable measure of the value of public services must be abandoned early in the game. Different goods and services may be added together meaningfully only if there exists some common denominator to which they can be reduced. In the market economy, prices provide a means whereby the values of separate goods and services can be added together to secure a total measure of gross national production or national income. But prices are not directly set for more than a small fraction of public goods and services; only divisible public services can be properly priced, and, as the last chapter indicated, these make up only one category of all public services. For the remaining public goods and services, the only meaningful way of adding up is that of using costs, in dollars. But it is at once evident that costs do not necessarily measure final values, since consumers cannot make the same adjustments as they can for private goods. The cost of a particular public service may seriously overestimate or seriously underestimate its value to the total economy.

The second quantity that may be measured, even if imperfectly, is the cost of governmental activity, not the value of governmental services. This cost should measure the value of the opportunities foregone by the community in securing the public services that are performed. These foregone opportunities may be conceptually measured by the values that are placed on private goods. Hence the value of the opportunity given up in order to secure a given quantity of public service is approximately measured by the market values of the private goods and services that could have been made available in the absence of the public activity. To be fully accurate here, we must assume that market prices reflect values set at competitive equilibrium and that resource suppliers are motivated solely by pecuniary considerations. Also, we must assume that the problem is one of measuring the opportunity cost of small changes in the size of governmental activity rather than the cost of total governmental activity.

MEASURES OF GOVERNMENTAL ACTIVITY

Total governmental expenditure

This is the one measure of governmental activity that comes most readily to mind. And it does provide a helpful, and readily available, index of the direct economic importance of government, especially when it is used to compare various levels over reasonably short time periods. Unadjusted figures for total public expenditure can provide the public with some measure of year-to-year changes in total governmental size. Such unadjusted figures will, however, reflect changes in prices along with changes in government's real share in economic activity. Hence, over any significant period of time, this difficulty must be eliminated. It can be by deflating the crude or unadjusted figures by some index of prices. This will produce a series for total governmental expenditures in dollars of constant values, sometimes called constant dollars. Such an adjustment has become more necessary with the onset of the more rapid rate of inflation since the late 1960s. Under high rates of inflation unadjusted expenditure totals will carry relatively little information content.

Population changes over time, and if more than a few years are to be compared, it may be desirable to adjust for changes in population. This second adjustment can produce a per capita measure of public spending.

Some series for government expenditure, as adjusted, should provide a good measure for the real cost of governmental activity during all periods except those characterized by significant unemployment of resources. Government expenditures are sometimes classified into two broad categories: *productive* expenditures and *transfer* expenditures. The first includes a measure for government's purchases of real goods and services, whereas the second includes transfers of purchasing power from the general taxpayer to specific individuals and groups. Hence, federal outlays for missiles are productive expenditures; social security payments are transfer expenditures. On the basis of this classification, it might be argued that the figures for total governmental expenditure tend to overstate the real costs of governmental activity and that this is better reflected in the figures for productive expenditure only. This view seems incorrect. The real cost of public activity is aimed at providing some measure of the value of private goods and services that are sacrificed in order to secure the benefits of public activity. Taxation imposed upon some members of the community is a real cost of securing the benefits arising from the direct subsidizing of other members even through explicit money transfers. This is as much a real cost as direct outlay for tanks, planes, and paper clips. For the purpose of estimating the real cost of government, the distinction between productive and transfer expenditures is not a useful one.

Governmental resource absorption

The exclusion of transfer expenditures from the total seems desirable, however, if the purpose of the measurement is that of determining the extent to which collectively made decisions replace private or individual decisions in the final allocation of resources in the economy. Although governmental transfers clearly affect the overall allocation of resources, as long as private individuals carry out the final act of spending, the organizing principles of the market economy are allowed to operate (within a specific regulatory framework). The principle of consumer sovereignty, as appropriately modified to account for real-world imperfections, remains in force. The transfer payments modify the distribution of economic power, but only secondarily do they affect the organization of economic activity. It is a useful and supplementary exercise, therefore, to examine the comparative growth of governmental resource absorption.

Government employment

It may also be desirable to measure the extent to which the market economy or the government actually organizes production of goods and services. This is slightly different from government resource absorption. Here the appropriate figures are those for the direct government employment of resource inputs. If the government purchases final goods and services from private firms, these goods and services are still produced in the organized market and the firms are presumably guided by the profit motive. Only if the government employs productive resources with a view toward its own production of final goods and services is this aspect of market organization replaced by collective activity.

The distinctions among total governmental expenditures, resource absorption, and government employment should not be overdrawn. By a simple reorganization of public activity, particular public services may be included in one or in all of these categories. A single illustration will indicate this, and, at the same time, clarify the distinctions.

We know that the federal government operates many veterans' hospitals throughout the country. Total expenditure on providing hospital services for veterans shows up in our accounts for total governmental spending; the value of goods and services directly purchased by the government in the performance of this function shows up in any measure of resource absorption, and the people hired at the hospitals are counted as governmental employees. Let us now suppose that a policy change dictates that all of the veterans' hospitals be sold to private firms who will then operate them under contract to the federal government, and that these firms will directly supply hospital services to qualified veterans. This change will serve to eliminate veterans' hospitals altogether from the third category, that of government employment. Employees will no longer work for the government, but for the private employers. As still a further policy shift, now let us suppose that the government decides to provide qualified veterans with hospitalization subsidies and then to allow these veterans to purchase the needed services directly from private hospitals. Here the veterans' hospital item would show up only in the total expenditure category. The payments listed would be transfer payments only; no governmental purchases of goods and services would take place.

The illustration indicates that the organization of the public service is all important in influencing its place in the accounting scheme. For this reason, the differences in the separate measures should not be overemphasized. Few people would argue that substantially different final results would be achieved in the three separate organizational forms suggested in the example. The organizational differences are, nonetheless, of some importance. The organizing forces of the market are utilized to a considerably greater extent in the third institutional structure than in the second, and to a considerable extent more in the second than in the first. In some cases, a shifting among such arrangements can produce major improvements in efficiency. Here is an area where present and continuing research by experts can lead to useful changes. This aspect of governmental expenditure policy will be discussed further in Chapter 18.

Government activity relative to gross national product

The measures discussed above provide some indication of the direct economic importance of governmental activity. Standing alone, they tell us little or nothing about the governmental sector of the economy relative to the private or market sector. In the progressive, growing economy, it is to be expected that the public sector will expand along with the private sector. The relevant question concerns the comparative rates of growth over time. For this purpose, it is desirable to reduce the absolute figures to percentages of national aggregates, for example, to reduce the figures for total public expenditures to percentages of *gross national product* (GNP) the best overall measure of the level of total economic activity.

Gross national product is defined as the total value of goods and services produced during the relevant time period. Of course, many measurement problems arise. Most of these need not concern us here. Some of the more difficult of these involve the way in which government services are to be counted. As has been indicated, no market value exists for many public goods and services in the sense that this applies for private goods and services. Government services can only be included at costs. But other issues arise. Should or should not transfer expenditures of governments be included in GNP? Should government services be treated as final consumption items or as productive services instrumental to the production of private goods? For the factual measures to be presented, we shall incorporate figures for gross national product as this is interpreted by the federal statisticians. This measurement includes in GNP only *productive* expenditures of governmental units; transfer expenditures are excluded (including interest on public debts). All productive expenditures are included. This amounts to assuming that all government services are either final products or else are intermediate items that are somehow not reflected in the final prices of private goods and services. While this classification is somewhat arbitrary, for the purposes of the rough comparisons to be attempted here, the possible refinements are not highly significant.

TOTAL GOVERNMENT EXPENDITURE

Having discussed the problems of finding appropriate measures, it is time to plunge directly into the hard facts. For fiscal 1977, total government expenditure is the United States was approximately $680 billion. Of this total, some $432 billion were expended by the federal government, and the remaining $248 billion by states and local governments. This figure for total governmental spending may be compared with an estimated gross national product for fiscal 1977 of some $1,887 billion. More than $3.60 out of each $10 earned in the national economy were channeled through the fiscal process for some government purpose. This very brief presentation of the current factual picture is perhaps sufficient to indicate the tremendous importance of the public sector of the economy, even when measured in the direct sense earlier discussed. But the magnitude of the governmental expenditure over the years is traced in Table 5–1.

Unadjusted figures for total governmental expenditures are given in Table 5–1, and these are illustrated in Figures 5–1 and 5–2. Several points may be noted on the basis of these very rough data. The first impression is one of the enormous rate of growth in total governmental expenditure over the century and two thirds that is covered. Although data for the 19th century are very spotty, even the roughest estimates indicate that the public sector of the American economy has been growing at an increasing rate almost from the beginning of history. Roughly speaking, governmental expenditures increased fourfold or fivefold during the first half of the past century, from 1800 to 1850. During the Civil War, federal expenditures surged above the $1 billion mark for the first time, but remained only one year at that level. Over the entire 50-year period, 1850–1900, total governmental spending increased somewhere between 10 and 20 times over; from 1902 until 1962, the increase was over 100-fold. And we are familiar with the veritable explosion in public spending that took place during the years after 1964. Total governmental outlay, at all levels, increased almost four times over during the 15-year period between 1962 and 1977.

A slightly different way of looking at these figures is in terms of

TABLE 5–1
Total government expenditure, federal expenditure, state and local expenditure (in current dollars), selected years, 1799–1980

Year	Total, all governments (in millions)	Federal (in millions)	State and local (in millions)
1799	$ 20–30*(est.)	$ 10†	$ nda*
1850	80–120(est.)	40†	nda
1902	1,660‡	572‡§	1,088‡§
1913	3,215	970	2,245
1919	22,882(est.)	18,448†	4,435(est.)
1922	9,297	3,763	5,534
1927	11,220	3,533	7,687
1932	12,437	4,266	8,171
1934	12,807	5,941	6,866
1936	16,758	9,165	7,593
1938	17,675	8,449	9,226
1942	45,576	35,549	10,027
1944	109,947	100,520	9,427
1946	79,707	66,534	13,173
1948	55,081	35,592	19,489
1950	70,334	44,800	25,534
1954	111,332	77,692	33,640
1958	134,930	86,054	48,876
1962	176,239	113,428	62,811
1966	224,813	143,022	81,791
1968	282,645	184,464	98,181
1970	332,985	208,190	124,795
1972	415,136	252,544	162,592(est.)
1974	478,325	295,147	183,178
1976	633,862	392,958	240,904
1977	680,329	431,980	248,349
1978		450,836	n.a.‖
1979		493,368(est.)	n.a.
1980		531,560(est.)	n.a.

* No data are available for state and local expenditure prior to 1900. The ranges of $20–30 million and $80–120 million for all governments in the years 1799 and 1850 are estimated on the basis of federal totals. From later data it does not seem likely that the federal government share ever exceeded one half of total government expenditure during this early period, and it probably was closer to one-third than one-half.

† Data for federal expenditure for 1799, 1850, and 1919 are taken from M. Slade Kendrick, *A Century and a Half of Federal Expenditures*, Occasional Paper No. 48 (New York: National Bureau fo Economic Research, 1955).

‡ Except where otherwise noted, data for total expenditure, federal expenditure, and for state and local expenditure from 1902 through 1971 are figures provided by the U.S. Bureau of the Census as reported in *Facts and Figures on Government Finance*, 19th Biennial Edition, 1977 (Tax Foundation, Inc.). Federal expenditures for 1978, 1979, and 1980 are taken from the Budget of the United States Government. It should be noted that the Census Bureau and the Office of Management and Budget use different accounting practices in computing federal government expenditures, Census totals are larger than Budget totals primarily because expenditures of such public enterprises as the U.S. Postal Service are included on a gross basis in Census accounts and a net basis in budget accounts.

§ State and local totals are adjusted downward by the amount of federal grants in aid since this appears in federal expenditure totals.

‖ Not available at time of publication.

FIGURE 5-1
Total government expenditure, federal expenditure, state-local
expenditure—1902-1977

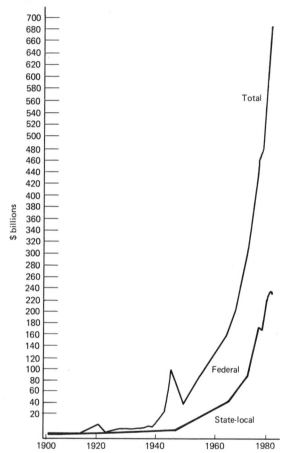

monthly, weekly, and daily rates of total governmental spending. All governments were spending in 1977 roughly $57 billion each month, or almost $13 billion each week, over $1.8 billion per day.

Another useful way of examining the growth of government expenditures is to examine them on a per capita basis. Certainly we might expect some growth in total expenditures to accompany population growth. However, the phenomenal increases in per capita expenditures which have occurred during the first seven decades of the 20th century indicate that population growth alone is capable of explain-

FIGURE 5–2
Total government expenditure—1902–1977—ratio scale

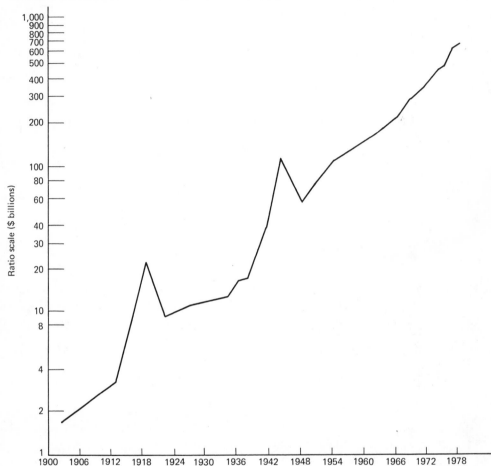

ing only a small proportion of the growth of the total public sector expenditures. General per capita expenditures of all governments increased from about $20 in 1902 to $750 in 1957. By 1977, this figure was slightly over $3,000. Between 1957 and 1977, population increases explained only about 24 percent of the total increase in government spending.

Another important relationship appears from a glance at Table 5–1. Except for war periods and for a short time in the depths of the Great Depression, state and local expenditures combined exceeded federal government expenditure up until World War II. Since World War II, federal expenditure totals have substantially exceeded those for the states and local units combined.

The state-local expenditure totals reveal a steady growth over the period covered. On the other hand, the federal totals seem to move by spurts. This is explained, of course, by the tremendous increase in federal government outlay made necessary by war. We need only to look at the isolated years of 1919 and 1944 in relation to preceding years to appreciate this fact. It is characteristic that the level of expenditure in postwar periods never falls to prewar amounts. Federal expenditure tends to grow in a stairlike progression, moving rapidly upward to meet wars and threats of war, falling back from prewar peaks, but remaining on upward slopes far above prewar plains. Thus, only in 1961 did the federal government spend up to the prior peak level of 1944, whereas, the 1919 totals were not actually achieved until the onset of World War II. The post-1964 upsurge in federal spending is partially, but not fully explained by the Vietnam War. Under the Johnson administration, nonmilitary outlays were allowed to accelerate sharply along with military spending, an experience unique in American fiscal history. Throughout the 1970s, it should be noted that inflation also added to growth of government expenditures measured in nominal terms.

Figure 5–1 provides a graphic picture of the growth of government expenditures and indicates the divergence between the growth pattern of federal expenditure and state-local expenditure.

The unadjusted data in Table 5–1 and the accompanying figures do not, however, tell us anything about the "real" growth of the public sector of the economy. It is conceivable, but not probable, that average prices could have moved up as rapidly as the expenditure totals over the period covered since 1799. In this case, the "real" size of the governmental sector might be no larger now than it was during our early history. The only way to find this out is to reduce the raw expenditure figures to some comparable real magnitudes. This is done, although the many limitations of the method must be recognized, by reducing the raw expenditure totals to some measure calculated in constant dollars. For example, if the figure for total expenditure should have doubled between a given two years, but the average price level had also doubled, the expenditure figure in terms of constant dollars should be the same for the two years. Technically, this process is carried out by deflating the raw data by some price index which is supposed to reflect the average price of goods and services in the economy. The results of such a calculation are shown in Table 5–2.

TABLE 5–2
Total government expenditure (in constant, 1967, dollars, selected years, 1902–1977)

Year	Total expenditures, all governments (in millions)	Year	Total expenditures, all governments (in millions)
1902	$ 5,461	1960	$159,419
1913	8,931	1962	185,906
1922	18,631	1964	207,424
1927	22,759	1966	225,264
1932	37,015	1968	275,722
1936	40,187	1970	301,617
1940	50,412	1971	326,431
1944	205,125	1972	336,184
1948	66,523	1973	324,259
1950	85,983	1974	298,766
1952	112,694	1975	318,090
1954	127,091	1976	346,373
1956	127,669	1977	350,323
1958	142,632		

Note: Figures in Table 5–2 have been adjusted using the producer price index as reported in *The Economic Report of the President, 1979.*

The figures in Table 5–2 show the growth of government expenditure independently of the increase in the average price level. Since average prices for the year 1967 provide the basis for the calculation, we may say that the series shows how rapidly government expenditures should have grown if prices throughout the century and a half were fixed at a level equivalent to that prevailing during that year

The figures in Table 5–2 indicate that real government expenditure has grown significantly during the 20th century, increasing by a factor of 64 between 1902 and 1977. In terms of interpreting the nominal figures in Table 5–1, the most significant adjustments have to be made for the period immediately following World War II and the nine years between 1968 and 1977. Both of these periods were characterized by significant price inflation. The growth in government spending during war continues to be reflected in the adjusted real data. For example, not until 1964 did real government spending surpass the total achieved at the peak of 1944. If we look at the growth of government expenditure between 1964 and 1977, it is clear that the nominal figures in Table 5–1 overstate the real growth in government spending by a considerable amount. However, adjusted real growth remains a significant 69 percent over that period.

Information concerning the growth of government outlay provides no indication of the *relative* importance of government in the economy. The next step in adjusting the data is, therefore, to compare the growth of the public sector with the growth of the economy as a whole. We may do this by computing the total public expenditure for each year as a percentage of gross national production. The results are indicated in Table 5–3, which begins in 1902, the first year for which reliable statistics are available.

Table 5–3 indicates that a considerable part of the expansion in the governmental sector of the economy is attributed to the overall growth in the economy. Whereas unadjusted total government spending increased more than 400-fold over the first eight decades of the 20th century, and even when adjusted for price changes, "real" government outlay has multiplied more than 64 times over, relative to GNP total government spending increased by a multiple of slightly more than four. This remains an extremely important increase. The governmental "share" of total production in the post-World War II period is more than four times as large as the governmental "share" in the first decades of this century. A continuing collectivization of the national economy has taken place as the 20th century has progressed.

Table 5–3 is useful also in comparing the relative efforts of the government in the two world wars. Whereas the public sector reached approximately one fifth of GNP in World War I, it reached almost one half in World War II. After an initial decline in the immediate aftermath of World War II in the late 1940s, the share climbed to about 26 percent during the Korean War, and has continued to increase, though at a reduced rate, since that time. Note that during all of this latter period, total public expenditure has comprised a larger share of GNP than during the peak spending years of World War I.

The sizeable increase in the percentage shown between the years 1927 and 1932 is explained by the onset of the Great Depression. As Table 5–1 shows, total government spending increased over this period by less than $2 billion. But the percentage figures of Table 5–3 reveal that the relative importance of the public sector increased by

TABLE 5–3
Total government expenditure as percent of
GNP (selected years, 1902–1978)

Year	Total expenditure, all governments, as percentage of GNP
1902	8.3
1913	8.8
1919	20.6
1927	12.6
1933	19.2
1939	19.4
1944	48.9
1948	19.5
1954	26.5
1958	28.4
1962	28.5
1966	28.3
1970	33.9
1972	35.5
1974	33.9
1976	37.3
1977	36.0

Note: Percentages calculated on the basis of total expenditure data contained in column 1, Table 5–1. Kuznets' data for GNP used for years prior to 1929; Department of Commerce data for years 1929–1977.

70 percent. This is due largely to the reduction of GNP which actually fell from more than $100 billion in 1929 to less than $60 billion in 1932.

RESOURCES ABSORBED BY GOVERNMENT

As stated earlier, total government expenditure, as adjusted, does provide the best measure for the real cost of public services. More limited measures may be helpful if one seeks to ascertain the extent to which collective decisions directly control the allocation of economic resources. For this purpose, some figures for total resource absorption are needed. This is obtained by subtracting from total expenditure that portion which represents transfer payments. Insofar as the fiscal structure merely transfers purchasing power from one group of individual citizens to another group, the government does not directly affect the organization of economic activity. Direct effects are exerted only when the government hires productive factors or purchases final goods and services. Government outlay for payrolls and purchases provides the appropriate measure here.

Table 5–4 shows how this outlay has grown over the half century covered. Only a few selected years are included, but these are sufficient to indicate the relative importance of direct resource absorption. At the start of the century, almost all government outlay was for payrolls and direct purchases. For the early years there is, therefore, little need to separate total resource absorption from total government expenditure, but transfer expenditures became an important part of total government outlay, especially during the Great Depression. This is indicated by the figure for 1939; government outlay for payrolls and purchases amounted to only $11.2 billion out of a total expenditure of $16.8 billion. Transfer expenditures (including interest) accounted for one third of total government outlay.

TABLE 5–4
Resource absorption through government (selected years, 1903–1978)

Year	Government outlay for payrolls and purchases, all units (in billions)	As percentage of total expenditure (percent)
1903	1.5	86
1929	8.5	82
1939	11.2	67
1949	37.0	64
1956	79.4	76
1960	100.2	74
1964	129.8	74
1968	198.7	74
1972	253.1	68
1974	302.6	66
1976	359.5	63
1977	394.0	63
1978*	434.2	64

* Preliminary figures.

Source: Data for 1903, 1929, and 1949, are taken directly from Solomon Fabricant, *The Trend of Government Activity in the United States since 1900* (New York: National Bureau of Economic Research, 1952), Table 7, p. 27, Department of Commerce figures are used for the years 1956–1972. as reported in the 1979 *Economic Report for the President*, pp. 268 and 269.

Although transfer expenditures remained important in the absolute sense, resource using expenditures increased in relative importance after 1950. However, these expenditures reached a postwar peak as a percentage of total government expenditures in the mid-1950s and exhibited a fairly persistent declining trend into the early 1970s. One possible explanation for this decline, especially as it occurred in the late 1960s and early 1970s, was the simultaneous decline in the relative importance of national defense expenditures, (almost all of which are resource using), as a component of total government expenditures. Should the international situation lead to a decision to increase the proportion of government expenditures made in the national defense category at some time in the future, the proportion of government expenditures which are resource using would probably increase.

GOVERNMENT EMPLOYMENT

One of the most useful measures of the actual scope of governmental activity lies in government employment. Direct government purchase of goods and services from the private economy does, of course, alter the pattern of resource usage. But under this arrangement the actual organization of production remains in the hands of private firms. Only when the government directly hires productive services from resource owners does the organization of production shift from the private to the public economy. Government employs all of the productive services, but we may get an idea of the growth of its overall employment by concentrating on the employment of personnel alone. In 1900, 1 out of 20 employed workers was employed by some governmental unit in the United State. By 1977, this had increased to one out of every six. Over the half century 1900–50, government employment increased, on the average, at an annual rate of 3.8 percent. Government purchases, by comparison, increased by an average of 5.6 percent per year. The relative importance of direct government employment within the public sector of the economy decreased. As both military and civil public services become more automated, the rate of increase in government employment relative to the rate of increase in governmental purchases should decrease. This trend may, however, be offset by the emphasis on utilizing government as the employer of last resort for those who fail to secure employment in the private sector.

CONCLUSIONS

What may we conclude from this brief survey of the growth of the public sector of the American economy?

1. The governmental sector has experienced phenomenal growth, whether this is measured on the basis of raw data or measured in "real" terms. In dollar terms, by 1977, government at all levels spent approximately 400 times as much as at the start of the 20th century. On a per capita basis, government spending has increased by a multiple of almost 300 over the 75-year period. In dollars of constant purchasing power, governments at all levels spend more than 64 times as much as at the turn of the century.

2. The governmental sector of the economy has also experienced significant increases relative to the growth of the overall economy. From less than 10 percent of GNP at the beginning of this century, government expenditure has grown to a position where it is about 36 percent of the GNP. The economy has undergone considerable collectivization over the years since the start of World War I.

3. Both the federal government sector and the state-local sector have increased steadily, but the largest growth has been experienced in the federal government sector. Federal expenditures now account for almost two thirds of the total government spending in the United States. Prior to World War II, federal spending did not normally exceed state-local spending, and at the turn of the century, federal spending was only one third of the total spending.

4. Direct resource absorption through governmental units has increased along with the total government expenditures, but at a slightly slower rate. Transfer expenditures have become more important, especially so during the depression of the 1930s, and again in the late 1960s and 1970s.

5. Government employment has increased rapidly, but not so rapidly as government purchases. Government employs almost one out of every six workers in the United States.

SUPPLEMENTARY READING

Solomon Fabricant, *The Trend of Government Activity in the United States Since 1900* (New York: National Bureau of Economic Research, 1952), and M. Slade Kendrick, *A Century and A Half of Federal Expenditures* (New York: National Bureau of Economic Research, Occasional Paper No. 48, 1955), may be consulted for more complete discussion of the growth of public expenditure in the United States over the periods covered. For an interesting and careful study which provides comparable data for Great Britain, see Alan T. Peacock and Jack Wiseman, *The Growth of Public Expenditures in the United Kingdom* (New York: National Bureau of Economic Research, 1961).

For the basic data over more recent years, the student should consult U.S. Department of Commerce sources.

For a useful survey comparing government growth in different countries, see Warren Nutter, *Growth of Government in the West,* (Washington, D.C.: The American Enterprise Institute, 1978).

6

Reasons for growth
of the public sector

$\mathbf{W}$e have seen how rapidly the
public or governmental sector of the American economy has grown,
and we have noted the particular acceleration of this growth after
World War II. More recently, we have emphasized the explosive increase in spending during the last half of the 1960s and the early
1970s. A more complete picture of this growth may be presented by a
functional classification of government expenditure at all levels. Detailed discussion of governmental budgets, by functions, will be reserved for later chapters, but some idea of the growth of the public
sector in terms of broad functional categories will be helpful here.

WAR AND WAR-RELATED EXPENDITURE

The single best explanation for the tremendous growth in the public sector of economy and also for the increased concentration of expenditure in the federal government is provided by the predominant
importance of expenditures, direct or indirect, made necessary by
wars or threats of wars. Federal expenditures have moved upward in
leaps, with the particular jumps occurring during war periods. Prior
to the Civil War, federal government expenditure did not exceed $75
million annually. But in 1865, federal expenditure reached a high of
$1,298 million. In the period following the war, federal expenditure

never fell lower than $200 million and rarely below $250 million.[1] This common failure of postwar federal expenditures to fall to prewar levels is explained, in large part, by war-related expenditures. The national debt is expanded during wars, necessitating a higher annual interest charge in postwar years. And veterans' benefits also loom as added expenditures in postwar periods.

Only in one year prior to World War I (except for the Civil War years) was total federal expenditure above $750 million. In 1919, a high of almost $18.5 billion was reached, and annual federal expenditure in the 1920s reached a low of $2.4 billion in 1924. Before 1940, federal government expenditure, even in the Great Depression, did not exceed $10 billion in any nonwar year. But in 1944 and 1945, more than $100 billion was spent. In the postwar period, federal expenditure dropped to $36 billion in 1947 and 1948, but since that time, because of the Korean War and the subsequent cold war, annual totals in the late 1950s and early 1960s moved upward beyond the $100 billion level. With the advent of the Vietnam War and the "Great Society" programs, federal spending after 1965 increased rapidly to a 1970 level of more than $200 billion. The 1970s were characterized by continued growth in federal outlays although at a much slower rate, in real terms, than characterized the latter half of the 1960s. Between 1965 and 1970, for example, federal government outlays expressed in constant (1967) dollars increased by 44 percent. Between 1970 and 1975, real outlays only increased by 5 percent.

Table 6–1 presents a breakdown between war-related federal expenditures and other federal expenditures for selected years. Total federal spending for national defense and international relations, for veterans' benefits and for interest on the national debt has been included in war-related expenditures. The inclusion of the last item, interest on the public debt, is not wholly correct. Although the largest share of the national debt was incurred during war periods, notably World War II, there was a significant increase during the Great Depression. This correction would, however, involve a relatively slight change in the overall totals, and it has been neglected in the preparation of Table 6–1. Also, all expenditure for international affairs has been attributed to the war-related category.

---

[1]Data taken from M. Slade Kendrick, *A Century and a Half of Federal Expenditures* (National Bureau of Economic Research Occasional Paper No. 48 [New York, 1955]), Table 6–1, pp. 74–77.

By a summary comparison of columns 2 and 3, up until the mid-1960s, the growth in federal government expenditure may be seen to have occurred primarily in the defense sector. This sector grew much more rapidly than the remaining items of federal spending. Since the Korean War years, federal civilian spending programs have grown at a more rapid rate than federal war-related expenditures. And during the 1970s the increase in federal civilian spending was roughly twice that of defense spending.

FEDERAL "CIVIL" EXPENDITURES

The pattern of growth in federal "civil" expenditures is of particular interest. Note that the figures in column 3 of Table 6–1 doubled in

TABLE 6–1
Total federal expenditure, war-related expenditure, civil expenditure (in millions, selected years 1799–1979)

Year	Total federal expenditure	National defense, veterans, interest	Civil (col. 1 –col. 2)
1799	10	9*	1
1850	40	23*	17
1902	572	335†	237
1913	970	450	520
1927	3,533	1,959	1,574
1938	8,449	1,900	6,549
1944	100,547	87,807	12,740
1948	35,592	23,154	12,428
1954	77,692	56,545	21,147
1958	96,054	59,388‡	26,716
1962	113,420	70,382	43,046
1966	143,022	77,116	65,906
1968	184,464	103,761	78,703
1970	208,190	110,854	97,336
1972	252,544	113,315	139,169
1974	478,325	124,880	167,311
1976	392,958	147,925	245,033
1977	431,980	158,361	273,619
1978 (est)	450,836	177,048	273,788
1979 (est)	493,368	199,910	293,458

* Data for column 2 for 1799 and 1850 taken directly from M. Slade Kendrick *A Century and a Half of Federal Expenditures* (National Bureau of Economic Research Occasional Paper No. 48 (New York, 1951), pp. 74, 75.

† Data for column 2 for years 1902 through 1954 computed from basic data contained in *Governmental Finances in the United States, 1902–1957.*

‡ Data for column 2 for years after 1954 computed from *Budgets of the United States Government.*

the single decade 1948–58, and almost tripled in the following decade 1958–68, and more than tripled during the 1968–78 decade. This accelerating growth in nonwar spending by the federal government is difficult to explain. Why have federal outlays increased so rapidly?

One of the most important reasons for this growth lies in the rate of change in outlays from the social security account. Between 1954, when some $3 billion was expended from this account, and 1970, there was a tenfold increase. Outlays tripled between 1970 and 1978 and further increases are projected for the future.

It seems useful to consider the growth of the federal "civil" sector with that of state-local spending which is, of course, exclusively "civil" in the sense used here. Note that prior to the 1970s, federal nondefense spending was never as large as total state-local spending. (Column 3, Table 5–1). This had been reversed by the late 1970s, however. Both as a result of an increased federal role in several traditionally state and local functions and because of the sharp increases in social security outlays, federal nondefense spending exceeded state and local spending by some $25 billion in 1977. It should be noted,

FIGURE 6–1
Federal "civil" expenditure and state-local expenditure (selected years, 1927–1977)

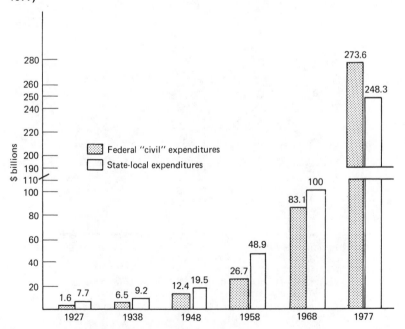

however, that the federal totals included grants-in-aid to state and local governments. Figure 6–1 compares federal "civil" expenditures with state-local expenditures for a few selected years.

Over the remaining fifth of this century, both federal spending and state-local spending will, of course, increase. It seems likely that the federal sector will expand more rapidly than the state-local sector. Two factors, both related to the changing age profile of the population, are especially important here. First is the expected growth in federal social security outlays due to increases in the number of beneficiaries and due to built-in increases in real benefit levels. Second, as the school age population stabilizes after the rapid growth experienced during the 1950s and 1960s, pressures for increases in this traditionally large component of state and local budgets will undoubtedly taper off.

STATE-LOCAL EXPENDITURES

State-local demands on financial resources take up almost 15 percent of GNP. These demands cannot be ignored even if they are sometimes overwhelmed in significance by federal programs. Expenditures made by the states and local units of government have shown steady increase over time.

The 1980s promise to be especially interesting in terms of potential changes on state and local spending patterns. Continued sharp increases in education expenditures seem unlikely for reasons already mentioned. In addition, although taxpayer discontent with government spending levels seemed to apply rather generally to all levels of government by the late 1970s, explicit action in the form of spending and taxing limits had been taken mostly at state and local government levels. The 1980s may be a decade in which growth in state and local spending is sharply curtailed.

WAGNER'S LAW OF INCREASING PUBLIC ACTIVITY

We have seen that a partial explanation for the growth of the public sector in the United States lies in the pattern of war and defense outlay over time. For the nonwar sectors, both at the federal and the state-local levels, many historical and institutional reasons may be adduced to explain why the national economy has become increasingly collectivized. But a more fundamental examination may be helpful; institutions are themselves patterns formed by individual decisions; and there are no immutable historical laws. Even war expenditures cannot properly be treated as wholly independent of individual choices.

Adolf Wagner, a noted German theorist of the 19th century, propounded an empirical law to the effect that governments inexorably grow larger, that the collective sector of an economy has an inherent tendency to increase in size and importance. Are there any logical reasons why this law, which does seem to have provided an accurate prediction of events, must hold true? Are there certain inherent tendencies for governments to grow larger and larger over time, not only absolutely, but relatively to the size of the economy?

Income elasticity of demand for public services

Such questions as these deserve consideration although they cannot be answered fully. The first step might be some examination of the *income elasticity* of demand for government services. As real income rises, the demand for all goods and services increases. This itself is sufficient to explain why people demand more public services in real terms. But this does not explain why government services have become more and more important relative to privately marketed goods and services. This would be explained only if the income elasticity for government services should be greater than the income elasticity for privately marketed goods.

Income elasticity is a measure of the responsiveness in demand to a change in real income. If real income goes up, an income elasticity of unity would indicate that, percentagewise, the demand for a good goes up proportionately with income. A 1 percent increase in real income would generate a 1 percent increase in the demand for the good in question. If we include saving as a means of using income, we can see that the income elasticity for all dispositions of income together must be unity. Therefore, if the governmental sector expands, relatively, as income expands, the income elasticity for governmental services must exceed unity. A 1 percent increase in real national income must generate a more than 1 percent increase in the quantity of public services demanded. There does seem to be reason for believing that income elasticities of demand for public services are rather high over certain income ranges. Few public services, beyond the barest protective legal structure, seem to be as essential as basic food and clothing. But as income rises beyond subsistence levels, governmental services become more important. Educational services, health services, highways, defense against aggression, and other services begin to loom large in the want patterns of individuals. But this effect may, in itself, extend only over some restricted range of incomes. At certain levels of real income, the elasticities of demand for public services may be quite high. But as real income increases beyond these limits, as individuals become affluent, basic needs for collectively provided services may also be met, and the public clamor for additional public activity may subside. Few generalizations can be advanced concerning the whole question of income elasticity for government services without detailed empirical investigation and inquiry.

Price elasticity of demand and differential productivity

If the forces of economic growth are such that productivity grows more rapidly in the private sector than in the public sector, the costs of public services will increase. If this differential growth of productivity in the two sectors is combined with a low "price" elasticity of demand for public services, total outlay on these services will rise relative to national product. This is a summary of the interesting thesis advanced by Professor William J. Baumol.[2] He argued that the provision of public services is characteristically immune from technological improvement at least by comparison with the private sector. One school teacher can supervise only 25 children, and technological improvements can change this ratio by little if at all. By contrast, the skilled technician, with automation, can supervise the operation of 100 machines where he or she previously supervised only 4. If the resource markets are such that the salaries for teachers must keep pace with those of skilled technicians, the community must spend an ever-increasing share of its total resources on educational services, even to maintain a constant absolute level of output. As the example suggests, Baumol's thesis may be subjected to criticisms, but its central proposition may provide considerable explanatory potential concerning the expanding role of government in the economy.

---

[2] William J. Baumol, *American Economic Review*, vol. 57 (June 1967), pp. 415–26.

Population growth, external diseconomies, and congestion

The single most important explanation for the increasing relative size of government in the economy may lie in the growth of population itself. As population grows relative to space, individuals necessarily become increasingly interdependent. The behavior of one person is increasingly likely to affect the utility function or the production function of some other person. External diseconomies of many sorts, all of which may be summarized under the single term "congestion," clearly become more important as population growth and the ensuing concentration of population in space proceeds. Collective or governmental action to prevent, reduce, or to eliminate the costs of congestion becomes increasingly necessary.

Collective decision processes and the provision of public goods

In the above paragraphs, discussion has been limited to "economic" reasons for the relative growth of governmental activity over time. A more fruitful approach may be that which contrasts the way collective choices are made with choice making in the private sector. By their very nature public services embody elements of indivisibility. They cannot, therefore, be directly "priced" when they are provided to individuals. Payments for public services must be divorced, wholly or partially, from the receipt of the benefits from such services. In the private economy, on the other hand, the receipt of a particular good or service is tied directly to the payment of a price as an integral part of the market exchange process. The individual is fully conscious of cost. The absence of this two-sided relationship in the fiscal process may tend to provide some logical support for the Wagner hypothesis. It will do so if public or collective "needs" are chosen independently of their costs, and if spending decisions are made prior to decisions on taxes. But the reverse might also be true in certain cases. Primary attention to costs, as these are reflected in tax burdens, may cause genuine collective "needs" to be overlooked.

Collective outcomes are, of course, political outcomes, and the final decisions on taxes and spending depend on the types of decision-making rules that are in effect. A careful evaluation of the rules for the reaching of financial decisions, followed by some attempts to predict the outcomes that will emerge, seems to be indicated. Surely the amount of collective spending will, in the normal case, vary with the decision-making rules, and, for this reason, cannot be predicted independently of these rules. This whole problem of collective decision making has, until very recently, been unduly neglected in public finance. We shall return to this topic in Part III.

In a more fundamental sense, Wagner's law, as such, cannot be said to have any logical basis. The decisions of a people concerning the share of total economic resources to be devoted to public rather than private uses cannot really be predicted in advance. Obviously, choices will depend, in part, upon the generally prevailing politico-economic philosophy. The role of government chosen by democratic society will be determined by the conception of the functions of government that is adopted by individual members of the community. During the late 18th and early 19th centuries, the regulatory functions of government were gradually reduced. For more than a century, the pendulum has swung toward more and more governmental regulation of economic life. Predictions are made with great caution here, but there may be signs that this swing will at least partially be stopped in the remaining decades of the 20th century. In the Soviet state, there has been noticeable shifting away from centralized controls over the economy.

DISPLACEMENT AND SCALE EFFECTS

In their study of the growth of public expenditure in Great Britain, Professors Alan Peacock and Jack Wiseman have developed some interesting hypotheses. They suggest that the failure of nondefense spending to return to prewar levels in postwar periods may be explained by what they call a *displacement* effect. In normal times, the possible extension of the public sector is broadly limited by what the general public considers to be a reasonably tolerable level of taxation. A major disturbance such as a war changes this tolerance limit, and invariably the economy is found to be capable of supporting heavier tax loads than had previously been deemed acceptable. In a world dominated by a politico-economic philosophy of expansion in the public services, governments will tend to utilize postwar or post-disturbance periods to expand ordinary services rapidly. And this expansion will be general throughout the public sector. This displacement effect will also be supported by other changes wrought by the major disturbance. Such periods create new and emergency demands on government, even in civilian sector. Governments gain experience in administration and regulation. The bureaucracy is increased in both size and in power. Vested interests emerge in bureaucracy itself, and people come to expect a greater degree of regulatory activity by government. This displacement hypothesis is supplemented by a *scale* hypothesis which suggests that the same factors tend to cause a concentration of financial responsibility in the central government.

These two hypotheses seem suggestive, and they do offer quite plausible explanations for observed facts about public spending over time. They suggest that, in the 20th century, major disturbances explain much of the increase in the relative importance of the public sector. On the other hand, in the absence of major disturbance the public sector may be predicted to increase only gradually and within reasonably prescribed limits. Taken independently, therefore, the Peacock-Wiseman hypotheses could not have predicted the genuine explosion in public spending that took place in the late 1960s. This "Great Society" spending boom took place alongside and not *after* the Vietnam War spending expansion.

SUPPLEMENTARY READING

For a collection of essays that examines in some detail the causes of the growth in government spending, see Thomas Borcherding (ed.), *Budgets and Bureaucracies: The Origins of Government Growth* (Durham, N.C. Duke University Press, 1975).

part II

Social goals
and fiscal
institutions

T he essential purpose of the fiscal
structure is to provide certain goods and services to the individual
members of society. In the modern economy, the quantity of resources channeled through the fiscal process in furtherance of this
purpose is proportionately quite large relative to the economy itself.
The magnitude of the "public sector" is such that important side effects may be exerted by the operation of the fiscal structure. The
question that is at once raised by the recognition of such effects is
whether or not the fisc should be used to further certain widely accepted "social" goals, quite apart from the mere provision of collective goods and services, narrowly defined.

To answer this question, we must first develop a "pure theory" of
government finance; that is to say, we must first discuss what the
fiscal system would look like if the provision of collective goods and
services were its exclusive purpose. What criteria determine how
much the public economy shall provide? How are the costs of public
goods allocated among individuals? There is general agreement that
this "pure theory" is the least satisfactory part of the whole subject
field of public finance, although important advances have recently
been made. In terms of the organization of this textbook, it is necessary that these "principles" be discussed before any more positive
detailed examination of fiscal institutions is undertaken.

69

Several points must be made at the outset. The discussion of the "pure theory" is the most difficult of the whole book. It is impossible to introduce complex ideas simply and accurately at the same time, but we have tried to simplify the argument to the maximum extent possible.

Fiscal theory in this pure sense is concerned with the role of the fiscal system in the political economy. As we define the pure theory here, it amounts to a description of the ideally neutral or ideally efficient fiscal structure. By this we mean that system which uniquely aims at providing the social group with some "optimal" or "efficient" quantity of collective goods and services, and doing so in an "efficient" manner. This description stems from the implicit assumption here that the system is organized solely to provide such goods and services. To use Professor R. A. Musgrave's terminology, the assumption is that the budget serves the allocative function exclusively.

Such an ideally neutral fiscal system would run afoul of other purposes which fiscal systems have, variously, been employed to promote. The discussion must, therefore, introduce a recognition of such conflicting norms for fiscal organization.

Perhaps the most important of these is the promotion of "social justice." The fiscal structure has been viewed as the appropriate instrument or mechanism through which income and wealth might be redistributed among individuals and groups in accordance with idealized norms for distributive justice. This role has been a traditional one for the fiscal system, but it has emerged with new vigor in the discussion of the 1960s and 1970s. To what extent should the budget be used to promote distributional objectives? To what extent can the budget be manipulated to serve such a purpose?

Such questions as these must be asked, and discussed, before any "principles" of taxation and of public spending can be derived. Traditional public finance has not been without its "principles." Hence, some attention must be paid to well-established "principles" for taxation and expenditures. Upon what bases are fiscal decisions now made, and can these orthodox principles be interpreted in recognition of the existing decision structure? How do the "principles" relate to the ways that collective decisions are reached? Can we suggest general rules that are suitable for the democratic process as it operates in modern Western nations?

7

Fiscal neutrality and economic efficiency

THE IDEALLY NEUTRAL
FISCAL SYSTEM

Neutrality has often been mentioned as one of the goals for the organization of a fiscal system, but the concept has rarely been defined with precision. We shall here define the ideally neutral fiscal system as one that provides collective goods and services "efficiently," noting that more than one system might satisfy this requirement. This definition is question begging, however, since "efficiency" itself requires definition.

Before proceeding further, it is best to dispel some false notions about fiscal neutrality. The neutral fiscal system is not one that exerts no influence on individual behavior. What is meant by no influence? There is nothing provided with which to make a comparison. Under a well-established fiscal order, individual behavior must be different from that in an economy which provides no collective goods and services, the no-government economy that we have introduced several times for comparative purposes. The point here can be made by way of a simple illustration. If no police protection were provided by government, private people would change their behavior by hiring more night watchmen, more private detectives. The provision of collective goods through a governmental unit allows for some substitution of these goods for private goods. The very idea of fiscal neutrality cannot, therefore, be conceived in terms of an absence of effect on private choices.

A more appropriate and useful conception may begin with an analogy with the market economy. If the fiscal system is conceived as the means through which collective goods and services are provided to members of the society without any subsidiary or supplementary social purpose, the market analogy comes to mind. We may begin, in this way, to get a better idea of what is meant by "efficiency."

Let us take any ordinary privately produced good, say, shoes. We say that this commodity is efficiently produced if the market price accurately reflects the marginal costs of production. If price equals marginal cost, the consumer is faced with a choice among alternatives which accurately reflects relative costs of this commodity and others. If, for example, a pair of shoes is priced at $20, and $20 equals marginal cost, the customer who purchases shoes is "directing" the economy to devote resources to shoe production which could, otherwise, be used to produce $20 worth in alternative employments. On the other hand, should the market price be $25 we could say that the consumer is not confronted with "true" alternatives. An artificial wedge would be inserted between selling price and genuine opportunity cost. A way could be worked out whereby both the consumer and the resource suppliers could be made better off. The shoes are not provided "efficiently" unless the price is $20.

A more sophisticated and more accurate way of stating this argument is to say that a necessary condition for the "efficient" organization of the market economy is that marginal rates of substitution among goods and services in consumption must be equal to marginal rates of substitution among goods and services in production. If this basic condition is not satisfied, it can be shown that at least one person in the group can be made better off without anyone else in the system being made worse off by some possible rearrangements. An "efficient" position, as defined in modern welfare economics, is a position from which no change can be made without someone being made worse off. There are, of course, many positions or situations that may qualify as "efficient" under this definition.

As we saw in Chapter 4, the characteristic feature of collective goods is the indivisibility of the services provided among the individual recipients. From this it follows that such goods and services cannot be directly "priced"; the market analogy cannot be fully applied (if it could be, there would be no need for government). The benefits from the lighthouse shine on all users indiscriminately, quite independently of the individual contributions or taxes toward its support. The same can be said of national defense. It is impossible to sell separate individuals divisible units of public services to the extent that these services are, in fact, indivisible. But some method of financing such services must be worked out, and this is the conceptual origin of the tax system.

In spite of the impossibility of "pricing" genuinely collective goods directly, some method of allocating or distributing the costs of such services may be worked out which is closely analogous to the pricing process in ordinary markets. The necessary conditions are the same as those which must be satisfied for private goods markets. Individuals must be placed in a position where the marginal rates of substitution among both private goods and collective goods in usage or consumption are equal to the marginal rates of substitution among both private and collective goods in production. For a single collective good, an "efficient" total quantity is provided when the aggregate marginal evaluation of that good by all citizens is equal to the marginal cost, that is, to the marginal rate of substitution between this good and money on the production side.

A simple example will clarify this. Suppose that we are considering a single island society with only the two citizens, Mr. Crusoe and Mr. Friday. The decision they confront is, say, whether to build a fishing net (a collective good) 10 feet long or 12 feet long. The difference in the total cost of building the two nets is six days' labor. Now let us say that the first citizen, Mr. Crusoe, estimates the additional length of the net to be worth four days' labor to him, personally. If the second citizen, Mr. Friday, considers the larger net to be worth, to him, as much as two days' labor time, the "collectivity" should decide to build the net to the longer size.

Even in such a simple example as this, however, there arise difficulties that are not encountered when we discuss efficiency in private goods markets. In the latter, since goods are wholly divisible as among final consumers, there is no distinction between what may be called satisfaction of the "aggregative marginal condition" and satisfaction of what may be called the individual marginal conditions. With the provision of collective goods, the first of these conditions may be satisfied without the second. This may be shown in our example. If the combined marginal evaluation of the added length of the fishing net exceeds six days' labor, the incremental addition should be made, on aggregative efficiency grounds, regardless of the way in which the two men share this cost; that is, regardless of the distribution of the "taxes" among them. So long as the summed marginal evaluation equals or exceeds the marginal cost of the incremental addition to the collective goods, the quantity of the collective good is not in excess of that which is "efficient." Neutrality is present, in one sense, when this aggregative marginal condition is met. Full neutrality is not present, however, until and unless each person has assigned to him a share in the cost that is equal to his own marginal evaluation. In our example, full neutrality is attained only when Crusoe is "taxed" at a rate of four days' labor and Friday is "taxed" at a rate of two days' labor. Here *both* the aggregative marginal condition and the individual marginal condition are satisfied. No change could possibly be worked out which would be to the benefit of both parties, and no member of the group would choose to cancel the decision that is made.

In this way it becomes conceptually possible for us to imagine an ideally "efficient" or "neutral" fiscal system. Each individual will pay an incremental or marginal tax for collective goods and services that is equal to the incremental benefits that he or she receives from these goods and services (the marginal evaluation that he places on them), and each collective good or service will be provided in sufficient quantity as to make total incremental benefits equal to the marginal cost of supplying the service. For example, if the citizens of the United States, taken together, should evaluate the benefits from an additional MIRV missile complex at $20 billion, this development should be undertaken if the added cost is less than $20 billion. These aggregate costs should then be distributed, through the tax system, in relation to individual marginal evaluations or benefits. If the incremental costs are estimated to exceed $20 billion under these conditions of demand, the development project should not be undertaken. The tax system that imposes on the people a higher aggregate cost, or which distributes this cost in some manner contrary to that determined by individual evaluation of the marginal benefits, must violate full fiscal neutrality in the sense here defined.

From the discussion to this point, it is clear that the "efficient" or "neutral" fiscal system must embody taxation on the basis of the so-called benefit principle. However, it should be noted that the proper interpretation of this principle in this connection is that taxes should be levied so as to equal *marginal* benefits of collectively provided goods and services, not *total* benefits. The failure to distinguish between these two possible interpretations of the benefit principle has been the source of much confusion. If taxes were levied such that total costs to taxpayers were equal to total benefits from public consumption, then "taxpayers' surplus" (the public sector analogue to consumers' surplus) would equal zero. This implies a public sector which is much too large relative to the private sector. Taxpayers would be indifferent between having public services provided at current levels or having no public services at all. If, on the other hand, marginal taxes and marginal public service benefits are equated, taxpayers' surplus is at a maximum. Net benefits from public consumption are as large as possible.

FISCAL NEUTRALITY IN THE PROVISION OF PUBLIC GOODS: A GEOMETRIC ANALYSIS

The preceding discussion can be presented in terms of the familiar supply and demand diagrammatics common to much of economic analysis. For some students, at least, such an exercise may help clarify the key concepts involved. For expositional simplicity and in keeping with the verbal discussion of the preceding sections, we will work with a very simple two-consumer model.

Suppose, in Figure 7–1, the quantity of some public, indivisible good, X, is measured on the horizontal axis. Individual marginal evaluations and the marginal cost of production are measured on the vertical axis, all denominated in money terms. The two curves labeled ME^A and ME^B are the marginal evaluation curves for our two consumers, A and B. The relationship depicted is that between the quantity of X being consumed and the marginal value placed on X by the individual. If income effects are assumed to be insignificant, these marginal evaluation curves are closely analogous to individual demand curves in market analysis. Although *individual* demand relationships are conceptually identical regardless of whether the good being demanded is divisible or indivisible, derivation of the *aggregate* demand relationships is very different. If the good in question is purely private and divisible, individual demand curves are horizontally summed to get aggregate demand. If the good is purely public, individual marginal evaluation curves must be vertically summed. This is because all individuals must jointly consume the same physical quantity of a public good. The summed marginal evaluations of

FIGURE 7-1

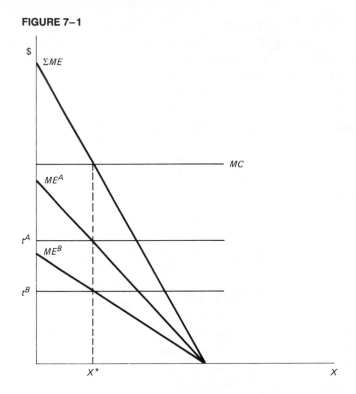

individuals thus reflects aggregate willingness to pay for marginal expansion in consumption of the good.

This can be clarified if we return to our simple two consumer model in Figure 7–1. The vertical summation of the marginal evaluation curves of the two individuals is that labeled ΣME in the diagram. The "aggregate marginal condition" referred to in the earlier discussion is simply a necessary condition for efficiency in public goods provision which states that the summed marginal evaluations of consumers be equal to the marginal cost of production. This condition is fulfilled at quantity X^* in the diagram as indicated by the intersection of ΣME and the marginal cost curve (labeled MC). If some quantity less than X^* is being provided, the aggregate willingness of the two individuals to pay for a small increment in consumption exceeds what it would actually cost to provide that increment. It is possible, in other words, to divide the cost of increasing consumption by one unit between the two individuals such that each would be better off paying his or her assigned share of the extra cost and enjoying the additional consumption. If some quantity greater than X^* is being consumed, it is possible to reduce production of the good and compensate each individual for his or her reduced consumption from the resulting cost savings.

Note that the aggregate condition says nothing about how cost shares should actually be assigned to the two consumers. The individual marginal conditions required for full fiscal neutrality in our framework are only fulfilled, however, when individual A is paying a marginal tax price of t^A and individual B is paying a marginal tax price of t^B. When this allocation of tax shares is in effect, each individual is in full marginal equilibrium vis-a-vis the public sector. Given the tax price, the public sector is just the right size from his or her individual perspective. The market analogy is complete. Just as the individual chooses to purchase that quantity of a private good in the market such that his or or her marginal evaluation of the good is equal to price, the individual is "purchasing" through the public sector that quantity of the public good for which marginal evaluation and marginal tax price are equal.

Wicksell's principle of taxation

As we know, and as we shall see, the ideally efficient fiscal system that has been sketched out briefly has never been put into practice, primarily because other purposes than efficiency have always affected decisions on fiscal organization. Because of this, little attention has been given to the problem of trying to put any elements of this purely neutral system into institutional reality. Until the last quarter century (during which exciting contributions emerged) Knut Wicksell, a distinguished Swedish economist who wrote near the turn of the century, was the only scholar to recognize this problem. He proposed a unique scheme for implementing the efficiency principle in taxation and spending. It will be helpful to discuss Wicksell's plan briefly.

The first step that would have to be taken to organize a fiscal system along efficiency lines would be to tie each decision on public expenditure to a decision on the distribution of the tax burden. No approximation to a "correct" quantity of collective services can be attained until the two sides of the budget account are joined in some way. Second, Wicksell proposed that the ordinary democratic decision-making rule of majority voting be suspended for fiscal decisions of the normal variety. Ideally, unanimity among members of the legislative body should be required, but Wicksell recognized the extreme limitations of this restriction. Accordingly, he stated that the simple majority rule be replaced in fiscal decisions by some rule of a relative unanimity. Relative unanimity was defined in terms of some qualified majority, perhaps five sixths of the members of the assembly.

When a new item of public spending is proposed, under the Wicksell scheme, a whole set of alternative distributions of the tax load required to finance the item of spending is drawn up. These are then taken up by the assembly in order. As soon as one of these distributions receives a required majority, the expenditure is to be adopted along with the tax bill chosen. If no tax distribution which can secure the required support exists, the proposed expenditure is to be rejected.

The Wicksell approach may be illustrated by an example. Suppose that a municipality is trying to decide whether or not to build a new civic auditorium. If the auditorium is really desired by the citizens, that is, desired more than alternative uses of the required funds, there must exist at least one, and possibly several, arrangements of the costs among the citizens upon which all of them will agree, or substantially so. If no such distribution exists, the auditorium is not valued as highly as the private goods and services that could be purchased with the tax dollars in its stead. Hence the project is not efficient, and it should be rejected. Wicksell was attempting, with these models, to suggest real-world institutions that might be required to ensure a neutral or efficient fiscal system.

There are, of course, difficulties in the Wicksell scheme. He did not appreciate adequately the costs of reaching decisions under the restrictive decision rules that he suggested, and he may have talked in terms of overly simplified fiscal structures. Nevertheless, his approach suggests that there are, and must be, sharp discrepancies between any modern fiscal system and that which would be required to satisfy the necessary conditions for efficiency. The fiscal system, as it exists, is clearly not neutral or efficient. There is little chance that collective goods and services are provided in any approximation to the "optimal" quantities that individual evaluations would determine. Some services are probably overextended; other services may be provided to less than "optimum" levels. The reason for this apparent inefficiency is that the existing systems were constructed and have evolved with relatively little, if any, regard for neutrality or efficiency in the sense here discussed. Other purposes have been dominant in shaping our fiscal structure. Subsequent chapters of Part 3 will discuss some of these other goals.

SECOND ORDER EFFICIENCY

The fully "efficient" fiscal system could serve as a norm for institutional reorganization only if the system were to be uniquely devoted to the provision of collective goods and services: that is to say, only if it serves an allocation function exclusively. Modern societies, however, have shown a willingness to sacrifice "efficiency" in the sense here discussed in order to employ the fisc for other purposes, most notably the redistribution of income. To what extent can economic efficiency, in the more orthodox sense, be retained as a criterion for actual fiscal organization?

When we say that collective goods and services are not provided efficiently, we are saying that taxes and public expenditures are not directly related in the decision making of the individual who participates in democratic choice institutions. Under these circumstances, then, taxes and public expenditures can modify the behavior of the individual in many possible ways. If an individual is faced with a tax bill that does not reflect his own marginal evaluation of the increment of public services being financed, this tax charge takes on the characteristics of a net withdrawal of real income. With reduced real income, the individual will modify his behavior with the direction of change depending on the precise nature of the tax.

The difficulties described above suggest an approach to second-order efficiency which is the result of moving to the other extreme from the position implicit in the previous discussion of the ideally neutral fiscal system. Suppose that instead of assuming that the fiscal system is organized solely to provide collective goods, it is instead assumed that no collective goods of any sort are provided. Individual taxpayers would regard tax revenues as net withdrawals from the economy with no benefits being provided in return. We know, that to some extent, taxpayers do think of the tax system in this way. Under these circumstances, the principle of "least price distortion" might provide a reasonable normative framework for organizing the tax system. Taxes affect relative prices in the private sector, with different types of taxes having different effects. Relative prices, in turn, exert an important influence on the behavior and choices of individuals. The norm of "least price distortion" simply requires that the tax system be designed to minimize the welfare loss resulting from any inefficient choices caused by tax-induced changes in the structure of relative prices.

At this point we must face up to a difficulty which cannot be resolved without a long and complex argument. Unless all parts of the economy are simultaneously adjusted, we cannot with full accuracy say that, under these conditions, the fiscal institution which distorts private choices the least necessarily increases overall "efficiency" in the private economy more than its alternatives. The fiscal principle of "least price distortion," which has often been advanced, is not fully correct. Under certain conditions, a tax that is used deliberately to insert a wedge between a selling price and a cost or supply price may lead to more efficient private decisions. The result depends in each case on the types and the extent of distortion already presented in the alternatives for private choice prior to the tax levy, as well as on numerous other relationships among economic variables. Modern theories of "optimal taxation" utilize the tools of sophisticated general equilibrium theory in an attempt to offer definitive results here. As mentioned, this elementary book is not the appropriate place to elaborate these models. It will be sufficient to say only that we may accept the principle of "least price distortion" as a "second best" or "second-order" approach to efficiency. We must recognize that the results arising from a rigorous application of this principle will not always be the desired ones. It seems reasonable, nevertheless, that application of the principle will normally lead to more efficient private choices.

What specific implications arise from this principle of "least price distortion?" First of all, when we consider the taxing side of the fiscal process, the principle indicates that normally the more general the tax, the less it will interfere with individual choices. The general income tax is preferred on these grounds to the particular excise or commodity tax. The former reduces income without placing a particular incentive on the consumer to modify his consumption in a specific manner. The tax imposed on several or all commodities will tend to be preferred over the tax on a single commodity.

The lump-sum tax

Somewhat interestingly, the "ideal" tax from the point of the principle of "least price distortion" is the lump-sum, or poll, tax. A tax levied upon the individual independently of a quantitative base can exert little influence on his behavior. Behavior will be modified only to the extent that the reduced real income of the individual reduces his consumption opportunities. The tax provides the individual with no incentive to economize on any form of consumption. The lump-sum tax is unimportant in actual fiscal systems. The conception is useful only in certain analytical models as this tax is contrasted with others which do exert more important effects on behavior.

The general proportionate income tax

Leaving the lump-sum tax, the tax that is levied proportionately on personal income satisfies the least distortion criterion quite well. The individual is attracted to consume more leisure than he would without the tax, but his general pattern of consumption is not greatly modified. His choice between methods of earning real income as between the riskier and the less risky ventures is not affected as would be the case with the progressive income tax.

The general sales tax

If taxation is to be placed on the purchase or consumption of particualr commodities, the least distortion principle indicates that one which is levied on the whole range of commodities is perhaps to be preferred over the tax which is concentrated on one or a few commodities. This tax is, of course, typical of many of the state revenue structures of the United States.

The lump-sum subsidy

Effects on the expenditure side are quite similar to those on the tax side. The "ideal" expenditure from the view of exerting the least distortion on individual private choice is the payment of lump-sum subsidies to individuals. These subsidies, which would be completely unrelated to the economic status of the individual, would influence behavior only to the extent that real income increases cause certain changes in the choice pattern.

The conception of general expenditure

Nothing on the public spending side corresponds closely with the general proportional income tax on the tax side. The idea of public expenditure being devoted to projects which are of general benefit to all members of the community is meaningful only to a certain extent. National defense expenditures are perhaps the closest modern equivalent. For the most part, however, expenditures are made for particular projects and the benefits from each of the collective projects undertaken will tend to affect specially situated groups in the economy. If this is true, significant effects on individual behavior must be expected. A single example will suffice. The decision to build the Tennessee Valley Authority affected private decisions in the Tennessee Valley.

Here we record an interesting phenomenon in the development of fiscal theory and policy. The principle of organizing the system so as to effect the least possible distortion in the structure of individual choices has been applied to tax distribution, but it has not been applied to the distribution of public expenditures. Yet, quite clearly, if the principle is applicable on the one side it is applicable on the other. There is no more reason for saying that a general tax is to be preferred over a specific one than there is for saying that a general expenditure program is to be preferred over a specific program, specific being defined geographically or otherwise.

This introduces a peculiar asymmetry in fiscal theory that we shall have occasion to refer to again later in the book. Fiscal tradition has been built on the idea that the least distortion principle applies only to the tax side of the account. This idea has affected the legal structure of the government. The courts have interpreted the U.S. Constitution to say that geographical uniformity of taxes is required. In other words, an individual in California must be accorded the same federal tax treatment as the equally situated individual in Virginia. But mention has rarely been made of the necessity for benefits from federal expenditures to be provided equally to equally situated individuals, either geographically or otherwise.

EQUITY AND EFFICIENCY

Equal treatment for equals

As suggested previously, the conception of fiscal equity, that is, equal treatment for equally situated individuals, has been applied to the distribution of taxes, but not to the distribution of expenditures in the same manner. This equity criterion, although motivated on grounds completely divorced from economic efficiency, does carry with it certain implications for efficiency in the structure of private choices. The equal-treatment-for-equals principle does not guarantee that private choices are not modified by the fiscal structure, but it does, if fully applied, serve to prevent differential effects on separate groups or individuals. The meaningfulness of this equity principle depends, however, on the way in which "equals" are defined for purposes of fiscal treatment. Differential taxes could be imposed without violation of the technical version of the equity principle if the group of "equals" is defined sufficiently narrowly. For example, a tax could conceivably be imposed on all redheaded, nonsmoking bachelors. To the extent that the same tax is applied on all persons in this category, the principle of equity could be applied. But common sense indicates that such a tax would be held to violate the real meaning of the principle. To be acceptable, a tax must be applied to rather broad groupings; in other words, "equals" for fiscal purposes must be defined in some reasonable and not wholly arbitrary manner.

To the extent that this is true, the general respect for the equity principle in the organization of the fiscal structure has been one factor tending to maintain general neutrality in its effects. The deliberate distortion of private choices in a differential way has been prevented, especially in the distribution of taxes. Much of the opposition to the erosion of the income tax base through numerous loopholes, tax shelter, and tax credit schemes stems from the fear that these violate the long-standing principle of horizontal equity. These devices tend to classify individuals, not in accordance with their ability to pay, but in accordance with the relationship of their private activity to some concept of "public interest."

This equity principle will be discussed in more detail in a later chapter. At this point it is suggested merely as one factor which, unintentionally, serves to prevent undue distortion of the resource allocation mechanism of the private economy by the fiscal structure.

EFFICIENCY AS A FISCAL NORM

Insofar as efficiency in the private economy has constituted a goal of fiscal organization, it has done so more or less negatively. That is to say, the principle of least resource or least price distortion, as reinforced by the principle of equity, has caused fiscal institutions to be constructed so as to allow generally free play for private economic decisions. A more positive role for the fiscal system in actually promoting economic efficiency has rarely been proposed or adopted.

There are two fundamental reasons why the tax expenditure structure should not be employed deliberately to promote economic efficiency. The first reason lies in the difficulty of defining and of distinguishing changes which will, in fact, produce greater "efficiency" in the total economy. We have briefly touched on the "second best" difficulty previously. But even disregarding this, no objectively determinate measure of economic efficiency exists that might be utilized to guide fiscal decisions. In some situations the maximization of real national income might appear to be an acceptable measure, but its limitations may be illustrated by a single example.

Suppose that a proposal is submitted to provide public subsidies for out-migration of individuals and families from areas of low average incomes. These subsidies will encourage some families to migrate to the areas of the economy with higher average incomes. As measured in terms of total national income, the national economy is made more "efficient" by the change. But actually the individuals involved may have been just as satisfied in the low-income regions; there is no objective way of measuring this sort of "income" except in terms of individual choices. Measured real income will tend to give a false notion of objectivity to the conception of "efficiency."

A second reason for saying that the tax expenditure structure should not be employed to promote overall economic efficiency in a positive way is based on a recognition of the actual process of decision making in a democratically organized society. The first objections may be disregarded in a despotism where all collective decisions are made by a single individual or a single-minded group. "Efficiency" in such a system may be defined as desired by the chooser, and the fiscal system may be used, along with other devices, to promote greater "efficiency" as defined. In a democracy, however, collective decision making is a complex process. Final decisions are the result of a whole chain of individual voting procedures, the debates and choices of representative assemblies, the exercise of executive leadership, the partisan activity of political parties, the conflicts of pressure group interest, and the intricacies of bureaucratic administration. At no place in this decision-making process can overall "efficiency" in the private economy be taken as the overriding aim, and fiscal devices cannot readily be geared to accomplish such "efficiency." Instead, if the efficiency-promoting purpose of the fiscal system is admitted as legitimate, there will likely arise a rather irresponsible and arbitrary set of fiscal devices, presented under the guise of "efficiency," which will serve to restrict the reasonably free operation of the market economy. In other words, the decision process represented, say, in the U.S. federal government, seems likely to be unable to distinguish "efficient" from "inefficient" changes, even in the broadest possible sense. Instead of providing subsidies to outmigration from depressed areas created by a declining resource base, the decision structure is likely to produce subsidies to industries and to individuals to remain in the uneconomic areas. In the name of securing greater efficiency, the actual decision process will tend to produce results like the tax depletion allowance for certain extractive industries which serves to attract an excessive quantity of investment into those industries. While good arguments can be advanced for particular subsidies and/or tax credits designed to accomplish specific objectives, there is genuine prospect of a Pandora's box of fiscal gimmicks being opened via the ordinary workings of the political process.

CONCLUSIONS

The ideally neutral or "efficient" fiscal system is one that has as a single purpose the provision of collective goods and services to individuals. This system will make the tax expenditure process as closely analogous to the market economy as is possible. But due to the indivisibility of benefits from collective goods and services, direct "pricing" is not available. Hence the tax structure must be made to reflect individual evaluations of the marginal benefits from government services, and the total quantity of public services provided must be based on some aggregation of these individual evaluations. In one sense, the "ideal" principle of taxation is the benefit principle. Until quite recently, Knut Wicksell has been the only economist who attempted to trace out the implications of the ideally neutral fiscal system in terms of decision-making institutions.

Many other goals are embodied in the actual fiscal systems of the modern world. Hence we can expect some external effects to be exerted on individual behavior by both taxes and public expenditures. Second-order efficiency can still be taken as a proximate goal for judging taxes and expenditure proposals, although the limitations must be kept in mind. Normally, other things remaining the same, when considered independently that tax or expenditure which affects the behavior of the individual the least should be preferred. This allows the principle of least price or least resource distortion to have some meaning.

Using the least distortion principle, in isolation from all others, the lump-sum, or poll tax may be taken as the proximate ideal. This tax exerts an influence on individual behavior only through its effects on real income. Applied more generally, the least distortion principle allows the general income tax to be preferred over the commodity tax, and the proportional tax over the progressive tax. It also allows a normative judgment favoring the general sales tax applied to all commodities over the specific excise tax levied on one or a few commodities.

Similar conclusions can be applied to the expenditure side, but we noted the asymmetry that exists here. The conception of general expenditure has never been rigorously formulated nor has the idea been translated into the actual fiscal structure.

Beyond the idea of least distortion, it is possible to use the fiscal system positively in actually promoting economic efficiency. We may cite instances of this usage, but we have argued against this extension of the system. Efficiency is a difficult concept to define at best, and the institutions for decision making are imperfect. Widespread departure from the ideal of least distortion, as supplemented by the principle of equity, would seem to open the door for all sorts of experimental tinkering with the tax expenditure structure, with dubious effects.

SUPPLEMENTARY READING

The student interested in Wicksell's early presentation of the pure theory of public finance and in his specific proposals should consult Knut Wicksell, "A New Principle of Just Taxation," contained in International Economic

Association, *Classics in the Theory of Public Finance,* R. A. Musgrave and A. T. Peacock (eds.) (London: Macmillan & Co., 1958). The work by Lindahl in this same volume is also relevant.

The most complete formal statement of the pure theory in recent works is to be found in the two basic articles by Paul A. Samuelson, "The Pure Theory of Public Expenditure," *Review of Economics and Statistics,* vol. 36 (November 1954), pp. 387–89, and "Diagrammatic Exposition of a Theory of Public Expenditure," *Review of Economics and Statistics,* vol. 37 (November 1955), pp. 350–56.

Chapter 4 in R. A. Musgrave's treatise, *The Theory of Public Finance* (New York: McGraw-Hill Book Co., 1959) should also be consulted.

James M. Buchanan, *Demand and Supply of Public Goods* (Chicago: Rand McNally & Co., 1968), treats the material discussed in the early parts of this chapter in monograph length.

8

Redistribution via the fiscal process

The fiscal process of taxing and spending offers a means through which the government can redistribute real income and wealth among individuals and families. To many persons, the redistributive aspects of the fiscal process loom as more important than the financing of public goods and services. Further, as the factual record suggests, fiscal transfers have become increasingly important in the government budget in the United States, and notably so after the middle of the 1960s.

INCOME DISTRIBUTION IN THE MINIMAL OR PROTECTIVE STATE

It will be useful to commence the analysis with reference to the principles of income distribution in an economy where government is limited to a protective role, where government's only duties are those of protecting private rights to life and property, and to enforcing contracts.

Resource owners in such an economy will be rewarded on the basis of the contributions to product value that are made by the resource services supplied. Traders or entrepreneurs will be rewarded in accordance with the net additions to resource values that their innovative insights generate. Rates of return to resource services will tend toward equality with the marginal value productivity of such services in the economy. The income shares of individuals will be determined by the amount of resources owned along with the value that the market places on these.

In such a pure market economy, individuals who possess no marketable resources and who do not have entrepreneurial talents will not be able to subsist except through the private charity of other persons who do possess either marketable resources or such talents. On the other hand, some individuals and families will probably receive extremely high incomes, which will, in turn, allow them to become very wealthy. And if wealth is allowed to be passed along through separate generations, the income prospects of individuals lucky enough to be born into such families are greatly enhanced. In the pure market economy, the actual distribution of the social product may involve significant differences among separate families. No generalized statement as to the proximate extent of inequality that would arise in such an economy can be made, and it is not even possible to say whether inequality would be greater or less than that which we might observe in the economy where government plays an active role.

THE ETHICS OF MARGINAL
PRODUCTIVITY DISTRIBUTION

The payment of resource services in accordance with marginal productivity serves an essential function in the market economy. The prices of such services cause resource owners to shift resource units into those employments where they are most productive, as determined by the buyers in the marketplace. Further, payments in accordance with marginal productivity tend to cause firms to combine different resources so as to produce goods at the lowest possible cost. For both of these reasons, marginal productivity payment leads to economic efficiency, to greater real national product. Insofar as higher real income is a desirable objective, marginal productivity distribution tends to have some ethical justification.

Other ethical ideals may come into conflict with that of higher real income. If income shares could be closely correlated with individual efforts, payment in accordance with marginal productivity might be difficult to argue against. Few persons, even those who might get the lowest incomes, could object to wide disparities in measured incomes if these disparities were seen to reflect the results of private choices.

This point is often overlooked and should be emphasized. And a considerable part of the observed differences in income and wealth can be explained to result from private decisions. A useful way of putting this is as follows: Even if everyone started adult life with precisely equal capacities, that is, with equal economic opportunities, the market system, by allowing full play for private choices, would produce significant differences in measured incomes in any given period of time. The richest persons in the system would be those who choose to work the hardest and to take the highest risks, those who are lucky, and those who choose to save and invest. The poorest persons, in measured income terms, would be those who prefer leisure to work, who desire security rather than risk, who are unlucky, and who prefer current consumption to future consumption.

The facts are, of course, that individuals are not equal in capacities to produce values and that persons do not confront genuinely equal economic opportunities. Therefore, some part of the observed inequality in the distribution of economic rewards results not from free private choices but from initial differences in endowments and capacities.

Equality of opportunity must be an important goal of any society that professes adherence to democratic or individualistic principles of social organization. The idea of a free society imposing upon itself certain broad and general constraints within which private individual choices are to be allowed to operate more or less presupposes that the decision-making individuals are afforded reasonably equal opportunities when the choices are made. There is, however, a vast gap between general acceptance of equality of opportunity as a desirable social goal and general agreement on the degree to which governmental action to achieve such a goal should be authorized. Equality of economic opportunity is almost impossible to define rigorously, and, even if an acceptable definition were possible, there would be wide dispute over the best means of attaining it. Further, any attempts to promote equality of opportunity through governmental action would conflict with competing ethical goals. Absolute equality of opportunity, however defined, remains as one of several aims of overall social policy.

What may we conclude from this brief discussion of the ethics of distribution? Four separate criteria have been mentioned: (1) the maximization of real national income, (2) the equation of effort and reward, (3) the equalization of endowments and capacities, and (4) the equalization of access to product values. The first two of these need not come into sharp conflict. But these conflict sharply with any overt attempts to promote (3) and (4). Traditionally, the compromise has been to make some effort to further (3). In the 1960s and 1970s, however, redistribution rhetoric, and to some extent redistribution policy, has shifted toward (4). At the same time, the costs imposed in the sacrifice of objectives (1) and (2) have come to be more widely recognized.

REDISTRIBUTION THROUGH AN IDEALIZED FISCAL PROCESS

Some income and wealth redistribution seems to be generally accepted as a desirable social goal. The fiscal system seems to offer one means through which this might be accomplished without imposing unnecessary costs in terms of efficiency losses. But a critical distinction must be made between the redistribution that might be accomplished through some idealized working of the fiscal system under the control of some benevolent government and the redistribution that might actually be predicted to occur under the operation of the governmental process that approaches the political reality we observe. It will be useful to examine redistribution under idealized politics initially. In the following part, the realities of politics will be introduced and the effects of this change in setting on the prospects for redistribution will be analyzed.

Even in the idealized political structure, the fiscal system necessarily involves redistribution, if for no other reason than that tax collections reflect coercive withdrawal of income from persons, and spending reflects provision of benefits to other persons in the economy. But there are several means through which the fiscal system may modify income and wealth distribution. We shall find it useful to discuss each of these separately.

DISTRIBUTION IN AN IDEALLY NEUTRAL STRUCTURE WHEN REDISTRIBUTION AS SUCH IS NOT A COLLECTIVE GOOD

Assume initially that a pure market economy is operating with distribution based strictly on marginal productivity. Government's role is limited to the protective function. Now assume that the provision-financing of a single public good or service is collectivized; a public sector is created. As the discussion in Chapter 2 emphasized, collectivization implies a shift toward equalization in the distribution of benefits from this good or service, regardless of the origins of the organizational change. Assume that the good or service is technologically such that common consumption is dictated. Let us further assume that the provision of this good or service is to be made economically efficient in the sense discussed in Chapter 7. The results will be that persons will receive equal consumption flows from the governmental provision of the good or service. In order that neutrality should accompany this equality in consumption flows, individuals must be charged in accordance with their differing marginal evaluations of the good or service. Since the nature of collective provision implies equality of consumption flows, persons cannot adjust differently to quantities of the good or service, as in the private market. Adjustments must be made in the tax prices paid for the good or service. Hence, even an ideally neutral fiscal structure must embody a scheme of marginal tax differentials.

If this elementary principle is recognized, an important principle emerges. When a mixed economy is evaluated, which includes goods and services provided through privately organized markets and through government, *the degree of distributional equality will be directly related to the size of the governmental sector, even if no direct attempt is made to promote greater equality, as such, through the fiscal process,* provided that economic efficiency is the objective for governmental action and provided that government operates in some fashion that approximates the ideal of benevolence. If either or both of these important provisions is not operative, the fiscal structure becomes an instrument through which particular groups in power may secure distributional gains at the expense of other groups. We shall discuss this prospect more thoroughly in the following main section.

REDISTRIBUTION AS A GENUINELY COLLECTIVE GOOD

A more comprehensive approach to the fiscal process suggests that income-wealth redistribution itself be examined and analyzed as a collective good or service. Empirical observation suggests that individuals do concern themselves with the well-being of others, and that they are willing to agree on tax-spending arrangements that are de-signed to alleviate poverty.

In one sense, the provision of funds to alleviate poverty is a classic example of a collective activity. The transfer of $1 to a poor person which improves his well-being is available to all persons in the col-lective group. The benefits are indivisible as among separate persons; individuals cannot readily be excluded. This suggests that even if all taxes should be levied on the basis of marginal benefits, that is, even if the attempt is made to achieve strict neutrality in the fiscal struc-ture, some funds would be devoted to income-wealth redistribution. Individuals, as taxpayers-beneficiaries, would probably be willing to reduce their own measured income levels in exchange for improve-ments in the well-being of others.

There are two distinct ways in which redistribution can be treated as a collective good. The extent to which each of these will be ob-served depends on the precise way in which individuals consider the interdependence that is involved. If individuals are interested in the utility levels of others, in some general sense, collective action may take the form of transfers of generalized purchasing power to those in need. No attempt would be made to restrict the freedom of recipients to choose among goods and services as they see fit. Many of the argu-ments in support of a negative income tax assume that the inter-dependence takes this form. Individuals may not, however, be specif-ically interested in the utility levels of others apart from the observed behavioral traits that relief of poverty promises. A potential taxpayer may be unwilling to support fiscal schemes designed to transfer generalized purchasing power to the poor, while at the same time he may be willing to support schemes which transfer specific income in kind to the poor. Examples of the latter may be programs to provide housing, food, medical care, recreational facilities, and so on. Experi-ence suggests that the income in kind transfer is more likely to be observed, although recent academic interest in negative income taxa-tion may well be followed by wide-spread political support.

Whether redistribution is or is not a collective good that is valued as such by individuals is an empirical question. But one important aspect of such a question is often overlooked. This aspect involves the *size* and the *characteristics* of the community of persons that are con-sidered. The "publicness" of redistribution may be very real, empiri-cally, if the persons who might be benefited are considered to be members of the "relevant community" by those who are taxed. By contrast, redistribution to persons who are considered to stand outside the appropriately-defined community may not qualify in any meaningful grounds of "publicness", at least in terms of evaluations. This aspect of the problem has important implications for the location of the redistributive function as among separate levels of government. Individual citizens who might enthusiastically support plans for the provision of poverty relief to needy persons in their town, may, at the same time, vigorously oppose generalized schemes for federal or central government welfare schemes. Taxpayers who might support income transfers to the poor within the United States may, at the same time, oppose international transfers in the form of foreign aid, even when it is recognized that those persons in developing nations are much more poverty stricken than any of the poor in America.

Constitutional redistribution emergent from social contract

In the two preceding sections, we have discussed possible redistribution of incomes and assets through the fiscal process on the implicit assumption that the prefiscal or initial set of individual claims to income flows and to stock of assets is acknowledged in the legal order, in the ongoing constitutional framework. This assumption may not, however, be fully legitimate, and redistribution through the fiscal process may be "explained" as an inherent part of the "social contract" in which individual claims and rights are settled. That is to say, individuals may acquiesce in the structure of private property rights only if they know that there is a continuing redistributive process generated via the fiscal system. In effect, the fiscal redistribution may embody the constitutional claims of individuals, claims which are as much a part of the genuine "social contract" in existence as the more directly measurable claims to privately held assets. We may discuss this sort of redistribution under four separate subheadings.

Rawlsian maximin principles of social justice.   Much of the discussion of income and wealth redistribution in the early 1970s was stimulated directly by the publication of John Rawls' book, *A Theory of Justice* (1971).[1] This work attracted widespread attention of

---

[1] John Rawls, *A Theory of Justice* (Cambridge, Mass.: Harvard University Press, 1971).

economists, philosphers, and other social scientists. Rawls asks: How can social justice be defined? He proposes to answer this question as follows: Suppose that each person imagines himself or herself to be behind a "veil of ignorance," in a setting where he or she has as much chance of being in any one position as another in the society. From such a setting, are there principles upon which all persons might agree? Rawls then suggests one such principle as a distributive rule, one that might emerge from such an idealized contract. This is the maximin principle, and one that has been much disputed since Rawls's book was published. This principle, or rule, states that income and wealth differences are acceptable only to the extent that such differences act to benefit the persons in the least advantaged positions in the social order. That is to say, the rich are allowed to retain higher incomes only if this retention serves the purpose, through added incentives for effort, for capital accumulation, and other means, of improving the lot of the poor.

Rawls himself does not specifically propose redistribution policy. He is suggesting the more positive proposition that some such "principle" does, in fact, inform the thinking of men in liberal society, and that the institutions which we observe may reflect some such redistributive aspirations. We need not fully accept the maximin criterion to recognize the value of Rawls's effort here. There is no need to be nearly so precise as to what sort of agreement might actually emerge from those who imagine themselves behind a veil of ignorance. Some precepts akin to those made specific by Rawls might well emerge, and insofar as individuals, in fact, do consider such principles important objectives for social policy, we might observe some attempts to put these objectives into action.

Insurance principles in constitutional contract.   In an earlier model which closely resembles that developed in more detail by Rawls, Buchanan and Tullock argued, in a more positive vein, that we might "explain" some of the fiscal redistribution we observe as a result of an insurance motivation embodied in constitutional contract.[2] They postulated that individuals, at some moment of decision on a whole set of constitutional arrangements, may have been largely uncertain about their own income positions in subsequent periods over which the contract agreed on was expected to be in operation. In

---

[2] See James M. Buchanan and Gordon Tullock, *The Calculus of Consent* (Ann Arbor, Mich.: University of Michigan Press, 1962).

order to ensure themselves against disaster should their own position be low in the income-asset scale, individuals might, in their own self-interest, agree on a scheme for fiscal redistribution, one that would tend to level postfiscal positions, at least to some degree. The insurance approach differs from that of Rawls in that it attempts to "explain" observed redistributional policy on a contractual basis without resort to normative precepts of justice; men are predicted to behave strictly in their own self-interest but the opportunity of ensuring against undesirable outcomes causes them to select, in advance, certain redistributional rules. The relative disadvantage in this approach lies in the recognition that individuals are never wholly uncertain about their own prospects, that the initial setting for such an idealized "social contract" has never existed.

Protection against revolution.   Geoffrey Brennan has advanced a somewhat different explanation for observed institutions of fiscal distribution, an explanation that also relies on the self-interest motivations of individuals, but which does not require the initial uncertainty present in the Buchanan-Tullock insurance model. In a position where individual endowments and claims differ greatly, redistributional policies may still emerge due to the fear of those who hold nominally large assets. They will agree to allow fiscal redistribution, within limits, because they may, in this way, protect their own claims against violence and revolution.[3]

Redistribution as the exercise of public property rights.   The three separate models sketched out above are all contractual in the sense that each attempts to explain fiscal redistribution in terms of an ongoing constitutional agreement, one in which precepts are laid down and followed in political reality. They rely respectively on the sense of justice, the uncertainty about income and wealth prospects, and the desire for protection of private property against violence and revolution. A somewhat different approach allows us to look at the fiscal process more directly as the working out of the "public property rights" which modern democracy necessarily involves. All citizens have the franchise, the right to vote, and this right to vote implies that they have a nominal claim, through the workings of the political process, on all income and assets in the community. The transfer of incomes and wealth that we observe to take place represents nothing

---

[3]See Geoffrey Brennan, "Parento Desirable Redistribution: The Non-Altruistic Dimension," *Public Choice*, vol. 14 (Spring 1973), pp. 43–68.

more than the cashing in of these claims, at least in part. In effect, this approach should object somewhat to the term "*re*distribution" here, since this word, in itself, implies that the nominal owner or recipient prior to transfer holds "legitimate" claims.

REDISTRIBUTION THROUGH NONIDEALIZED AND POTENTIALLY OBSERVABLE FISCAL-POLITICAL PROCESS

In the preceding main section, we have discussed income and wealth redistribution as it might ideally be carried out in furtherance of ultimate social objectives (such as economic efficiency, social justice, income insurance, and self-protection), ideally carried out by a governmental or political process that is totally responsive to the expressed demands-desires of the voters-citizens-taxpayers-beneficiaries. In a sense, the whole discussion was based on the presumption that "government," as such, did not exist. But, whether we like it or not, government does exist as an independent entity, and when it is authorized to engage in income and wealth redistribution we must analyze the operations of government as it might actually work. Once this elementary point is recognized, it becomes apparent that the fiscal process may not yield the results discussed in the preceding section, regardless of the intent of the citizens. Political structures may generate transfers of income and wealth that do not accord with any of the plausibly accepted norms. Unless there are overt constitutional restrictions, effective transfers will tend to be made for the benefit of those who are the members of the decisive political coalition, whether these be members of a legislative majority, a ruling party, or a committee of elders. Fiscal redistribution will, to some extent, be aimed to benefit the members of the ruling coalition along with its favored constituents.

Consider a simple example. Many dollars are collected in taxes from American citizens for the express purpose of poverty relief (for welfare programs). But it is well known that those persons who are actually poor get only some fraction of each dollar collected in taxes. Where does the difference go? The difference reflects redistribution from the taxpayers to the members of the political bureaucracy, whose high salaries and perquisites could not be justified by any conceivable purpose of a redistribution program.

Much of the income and wealth transfer that takes place in modern fiscal systems reflects little more than direct political profiteering. Rent-seekers have, quite correctly, recognized that opportunities exist for exploitation via the fiscal system. And divergent groups have sought, and received, their own redistributive handouts at the expense of the taxpayers, with generous "bribes" for the legislative and executive bureaucracy in the bargain.

Since the "rich" are always in the minority, it would seem that the "non-rich" could always be organized so as to capture governmental decision-making and to exploit the "rich" to the maximum extent. Experience suggests, however, that this direct exploitation of the rich is more limited than simple political models might predict. Why? There are several answers. In the first place, the "very poor," like the "rich," are few in number. In order to form an effective anti-rich coalition, the poor must join forces with large numbers from the middle-range, median-income levels. But it is precisely this middle-income group that is singularly uninterested in helping the poor, and the transfers that emerge are more likely to be those that benefit middle-income groups, with both the rich and the poor being exploited in the process. Observation suggests that much of the fiscal redistribution that takes place is of this variety rather than that which would be dictated by any of the norms previously discussed.[4] In the second place, so long as social mobility is high there are widespread expectations of being able to move up in the income scale. This places limits on the degree to which persons will deliberately choose to use the fiscal process to improve current income distribution. Finally, those who might seek to exploit the rich will recognize that the revenue maximizing rates of tax may not be so high as naive estimates might indicate. Incentives to work, to invest, to take risks are very important in generating economic growth and development.

PUBLIC SPENDING AND EQUALITY OF OPPORTUNITY

A distinction must be made between measures designed to equalize incomes and wealth once these are earned and accumulated, and measures designed primarily to equalize the opportunities of persons to earn incomes and to accumulate wealth. Various programs of public spending may be initiated that have as their main effects the

---

[4]See George J. Stigler, "Director's Law of Public Income Redistribution," *Journal of Law and Economics*, vol. 13 (April 1970), pp. 1–10.

equalizing of opportunities. Expenditures for education come to mind as perhaps the best example here. To an extent at least, individual opportunities for the earning of income in the market tend to be equalized as educational services are financed publicly and made available to all children of the community.

Additional spending programs can be placed in this category. For example, public spending to train or to retrain displaced workers so that they may find and keep new job opportunities seeks to equip persons to earn incomes rather than to transfer income directly to them. Labor exchange outlays serve the same purpose.

To the extent that such spending programs can equalize opportunities, direct income transfers via the fiscal process become less justifiable. If the teen-age dropouts can be encouraged, through spending programs, to equip themselves to earn socially acceptable levels of income, they are removed as a potential relief charge on the community. To the extent that the displaced strip miner can be retrained to become an insulator, the miner's family may be removed from the dole. In terms of individual morale, if for no other reason, public spending on such programs as these, insofar as they are substitutes, are preferred to direct transfers.

REDISTRIBUTION BY NONFISCAL MEANS

If income and wealth redistribution is desirable, and if the governmental appetites towards perverse transfers can be constitutionally constrained, it will be more effective to accomplish this objective through the fiscal system than through alternative methods. Differential taxes and benefits can be super-imposed on an operating market economy; the effects on individual behavior are largely indirect. Behavioral distortions can be minimized. On the other hand, more direct attempts to modify the distribution of income may affect individual behavior more significantly. There may be a greater cost in efficiency. In addition, there is no real assurance that the direct methods will achieve redistribution in the direction desired in the first place.

Numerous examples could be employed to illustrate the redistributive ineffectiveness of direct interferences with market processes. Minimum wage laws provide perhaps the best of these. Such laws are supported on the argument that the effects will increase the overall equality of income distribution, because the wages of the lowest income workers will be increased. But it is clear that, if the minimum wage is at all effective, those workers with the lowest productivity will be thrown out of work. Their real incomes will be lowered rather than increased. The effects may be to increase the incomes of some wage earners who remain employed, but the achievement of greater equality in overall income distribution is not necessarily produced, and the whole wage-setting process in the labor market is seriously affected by the wage floor imposed. If the lowest wage workers are to have their real incomes increased, a system of subsidy payment supplementing earned incomes and financed out of general tax revenues will accomplish this purpose more certainly, and without undue interference with ordinary operation of the market economy.

CONCLUSIONS

The free enterprise economy distributes real income produced in accordance with the principle of marginal resource productivity. Resource owners tend to receive income roughly equivalent to the marginal contribution of resources put on the market. Despite the many departures from the perfectly working market economy that are present in the United States, the distribution of real income in the private economy can still be said to be based on the marginal productivity principle in a first approximation.

The exclusive reliance on marginal productivity distribution of real income would be unacceptable to many people in the modern world. The need to modify this distribution in the direction of achieving greater equality in personal incomes and wealth has been widely recognized for many years. The fiscal system provides the appropriate mechanism in the modern economy through which some redistribution can be effected. This redistribution can be carried out in several ways with differing effects. Purely redistributive measures consist of net transfers among individuals or groups. These transfers can be generally imposed on such criteria as income or wealth, or they can be quite specifically imposed on arbitrary criteria. A more important way in which the fiscal system accomplishes income redistribution is through transfers of income in kind. Individuals who qualify are provided with specific goods and services rather than generalized purchasing power. Even if redistribution is not explicitly considered as a collective good, the collectivization process itself ensures that real income equalization be increased due to the differentials in marginal tax prices that equilibrium adjustment requires.

If income redistribution is accepted as a social goal, it is considerably more efficient to achieve this through the fiscal process than through alternative methods. These alternative methods will normally take the form of direct interferences with the market economy. Not only will overall efficiency in resource use be reduced to a greater extent, but there is no assurance that the desired redistribution will be achieved at all.

It must always be kept in mind, however, that fiscal redistribution is also political redistribution. That is to say, fiscal transfers must be based on political decisions, and not on those of the economist or social philosopher who lays down idealized schemes for distributive justice. Observation of political reality suggests that rarely, if ever, will the actual redistributive process be close to the ideal. And in many cases, the results may be contrary to the purposes which may offer the initial motivation for the plans.

9

Traditional principles of public finance

$\mathbf{W}$e have discussed economic effi-
ciency as a possible goal for organizing a fiscal system, and we have
examined the use of the fiscal structure to promote distributive objectives.

Existing fiscal systems have not, of course, been organized on the
basis of the objectives discussed, even if the nonrational aspects of
institutional history could be eliminated. The pursuit of economic
efficiency, even as tempered by distributive and other goals, has not
been explicit in the derivation of policy, and the development of fiscal
institutions reflects little adherence to such principles. But in order
to understand existing fiscal institutions we must now examine the
set of principles that has been explicitly proposed for fiscal organization in the past, because these principles have influenced, and continue to influence, public thinking on current policy issues and,
through this, policy formation itself. This chapter, therefore, will be
devoted to a brief review of what may be called the traditional, or
orthodox, principles of public finance.

THE FUNDAMENTAL FISCAL ASYMMETRY

As mentioned earlier, a rather singular asymmetry has been
present in the development of both fiscal principles and institutions,

especially in Anglo-Saxon countries. We find that tax legislation has been discussed in terms of the various "principles of taxation." But we find extremely little discussion until quite recently on "principles of public expenditure," and when such principles are found, they are based on a wholly different philosophical conception of the state. This asymmetry seems to stem from an early misconception by the classical economists. Public expenditures were assumed to be wholly unproductive; therefore, the task of public finance theory was that of showing how the necessary tax load could be distributed so as to cause the least possible damage to the private economy. Hence, "principles of taxation" were developed that have provided certain rough norms for the distribution of the tax load among individuals and groups. No attention, or almost none, has been paid (again until quite recently) to the relatively more important question concerning how much the tax load should be, that is to say, how the total resources of the economy should be divided between the public and private sector. Both the amount and the distribution of public expenditures have been considered, by and large, as being determined outside the limits of public finance as a subdiscipline of economics. Some writers have explicitly stated that these decisions are to be taken as political in nature and, presumably, not subject to reasoned discussion and analysis. The same logic could, of course, be applied to the distribution of taxes. All problems in public finance are political since they directly involve some decision making by the collective authority. But this is no reason why objective discussion and analysis cannot be helpful to those who do ultimately decide on policy, and the exclusion of public expenditure norms has severely and unduly limited the usefulness of traditional public finance theory.

THE PRINCIPLE OF HORIZONTAL EQUITY

One of the most widely accepted principles or norms for the distribution of taxes among individuals states that *individuals in similar situations should be treated similarly*, or, in other words, *equals should be treated equally*.

The origin and general acceptance of this principle in democratic societies is not difficult to explain. Its source is the principle of the equality of individuals before the law, tax treatment being legal treatment in essential respects. Arbitrary and capricious treatment of individuals by legal institutions is prevented by constitutional law, and this constitutional protection against arbitrary or discriminatory treatment by government has been extended to apply to the distribution of taxes.

On ethical grounds, little objection can be raised to the equity principle. Arbitrary taxation of particular individuals would violate the value sense of most members of Western society. There are, however, some difficulties with the practical interpretation and application of this principle. For example, if individuals have widely divergent tastes, almost any tax is likely to be characterized by horizontal inequity in the sense that individuals who are equally well off before the tax is imposed will probably occupy unequal post-tax positions. Suppose, for example, that two individuals have identical earnings opportunities, but that one has a stronger preference for leisure than the other. In a world with no taxes, the two might achieve roughly comparable levels of satisfaction or well-being though one would achieve this satisfaction by consuming more leisure and less money income than the other. Suppose now that a tax is imposed on money income. The individual with the stronger preference for leisure would bear a disproportionately light tax burden and thus occupy the better post-tax position. This problem is clearly also present with any tax on a commodity or group of commodities for which some individuals have stronger preferences than others.

The imposition of equal taxes on all individuals would, in one extreme sense, seem to fulfill the equity criterion. However, an important corollary of the equity principle is that unequals should be taxed unequally. This corollary is clearly violated by equal taxation of everyone.

The principle of taxing equals equally and unequals unequally requires that certain criteria be established for classifying individuals for tax purposes. Unless all persons can be presumed to have identical tastes, the impossibility of measuring and comparing utilities interpersonally makes unavoidable the type of horizontal inequities discussed previously. However, certain traditions seem to have been established concerning objectively measureable critera to be employed in classifying individuals for tax purposes. These criteria seem to be generally accepted and broadly consistent with the spirit of the equity norm's prohibition against arbitrariness. For example, tax discrimination based on income or wealth is widely accepted. Also, tax discrimination on the basis of the consumption of particular products or services is not held to violate the equity principle. These appear to be *reasonable* classifications, broad enough to contain many individuals within each grouping, the reasonableness in each case being determined finally by constitutional procedure.

It seems important to note that the equity principle can be used to evaluate the overall design of a tax structure, but is also important in considering marginal changes in that structure. Tax reform can raise serious issues of transitional equity because many forms of preferential tax treatment are reflected in the value of real assets. Removal of such tax preference, to improve either the efficiency or the long run equity of the tax system, may cause an immediate readjustment of asset values in which some individuals suffer a significant wealth loss which is not experienced by equally well-situated persons who happen not to be holding those particular assets.

The broad acceptance of the equity principle seems to prevent particular individuals or small groups from being subjected to differential tax treatment. A tax levy upon the residents of a particular urban street would be held unconstitutional unless the revenues should be devoted to the improvement of that street. A tax base defined so as to include only one individual would clearly be unacceptable, for example, a tax on all redheaded men over 50 years of age working as attendants in a particular drive-in theater. Criteria of reasonableness would also preclude taxation based on racial, religious, or geographic groupings.

The primary objection to the application of the equity principle lies in the fundamental asymmetry discussed previously. The equity principle has never been applied to the distribution of public expenditures, although the reason for such application would seem equally valid. Limitation to the distribution of taxes stems from the implied assumption that public expenditures are wholly unproductive or else benefit all groups equally. If differential benefits to separate individuals and groups are recognized, there is little ground for the application of the equity principle on the tax side. Or, considering the problem from the other extreme, there is equal justification for applying the equity principle on the expenditure side. Actually, fiscal systems exhibit rather arbitrary discrimination in expenditure distribution. Particular occupational groups are differentially provided with subsidies (for example, farmers), and residents of particular geographic regions (for example, the Rocky Mountain states) are differentially benefited. The provision of public service to an individual or family does not imply any legal or ethical claim of all individuals equally situated to receive the same service. Because a federal government irrigation project differentially benefits landowners in one valley, farmers in adjacent valleys are given no legal claim for similar treatment.

An attempt to extend the equity principle to apply to the expenditure side in a way similar to its application on the tax side would stifle many public expenditure programs. A more useful development would appear to be a recognition that differential expenditure justifies differential taxation and that the equity principle is acceptable only for the distribution of those taxes required to finance genuinely general public expenditures.

THE ABILITY-TO-PAY PRINCIPLE

A corollary of the equity principle states that *unequals should be treated unequally.* This has been widely referred to as the principle of *vertical equity.* But the question as to how the total tax bill shall be distributed among the different classes and groups of taxpayers presents many difficulties. To what extent shall discrimination in tax rates among separate classes and groups of the population be accepted?

One thing requires stating at the outset. There are no agreed-on or widely accepted answers to these questions. Different experts disagree, even if this is recognized as a field where expert opinion is better than any other, a highly questionable recognition in itself.

Nevertheless some decisions must be, and have been, made in distributing taxes among separate groups. These decisions have not been made on the basis of purely expedient considerations. Some "principles" have been used, at least in the discussions of alternative tax programs.

The single principle that has been most widely accepted in the modern fiscal system states that taxes should be distributed in accordance with the ability of the individual to pay. This has been a very effective principle because it provides a rough guide to tax policy without at the same time specifying precisely the actual distribution to be adopted. Within the limits of this principle, many conceivable tax distributions can be, and have been, adopted.

Ability to pay has normally been measured by incomes and wealth. The higher the income of an individual, the more able that person is to pay taxes; similarly, the greater the amount of wealth possessed, the higher the ability to pay. This preliminary definition of ability to pay suggests that, in any distribution of the tax load, taxes paid must vary directly with incomes and wealth.

But this preliminary definition does not get the tax commission very far in planning its tax program. The hard question remains: How much more should the rich individual pay? The imposition of tax rates proportional to income would guarantee that the rich pay more than the poor. For example, a tax rate of 10 percent would take only $100 from a net income of $1,000 and $1,000 from a net income of $10,000.

Ability to pay has been defined more specifically than this, or rather, attempts have been made to define it, so as to justify progressive taxation. That is to say, it has been argued that the ability-to-pay principle has not been met unless the high-income groups pay proportionately more than the lower income groups. For example, the $10,000 net income must be taxed at, say, a 20 percent rate in comparison with the 10 percent rate on the net income of $1,000.

Several so-called theories have been developed to justify income tax progression. The most sophisticated of these, and the only one which necessarily points toward a progressive rate structure, is the *principle of minimum aggregate sacrifice.* This approach assumes, first of all, that individual satisfaction or utility is a measurable magnitude and, more significantly, that this magnitude is comparable among separate individuals within the social group. An implication of this assumed measurement is that the maximization of total utility for all individuals is an appropriate goal for social policy.

Here, again, all public expenditures have been assumed away, so to speak, and the principle applied only to the tax side of the account. If public expenditures are considered always to constitute net drains on the private economy, the conceptual framework here suggests that taxes should be so distributed as to cause a minimum reduction in total utility of all individuals jointly considered. Hence the name, *principle of least sacrifice or minimum aggregate sacrifice.*

Before the principle can lead to an actual distribution of taxes, some assumption must be made about the change in individual utility as income changes. Here the more normal assumption is made that total utility enjoyed by each individual increases at a decreasing rate as more income is received. Or, in other words, the marginal utility of income declines as more income is added. The extra dollar provides the man with $1,000 less additional enjoyment than was provided him by the 999th dollar. Therefore, if individual utilities may be compared among persons, the collection of a dollar in tax from the high-income receivers will reduce their total satisfaction less than a similar collection of a dollar from the low-income receivers. Hence, the major portion of the tax bill must be placed on the high-income classes. Incomes must be leveled down by taxation in order to meet fully this principle.

Modern economic thought does not accept this principle as possessing any validity. First of all, individual utility is not now considered to be a cardinally measurable magnitude. Even if it were, utilities could not be compared among separate individuals. This fact alone prevents the principle from having any "scientific" basis.

The ability-to-pay principle can lead to no specific configuration of taxes apart from the simple proposition that higher income receivers should pay higher taxes. Progression in the rate structure must be defended on quite other grounds. Nevertheless, it should be fully recognized that the false correlation between ability to pay as a guiding principle and progression in rates as a policy continues to exert important influence on the thought of policy makers.

Progressive tax rates, based on income, must be defended or explained on grounds of efficiency, distributional norms, or of political coalition formation. If the utility functions of individuals are such that marginal valuations of public goods tend to be directly and disproportionately related to income levels, a progressive rate structure would be required for full neutrality. Since we have little evidence on the actual evaluations, this says little more than that progression in taxation is not necessarily inefficient. A slightly different defense of progression emerges when the tax structure is recognized as quasi-permanent and when uncertainty about individual income levels is introduced. Here individuals may choose to pay taxes under a progressive structure in order to concentrate payments during periods when the marginal utility of income is relatively low. If neither of these defenses for progression can be used, the widespread use of this rate structure may be explained as the working out of some of the norms for fiscal redistribution discussed in Chapter 8. Or, finally, progressive income taxation may be explained purely on political grounds. In this case, progression represents one part of a process through which gains are secured by one group at the expense of remaining groups.

At its best, the ability-to-pay principle can provide some very rough guideposts to the distribution of a given or predetermined tax load. It offers no guidance at all in the more important fiscal decision: How much should the tax load (and public expenditure) amount to? Again we find the asymmetry that we have so frequently mentioned.

THE BENEFIT PRINCIPLE

An alternative principle for the distribution of the tax load among separate individuals and groups states that tax obligations should be based on the benefits received from the enjoyment of public services. At the outset it should be noted that this principle has the logical advantage of tying together the collective decisions on taxes with those on public expenditures. The whole fiscal process is incorporated, and a comparison between taxes and expenditures becomes possible.

But the benefit principle, as stated previously, remains ambiguous. Several interpretations may be placed on the principle, and it will be useful to discuss each of these in sequence.

The first, and least acceptable, interpretation of the principle states that the *total* tax bill for each individual should be equated to the *total* real benefits that the individual receives from the provision of public services. This interpretation is clearly misleading; there should be, in all cases, a sizable "taxpayers' surplus" left over in terms of real benefits after all tax obligations are met. For example, it is evident that the total benefits provided by the availability of a municipal police force are far in excess of the *total* cost of providing the police protection. The benefit principle of taxation should never be stated in *total benefit* terms. To do this is to repeat the age-old confusion in economic thought between value in use and value in exchange.

A second interpretation of the benefit principle states that taxes should be distributed *proportionately* with total benefits received. The tax obligation to be charged to a particular individual depends, in this formulation, on the total benefits enjoyed, but need not be equal to this total. If some "taxpayers' surplus" is produced through the fiscal process, each individual taxpayer may expect to find his or her real income increased as a result of the combined tax expenditure process. This version of the benefit principle has some merit in the abstract if the total public expenditure (and tax load) is determined independently outside the fiscal decision process itself. But even in these cases no possible means would seem to exist, even conceptually, of measuring total benefits and of allocating tax obligations proportionately to these.

A third interpretation of the benefit principle is the most appropriate, especially from an analytical point of view. This states that taxes should be allocated among separate individuals on the basis of *marginal benefit or incremental benefit* received, not total benefit. The principle, stated in this manner, involves the setting of taxes in a way that is strictly analogous to the setting of prices in the private market economy. This process has already been discussed in some detail in Chapter 7. The ideally neutral or the ideally efficient fiscal system that was discussed there incorporates taxation in accordance with the principle of incremental benefit. A particular individual would be required to pay a "tax price" for each unit of a given public service that is equal to the marginal or incremental benefit he receives from a unit of this service. This appropriately set "tax price" would be independent of total benefit received from all units of the public service.

This version of the benefit principle allows the total amount of public services to be conceptually determined. Thus it is the only "complete" principle in a methodological sense. If each taxpayer is paying for each public service on the basis of the marginal benefits actually enjoyed, the total tax collection from all individuals provides a useful measure of the marginal evaluation of the public service. The provision of this service can then be extended as long as this total marginal evaluation exceeds the marginal cost of providing the service. Again, a simple two-man example may be used to clarify this point. Suppose our island society with Crusoe and Friday, and suppose further that the decision to be made concerns whether or not to build the lookout tower 2 feet higher than it is at present, the tower being a collective good. If Crusoe estimates that the *marginal benefit* of the additional 2 feet in height will be 10 days' labor, and Friday estimates a *marginal benefit* of 5 days' labor, the addition should be made if the cost is less than 15 days' labor, and taxation is based on the principle of marginal benefit. If, on the other hand, the cost should be 20 days' labor, no distribution of taxes could possibly be justified. The addition should not be undertaken.

As concluded in Chapter 7, a fiscal system that incorporates the principle of marginal benefit is useful as a conceptual model. It allows a "solution" to the collective choice process to be defined that is "efficient." But when we come to consider real-world fiscal systems, the principle of marginal or incremental benefit provides little assistance. Decisions as to the total amount of expenditure and as to the distribution of taxes must be made, and policy makers cannot "read" individual evaluations of public services. Furthermore, individuals, if they are to be taxed on the marginal benefit principle, will have a strong incentive to conceal their true evaluations from the decision-making authorities.

It is possible, however, that basic changes in the institution of decision making itself could allow a reasonably close approximation of the principle of marginal benefit to be achieved. This is the plan suggested by the famous Swedish economist, Knut Wicksell, that has already been briefly discussed in Chapter 7.

The difficulties of applying the principle of marginal benefits in imposing taxes in real-world structures are, of course, immense. There is no means of determining, even to some first approximation, the relationship between marginal benefits and tax payments. At best, some overall, or general, criterion may be introduced, such as income, which carries the presumption that it indirectly measures marginal benefits from the whole package of public or collective goods contained in the governmental budget, including the implicit redistribution of real incomes that the budget accomplishes.

These limitations are fully applicable only when we treat the fiscal structure of the central government. If individuals are free to migrate among different local government jurisdictions, the "voting with the feet" acts to constrain fiscal departures from the efficiency criterion.

In one important application, the benefit principle can be used somewhat more explicitly. The principle of *differential benefit* from *particular* public services may be helpful in imposing special taxes. This principle does explain some of the special levies that are to be found in the tax system. If particular consumers of a commodity are held to receive some special benefits from government, it is appropriate that the taxes required to finance this service be imposed on these consumers. In this way, the financing of the highway system by gasoline and motor vehicle license taxes has been justified, and this has become an important part of the overall fiscal system of the United States. This use of the benefit principle is applicable when no redistributive purpose is desired. Thus, special assessments are imposed on residents of particular urban streets to finance street improvement or sewer line connections. License fees of all sorts are charged to finance the administrative costs of providing particular services.

CONCLUSIONS

Three major principles of public finance have been discussed. Traditional public finance theory, however, has been characterized by a fundamental asymmetry. "Principles" have been developed primarily in regard to the distribution of taxes among individuals and the distribution of public expenditures among separate individuals and groups. Little attention has been paid to "principles" for the determination of the appropriate amount of resources to be devoted to public as opposed to private uses.

The principle of horizontal equity states that equals should be treated equally. This principle has been widely applied in the distribution of taxes, and its acceptance in legal institutions has prevented arbitrary discrimination among individuals and groups. But the line between arbitrary and nonarbitrary discrimination remains ill-defined, and little attempt has been made to apply the same principle to expenditures.

A corollary to the horizontal equity principle states that unequals should be treated unequally. This is known as the principle of vertical equity. Incomes and wealth have been generally accepted as a basis for distinguishing groups. But the difficult question concerns just how unequal the treatment shall be. The second major principle discussed embodies an attempt to answer this question. The principle of ability to pay suggests that tax rates should vary directly with income and wealth. But the principle has also been used to justify progressive tax rates in relation to income. This extension of the ability-to-pay principle is not supported on scientific or analytical grounds. The justification or explanation for progressive taxation must rest on different grounds. The ability-to-pay principle cannot be at all helpful in determining the appropriate amount of public expenditures to be undertaken.

The third principle discussed was the benefit principle of taxation. This principle has several interpretations, and much confusion has been based on failure to distinguish these. The most acceptable of the interpretations states that taxes should be allocated among individuals in accordance with the marginal or incremental benefits received from government services. This is the principle incorporated into an "ideally efficient" fiscal system that was previously discussed. The principle does have the advantage of providing a complete solution to the collective choice process; tax and expenditure decisions are tied closely together. The principle has its greatest specific applicability in the real world for those fiscal decisions incorporating differential taxation on groups differentially benefited by public services where such groups have no claim for additional real income on distributional grounds.

The traditional "principles" of public finance leave much to be desired in the way of providing a set of norms upon which fiscal decisions may be made. The fundamental asymmetry has caused the principles to be confused and, in many cases, misleading. Nevertheless, such principles as ability to pay have been important in shaping public attitudes, and because of this, the student can neglect them only at the peril of failing to understand the existing fiscal process.

Norms for organizing the fiscal structure must reflect the existence of competing goals. The analytical apparatus of the economist can do little more than to indicate the results of alternative proposals. Attempts to make norms "scientific" are doomed to failure; but given an explicit statement of criteria for fiscal organization, much progress may be made toward developing genuine "theories" of public finance.

SUPPLEMENTARY READING

For a more advanced discussion of both the ability-to-pay and the benefit principles, the student is advised to consult R. A. Musgrave, *The Theory of Public Finance* (New York: McGraw-Hill Book Co., 1959), chaps. 4, 5.

A useful discussion and critique of the equity norm is contained in a paper by Professor Martin Feldstein, "On the Theory of Tax Reform," *Journal of Public Economics* (July–August, 1976).

part III

The fiscal decision process: The theory of public choice

As a subdiscipline, public finance has undergone a major change since the first edition of this textbook was published in 1960. Before that time, little or no attention was paid to the processes of collective decision making. A discussion of "principles," that is, a normative treatment of how fiscal systems "should" be organized, was followed by an analysis of the way in which taxes and spending programs affect individual and group behavior. As we have noted, however, fiscal decisions are not made strictly in accord with the economist's normative principles. These emerge from a very complex political structure in which many participants are involved and at several levels. The whole subject of public finance was incomplete. Fortunately, in the 1960s, "public choice," the theory and analysis of collective decision making, was increasingly incorporated into public finance. The third edition of this textbook, published in 1970, was the first to incorporate a whole section on the decision process. Several textbooks have followed this lead; "public choice" has taken its place as an inherent aspect of public finance.

Part III represents an extended and revised set of chapters devoted to the decision process. Perhaps the single most outstanding feature on the public finance "landscape" in the late 1970s was the apparently burgeoning "taxpayers' revolt." This was manifest in widespread interest in and, in several instances, formal imposition of constitutional limits on government taxing and spending. An attempt has been made in this section, most notably in Chapters 13 and 16, to provide an elementary analytical framework within which this phenomenon might be examined.

It should be recognized that the models discussed in this section generally remain extremely simple and abstract. However, the whole content of public choice as a newly independent subdiscipline could scarcely be incorporated here. Our purpose is instead to offer the student some feel for the complex set of issues opened up for analysis when the fiscal decision process is critically examined.

10

The political basis for fiscal decisions

Goods and services are demanded by individuals as consumers in the marketplace and as participants in a political decision process. In response, firms emerge as suppliers in the marketplace, and governments become economic units. The "public economy," the "public sector," involves the governmental provision of goods and services to beneficiaries. These are financed through the tax revenues that are collected from individuals coercively. Despite the proclivity of the economists to do so, the fiscal process cannot be divorced from the political structure.

How do individual demands for public goods and services translate themselves into action? To what extent does the budgetary pattern observed on both the tax and spending side accurately reflect individual desires? The answer to these and similar questions requires a theory of demand for public goods and services. But such a theory cannot be approached until and unless the political process itself is analyzed. This process involves the participation of individuals in several capacities, and its complexities are widely acknowledged. The linkage between the individual choice inputs and the collective choice outputs is not a direct one. Nonetheless, a start must be made toward understanding.

The central problem was summarized in Chapter 3. What is government? How is it to be conceived? If we are willing to think of government as an entity that is separate and apart from its citizens, we can develop theories of governmental choice making that are similar in basic respects to the theory of individual choice making in the marketplace.

GOVERNMENT AS A BENEVOLENT DESPOT—AS A MAXIMIZER OF THE PUBLIC INTEREST

There are two quite different models of government as an "individual," as a monolithic utility-maximizing entity, that might be introduced. These two models lie at opposing ends of an analytical spectrum, and various in-between models might also be constructed.

Much of traditional public finance theory, especially in its normative variants, has been implicitly based on what may be called a "benevolent despot" model of government and governmental process. In this conception, government is a single-minded entity, and the "public interest," the interest of the citizens, is the maximand in its utility or objective function. The constraints faced would be the familiar trade-offs among resource units, along with the reactions of individuals to fiscal burdens and benefits. The government would try to take such reactions into account. Taxes would be adjusted so as to minimize negative individual responses. On the tax side alone, and treated independently from the spending side of the fiscal account, government's action in this model would be similar to, although at base different from, the traditional neoclassical principle of taxation in accordance with least aggregate sacrifice, discussed briefly in Chapter 9. The latter principle, presumably, involves minimizing genuine sacrifice imposed on taxpayers, as measured in some ex-post sense. But felt sacrifice or utility loss may not be the same as anticipated loss. And a government, even if its objective is strictly that of minimizing the utility losses of taxpayers, could only try to compute or to estimate what individuals might actually suffer from tax imposition.

On the other side of the account, the benevolent government would find it advantageous to distribute benefits in accordance with some estimates of the utility gains of individuals in the community. Such governmental estimates may or may not come close to matching the genuine utility gains that any distribution of public outlays would generate.

Quite apart from the difficulties such a "public interest" government might have in estimating or computing individual utilities, there is also the major, and unresolved, problem of "adding up." Let us suppose, for purposes of discussion here, that government could estimate the prospective utility gains and losses of an individual accurately. But how are the gains and losses in utility for separate individuals in the community to be added up so as to maximize the "public interest"? What weights are to be put on the separate utilities of various persons? Are such weights to be arbitrarily assigned? Or are all persons to count equally?

Welfare economists have worried over such problems as these for a half-century and without satisfactory resolution. Even if government should really want to maximize the "public interest," there would be almost as many versions of what the "public interest" is as there are persons in the community.

GOVERNMENT AS LEVIATHAN

In the preceding section government was discussed in terms of what is often called the "benevolent despot" model. The entity of government is conceived or modeled as a single-minded decision maker which, nonetheless, has the interests of the citizenry, as it conceives such interests, as its central objective. This benevolent despot or "public interest" model of government and politics has been subjected to increasingly sharp criticism within recent decades, and an opposing model has seemed to be more useful in analyzing governmental process, at least within the set of utility-maximizing assuptions.

If government is to be conceived or modeled as a single decision-maker that may be analyzed in a utility-maximizing framework, an alternative formulation would attribute to government straight-forward self-interest rather than benevolence. Government modeled as a Leviathan would maximize its own utility by exploiting citizens to the maximum possible extent. If such a model is limited to fiscal behavior, utility maximization would require that government try to maximize the "fiscal surplus" that it receives. This surplus is defined as the difference between the total of tax revenues collected and the amount of outlays made toward the provision of goods and services valued by citizens. This difference or surplus is available for the disposition of the government, for usage as it sees fit, presumably to provide lavish living (the courts of the kings), plus perquisites of office, and the pleasure of a secure and quiet life.

A government that behaves as Leviathan would not necessarily impose heavier taxation than governments subject to normal electoral controls. Especially if Leviathan's time or planning horizon is extended over several years, surplus maximization would not involve a sapping of the sources of economic progress. Clearly, the present value of fiscal surplus will be maximized by maximizing the rate of growth in the economy. Nor would Leviathan necessarily tax citizens without providing something in return. Revenues might be related to the return flows of goods and services provided, and fiscal surplus may be increased by some provision of goods and services.

The model of government-as-Leviathan is not normally discussed and analyzed in public-finance textbooks, although similar models were widely discussed in some of the early Italian writings. Standard textbooks have embodied the implicit assumption that democratic electoral constraints operate to prevent governmental "misbehavior." More and more such an assumption has come to seem naive and simplistic. The explanatory value of the government as a Leviathan model is only beginning to be explored.

Even if, empirically, governments rarely behave as Leviathans, the model can be helpful in generating normative judgments concerning the imposition of constraints within which governments are allowed to operate. Even if it should be acknowledged that governments will rarely, if ever, act just as the surplus-maximizing Leviathan would act, realistic evaluation of the factual record suggests that some such behavior may occur on occasion, and at least that such behavior is enough of a danger to suggest constitutional constraints on governmental process. The logical basis for imposing constitutional tax and spending limits arises from just such a modeling. Tax and spending institutions may be designed for the express purpose of keeping government's natural taxing and spending proclivities from extending beyond those limits dictated by plausibly realistic "public interest" percepts.[1]

---

[1] For introductory analysis based on the Leviathan model, see Geoffrey Brennan and James M. Buchanan, "Towards a Tax Constitution for Leviathan," *Journal of Public Economics,* 8 (1977), 255–273; "Tax Instruments as Constraints on the Disposition of Public Revenues," *Journal of Public Economics,* 9 (1978), 301–318.

GOVERNMENT AS A RULING COMMITTEE, CLASS, GROUP, OR "ESTABLISHMENT"

In either of the two models of government described in the two preceding sections, government is modeled as a single utility-maximizing unit. Strictly speaking, such a model could be plausible only with a one-person, single-ruler government. At best, the models must be treated as such, as models for a much more complex reality, rather than as representations of such reality. In many cases, it is useful to proceed analytically on the basis of "as if" assumptions even where gross violations of reality are acknowledged.

Even in the most extreme totalitarian regimes, government is not one person. A more familiar pattern is for governmental decision-making power to be limited to a small group of individuals, a committee. As this committee size is extended, we get into situations where there exists a clearly defined ruling class or an elite.

For our purposes, we note only that such group models for government fall between the utility-maximizing models briefly discussed above and the large-group democratic models to be discussed below. Strictly speaking, only individuals have utility functions, and different members of a ruling committee or group, no matter how small, will have different utilities. While the group may, as a unit, be conceived as maximizing some commonly shared function for "group utility," as against the constraints imposed by the reactions of nonmembers, within the group itself each person will act to further his or her own utility, which must diverge at significant points from any group defined function.

This basic model of government is immensely important in reality, and notably in all communist or one-party regimes. Analysis of its decision-making processes remains in its infancy. If the group is small, some aspects of its decision-making can be analyzed in terms of the theory of committees, as developed primarily by Duncan Black. Alternatives to be considered are likely to be different in terms of the responses of nonmembers; hence, these differential responses can modify the relative costs of programs. For this reason, those who remain outside the ruling committee are not without influence on final outcomes. By their behavior, persons outside the group of rulers can make some courses of action more costly than others. Ruling committees cannot simply proceed as if response mechanisms are identical over all relevant alternatives.

As the ruling committee or group expands in size and becomes a "class" or a loosely-knit, perhaps open-ended "establishment," any analysis of its decision-making process becomes exceedingly complex. Needless to say, the public-finance textbook appropriate for such governmental process remains to be written.

GOVERNMENT AS DEMOCRATIC PROCESS

We shall devote most of this part of the textbook to the democratic model of government. This model is based on the presumed participation of *all* members of the community in the political decision process. In many respects, the democratic model remains less than fully descriptive of reality, even in those politics with nominally democratic institutions. Some individuals participate scarcely at all in politics; they abstain from active voting, even on the occasional election of representatives. Many, indeed most others, participate only in such elections of representatives who are empowered to make decisions for the whole group. As agents for the citizens, representatives have interests that may be quite different from those of citizens, and they may have considerable leeway to further their own interests. Nonelected bureaucrats may be immune in many respects to the controls of the legislative authorities, and especially in regimes that have permanent civil services. As governmental size grows, decisions must increasingly be shifted away from elected legislators and into the hands of nonelected bureaucrats.

Nonetheless, analysis must start somewhere, and by building up from simple and unrealistic models we may be able to reach meaningful statements about the real world. At the least, we can claim that the use of the simple models to be discussed in the next two chapters provides a more effective insight into the workings of the fiscal process than that which has informed the benevolent despot model. As noted earlier, the Leviathan model is in its early states of development. Some combination of a Leviathan model and the democratic process models to be discussed seems to offer the avenue for the most fruitful developments in public-finance analysis over the remaining decades of this century.

SUPPLEMENTARY READING

For elaboration of the discussion of several points in this chapter the student should consult: James M. Buchanan, *Fiscal Theory and Political Economy* (Chapel Hill, N.C.: University of North Carolina Press, 1960); James

M. Buchanan and Gordon Tullock, *The Calculus of Consent* (Ann Arbor, Mich.: University of Michigan Press, 1962; paperback, 1965); Geoffrey Brennan and James M. Buchanan, *The Power to Tax: Analytical Foundations of a Fiscal Constitution,* (Cambridge University Press, forthcoming).

11

Simple models of
majority voting

As we have noted, individuals do not participate equally in the decision-making processes of even the most democratic of collectivities. The role of the individual is often extremely limited, and his or her share in the making of a final decision may be very small. In large-number groups, it may indeed be shown that any form of participation by an individual is privately irrational in the strict cost-benefit sense. Nonetheless, even disregarding this, the person may vote for a candidate periodically, and the winning candidate may or may not represent his or her interests effectively. Referenda on specific issues, fiscal or otherwise, may be few and far between. Participation beyond such periodic voting for candidates may be restricted to the general avenues of protest open to the public such as letters to congressmen, letters to editors of local newspapers, and expression of opinions in polls. Some individuals possess, of course, much greater power in shaping decisions. Persons who work in the mass media share in shaping opinion, at least to some extent. Scholars who make policy proposals may provide leadership indirectly through their influence on both political leaders and on the media. Bureaucrats concerned with the actual working of governmental programs may modify the course of program operations. And elected and appointed politicians themselves retain an important area of discretionary control, despite their attempts to maintain positions of power through satisfying voters in some ultimate sense.

These many and varied roles assumed by different individuals in the political process make simple analysis very difficult. Any model that is tractable, that can be employed rigorously in analysis, must seem descriptively to be a caricature of reality. The abstraction of the competitive model for economic activity is comparable here, but its connection with actual economic process is much closer than any plausible model for political interaction. Nonetheless, we shall proceed bravely here. We shall adopt the simplest model of majority voting, despite the acknowledged limitations.

SIMPLE MAJORITY VOTING—THE CYCLICAL MAJORITY POSSIBILITY

We commence with the simplest possible model. Consider a community in which there are only three persons, each of whom has an equal share in community collective decisions. All such decisions are reached after approval by a majority of the members.

As the work of Kenneth Arrow, Duncan Black, and others has emphasized, governmental decisions even in so simple a community as this may not be consistent, one with the other. If each of the three persons has a utility function that exhibits the standard properties, a majority voting rule may still produce inconsistent or intransitive results. This well-known possibility is known as the *paradox of voting*, and it stems from the problems involved in combining individual values into collective outcomes. A simple example will make this clear. Suppose that we name the three persons, 1, 2, and 3, and that there are three alternatives to be voted upon, only one of which is to be selected. Let us label these alternatives as *A*, *B*, and *C*. These might be candidates for office, proposals for public spending, or anything else. Let us suppose further that each of the individuals ranks the three alternatives in the following way:

$$
\begin{array}{ccc}
1 & 2 & 3 \\
A & B & C \\
B & C & A \\
C & A & B
\end{array}
$$

Now suppose that alternative *A* were to be put up against alternative *B* in a straight majority vote on these two issues or candidates alone.

From the ranking, it can be seen that 1 and 3 would vote for *A*, hence *A* would be selected. Now suppose that this vote is followed by one in which *A*, the winning issue, is put against *C*. Note that individuals 2 and 3 would vote for *C*. But following this, suppose that *B* is put up against *C*. From the ranking, it can be seen readily that 1 and 2 would vote for *B*. If alternative *A* were again put up against *B* in a pairwise comparison, it would once again secure majority support, and so on in a continuous cycle.

In this situation, there is no motion, issue, or candidate that can secure a majority over all others if taken in a series of pairwise comparisons. There is no genuine majority motion, and the voting process will continue to cycle as between various alternatives until and unless some arbitrary rule is adopted which stops the procedure. This phenomenon has been called a *cyclical majority*.

In the intellectual history of analyzing democratic governmental process, this phenomenon has been important. It has been employed to demonstrate that democratic process, even in the most abstract models, need not produce results that can be classified as rational or consistent. This proof, in itself, has undermined much of an ill-founded and early naïve faith in democratic procedures as such. For several reasons, however, the real-world importance of the paradox is limited. The relevant question here is the frequency of occurrence of the paradox. This depends on the way in which individual voters rank the alternatives before them, and the rankings need not be such as to produce a cyclical majority. If rankings are equally likely over all of the alternatives for all persons, and if the number of voters becomes large, in the three-candidate or three-alternative model, the probability of a cyclical majority occurring approaches 9 percent. Considerable work has been done in computing the likelihood of occurrence of the cycle with differing numbers of voters and differing numbers of alternatives. There has also been much sophisticated research on the limits or constraints that must be placed on individual rankings in order to ensure that the paradox does not occur. In one sense, the existence of the paradox suggests that some members of the group hold "extreme" or "bizarre" preferences.

Simple majority voting—single-peaked preferences

If individual preferences are *single-peaked*, the paradox does not occur, and simple majority voting will produce a unique result. The notion of single-peaked preferences is important for our purposes because, as we shall show, fiscal alternatives are such as to make the occurrence of single-peaked preferences highly probable. It is perhaps worth noting that the analysis of single-peaked preferences was initially developed by Duncan Black, who himself had previously worked in public finance theory.

Consider a slightly modified example of our three-person community with individuals 1, 2, and 3 as before. Instead of the alternatives A, B, and C as unspecified, let us now consider three fiscal alternatives:

X—Spend $1,000 on a school.

Y—Spend $500 on a school.

Z—Spend nothing on a school.

Given these alternatives, it becomes relatively easy to see that the individuals would normally rank these so that the cycle would not occur. An XYZ ranking, comparable to the ABC ranking above, is certainly plausible. So is an YZX ranking, comparable to the BCA ranking above. But look more carefully at the CAB ranking above. In our fiscal example, such a ranking would be ZXY, which seems wholly implausible. This requires that one person prefers no spending as the alternative and maximum spending as the second alternative. It is on the basis of predictions that this sort of "absurd" rankings will not frequently occur that majority voting secures a stouter defense.

The term "single-peaked" preferences is taken from the graphical illustration of the simple majority voting problem. Refer to Figure 11–1. On the abscissa, we measure spending on the school. The three discrete proposals labeled as X, Y, and Z above are depicted accordingly. On the ordinate, we measure the preferences of the three persons, 1, 2, and 3, with these being measured only in ordinal units. As drawn, note that individual 1 prefers X, the high-spending proposal, to each of the others, and prefers the middle proposal to no spending at all. Individual 2 prefers the middle-spending proposal to each of the other extremes, while individual 3 prefers no spending at all, but also prefers the minimum of the remaining two propositions. Single-peakedness means only that the middle-range alternative must stand between the two extremes for both 1 and 3.

The effects of the existence of single-peaked preferences on eliminating the paradox or the cyclical majority can be seen readily from Figure 11–1. Note that proposition Y will secure a majority ap-

FIGURE 11-1

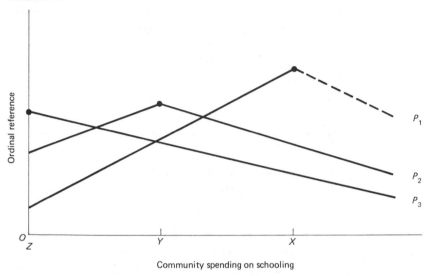

Community spending on schooling

proval against all other proposals. If put against X, both 2 and 3 will vote for Y. If put against Z, both 1 and 2 will vote for Y. Hence, Y is a majority motion or proposal in the genuine sense that no other proposal can possibly secure majority approval over it.

From looking at Figure 11-1, it can be seen that no arbitrary limits need be put on the number of possible alternatives. As drawn, the spending proposal represented at Y would secure majority approval over any other proposal for budgetary outlay. In the real-world fiscal process, it seems best to think of continuity among a whole set of spending proposals rather than limitation to a few discrete alternatives.

The single-peaked preference model allows us to develop one important principle about voting outcomes under simple majority rule. Note that if preferences can be arrayed as they are in Figure 11-1, the alternative that is finally chosen by majority voting will be that which is preferred by the person whose preferences are *median* for the whole group. The effect of majority rule decision making is to convert the person with median preferences into the effective or decisive party in the community. This result is, of course, little more than common sense, but it is useful to remember in more complex applications.

MAJORITY VOTING AND THE DEMAND FOR PUBLIC GOODS

To this point, we have discussed majority voting models using fiscal alternatives without specifying these alternatives fully. In the preceding section, we employed three spending proposals as alternatives without specifying the source of the revenues that were to be used in financing. But all fiscal decisions are two-sided; either explicitly or implicitly, a vote for or against a spending proposal implies something about the levy of taxes to finance that spending. The next step is obviously one of introducing this two-sidedness of the fiscal or budget account into our simple analytics.

Let us remain with the example where the alternatives are various amounts of spending on schooling in our three-person community. But now let us assume explicitly that the three persons (families) are to share equally in the cost. In Figure 11–2, we measure schooling in dollars' worth of inputs on the abscissa, as before. On the ordinate, we measure the demand and costs for schooling for 1, 2, and 3. The cost per unit faced by each person is shown at T. As drawn, individual 1, the "high spender," optimally prefers X dollars' of spending, making his behavior as depicted here consistent with that shown in Figure 11–1. Individual 2 optimally demands Y dollars' worth of schooling; individual 3 optimally prefers no outlay on schooling. Note,

FIGURE 11–2

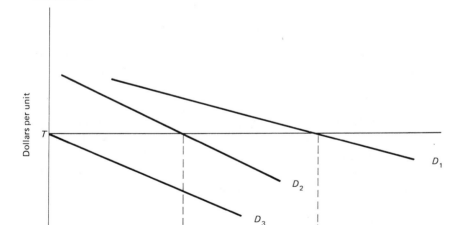

Spending on schooling

however, that at some lower share in costs, individual 3 would be willing to support schooling outlay.

The construction of Figure 11–2 allows us to bring out one feature of collective decision making that distinguishes it sharply from decision making in the private market. In the latter, when faced with a uniform price, persons adjust to their optimally preferred quantities. If the good depicted were a privately marketed good, fully divisible as among persons, there would be no difficulty in the three persons adjusting to separate quantities, as indicated. With a good that is supplied collectively or governmentally, however, all members of the community must adjust to the *same quantity*. This is the characteristic feature of collective supply, as we have emphasized at several points in this textbook. Hence, regardless of what the final outcome of a voting or decision process may be, some persons will be disappointed insofar as their optimally preferred demands are not met. As discussed in Chapter 7, it is possible to think of a differential "tax price" structure such that agreement on a common quantity could emerge. For present purposes, this ideal collective solution can be neglected. Given any tax-sharing scheme along with any rule for making collective decisions, some persons in the group will want more than that quantity chosen, others will want less. As shown in Figure 11–2, only the person with median preferences for the good, individual 2 in our example, will be "on his or her demand curve" for the collectively supplied good, at the specified sharing arrangement.

Under the conditions depicted, the outcome at Y will be an equilibrium one, so long as the majority voting rule remains in effect, and so long as other issues are treated separately. Despite the obvious unhappiness that individuals 1 and 3 both feel about the outcome at Y, despite the inefficiency of this outcome from their respective points of view, the median preferences remain controlling under majority voting. This conclusion remains true regardless of the relative intensity with which the separate persons evaluate the alternatives. Individual 2 may, for example, be relatively insensitive as among all three alternatives, only slightly preferring Y, while individual 1 may have very strong feelings about the relative desirability of X. However, so long as this set of proposals is considered in isolation from all others, so that all side payments are excluded, even those that represent political "trades," the relative intensity of preferences cannot be manifested under simply majority voting processes.

PUBLIC GOODS DEMAND AND RELATIVE INCOMES

The inefficiencies present in the majority voting solution as depicted in Figures 11-1 and 11-2 may be reduced by a shift in the tax-sharing scheme. In a small-number setting, such as our three-person community here, we might expect a process of bargaining on relative tax shares to take place. These small-number models are useful, however, only to the extent that they allow us to isolate and to discuss features that remain present in large-number settings. And, in the latter, bargaining among individuals and groups could not be expected to produce agreement on tax-sharing arrangements. Overall "constitutional" decisions must be made on the tax structure more or less independently from decisions as to budgetary outlays on specific goods and services financed under that structure.

How should the tax structure be organized? We have already discussed this in Chapter 7, but it will be useful to examine this question again in the context of simple voting models. If the demands of the separate persons can be related in some manner to externally observable criteria upon which tax shares may be levied, some shift toward greater efficiency in results can be made. If the demands of individuals for publicly supplied goods and services should be related directly to relative incomes, and if this relationship can be specified with some precision, a tax-sharing scheme may be implemented that will reduce substantially the inefficiencies generated by the operation of majority voting rules. The presumption that such a relationship can be specified lies at the basis of proposals to employ income and wealth taxation as major revenue sources.

Let us now apply this to our geometrical constructions. If individual 1, who desires the high rate of spending is the high-income receiver in the group; if individual 2 is the median-income receiver, and if individual 3 is the low-income receiver, tax shares can be adjusted to some income-related base. Hence, in lieu of equal shares as depicted in Figure 11-2, suppose that the tax shares are as shown in Figure 11-3, with T_1, T_2, and T_3 representing the tax prices faced by the three persons. Note that, at any output, these add vertically to equal three times the T of Figure 11-2. With this tax structure, and with unchanging demands, the degree of dissatisfaction is greatly reduced. Unless the relative tax shares are perfectly adjusted to differing demands, majority voting will not likely produce full efficiency.

But clearly the adjustment in the tax shares can move the group toward agreement on spending proposals.

As drawn in Figure 11–3, the low-income person 3 continues to prefer a smaller quantity than Y (in this case Z'), the continuing equilibrium outcome under majority voting, while the high-income person 1, continues to prefer a larger public goods quantity than Y (in this case X'). This suggests that, even though the low-income person is securing a differentially favorable "price" in the purchases of the public good, the necessity of adjusting to a commonly shared quantity involves an excessively large budget from 3's point of view. Similarly in converse for the high-income person. Despite the differentially unfavorable "price" which the tax system imposes upon 1, the necessity of adjusting to a commonly shared quantity involves the high-income person in a budget that is smaller than optimal. As before, only the median person is fully satisfied. In this particular configuration, the tax rate structure is insufficiently progressive to generate full efficiency.

This result can, of course, be reversed with changes in the rate structure. Suppose that the tax shares should be represented by T_1', T_2, and T_3'. In this case, the low-income person would desire a larger budget than Y, while the high-income person would desire a smaller

FIGURE 11–3

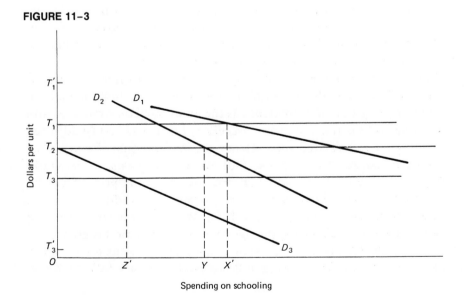

budget than Y. The tax rate structure would be overly progressive for full efficiency.

EMPIRICAL TESTS FOR TAX STRUCTURE EFFICIENCY

The analysis here is extremely abstract and overly simplified. Nonetheless, it does suggest certain empirical tests for the overall efficiency of a tax structure. The construction of Figure 11–3 suggests that the direction of dissatisfaction concerning budgetary size may be indicative of the efficiency of the tax rate structure. We recognize that, in real-world fiscal systems, a large share of revenues is collected from income taxes, which are normally progressive. Does the degree of rate progression accurately reflect the differential levels of demand for public goods and services by individuals at different income levels? Is the existing system unduly progressive? Or is it not progressive enough? This question may be answered by reference to the relationship between levels of income and attitudes toward total budgetary outlays. If we should find that, systematically, persons with lower incomes tend to favor larger public spending programs, financed with existing tax systems, while at the same time, persons with higher incomes tend to favor smaller public spending programs, this would provide evidence that the tax rate structure is overly progressive, as evaluated in strict efficiency terms. Conversely, if we should find that persons with lower incomes tend systematically to favor smaller budgets while persons with higher incomes favor larger budgets, we could say that the rate structure was insufficiently progressive. If no systematic relationship between income level of persons and attitudes toward budgetary size should be found, this would provide some indirect evidence that the tax rate structure is at least not grossly violative of efficiency norms.

Evidence exists only in bits and pieces. Persons at the very lowest income levels systematically tend to desire larger public spending programs; persons at the very highest income levels do not systematically oppose larger budgets. This combination suggests that the tax rate structure is perhaps overly progressive at the very lowest income ranges and insufficiently progressive at the highest income ranges. Over the broad median ranges of incomes, there appears to be no systematic relationship between income level and attitudes toward budgetary size. These conclusions are broadly suggestive, but they are based on very limited evidence. This is an area for useful and imaginative empirical work upon which more definitive conclusions might eventually be based.

SUPPLEMENTARY READINGS

The standard works in discussion of cyclical majorities are : Kenneth Arrow, *Social Choice and Individual Values* (New York: John Wiley & Sons, Inc., 1951, 1963), and Duncan Black, *The Theory of Committees and Elections* (Cambridge: Cambridge University Press, 1958).

.The application of majority voting models to fiscal decisions is discussed in James M. Buchanan, *Public Finance in Democratic Process* (Chapel Hill, N.C.: University of North Carolina Press, 1967).

12

Complex majority voting models

$\mathbf{I}$t is not difficult to construct complex models that appear superficially to be more descriptive of reality than the grossly simplified majority voting models examined in Chapter 11. The question is whether or not the more complex models yield additional predictive value sufficient to justify their derivation. This can never be fully answered, and the analyst or the student must somewhere make his or her own choice as to the appropriate stopping point. For our purposes in this basic textbook, one additional step will be taken. We shall discuss two-dimensional rather than uni-dimensional political choice. But even after this, our models of fiscal process will remain extreme simplifications.

In the simple majority voting models of Chapter 11, we assumed implicitly that there is only one issue to be voted upon. The collective decision involves the selection of a single candidate, a single-fiscal alternative, a single size of investment in schooling for the community. In elaborating on the fiscal decision alternatives, we found it necessary to bring in the tax side of the account, but we simply plugged this in, so to speak, and we did not allow this to enter the analysis as a set of alternatives among which a collective choice must be made. In this chapter, we shall explicitly make this type of extension.

MAJORITY VOTING AND A TWO-SECTOR BUDGET

Initially, it will be helpful to discuss this model in terms of a two-sector, or two-program, budget, with the tax institutions assumed to be fixed as before. Assume that the total budget in our simple three-person community is to be devoted to expenditures on schools *and* on police. The community must determine how much total spending is to be done publicly and how this total is to be allocated as between these two programs. If the collective decision on each item were to be made in complete independence from the other, the earlier results would not be modified. In this case, the person whose preferences are median for the group on each program separately considered would be controlling under simple majority voting. The budgetary combination would then reflect the two-median levels of outlay, given the taxing institutions. The median voter may be, but need not be, the same individual under each item.

It is possible to develop a simple geometric model of majority voting on a two-sector budget. In Figure 12–1, budgetary outlay on

FIGURE 12–1

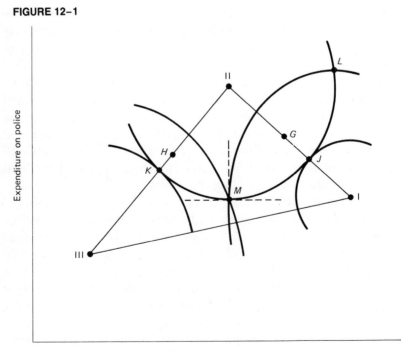

Expenditure on schooling

schools is measured on the horizontal axis and budgetary outlay on police is measured on the ordinate. Each of our three citizens will have some most preferred combination of spending on these two programs, given the assumed tax structure. Individuals 1's most preferred combination is shown at the point I in the diagram. Individual 1 prefers a relatively large outlay on education and a median outlay on police. Individual 2's most preferred combination is that labeled II and is characterized by a relatively large outlay on police and a median outlay on education. Finally, individual 3 prefers a relatively small outlay on both education and police as indicated by the optimum labeled III in the diagram.

The budget most preferred by an individual as represented by the optimum point is that which provides the individual with the utility maximizing combination of education, police protection and, implicitly, private consumption given the individual's gross income and his or her share of public sector costs as determined by the taxing institution. A departure from this optimum in *any* direction will result in lower utility for the individual. This suggests that the individual indifference curves in our two-sector diagram will surround the optimum point. The closer an indifference curve is to the optimum point, the higher the utility provided by the budget combination through which it passes. If each individual's preference for school spending is unaffected by outlays for the police function and vice versa, then the indifference curves surrounding his or her optimum point will be symmetrical. We shall make the assumption that the curves are perfect circles to keep the analysis relatively simple.

Given this assumption that the two budget items are independent within the preferences of each individual, the budget combination shown at M will be chosen if each of the two spending programs is considered in isolation from the other. Individual 2 will be the median voter with respect to school expenditure and individual 1 will be the median voter with respect to spending on the police function. However, there is an important difference between the one-dimension and the two-dimension cases which becomes clear with closer examination of the preference mappings in Figure 12–1. Note that for each budgetary item considered separately, individual preferences are single-peaked. The analysis of Chapter 11 suggested that when single-peakedness exists, the cyclical majority vanishes and a unique majority solution is guaranteed. This is not the case, however, when the budget has two or more spending components rather than just one. The indifference curves in Figure 12–1 indicate the willingness of the individual voters to make tradeoffs between the two spending programs. As a result, the budgetary solution at M in the figure is not a stable majority solution. Individuals 1 and 2, for example, will vote for a proposal to change to the budgetary combination at point G. But, if we suppose that G is attained, then individuals 2 and 3 will vote to shift to a combination such as that labeled H in the diagram. Despite the existence of single-peaked preferences on each issue taken separately, the cyclical majority problem emerges with full force when more than one variable is considered.

More generally, the lines connecting the various points of optima in Figure 12–1 have the following characteristics. At each point on the line connecting the optimum points of two voters, the indifference curves of those two voters are just tangent to one another as, for example, at points J and K in the diagram. If any two voters form a majority coalition to control budget choice, the budget upon which they agree will tend to be somewhere on this contract locus connecting their two points of optima. If a budget is not on their contract locus, then there is some budget on the locus which is preferred by both voters. Cycling occurs because if, for example, voters 1 and 2 have formed a coalition and agreed on a budget somewhere on their contract locus, voter 3, the minority voter, can offer either of the majority voters an alternative budget which may, for example, be on the contract locus connecting 3's optimum point with that of voter 1 or 2 and which would be preferred by both that voter and voter 3 to the budget agreed upon by the old coalition of 1 and 2. And, of course, alternative coalitions could once again secure majority approval over that one. Cycling will be continuous under the conditions depicted and, for our purposes, may be considered to be among points on the three contract loci.

CYCLICAL MAJORITY AND PARETO OPTIMALITY

Once again, however, there are reasons why the prediction of cyclical majorities should not be disturbing. First of all, the set of positions among which majority voting results cycle will tend to be coincident with the set of positions that are Pareto optimal or efficient, given the two dimensional limits imposed on the model. In the construction of Figure 12–1, the Pareto optimal set of positions is defined by the boundaries and internal part of the triangular area marked off by the contract loci connecting optimum points I, II and III. From any point within this set, no budgetary change can be made which does not harm at least one of the three voters. When the budget changes from M to G, for example, voter III is made worse off. On the other hand, any budget outside the triangular area is dominated by at least one budget on or within the boundaries of the triangular area which at least one voter regards as more satisfactory and which no voter regards as less satisfactory. For example, both voters 1 and 3 would prefer the budget at point J to that at point L while voter 2 is just indifferent between the two budgets.

As was discussed in the preceding section, majority vote cycling will tend to involve budgets on the contract loci or outer boundaries of the Pareto optimal region. Hence, from the point of view of economic efficiency as defined in the strict Paretion sense and limited to two dimensions, there need be no cause to worry about majority voting cycles. Aside from the costs that are involved in change itself, which may, of course, be significant, the shift from one optimal position to another cannot be judged as either good or bad in an efficiency sense.

CYCLICAL MAJORITY AND MANY-PERSON GROUPS

To this point, the analysis has been represented in terms of very simple three-person models. These have considerable explanatory relevance, but the effects generated by changing to a model that involves many actors should be noted. Consider the two-dimensional diagram of Figure 12–1. Instead of three persons, assume that there are many persons, and that their respective points of optima are scattered throughout the surface of the figure. It is relatively easy to trace out the effects of this single change on the results. The majority voting combination will still be determined by the intersection of middle lines of optima if the two issues are considered independently of each other. Also, there will tend to be an area within which the cyclical majority phenomenon exists. But as the number of persons becomes large, this area will become quite small, in fact trivially so, as the number of voters becomes very large. We shall not trace this result out in detail, but it may provide the student with a useful geometrical exercise. It suggests yet another reason why we should not become overly concerned about the instability created by the presence of the cyclical majority.

MAJORITY VOTING AND EXPLICIT VOTE TRADING UNDER TWO-ITEM BUDGETS

In Figure 12–1, the combination shown at M will be selected by majority voting if the two variables or issues are settled independently of each other. As we showed, however, the position at M will not be stable in that proposals can be made which will be preferred to M by a majority of the voters. This involves the necessity of considering the two issues simultaneously or as a combination rather than independently. By shifting from M to G, for example, both components of the position must be taken into account. In an indirect sense, therefore, the two members of the majority that approve the shift can be said to be "trading" or "exchanging." They are not, however, explicitly trading or exchanging votes as such. Instead they are exchanging agreements on a combination that embodies two elements.

The distinction between this and explicit vote trading, as such, can

FIGURE 12–2

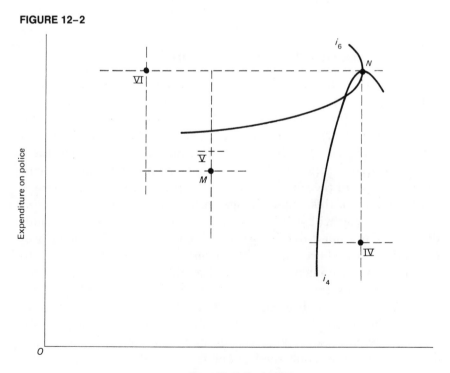

Expenditure on schooling

be shown by reference to Figure 12–2. As before, assume that the optimally preferred position for three persons are shown at IV, V, and VI. In this case, however, we must introduce differential intensities of preference for at least one of our participants. Individual 4, whose optimal position is shown at IV, is, we shall assume, relatively indifferent as to the level of outlay on police, but is intensely interested in a relatively high outlay on schools. The indifference contours surrounding IV tend, therefore, to be elongated in a vertical direction. Individual 5, whose optimal position is shown at V, is not intensely interested in any one of the two budgetary items but rather, prefers a median outlay on police and a median outlay on schools. Individual 6, whose optimal position is at VI, is relatively indifferent as to the outlay on schools but is intensely interested in having a large outlay on the police forces. The indifference contours surrounding VI tend to be elongated in a horizontal pattern.

As in the earlier construction, if each issue or item is voted upon independently, the majority rule outcome will be at M, where the middle lines of optima intersect. In this case, note that individual 5 is the voter with median preferences on each issue. Hence, the majority voting outcome will fall precisely on 5's optimal position. M and V will coincide.

This position is likely to be very unstable, however, even if the two items continue to be voted on separately. With relatively intense preferences, explicit vote trading may emerge. Suppose that individual 4 offers to turn over to individual 6 a vote on the public outlay item in the budget in exchange for 4's vote on schools. With this explicit vote exchange, the majority voting outcome will shift dramatically from M to N, outside the Pareto-optimal set of points, and perhaps far removed from M. Despite holding a seemingly advantageous position, individual 5 will be unable to do much about this.

This overly simplified geometrical illustration is helpful in providing an elementary beginning of the analysis of the complex vote-trading processes that take place in representative assemblies. This process, familiarly known as logrolling, is widely recognized to occur. As the construction shows, it provides a means whereby the person or group with relatively intense preferences on one particular issue from among a set of issues can secure some satisfactory meeting of its desires on that issue by sacrificing its own power of decision on other issues. The vote-trading process also allows demands that satisfy less than a majority of the group to be met.

TAX CONSTRAINTS IN A TWO-SECTOR BUDGET
UNDER MAJORITY VOTING

To this point we have discussed the allocation of budgetary resources as between the two expenditure categories, schools and police, without specifying the revenue sources. This omission must be corrected. The derivation of the individual preference maps requires, of course, that some means of raising the required revenues exists that is known by each citizen. In his internal tradeoffs as between outlay on schools and police, each person knows precisely how his tax bill will change from position to position on Figure 12–1 or 12–2. Each person must know how much tax he or she will be required to pay to finance each and every budgetary combination that is possible. With this assumption, the analysis above is unobjectionable, provided we assume that total rates are allowed to be set residually. That is to say, majority voting on alternative budgetary combinations will produce some position, say M in Figure 12–1, which implies a specific budgetary total. If tax rates are then adjusted so as to produce this amount of revenue without the necessity of a specific tax rate decision, there is no new problem created by recognizing the tax constraints. In local or municipal government financing, this model of fiscal decision is descriptively realistic. Taxes are largely levied on real property, and the actual rates of tax are allowed to be settled residually after the required budgetary expenditures are known. The allocation of funds within the budget sets the level of tax rates required to produce the necessary revenues. This has been the model traditionally used in much public finance discussion, and the collectivity has often been contrasted with the individual economy in this respect. The model suggests that the income of the collectivity, the revenue collected, is the dependent variable, with the "needs" representing the independent variable. By contrast, for the family or the individual, the income, or revenue, is presumed to be the independent variable, with "needs" being the dependent one, at least as these are met in the marketplace. The limitations on this contrast seem evident, but frequent reference to it should be noted.

For many fiscal structures, it is clear that the tax rates are not residually determined by the budgetary allocation decisions. Specific decisions may be made as to rates of tax, and hence as to the total budgetary commitments. And budgetary allocation among separate components may be made *after*, not before, the specific decision on tax rates. We need to expand and to modify the analytical models of majority voting rules to discuss this type of fiscal decision process.

Consider Figure 12–3. As before, we measure spending on schools on the abscissa and spending on police on the ordinate. Since we measure spending in dollar units, a diagonal line running from northwest to southeast at 45° with the axes will represent various possible combinations within the limitations of a fixed total budget. We may label such lines as isobudget lines; only a few such lines are drawn in Figure 12–3, representative of the whole family. If a total budget is set independently of the allocation among the two spending items, majority voting rules may then determine which among all the possible combinations will be selected. The problem is, in a sense, converted to one dimension. Consider isobudget line labeled as BB. Individual 1 will, from among these attainable combinations, prefer position b_1; individual 2 will prefer position b_2, and individual 3 will prefer position b_3. As the construction indicates, the median prefer-

FIGURE 12–3

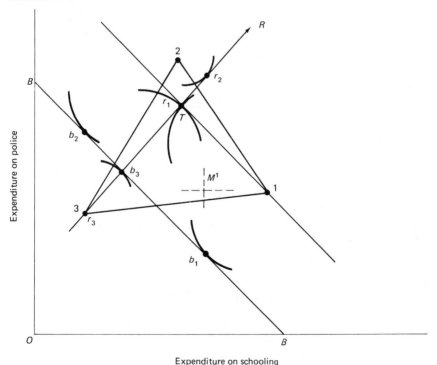

Expenditure on schooling

ence will be that of individual 3, and single-peakedness will ensure that b_3 will result from the application of majority voting rules. For any isobudget line, we could trace through a similar exercise and determine the allocation within the budget total that would secure majority approval. We can then trace out the locus of such majority allocations over the whole family of budgetary levels. Such a locus is shown by the ray R in Figure 12–3.

If individual members of the community know the general shape of this budgetary locus, that is, if they know roughly how the budget will be allocated as between the two public services at all possible levels of spending, we can then determine which budgetary level majority voting will produce. This can be shown readily from the same construction in Figure 12–3. Movement along the locus R becomes a second one-dimensional majority voting problem, and single-peakedness ensures the existence of a stable outcome. Note that individual 1 will, when faced with the prospect of choosing among the combinations along R, prefer r_1; individual 2 will prefer r_2; individual 3 will prefer r_3. The budget level that will be selected is shown at T.

The intersection of locus R with the isobudget line at T is analogous to the intersection of the middle lines of optima at M in the construction of Figure 12–1. If the collective decision process proceeds as here indicated, that is, with the tax rate chosen independently (which in turn determines the size of the budget) from the allocation of spending as between the two budgetary components, the position at T will be stable.

This allows us to state one important principle. The position at T, attained under this decision-making process, will not be the same as that attained at M^1, under the different process, despite the fact that the preference mappings of the three persons remain unchanged. The majority voting outcome that will emerge will depend on the procedures that are employed. The decision-making institutions become relevant variables in generating the outcomes that are chosen.

TAX ADJUSTMENTS AND POTENTIAL AGREEMENT UNDER TWO-SECTOR BUDGETS

Recall that, in the discussion of Chapter 11, we demonstrated that the range of individual differences concerning the preferred quantities of public spending in the one-good or one-sector model could be reduced by adjusting tax shares among individuals. It will be useful to examine the possible application of a similar exercise in the two-sector budget model.

In all of the discussion here, we have implicitly assumed that the basic tax structure is settled. Assume that taxes are levied on income. If the areas of disagreement, as indicated in Figure 12–4, where the three most preferred positions 1, 2, and 3 are identical with those of Figure 12–3, are due to differences that can be related to income levels, general tax adjustments can narrow the range of discord, just as in the one-dimensional model. If individual 3, who prefers a small budget, does so because of a relatively low income, a change in the tax to increase the degree of progressivity may shift his preferred position to 3′, reducing Pareto-optimal set of positions as indicated. In summary, general tax rate adjustments may, in some cases, reduce the area of potential agreement in the two-sector budget diagram to an area elongated along an isobudget line. General tax adjustments cannot reduce the range of disagreement between those who prefer quite different budgetary combinations.

FIGURE 12–4

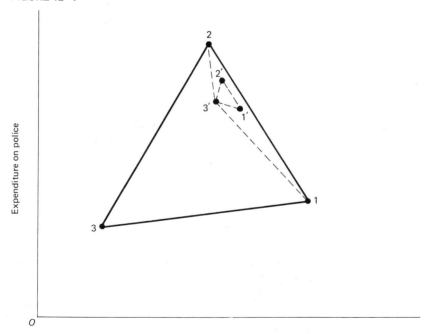

Expenditure on schooling

This range of disagreement can be reduced by introducing special tax rate adjustments for specific budgetary items. If, in whole or in part, earmarked taxes should be placed on direct beneficiaries of school outlay or on police outlay the range of disagreement may be reduced to that illustrated by the triangular area shown by 1′, 2′, and 3′ in Figure 12–4. Tax adjustments reduce the size of the Pareto-optimal set of points or positions, when these are defined in two dimensions. This illustrates the more basic proposition that the possibilities for improvements that are mutually agreeable to all parties increase as more and more variables are allowed to change.

AGENDA CONTROL AND BUDGETARY OUTCOMES

The influence of decision-making institutions on budgetary outcomes noted previously suggests that one way in which interested parties might seek to manipulate those outcomes to their own advantage is to capture control of the agenda or set of rules governing the collective decision process. Recall from the earlier discussion that a different budget was chosen when the two budgetary components were voted on independently than was chosen when total spending and allocation of that total were the two separate agenda items put before the voters. Different budgets provide potentially different levels of satisfaction for individual voters. Thus, some voters can gain and others lose from a change in the agenda. In this section, we shall examine two ways in which control of the agenda might be used by relatively high demanders of public services to extract majority support for budgets which are significantly larger than those which would be approved in the absence of such agenda manipulation.

Suppose that in every budget period, voters are asked simply to approve or disapprove a proposed budget. If the budget proposal is voted down, some predetermined alternative budget labeled the *reversion budget* is automatically adopted for the period in question. Thus voters, in effect, are asked to choose between the formal budget proposal and the reversion budget. If the reversion budget is below that budget which is most preferred by the median voter, the maximum new budget proposal which can receive majority support will be significantly above the median voter's most preferred budget.

This method of agenda control can be employed in budgets which allocate funds among two or more functions. For simplicity, however, the single-function budget will be examined here. Figure 12–5 illustrates the ordinal rankings of three voters over various levels of public spending. Voters 1, 2 and 3 are the respective low, median, and high demanders of the public service in question. If the voters had the opportunity to consider all possible spending proposals, only one budget could receive majority support over all others. That budget would be, of course, B^*, the budget most preferred by voter 2, the median voter. In a vigorously competitive and relatively unconstrained political process, B^* would seem to be the most likely budget choice.

Suppose, however, only one budget is to be offered to the voters for their approval or rejection with the reversion budget, labeled B_r in the diagram, to be automatically adopted in the event of rejection. The range of budget proposals which could potentially receive majority approval as alternatives to B_r includes all spending levels between B_r and B_m. If a proposal is advanced which either exceeds B_m or falls below B_r, the median voter and one of the others will vote to reject it

FIGURE 12–5

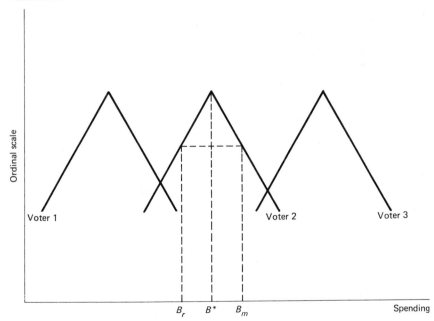

in favor of B_r. Suppose also that voter 3, the high demander, has succeeded in controlling the choice of which proposal is to be advanced. This control is a valuable perogative. Voter 3 wants to propose the largest budget possible, subject to the constraint that it not be too large to obtain majority approval. This budget, is of course, B_m. By obtaining an effective monopoly over the choice of budget proposals, voter 3 has succeeded in obtaining majority support for a budget which is larger than that which would be chosen in a more competitive political process.[1]

When the total budget is to be allocated among two functions, a second potential means of manipulating the final outcome is that of controlling the mix of spending on the two functions. Voters are allowed to vote directly only on the total level of spending with the proportionate allocation of that total having been predetermined. To clarify, consider Figure 12–6. In the figure, the most preferred combinations of spending on education and police for our three voters are as indicated by the optimum points I, II and III, with the corresponding circular indifference curves surrounding each voter's optimum.

Suppose the budget mix has been set at the relative proportions indicated by the ray labeled A in the diagram. If voters are asked to vote on a total level of spending given the knowledge that the final allocation will lie on A, that level of spending associated with the budget labeled a will receive majority support. If the spending mix were instead that reflected in ray B, total spending to provide budget b would be chosen. A fixed budget mix along ray C would result in budget c, and so on. Let the heavy line labeled XX in the figure depict that actual budget choices associated with the various budget mixes. It can now be seen that control of the budget mix provides a means of manipulating budgetary choice. If, for example, voter 2 were to control the mix, that mix associated with ray B will provide 2 with the most satisfactory budget from among the set of feasible alternative along XX. If voters 1 or 3 were to gain control of the mix it is obvious that different budgetary outcomes would result.[2]

---

[1] A detailed presentation of this model, is given by Thomas Romer and Howard Rosenthal in a paper entitled "Political Resource Allocation, Controlled Agendas and the Status Quo," (Public Choice, forthcoming).

[2] This model is developed in detail by Robert Mackay and Carolyn Weaver in a paper entitled "Commodity Bundling and Agenda Control in the Public Sector" (unpublished manuscript).

FIGURE 12-6

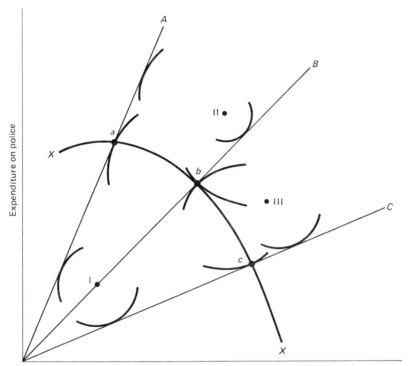

CONCLUSIONS AND SUMMARY

The geometrical constructions developed in this chapter, although they remain extremely simple in one sense, may seem to be more complex than their predictive, explanatory value warrants. In the real world, budgets involve many dimensions of both the spending and the tax sides of the account. Any descriptively realistic model of the process through which collective decisions on the many variables of a budget are made would prove far too complex and cumbersome for useful expository treatment. It is hoped that the models of this and the preceding chapter provide an understanding of budget decision processes which could not be secured by concentrating on the descriptive complexities of modern budgets. The latter complexities will become apparent when we look at federal spending programs in the next part of the textbook.

SUPPLEMENTARY READING

For an early treatment of some of the basic geometry, the student may consult Duncan Black and R. A. Newing, *Committee Decisions with Complementary Valuation* (London: William Hodge, 1951). Other treatments of certain aspects of the material discussed is found in Gordon Tullock, *Towards a Mathematics of Politics* (Ann Arbor, Mich.: University of Michigan Press, 1967), and in James M. Buchanan, *Demand and Supply of Public Goods* (Chicago: Rand McNally & Co., 1968).

13

The fiscal "constitution"

We have raised such questions as: What share of national product shall be allocated through governmental rather than market process? How large shall the total governmental budget be? How shall this budget be factored down as among separate spending components or categories? In this part of the textbook, we have tried to explain how the answers to such questions as these emerge from a democratic decision structure. But one significant fiscal question is not present in this listing: How shall taxes be levied? In the brief references made to taxes in the preceding chapters, we have merely assumed specific tax institutions to be existent.

TAX SHARES, DIVISIBILITY, AND ZERO-SUM GAMES

The reason why the tax question has been relatively neglected is that it is characteristically different from questions concerning budgetary size and allocation. The nature of taxation itself ensures this. Given any specified tax structure, one which relates tax obligations to an economic base or one which assigns tax shares among different persons and groups, we can analyze the fiscal decision process in terms of areas of agreement on the part of all persons or on the part of persons in a dominant majority coalition, agreement concerning the budgetary variables. This was the procedure followed in Chapters 11 and 12. Agreement here consists in the settlement on values for variables which all persons must commonly share. The final values chosen for budgetary size and composition must be available equally to all members of the community; these are indivisible in this sense.

We cannot, however, proceed in reverse order. We cannot, that is to say, assume that these budgetary variables, both as to size and composition, are fixed in advance and then proceed to analyze the process of group agreement on the allocation of tax shares among individuals and groups. The reason is that tax shares are measured in monetary units that are fully divisible as among separate persons. There is no area of agreement on such sharing, at least in simplified models where persons are assumed to be motivated primarily by their own economic well-being.[1] Taxation takes on aspects of a zero-sum game. If one person succeeds in reducing his tax liability by a dollar, some other person or persons finds his or their liability increased by $1. Taxation takes on properties of either/or; either one person or the other pays.

When this very simple fact is recognized, the difficulties of securing any agreement at all on the allocation of tax shares becomes apparent. Collective decisions on tax systems and changes in these systems become extremely costly, and we may wonder that existing systems, once established, are ever changed. And we should not be at all surprised by continual agitation for so-called "tax reform" while observed tax institutions remain relatively stable. At a naive level, any chosen allocation of tax shares would seem to represent the exploitation of the politically weak by the politically strong. In such a simplistic game theory model of taxation, we should expect that members of the dominant political coalition would pay little or no taxes while imposing heavy burdens on members of the powerless minority.

HOW CAN GENERAL TAXES BE EXPLAINED?

Observations of fiscal structures falsify the predictions which the simple game theory model makes. Taxes are observed which are general in their imposition. All persons and groups, or substantially all, pay taxes, and individual shares seem to depend upon reasonably

---

[1]As discussed earlier in Chapter 8, modifications on these simplified models will allow for some agreement on taxing schemes even for purely redistributive purposes, but these complications are ignored in this chapter.

explicit criteria of economic status such as incomes, property holdings, and consumption spending on all or on particular products and services. Can we possibly explain the generality of taxation by resort to simple and abstract models of democratic decision process?

Reconciliation is achieved when we recognize that collective decisions on taxing institutions are temporally different from those involving budgetary size and composition. Budgets are made within the restrictions of existing tax institutions. This is descriptively true, and the simple majority voting models yield fruitful insights. But tax-share decisions are not made with the restrictions of existing budgets. Tax-share choices are made independently, and they are made to be applicable over a much longer period of time than budgetary choices. The tax-share choices are essentially constitutional in the descriptive meaning of this term. That is to say, tax institutions, which embody specific tax-share allocations as among separate persons and groups, are collectively chosen as quasi-permanent fiscal devices, designed to yield revenues over a long sequence of budgetary periods and over many possible budgetary compositions. For this reason, it is appropriate that tax structures be conceived as inherent parts of a "fiscal constitution" that is changed only occasionally and then not in direct response to short-run modifications in the budgetary variables.

In referring to the "tax constitution" or "fiscal constitution" here we emphasize the quasi-permanent nature of tax-law changes. We do not necessarily suggest that tax laws should be explicitly incorporated in the constitution document and thereby made immune to legislative tampering. The advantages of tax-law stability through time should not, however, be overlooked, and there may be strong arguments for more explicit recognition that such laws should indeed be treated in constitutional terms. The apparently growing support for imposing constitutional tax limits will be discussed in Chapter 16.

Consider the idealized selection of tax-sharing arrangements under a constitutional approach. Individuals are asked to select, to "vote for," tax-sharing alternatives on the assumption that the structure finally chosen will be used to finance budgets at all possible levels and of all possible combinations of spending items. If individuals are uncertain as to their own specific private economic status during future periods of time and also uncertain as to their own desires for specific public spending programs, they may think in terms of general taxing schemes, those that might be broadly acceptable over wide ranges of individual positions. In this choice setting, the conception of "fair" or "equitable" taxation takes on a meaning that is relevant for individual participation in such collective choice processes. The approach to taxation here is akin to that discussed in Chapter 8 with respect to contractual or constitutional fiscal redistribution. Criteria for tax "justice," or "fairness," here are closely related to the more general precepts for "justice" discussed by John Rawls.

Even at this constitutional level of decision, individuals will, of course, have differing notions as to preferred tax-sharing schemes. But a range of agreement does seem possible in this setting, and the zero-sum aspects of taxation in the single-period fixed budget setting largely disappear. The selection of a set of tax institutions here becomes analogous to the selection of rules for a game, by participants who do not fully know what their own positions will be in subsequent rounds of actual play. Each person will, in his own interest, be led to select a set of rules that he considers broadly "fair," so as to prevent undue penalization for those who may be, unpredictably, in unfavorable positions.

WHY MUST ALL PERSONS PAY TAXES IN THE SAME WAY?

The central question of this chapter is: How are taxes to be paid? As we have noted, tax payments made by an individual are measured in money, generalized purchasing power, and this is fully divisible as among persons. How is the question as to how taxes are to be paid any different from the question as to how prices are to be paid in the private economy? The essential difference here is that tax arrangements which are applicable to one person must be applicable to all persons in the community. Individuals cannot individually choose how they are to meet their obligations to the government. Ideally, this might seem to be an optimal arrangement. Suppose that each person owes a share in government financing amounting to $1,000. Why could we not allow each person to pay this sum in any way that he or she chooses? This procedure could, in fact, be followed if the size of the financial obligation should be fully independent of the means of payment. However, if we want to adopt tax-sharing institutions that are not directly related to budgetary size and composition, the means of payment become, in turn, a means for determining relative shares.

PROGRESSIVE TAXATION AND
DEMOCRATIC CONSENSUS

We observe that progressive income taxation is an important revenue producer in the United States. Is it possible to explain the origins of this important tax institution in terms of the approach that is examined in this chapter? Opponents of progressive income taxation often denounce this institution as demonstrable exploitation of the rich by the poor who make up the dominant political majority. Proponents often defend this institution on purely ethical grounds without reference to any economic origins.

It seems probable that at least some support for progression, as a sharing scheme, does lie in the type of calculus suggested here. If individuals are faced with the choice among several taxing institutions, in the knowledge that the alternative selected will remain in effect over a long period of time, and if they themselves are uncertain as to their own economic status over this period of time, they may well "vote for" progressive taxes on income. Under this institution, they know that they will be subjected to heavy taxes only if they are fortunate enough to receive large incomes; if they are unlucky in the economic game and secure only a small income, they are assured that their taxes will be more than proportionately reduced. On the basis of this sort of calculus, and quite apart from any fellow feelings for others, feelings which can be partially translated into demands for explicit redistribution as a "public good," a certain logic of progressive taxation can be developed. Individuals may agree, within certain broad limits, on progressive income taxation as a part of their fiscal constitution. Progressive income taxation will be further analyzed for its economic effects and for its actual institutional form in the United States, but it is useful that its place in a democratic social process be recognized. To the extent that progressive rate structures are viewed by high-income earners and low-income earners alike as means through which the former are exploited by the latter through the fiscal process, democratic consensus has broken down.

DIRECT VERSUS INDIRECT TAXATION

The constitutional approach to the choice among tax institutions offers interesting insights into the age-old question concerning the desirability of direct versus indirect taxation. Direct taxation is defined as taxation imposed upon the person who is intended to be the final bearer of the burden of payment. Indirect taxation is defined as taxation imposed upon others than the person who is intended to bear the final burden. When participating in a choice among fiscal instruments, in the knowledge that the instrument selected is to remain in force over a whole sequence of budgetary periods, why should an individual prefer to pay a tax indirectly? Such a tax, which would normally be imposed on the purchase of a particular product or products, clearly distorts the individual budgetary allocation in the private market. (We shall discuss the familiar excess burden argument in detail in a later chapter.) Why should individuals choose this tax if they recognize the presence of this predictable distortion?

A person may, quite rationally, select a tax which imposes such a distortion for the very reason of such distortion. This is the very essence of what is often called *sumptuary taxation*, defined as taxation that is designed to discourage the consumption of certain products and services. There are two separate elements involved in such taxation. By "voting for" a tax on a particular product, an individual may be indicating a preference for a scheme that discourages *others* from consuming products which he or she thinks they should not consume. (Taxes designed for this purpose will be separately examined in Chapter 27.) This is the traditional interpretation that has been placed on the support for sumptuary taxation. However, the individual may select the indirect tax here in order to discourage his or her own consumption of the product in future periods. The constitutional approach allows us to isolate this second explanatory feature which the more traditional approach tended to ignore.

A second reason why the rational person may deliberately choose the taxation of specific consumption items is equivalent to the explanation of the support of progressive taxation outlined above. Certain consumption items may be quite closely correlated in usage with high-income levels; in addition, these items may be known to be displacable in time. Individuals who are uncertain as to their income earning prospects may not be at all averse to placing a heavy burden of taxation on the consumption of items that they expect to demand only during periods of relative affluence.

TAX SHARES AND TOTAL TAXATION

Our discussion of the constitutional approach to taxation in this chapter has been largely devoted to tax-share distribution. To this point, we have not examined the question of the level or total of taxation. But these two aspects may be closely related. The tax-share distribution may influence the level of total taxation that governments might impose. Recognizing this, individuals may want to restrict governmental revenue-raising indirectly by the specific selection of certain tax-sharing institutions. For example, for a given base, progressive taxation will raise less revenue than proportional taxation. Or, a less comprehensive tax base will produce less total taxation than a more comprehensive base. Some of these considerations will be examined in Chapter 16.

CONCLUSIONS AND SUMMARY

We have done little more than sketch out a beginning of a constitutional approach to the selection of tax-sharing institutions in this chapter. The summary treatment covers material that has been developed in more detail in other works. The whole approach is not traditionally included in elementary textbooks and there remain many aspects of the "fiscal constitution" that have not been analyzed satisfactorily.

SUPPLEMENTARY READING

The student interested in pursuing the discussion of this chapter further is referred to James J. Buchanan, *Public Finance in Democratic Process* (Chapel Hill, N.C.: University of North Carolina Press, 1967), and to Geoffrey Brennan and James M. Buchanan, *The Power to Tax: Analytical Foundations of a Fiscal Constitution* (Cambridge University Press, forthcoming).

14

Bureaucracy and the supply of public services

$$T$$he discussion in the preceding chapters of this part focused on the demand for public services. Analysis of the collective decision rules under which the actual nature and quantity of public services are determined was of primary concern. This chapter is concerned with the supply of public services and specifically the implications of different institutional organizations of that supply. Specifically, is it necessary for public agencies to be formed to produce public services, or can private enterprise be relied upon to perform that function?

Bureaucracy is the social institution through which publicly provided services are publicly produced. It is an institution of increasing importance in American society. While some public services are purchased directly from private enterprises, most are supplied by government bureaus. The expansion of the public sector discussed previously in this text has been accompanied by substantial expansion of the bureaucracy. Consider, for example, that in 1900, only 1 of every 20 members of the U.S. labor force was employed by a governmental unit. By 1977, this figure had risen to one in six.

The choice to supply a public service through a government bureau rather than private enterprise, or vice versa, can have significant implications for the efficiency with which the service is supplied. This decision is, therefore, also an important component of public choice.

It may be as relevant to determining public sector outcomes as the choice of the collective decision rules under which citizen demands for public services are expressed. This chapter will attempt to clarify the relevant differences between public and private supply.

MODELS OF BUREAUCRACY

Almost everyone has some opinion on how well or how poorly bureaucracies function. The two points of view which are probably the most widely held are diametrically opposed in the sense that in one, bureaucrats tend to do almost everything right, while in the other, they do almost nothing right. In the first model, bureaucrats automatically perform the tasks assigned to them under various public expenditure programs in an efficient, effective manner. Pursuit of the public interest is assumed to be their only objective. The latter model tends to view bureaucrats as stupid or venal, or perhaps both, but, above all, incapable of performing the tasks assigned to them in anything even approaching an efficient manner. Both of these models suggest a futility of further analysis of bureaucratic institutions: one, because no improvement is necessary in the performance of public bureaus; the other, because such improvement is a hopeless task.

An alternative and more fruitful approach to the study of bureaucracy views bureaucrats as rational, utility-maximizing individuals, reacting to the constraints and incentives present in the bureaucratic institutions in which they operate. With this approach, it becomes possible to develop a predictive theory of bureaucratic behavior and, perhaps more importantly, to think in terms of designing bureaucratic institutions so as to provide stronger incentives for bureaucrats to pursue the public interest while simultaneously seeking their own self-interest.

Because the alternative to bureaucratic supply of public services is the purchase of such services from private firms, the most useful framework for analysis of bureaucratic institutions is one which allows easy comparison of different supply characteristics which emerge from public and private production. Here the important issue to examine is that of what differences exist between the two institutions with respect to the incentive structure which can result in differences in actual supply. The three differences which are most commonly noted in this respect are: (1) the lack of competition among several public bureaus engaged in supplying the same service, (2) the structure of public bureaus which prevents their being operated for profit, and (3) the fact that public services are usually not sold for a price, but rather produced with lump-sum appropriations.

Unlike the market, in which several firms are usually engaged in supplying the same good or service, a government bureau is typically given exclusive responsibility for providing a particular public service. What are the implications of this lack of competition? Perhaps the most obvious is a reduced incentive for that service to be provided efficiently. If several bureaus were to compete for funds to produce a particular service, for example, each would probably have an incentive to prove to the agency responsible for allocating such funds (the Congress or the Office of Management and Budget [OMB], for example), that it could provide the service more efficiently than the others.

The existence of competing bureaus makes it easier for the agency allocating funds to police or measure their efficiency. Suppose, for example, that only a single bureau was engaged in producing some service and that it requested an appropriation of x dollars to provide a certain level of the service. Without detailed knowledge of the production function, the cost of resources, and so on, it is impossible for a congressman or an OMB analyst to know whether x dollars is really necessary to provide that amount of service, or whether it could be provided with a smaller expenditure. The existence of several bureaus providing the same service provides some bench marks for the decision maker in that he can compare the performance of any one bureau to that of the others.

Private entrepreneurs pursue profit; bureaucrats are forbidden to do so. This difference may also be significant in attempting to predict differences in supply by firm or bureau. Again, the argument most commonly advanced is that the goal of profit-maximization is accompanied by strong incentives to minimize production costs. Because private entrepreneurs capture any excess of revenue over cost as income, there is an obvious incentive for them to seek to produce their product in the least costly manner possible. In contrast, should a government bureau ever spend less than its appropriation, the funds would either be carried over into the next year with the new appropriation reduced accordingly or simply returned to general funds. They could not be used to reward the bureaucrat whose innovation or administrative ability enabled the savings to be made.

If bureaucrats do not maximize profits, what do they maximize, and how does the choice of a maximand affect the supply of public services? The simplest answer is, of course, that bureaucrats maximize utility. However, this answer does not yield any useful insight into the operations of bureaucracy unless or until the arguments in the utility function are identified. In other words, what specifically do bureaucrats seek to attain?

It has been argued by some that because bureaucrats are prevented from increasing their incomes by operating their bureaus profitably, they will instead seek to supplement their incomes by increasing the nonmonetary emoluments of their offices. They will seek to include in their appropriations such things as plush offices, chauffered limousines, extensive "business" travel, and so on. This type of behavior is probably difficult to police effectively, but the amount of actual inefficiency which results is probably quite small. Assuming a competitive supply of bureaucrats, in the long run these non-pecuniary benefits may simply replace some of the monetary income, or salary, which must be offered to attract individuals to the civil service.

Niskanen has advanced a model of bureaucracy with more serious implications for the efficiency with which public services are provided.[1] He assumes that bureaucrats are primarily interested in obtaining such things as higher salaries, prestige, power, and patronage, and that the ability of any bureaucrat to obtain these things is positively correlated with the size of the budget which he administers. It follows that bureaucrats will be primarily interested in maximizing the budget of their bureaus.

Given budget maximization as a bureaucratic objective, what are the implications for the supply of public services? Niskanen argues that the objective of budget maximization combined with the position of most bureaus as monopoly suppliers of some public service will result in an excessive supply of such services. Primarily because of their monopoly position, bureaucrats are able to confront the agencies responsible for appropriating funds to them with all-or-nothing offers to supply public services rather than simply offering a per unit price and allowing the agency to choose a preferred quantity at that price.

The rationale of all-or-nothing offers can be clarified by considering the following example. Within limits, individuals can be offered a

[1]William Niskanen, *Bureaucracy and Representative Government* (Chicago: Aldine-Atherton, Inc., 1971).

certain number of units of any good for some total expenditure and will accept the offer rather than forego consumption of that good completely. They can be forced to buy a larger quantity of the product when confronted with such an offer than they would buy if they were instead simply allowed to buy as much of the product as they desired at a per unit price equal to the average price implicit in the all-or-nothing offer. Obviously, purchasers of any service are better off when allowed to quantity adjust in response to offered prices than when forced to respond to all-or-nothing offers. In Niskanen's model, the ability of bureaucrats to confront the appropriating agency with all-or-nothing offers to supply public services enables them to secure much larger appropriations than are consistent with economic efficiency. If sponsors can be exploited fully in this way, public services will be provided in such large amounts that there will be no net benefits from their provision.

Lindsay has developed an interesting model of bureaucratic performance which differs somewhat from the Niskanen approach.[2] He argues that a crucial difference between market and governmental provision of a good or service is that, in the latter case, the persons responsible for appropriating funds to finance the service are often not direct users or consumers of that service. Education and welfare services provide examples of this phenomenon. Many potentially desirable attributes or characteristics of services can not be easily detected or measured by nonusers. Inability of legislators to monitor such attributes makes it difficult, if not impossible, for bureaus to be rewarded for providing them. As a consequence, bureaus have no strong incentive to provide these characteristics even though direct consumers of the service have a latent demand for them. Instead, governmentally financed and produced services are characterized by a relative overabundance of those attributes which can be easily monitored by the legislature. For example, legislators may find it difficult to carefully monitor quality, but can more easily monitor cost per service unit. This makes it difficult for a bureau to improve the quality of its service because the legislators will observe the increase in cost but not the improved quality.

---

[2]C. M. Lindsay, "A Theory of Government Enterprise," *Journal of Political Economy* (October, 1976).

CAN BUREAUCRATIC PERFORMANCE BE IMPROVED?

The preceding discussion was essentially a critical one. Emphasis was on the shortcomings of bureaucracy. The obvious issue which remains is whether or how bureaucratic performance can be improved. Some suggestions are obvious from the preceding discussion. Substantial improvement in the supply of public services would probably occur, for example, if several public bureaus were forced to compete for the appropriations necessary to supply it. The only possible source of an argument on grounds of economic efficiency for having a single bureau supply a particular public service would be the existence of significant economies of scale for production of the service. Whether such a cost function does, in fact, characterize the production of most public services is an empirical issue. However, it seems unlikely to be the case for most public services. Even if economies of scale were a relevant factor, the benefits of increased competition could conceivably outweigh the more direct efficiency loss in the production process from allocating production responsibility among two or more bureaus.

It should be noted that while placing bureaus in a more competitive environment, perhaps allowing them some profit incentive, and so on might improve their performance appreciably, all that is really being done is making bureaus more closely approximate private firms. Once this is recognized, the most obvious question to ask is: Why have public bureaus at all? Why cannot private firms supply public services?

Conceptually, public provision of a service does not require public production. The decision to collectively *finance* a service does not preclude its actual purchase from private suppliers. In fact, many of the services provided by government were, at some time in history, supplied to the government by private entrepreneurs. Even national defense, the most traditional of all government functions, was at various times and places in history provided by mercenary armies. Today, few would argue that the defense industry should be nationalized to the extent that the government itself go into the business of actually producing the various missiles, jets or even rifles utilized by the Armed Forces. Today, private supply of some public services is being utilized by some local governments. Public service contracts are negotiated with private firms for provision of such services as garbage collection and fire protection.

It is perhaps the case that some public services cannot be satisfactorily supplied through government contracts to private entrepreneurs. The intangible nature of many services may be difficult to specify in contractural form thus making more direct, day to day supervision by government officials an unavoidable necessity. However, at least some expansion in the role of private firms in the production of public services seems a possibility worthy of serious consideration.

EDUCATION—AN EXAMPLE

Education provides an excellent case study of a rather complete failure to make the distinction between public provision and public production of a service. It is, therefore, useful to examine the provision of this service in some detail. Arguments supporting some governmental financing of education will be discussed later in Chapter 31. Here, it is sufficient to note that such arguments would provide no support for or against public operation of educational institutions.

The distinction between public financing and public operation is of considerable importance in education because popular opinion has tended to accept the view that public operation as well as public financing is essential. The public school system is rarely subjected to question in terms of its comparative efficiency with a publicly financed but privately operated system. Many noneconomic considerations enter into choice here and an argument can be made for public school systems on the "melting pot" basis. However, the point to be made here is that there is no economic basis to the public school argument and, especially in view of the preceding discussion of this chapter, there is no reason to think that, a priori, public operation is more efficient than private operation.

The so-called voucher plan for education provides an example of an institutional arrangement in which public financing and private supply of a service might coexist. The central principle of any voucher scheme is that the governmental payment is made directly to the family of the child to be educated. The family is then allowed to choose its own preferred school, provided only that the school meets accreditation standards laid down by educational authorities. The competition among suppliers of education that this scheme would introduce should increase efficiency, and families who choose to do so could supplement governmental financing more easily than under a monopoly system of publicly managed schools. The size of vouchers could be inversely related to family incomes, reflecting a substantial social interest in the education of underprivileged children (at the margin of independent provision).

CONCLUSIONS

Bureaucracy is a major institution in our society. Most of our public services are presently being supplied by government bureaus. There is considerable dissatisfaction with the performance of most bureaus. The discussion in this chapter has tried to indicate some organizational characteristics which seem likely to hinder the effective performance of bureaus.

Perhaps the most important point made in this chapter is that the choice of how public services are to be supplied is an important one. Given the difficulties with bureaucratic supply, the possibility of increasing the importance of private enterprise in the supply of public services is worthy of serious consideration.

SUPPLEMENTARY READING

William A. Niskanen's work has generated important contributions to the theory of bureaucracy. For a more thorough discussion of many of the points made in this chapter, and of some further aspects of bureaucracy not discussed here, the student is referred to his book, *Bureaucracy and Representative Government* (Chicago: Aldine-Atherton, Inc., 1971); or to *Bureaucracy: Servant or Master* by William A. Niskanen with commentaries by Douglas Houghton, Maurice Kegan, Nicholas Ridley, and Ian Senior (London: Institute of Economic Affairs, Ltd., 1973).

Gordon Tullock, *The Politics of Bureaucracy* (Washington, D.C.: Public Affairs Press, 1965), also provides an interesting approach to the study of bureaucratic institutions.

15

Public choice and budgetary size

$\mathbf{A}$s we have noted earlier, one of the major problems in modern public finance is the explanation of the rapid growth in the public or governmental sector of the economy. In Part II, we traced the factual record of this growth in the United States, and we examined some of the familiar reasons adduced by way of explanation. In this chapter, we adopt a public choice approach in an attempt to determine whether or not additional explanatory hypotheses might be developed to explain the observed expansion in governmental size. Are there structural elements in the decision process which ensure the empirical validity of Wagner's law of an expanding public sector? What institutional biases are present in the making of fiscal decisions?

THE SEPARATION OF EXPENDITURE AND TAX CHOICES

In the simplified models of collective decision making previously examined, we have assumed that individual preferences about levels of outlay, or expenditure, on specific budgetary components (police and schools) were based on fully informed and accurate estimates of the tax costs that each level of outlay would imply, for the individual as well as for the whole community. This is an heroic assumption; individuals are not likely to be informed about their own tax shares in any proposed increment to budgetary spending. If, however, a tax or financing decision is tied to the spending choice, if the tax decision must be made *simultaneously* with the spending decision, the two sides of fiscal choice, the costs and the benefits, may be brought into some sort of rough-and-ready comparison, both by the individuals who must pay the taxes and who expect to get some of the benefits, and by their representatives in legislative assemblies. Even here, fiscal illusions may be present, in either direction, and there is no assurance that major errors will not be made. At a minimum, however, the costs of fiscal action are included in the composite budgetary choice made for the whole community.

A different dimension of potential error, and one that can be directionally identified, emerges when the two sides of fiscal choice are divorced one from the other. If political process allows decisions to be made on budgetary spending in apparent separation from decisions on financing this spending, it seems clear that a bias is introduced toward inefficiently large budgets.

Consider a family analogy. Suppose that an agreement is made between husband and wife to the effect that the wife does all the shopping while the husband pays the bills at the end of the month. It may be predicted that, under this arrangement, the family spending will tend to be larger than it would be if both the spending and the bill-paying chores should be assigned to the wife. If she is not confronted with the cost side of a purchasing choice, the wife will tend to overestimate the relative desirability of available commodities and services and she will tend to overextend family purchases. (No sex discrimination is involved here; the results hold equally if we reverse the husband-wife roles in our example.)

The institutions of fiscal decision making in most democratically organized governments are analogous to the family example suggested. Those legislators who are charged with the responsibility of making decisions about the size of specific budgetary outlays are not the same subgroup of legislators who are charged with making decisions about the level of taxes to be imposed. Those members of appropriations or budgetary committees, the first group, will tend to overestimate the desirability of additional government spending because they will not be fully conscious of the costs that such spending necessitates. This proclivity to spend is reinforced by the political process itself. Legislators want to secure reelection, and they know that voters want spending projects.

Spending proclivity and budget balance. The separation of expenditure and financing decisions, whether within the calculus of a single decision maker, or among different decision makers, or groups of decision makers in a legislature, need not exert a major upward bias on budgetary size over the long run if overall budget-balance constraints are severe. Return to the family example. Even if the wife does all of the spending while the husband pays all of the bills, the income constraint will keep the household budget within fairly narrow limits. No matter how much the wife might be inclined to spend, only so many bills can be paid, given the income and wealth position of the family. A similar budget-balance or income constraint applies to most local governments, with some qualifications. Taxes are not simply adjusted upward without limit to meet whatever expenditure commitments are made through the community choice processes. Some residual adjustment of this sort may take place, and notably so with the local property tax, but there are effective bounds on this type of adjustment.

The separation of spending and taxing decisions may, however, exert a significant expansionary influence in those governmental units where no strong budget-balance constraint is operative, where residual financing instruments are readily available. This characterizes the federal government, which does possess both money-creation and debt-issue authority much beyond those possessed by any local government jurisdiction. If the Congress, and the Executive, approve a level of federal spending in excess of the revenues generated under the legislatively approved tax structure, the budgetary deficit may be readily financed either by the issue of new public debt or by the issue of new money, or both. (In practice, money is issued under the guise of issuing debt.) The revenue limits created by the productivity of approved tax rates exert only an indirect control feedback on the spending proclivities of politicians.

Balanced-budget rules and Keynesian fiscal policy. For the central government, or for any government with unlimited money creation or debt issue authority, the overall budget-balance constraint could exert an influence only in the form of some established and respected rule for "fiscal responsibility." If political leaders, and the public generally, should consider it to be irresponsible to allow the budgetary decision process to generate continuous deficits, and if any departure from budget balance should be treated as a temporary phenomenon to be corrected as soon as possible, there need be no long-run effect on the size of the public sector exerted by the separation between the two sides of the fiscal account in the institutional structure of collective decision making.

Roughly speaking, some such rule did exist prior to the onset of Keynesian economics along with its implied norms for using the government budget as a primary instrument for achieving macroeconomic objectives such as full employment, economic growth, international balance, and price-level predictability. In order to secure widespread popular and political acceptance of the view that the budget might properly be used instrumentally for other than traditional purposes, it was necessary to destroy or to undermine the budget-balance rule or myth in the public mind. Economists, and following them, journalists and political spokesmen, argued that the generation of budget deficits (financed by money or debt) need not reflect fiscal irresponsibility. Indeed, quite the opposite; in a regime of widespread and continuing unemployment (the economy of the 1930s), the generation of large budgetary deficits, financed by money issues, would have reflected sophisticated social and fiscal responsibility and might have promoted the attainment of widely accepted social objectives.

Unfortunately, however, these early advocates of the abandonment of the budget-balance rule did not fully reckon on the predictable behavior of the politicians and their constituents to the newly developed arguments. They neglected to approach the problem in a public choice framework of analysis; they overlooked the fact that all fiscal policy must be implemented through the political choice process. These early advocates did not consider what might happen during periods when Keynesian norms for fiscal policy might dictate either budgetary surplus or budgetary neutrality (many of the years since World War II). Once budget balance, as a behavioral constraint, was abandoned, the proclivity toward expenditures emerged quite predictably. Political leaders, responding directly to the desires of voters, who are potential beneficiaries, found it advantageous to increase programs for federal outlay. The promised benefits seemed quite tangible, and these took on explicit meaning for the congressman who sought reelection. For the same reasons, taxes were not popular with citizens, and this unpopularity was not lost on the potential or aspiring legislators. Once the rule or myth that tied the two sides of the fiscal account together was eroded, the direction of budgetary bias seems clear. The history of the period since World

War II corroborates this hypothesis; budget deficits have become the order of the day. During the 35-year period, 1945–80, there were only nine years when the federal budget was not in deficit. And, perhaps more significantly, during the 20-year period, 1960–80, there was only one year, 1969, when the federal budget was not in deficit. These data suggest that the bias discussed here has been operationally significant. The effects are probably most important in explaining the veritable explosion in federal spending that took place in the late 1960s. Keynesian norms for fiscal policy were first advanced in the 1930s, but their full impact on political and public opinion was not exerted until the 1960s. By the late 1970s there was some evidence that the balanced budget rule was regaining some of its former prominence. By early 1979, legislatures in several states had passed resolutions calling for a constitutional amendment to require the federal budget to be in balance except during periods of serious economic dislocation. Constitutional constraints on government spending including the balanced budget rule, will be discussed in greater detail in Chapter 16. It can be noted here, however, that such efforts can, in a sense, be interpreted as acknowledgement of the expansionary bias created by the divorce between sides of the fiscal account both structurally and attitudinally.

FRAGMENTATION OF BUDGETARY DECISION MAKING

The directional bias toward governmental growth discussed above would be present even if only one public good or service should be provided. An additional element is present in a budgetary process that incorporates spending on several public goods and services, which is, of course, the appropriate model for describing political reality. To the extent that budgetary decisions are made on the components separately, and the budget is considered incrementally, *fiscal externalities* may arise. Decisions taken with respect to a single budgetary component may affect the setting for decisions on other components and these spillover or external effects may not be considered. In principle, the externalities here can run in either direction; in practice, external diseconomies seem predominant.

Consider the following example. The federal highway trust fund provides some funds for highway construction in urban areas. The federal government also subsidizes urban mass transit systems in many cities of the country. By providing additional public highways, the relative cost of transit via private automobile is lowered relative to use of mass transit facilities. The benefits of subsidization of mass transit are likely to be directly tied to the extent of subsidization of highway construction. Suppose that a highway construction project is calculated to yield net benefits of $1 directly to highway users but will simultaneously lower the returns of a proposed mass transit project from $5 to $3, because the number of users of the transit system is lowered. If both projects are considered separately without consideration of the benefit spillovers, both projects will be adopted. Net benefits from the two projects will be $4. However, if only the transit project were adopted, net benefits of $5 would accrue.

This phenomenon is familiar to economists in the analysis of private sector decisions. It has not, however, been applied widely to the choices that apply to the public sector, whether these choices be treated at the level of voters, legislators, or bureaucrats. So long as differing sectors of the government budget finance differing bundles of goods and services, and so long as the decisions on these components are treated separately, the results suggested in the example seem to apply.

The fiscal externalities may be "internalized" if the whole budget is considered as a package. In the federal government, this was one of the purposes of the legislation in the 1920s which established the office of the budget in the executive branch (now the Office of Management and Budget formerly the Bureau of the Budget). The Office of Management and Budget (OMB), in examining all of the spending components simultaneously, can take the spillover effects into account. The effects can reappear, however, if the Congress considers various spending programs in a fragmented manner. Prior to 1974, this was the case. Legislation enacted in that year significantly altered the manner in which Congress makes spending decisions. New committees were created with responsibility for examining and proposing overall expenditure targets and examining programs in broad functional categories rather than singly.

The 1974 budget reform legislation may help to alleviate the expansionary bias resulting from the separation of the taxing and spending decisions as well as that resulting from fiscal externalities. This is because the Congress will now set target ceilings for expenditures in broad functional categories prior to considering specific legislation. If overall spending should exceed the targets, legislation altering either appropriations or the ceilings must be passed before the start of the fiscal year. Some problems remain. The possibility exists for the Congress to simply adjust the ceilings ex post to conform to actual appropriations. The weakness of the constraint on the size of the deficit also remains. However, to the extent that the Congress is forced to operate in an environment which requires explicit consideration of overall spending totals, some of the expansionary bias discussed earlier may be removed.

Controllability of outlays and budgetary size

Actual outlays under many government programs are relatively uncontrollable, at least in the short-run, because the programs involve long-term budgetary commitments. Increasing importance of these types of programs in government budgets may be important in explaining the growth of total expenditures and the inherent difficulties associated with trying to slow down the growth of budgets or even trying to reduce them.

The federal government's experience with uncontrollable outlays provides a useful example. According to the 1980 budget, uncontrollable outlays accounted for 75 percent of total expenditures and had been rising not only more rapidly than federal receipts, but even more rapidly than the rate of growth of gross national product. Most of the programs in the federal budget involve payments to individuals under such programs as social security, Medicare, veterans' benefits, and so on. Obviously, once these programs are instituted the government can do little to control increases in the number of recipients and is legally committed to increase outlays sufficiently to cover these persons.

Many of these programs require long-term commitments in order to be effective and equitable. One need only imagine the chaos that would result if the social security program were subject to full congressional review and authorization each year. However, as such programs increase in relative importance, the degree of short-term discretionary control over government outlays declines. Politicans may perceive a fairly universal desire among their constituents for tax reductions and reduced budgetary size. However, the number of programs that can be cut in the short run may be severely limited and those programs may not, in fact, be the most desirable programs to cut.

Perhaps an even more serious problem results because of an absence of strong incentives for politicians to subject the "uncontrollable" programs to critical review even in the long run when outlays could actually be reduced. This is because a politician may never be able to capture any benefits of a decision to gradually phase out such programs. The actual reduction in outlays would occur several years after the phasing-out decision was made. Politicians are necessarily somewhat shortsighted in the sense that they always must be concerned about retaining office in the next election. They will, therefore, tend to concentrate their efforts on programs and policies which will directly aid in their reelection. The benefits of phasing-out certain relatively long-term programs may well not begin to be felt until some period well after the election following the decision to halt the program. By that time, the concerns of politicians and their constituents may have changed drastically.

MAJORITY RULE AND BUDGETARY SIZE

We have suggested that possible biases toward relatively excessive growth rates in public spending arise from the structure of fiscal decision making, as such. To this point we have not examined the rules for making collective or political decisions. Even if legislatures should operate under an effective rule of unanimity, we might still get the results previously suggested. We must now examine the implications of nonunanimity decision rules.

The most familiar of these is the rule of simple majority. It will be helpful to look at this rule in its simplified form, even if we recognize that the relatively complex structure of actual political process may require either less than or more than a simple majority for final action on collective alternatives. Again it is useful to develop a simple numerical example in a three-person context. Assume that a collectivity of three persons, M_1, M_2, and M_3, finances public goods and services from the imposition of a general tax which is imposed equally on all persons. Assume, further, that all decisions are made by a simple majority vote on an item-by-item basis.

Three spending projects are under consideration, each one of which is estimated to cost $100, including collection and enforcement. For purposes of simplification, we assume that the fiscal externalities of the sort previously examined do not exist here. For each of these projects, therefore, the tax bill per person will be $33.33. The benefits of the three projects, I, II, III are arrayed as follows:

	Project I	Project II	Project III
Benefits to M_1	$35	$35	$ 0
Benefits to M_2	35	0	35
Benefits to M_3	0	35	35

Note that, with simple majority voting, each one of the three projects would secure approval, despite the fact that, on each project considered separately, the aggregate benefits fall short of the costs. This is because the required balance under this voting rule is not that between benefits and costs for the whole group but only that for a majority of its members. For two members of the group, each project yields benefits in excess of costs, and will, for this reason, tend to secure majority approval. The total budget will tend to be overexpanded even without the fiscal externalities discussed above.

As in the other case, however, this bias may be removed if all three projects are treated simultaneously as a combined budgetary package. For all three projects, the total benefit to each person ($70) falls far short of the total cost ($100). However, to the extent that separate decisions are made on spending projects by majority voting, the results seem likely to be in the direction indicated. Unless side payments or compensations are somehow allowed to take place, there is no assurance that majority voting rules will not select projects whose aggregate costs exceed aggregate benefits.

The features of the model which produce these results should be identified. Note that we assumed that a general tax was imposed equally on all persons, while the benefits from each project were assumed to be concentrated on only two of the three persons in the hypothetical community. If, by contrast, the benefits should be more equally and more generally shared than the taxes, the opposing bias would be present under majority voting. General-benefit projects would tend to go unapproved, despite the excess of aggregate benefits over aggregate costs. And, in converse, differentially based taxes would tend to be reduced, even at the expense of cutting back on general-benefit-spending projects.

Does majority voting tend to bias budgets upward or downward? The model suggests that the answer is basically an empirical one, and it depends on the relative generality of taxes and benefits. To the extent that taxes are more general than spending benefits, the bias is clearly upward. This seems to be empirically supported. We have noted the asymmetry which allows public expenditure programs to be directed toward specific subgroups of the population but which does not allow departures from uniformity in taxation save within narrow limits. It was possible for the federal government to spend funds to build the Tulsa ship canal. It would not have been constitutional for the federal government to tax the citizens of the Arkansas River valley differently.

Within the budget itself, the model suggests that majority voting tends to bias adjustments in favor of special-benefit projects and against general-benefit projects. Similarly, to the extent allowable under law, within the tax system itself the effects of majority voting are to bias collective decisions toward discriminatory and away from general taxation.

VOTERS, POLITICIANS, AND BUREAUCRATS

Public choice models are helpful in pointing toward directional biases in the political process even if many of the complexities of governmental structure are neglected. For any degree of sophistication, however, we must move beyond the level of voters and examine, even if briefly, the behavior of politicians in elective positions as representatives of the voters. Individual citizens, as voters, do not make actual choices on taxes and on public expenditures. Voters select among candidates who hope to represent them in legislative assemblies and in executive positions. The budgetary choices are actually made by these politicians. To the extent that these representatives desire reelection, they are constrained in their behavior by what they think are the desires of voters. But these constraints, at best, allow for considerable flexibility of choice on the part of the politicians. When this element is added to our models, what can be said about the directional bias on budgetary decisions?

Within the constraints that they recognize, the politicians will seek to maximize their own utility from participating in collective or group choices. We may get some idea as to the directional bias here by looking more carefully at the utility function of the politician. To do this, we may think of three separate types: the ideologue, the pure politician, and the profiteer. Each of these may be discussed in turn.

Politics offers an opportunity for the person who has a consuming ideological passion to modify the structure of society. But politics seems to be an unlikely career for the person whose ideology calls for a severely limited public or governmental sector of society. The rugged individualist, the proponent of strict laissez-faire, is less likely to be attracted to politics as a career than the person whose ideology is basically socialist, who desires reform in the direction of an expanded public sector. To the extent that more of the latter group than the former tends to seek and secure public office, the prediction can be made that the bias is toward large rather than toward small government.

Consider now the pure politician: the person who has little or no fundamental ideology; who really has no clear ideas as to how society might be reformed, but who does enjoy the emoluments of public office; who enjoys the power and prestige involved; and who finds the career of politics personally pleasing. This person will be somewhat more responsive to what he or she thinks are the desires of constituents than the ideologue, and this person will pay somewhat more attention to the constraints posed by the prospects of alternative candidates in subsequent elections. There will be no inherent bias toward large government in choice behavior except insofar as this sort of bias is inherent in the demands made by constituents. As suggested in the earlier models, however, there may well exist such a constituency bias. Individuals can secure the benefits of spending projects directly and in a discriminatory fashion; the costs can be levied generally on all taxpayers. The pure politician knows this, and will be much more inclined to stress the spending record than the taxing record in appeals to the home district.

Finally, there is the profiteer, the person who seeks political office largely for the pecuniary profits that it promises. Here the directional bias seems self-evident. Political profits, available through kickbacks, payoffs, contributions, by-product deals in the private sector, and so on, are much more likely to be available through large programs of public outlay than under small programs. Furthermore, these opportunities are more likely to appear under newly enacted programs of public spending, and before established standards are laid down, than under old and continued programs. The political profiteer will tend to urge new and larger programs.

The differentiation of these three separate models of the politician is helpful in discussing budgetary choice biases. There are not likely to be good examples of persons fitting any one model perfectly. But most politicians represent some combination of the three attributes noted, and the weights will vary significantly from person to person. But straightforward utility maximization on the part of the average politician probably does impute a bias toward expanding the size of the public sector rather than its opposite.

Elected politicians in democracy make the basic decisions on budgets. But these decisions are implemented by appointed bureaucrats. These persons are also utility maximizers, and they will try to secure their own best advantage within the constraints they face. We may predict that, within the limits imposed on them, bureaucrats will seek expanded public spending. Career advancement depends on program size, and those attracted into the governmental bureaucracy will, in any case, be inclined toward the collective sector. Some of these aspects of the bureaucracy were discussed more fully in the more general treatment of the preceding chapter.

CONCLUSIONS

One of the major problems in modern public finance is that of explaining the rate of growth of government, and notably during the period since 1965. The more traditional explanations, discussed briefly in an earlier chapter, do not seem adequate. In this chapter, we have attempted to apply the tools of public choice theory to this issue. We have examined some of the possible biases which emerge from the institutional structure within which fiscal decisions are made. It seems possible to explain some of the growth that we observe empirically by the biases in the collective choice process. These biases stem from many sources, including the divorce of the two sides of the budget account, and notably, in the post-Keynesian period, the fragmentation of the budget. Difficulties also arise because of the existence of fiscal externalities or spillovers that are not fully internalized, the noncontrollability of spending programs, and the greater generality of taxation than of public spending. These structural features of modern government combine with less-than-unanimity voting rules in legislative assemblies and with the utility maximizing of elected politicians and bureaucrats to impose an upward spending bias on budgets. Correction of this bias may be expected only to the extent that it is recognized and that steps are taken toward "internalization," by constitutional precepts and other means.

SUPPLEMENTARY READING

For an early and effective argument for combining the two sides of the budget, see Knut Wicksell, "New Principles of Just Taxation," in R. A. Musgrave and A. T. Peacock (eds.), *Classics in the Theory of Public Finance* (London: The Macmillan Co., Ltd., 1958). For an elaboration of some of the public choice aspects of fiscal choice, see James M. Buchanan, *Public Finance in Democratic Process* (Chapel Hill, N.C.: University of North Carolina Press, 1967). For an incorporation of some of these aspects into an explanation of government growth, see Thomas Borcherding (ed.), *Budgets and Bureaucrats: The Sources of Government Growth* (Durham, N.C.: Duke University Press, 1975).

16

Constitutional limits on taxing and spending

INTRODUCTION

Preceding chapters in this part of the book have discussed, in very simple models, some of the operating characteristics of governments in the making of budgetary allocations. The objective for analysis was the making of rudimentary predictions about the level and the composition of budgetary outlay under differing rules, institutions, and procedures that might describe political structures. Chapter 13 introduced the notion of a "fiscal constitution," and notably with respect to the quasi-permanent nature of tax laws or tax rules. In this chapter, we propose to discuss the "fiscal constitution" more specifically, and especially with reference to the intense activity represented in various efforts to impose constitutional tax and spending limits, activity that characterized the American political setting in 1978, 1979, and 1980. We shall briefly examine the basic logic of fiscal limits. Following this section, we then shall discuss alternative means through which constitutional provisions may place boundaries on the taxing and spending powers of governments. In concluding sections of the chapter, we shall make some assessment of the "tax revolution" of 1978–79, along with tentative predictions for the 1980s and beyond.

THE LOGIC OF TAX LIMITS

Why should voters desire to impose constitutional restrictions on government's power to tax? This question assumed a position of importance in the United States only in the late 1970s. Prior to that time, the prevailing or orthodox opinion seems to have been that the electoral politics of democracy offered sufficient protections and guarantees against excessive taxation and excessive public spending, with "excessive" here being defined or measured by the preferences of voters themselves. If, for example, elected legislators and executives should enact budgets, financed by accompanying taxes or by inflation, far beyond the levels demanded or desired by their voting constituencies, these same politicians would court defeat by potential tax-cutting, budget-slashing candidates for office at the next election. So long as elected politicians are required to run on their fiscal record, which is available for all to see, and so long as they must submit themselves for re-election at periodic intervals, fiscal exploitation is held in check. Or so the traditional argument was made, either explicitly or implicitly.

In the context of such an argument, any overt constitutional restraints on the behavior of legislative or executive representatives in fiscal matters would be either unnecessary or unduly inhibiting. Such restraints might actually prevent the true demands of citizens from being met by government. Constitutional limits might be viewed as the "dead hand of the past" that prevents flexible responses to the changing fiscal needs of the future.

We cannot discuss the flaws in the traditional argument in detail. As the analysis of the preceding chapters should have suggested, however, the very limited controls exercised by electoral competition should be clear. The traditional argument assumes that the bureaucracy is totally passive and disinterested, and that this bureaucracy exerts no influence on budgetary outlays. The argument also assumes implicitly that the whole fiscal process is symmetrical in the generality of taxes and benefits. That is, the argument does not allow for the prospect that program benefits might be more concentrated than tax costs, with the predictable profitability of pressure group politics aimed at promoting spending rather than at cutting taxes. The familiar argument also leaves no room for "fiscal illusion." There is no recognition that potential taxpayers may not fully realize the real costs of spending programs. The argument does not incorporate the effects of coalition formation in democracy, where members of a dominant majority may use their taxing-spending powers to exploit members of a minority, and in so doing, effectively "bribe" a sufficient number of voters to retain elected office.

These flaws in the traditional argument are essentially logical in nature. They weaken very substantially the view that competitive electoral politics is sufficient to keep the fiscal powers of government within bounds. But these logical flaws are accompanied by an accumulating historical-empirical record of continuing and accelerating growth in levels of taxation and of public spending. Those who offer the electoral politics of modern democracies as the guarantor of taxpayers against fiscal exploitation would be hard put to "explain" the changes in voters' preferences or desires for public-sector activity sufficient to have generated the observed growth rates in the period since World War II, and notably in the late 1960s and the 1970s. A realistic look at this evidence on the increasing size of the public sector, in either relative or absolute terms, measured either by tax collections or by total budgetary outlays, must suggest that the electoral process has not operated in any manner akin to that implicitly claimed for it in the orthodox argument sketched out above.

If this point is acknowledged, the logical grounds for constitutional fiscal limits are established. No one would argue that unchecked fiscal authority is a desired attribute of government in any well-functioning social order.

PROCEDURAL CONSTRAINTS

If the desirability of establishing or maintaining some limits or boundaries on the taxing-spending proclivities of government is acknowledged, and, further, if constitutional stipulations of such limits are assumed to be effectively enforceable, the question then becomes one of selecting or choosing the form or type of limit that might be imposed. In this section we shall examine several *procedural* constraints, by which we mean that the levels of taxation and outlays are controlled indirectly by the structure of the rules and procedures through which political decisions are made. In the next section, we shall examine the more direct limits, those that impose *quantitative* constraints on either taxation or spending levels, or both.

Before examining alternative procedural constraints, however, we should note once again that there do exist legal-constitutional constraints on governmental taxing powers in the United States. Governments, whether central or local, have never been able to levy taxes on citizens in a wholly arbitrary or discriminatory fashion. Criteria for generality must be met in order to satisfy the due process requirement of the Constitution. The absence of symmetry between taxation and spending in this respect is worth noting. There are no criteria for generality in public spending programs that are at all comparable to those that exist on the taxing side of the account. For the first century and a half of our national experience, the uniformity clause in the Constitution effectively prevented the imposition of progressive rates of tax on income. Only with the adoption of the 16th Amendment in 1913 did the potential for fiscal exploitation inherent in the progressive tax instrument become available for use by government.

Special majorities for taxing and/or spending legislation

The first type of procedural constraint may be handled briefly. The Wicksellian "fiscal exchange" theory of the public economy was introduced in Chapter 9. Wicksell's ideal for political decision-making was one that required unanimous approval of all taxing-spending projects, at least in the legislative assembly. Wicksell argued that, only with a unanimity rule could citizens be sure that publicly-financed projects were really worth the tax costs involved. Any departure from the rule of unanimity opens up the possibility for fiscal exploitation. Inefficient projects may be financed, and taxpayers may be coerced into payments for project benefits that they do not desire.

Even Wicksell recognized, however, that the unanimity rule was highly impracticable. His basic logic can, however, be translated into practical proposals for political reform that require special or qualified majorities for budgetary legislation. There is nothing at all sacrosanct about the requirement that simple majority approval must be sufficient for all political decisions. And constitutional requirements could surely be laid down that stipulate two-thirds, three-fourths, or five-sixths majorities for passage of specific financing bills. Any such shift away from simple majority rule toward more inclusive or qualified majorities will reduce the potential for fiscal exploitation.

Qualified majority voting rules are found in existing state constitutions, and notably with application to the incurring of bonded indebtedness by local governments. Referenda are often stipulated and the approval of more than a simple majority of voters is required before bonds can be issued. In some instances, a simple majority of qualified electors rather than a majority of those persons voting is stipulated; this restriction becomes significant when normal voter turnouts are small.

The popular discussion of Proposition 13, approved by California voters in June 1978, was concentrated on the quantitative limit on property tax rates. We shall discuss this limit later in this chapter. The accompanying procedural restriction contained in Proposition 13 was often neglected. New taxes must be approved by a two-thirds rather than a simple majority of the state legislature. This feature may well prove to be more restrictive in effect than the direct lid on property tax rates.

Generality in taxation and spending

A second procedural change that would impose constraints on government's exercise of its fiscal authority arises, not at the level of decision rules, but from the types of fiscal activities that are allowed. As noted above, there exist legal-constitutional restictions against arbitrary taxation beyond certain limits. Criteria for generality in tax treatment must be met. Some legal philosophers, notably Professor F. A. Hayek, have argued that progressive taxation violates the basic precept of fiscal generality, whereas proportional taxation would not do so. By implication, the argument here suggests that repeal of the 16th Amendment might be all that would be required to keep federal government taxing-spending proclivities within tolerable boundaries. The willingness of members of dominant political coalitions to impose taxes might be dramatically reduced if these persons should be required to choose in the knowledge that they, themselves, would also be faced with tax shares proportional to their own income-wealth positions.

As noted earlier, criteria for generality have never been extended symmetrically to the spending side of the fiscal account. And, unless some such extension should be made, the shift from progressive to proportionate rate structures for taxation might not have the constraining effect that initial analysis suggests. A constitutional requirement to the effect that public programs must supply benefits generally or uniformly would be extremely difficult to implement in practice. Obviously, such a requirement would make direct transfer programs almost impossible.

In terms of the "taxpayers' revolution," there seems to have been little or no impetus to shift from progression to proportionality in taxation. Income tax progression is probably imbedded so deeply in the American fiscal structure that any changes in the "fiscal constitution" would have to incorporate this element of potential conflict rather than eliminate it.

Simultaneous consideration of spending and taxation

If plausibly rational spending-taxing outcomes are expected to emerge from the deliberations of a legislature, the benefits and the costs should be simultaneously estimated. Budgetary processes which allow for a political separation between legislation on spending and legislation on taxation, as for example through the separate committee structures of the congress or state legislatures, tend to make such simultaneous estimation difficult. One of the central constitutional reforms proposed by Wicksell was that no spending authorization be made except as accompanied by legislation authorizing the taxation required to finance the anticipated outlay. The budget is necessarily two-sided, and legislatures should be constitutionally required to consider it as such.

This relatively simple and straightforward constitutional restriction might reduce significantly the proclivities of legislatures to generate excessive expenditure. If required to finance each and every outlay through taxation, legislatures would be much more reluctant to approve proposed spending projects.

To a limited extent, the Federal Budgetary Reform Act of 1974 was motivated by a recognition of some need for coordination between the two sides of the United States federal government's budget. This act did not require that taxes match spending, item by item, or in any overall sense, but it did set up procedures that allow Congress to consider the budget in the large, rather than piecemeal. Preliminary results suggest that the 1974 changes have had some effect in reducing the explosive rate of growth in federal outlays. This legislation is not, however, *constitutional*, and there is no guarantee at all that future Congresses might not abandon its precepts.

Earmarked taxes — sectoral budgeting

An indirect means of relating governmental outlays to the taxes required to finance them is provided by earmarking, an institution that is present in several state constitutions, and, legislatively-generated, also at the federal level. The proceeds of a particular tax are "earmarked" for spending on a particular governmental service or set of services. The most familiar example is provided in the requirement that revenues from highway or road use taxes (on gasoline, tires, etc.) be expended exlusively on the construction and maintenance of roads. This sort of earmarking need not reduce or restrict governmental proclivities to spend, and indeed under certain conditions, spending may be encouraged. The device does, nonetheless, force political decision makers to examine the two sides of the fiscal account simultaneously. It is much easier to compare the benefits and costs when a single public service is financed by a single tax than when a whole array of services are financed by a whole set of taxes. Although it is not constitutionally required, the most important example of earmarking quantitatively is the financing of social security benefits from the combined employee-employer payroll tax.

Budget balance

In the policy discussions of the late 1970s, the possible constitutional requirement for budget balance was the center of much attention. In early 1979, 27 state legislatures had enacted resolutions calling for an amendment to the United States Constitution that would require budget balance on the part of the federal government. Attempts were being made to secure the required approval of 34 state legislatures, in which case, a constitutional convention would be indicated, provided that Congress did not itself initiate such an amendment. Many of the state constitutions contain balanced-budget provisions.

A basic difference between state governments and the federal government in relation to budget balance should be noted. State governments do not possess independent powers of money issue in the United States; budget imbalance will, in such case, necessarily involve the issue of genuine debt obligations. The federal government does possess money creation powers; it may, therefore, unbalance its budget by resort to money issue (indirectly, via the Federal Reserve system) as well as by issue of genuine debt obligations. For reasons of this basic difference in money-creation powers, therefore, a constitutional requirement for budget balance may seem more important at the federal government level than at the state or provincial government level.

The upsurge of support for a constitutional amendment for federal budget balance emerged directly from the record of fiscal irresponsibility over the period 1960–1980. Only in one year, over this two-decade span, 1969, did the federal budget balance; all other years recorded deficits; and the size of the deficits grew at an increasing rate over time. It seemed clear that something had gone wrong with the basic Keynesian policy logic, which called for deficits in years of recession, and for budget surpluses in years of inflation and boom. The Keynesian presumption for fiscal policy had ignored the workings of democratic politics.[1] And the "old-time religion" of budget balance no longer seemed to exert an influence on budgetary outcomes.

More explicit constraints on the form of a constitutional amendment seemed to be needed, and, symbolically, budget-balance was easy to understand. This proposal for change in the American fiscal constitution seemed to generate much more extensive public support than any of the alternatives suggested.

Separation of tax bases or sources and of governmental functions among levels of government

A final constitutional means of limiting the taxing and spending proclivities of government is provided in a recognition of the explicitly *federal* nature of a political system. If effective and enforceable means of separating the power of the central (federal) government and the state governments can be constitutionally defined, the taxing-spending authority is necessarily limited. To the extent that the central government is precluded from entering into functions reserved for state-local governments, then central government outlays for such purpose have no reason for existence. And, total outlays will tend to be limited by the operation of certain competitive forces as among the separate state or provincial units. Gross inefficiencies in

---

[1] For an elaboration of this point, see James M. Buchanan and Richard E. Wagner, *Democracy in Deficit* (New York: Academic Press, 1977).

the fiscal operations of state governments (or local governments within states) will generate resource migration and mobility, and, in recognition of this predicted result, taxation and spending will tend to be maintained within tolerable limits. No such controls are operative for the central or federal government, which is coincident in impact with the total economy.

QUANTITATIVE CONSTITUTIONAL CONSTRAINTS

None of the procedural constraints discussed above is aimed at laying down precise quantitative limits on the size of the public or governmental sector of the economy, defined in budgetary terms, that is in terms of total tax revenues or total outlays, either in a relative or an absolute sense, or in respect to some total or its rate of change. The procedural constraints are aimed to modify the structure within which fiscal decisions are made; they are not designed to operate directly on the *results*.

A different set of constitutional proposals, all designed to impose limits on revenues and/or outlays, involves attempts to affect results directly rather than through modification in the political decision structure.

Outlays or revenues as a designated share of GNP or GSP

The proposal that was made in the 1970s, and which seemed to attract the most widespread support among professional economists, was aimed at maintaining total outlays of government within a constitutionally specified share or proportion of national or state product or income, as measured. Tennessee was the first state to amend its constitution (in April 1978) along these specific lines. Several other states adopted comparable constitutional constraints, and, in early 1979, an amendment to the United States Constitution was suggested along similar lines.

The motivation and support for these quantitative limits on the size of the governmental sector stem from the observed rates of growth, in both relative and absolute terms, and the recognition of the desirability of slowing down these rates. The ratio-type proposals, with total governmental tax revenues or total outlays, tied to GNP, national income, or state income, have the advantage that they allow for increases in revenues-outlays as the supporting economy grows. One variation on the straightforward ratio-type proposal ties rates of increase in the government's revenues and/or outlays to rates of increase in the supporting economy, to GNP, national, or state income.

Initial and somewhat preliminary experience suggested that ratio-type proposals to restrict revenues and/or outlays constitutionally might be more difficult to implement politically than either some of the procedural constraints discussed above or some of the more direct, and more readily understood, quantitative constraints to be discussed below.

Tax base constraints

An indirect means of restricting the quantitative levels of potential revenue extraction, and, through this, of governmental resource use, lies in constitutional limits on allowable bases for taxation. By an appropriate selection of tax bases, the total potential revenues can be controlled. State governments often restrict the taxing powers of local governmental units in this way.

A general example might be a constitutional provision that allows the federal government to levy a progressive tax on personal incomes, but restricts this tax to a money-income base. Nonmoney income might be explicitly excluded from the allowable base of the tax, hence allowing persons to "opt out" of the money-earnings nexus if tax rates get excessive. In the knowledge that such "opting out" would indeed take place, government would be encouraged to hold rates of tax below certain threshold levels. The argument here suggests that comprehensiveness in the base of taxation need not be a desired objective for tax reform, which, of course, was counter to the discussion of the "best" tax arrangements often found in a nonconstitutional policy framework.[2]

Direct constitutional constraints on specified rates of taxation

The most widely discussed political event of the late 1970s was

---

[2]For further discussion, see Geoffrey Brennan and James Buchanan, "Towards a Tax Constitution for Leviathan," *Journal of Public Economics*, Vol. 8 (December 1977), pp. 255–74.

Proposition 13, and the most familiar feature of this change in California's constitution involved the imposition of a maximum rate of 1 percent of tax on the market value of real property. This type of constitutional constraint is much more specific, and much more readily amenable to general public and voter understanding, than either the procedural constraints discussed or the more general ratio-type proposals variously advanced. Property owners, existing and potential, could predict the results in quantitative terms. This fact accounts, in part, for Proposition 13's widespread support. The disadvantages with such proposals arise from their specificity, however. To the extent that a specific tax or tax source is singled out, the overall purposes of keeping governmental taxing-spending proclivities in line may be subverted by allowing recourse to alternative tax sources, upon which rate limits are not imposed, including, of course, shifting of taxing authority to higher-level jurisdictions. The likely result of Proposition 13 over a long term will be the concentration of more taxing power at the level of the state as opposed to the local government level.

CONCLUSIONS

In this chapter, we have attempted to discuss briefly alternative constitutional limits on governmental powers to tax and to spend. The subject matter of this chapter would have seemed to be, and would have been, almost totally irrelevant in the first and second editions of this textbook published in 1960, and 1965 respectively. The "tax revolt" or "taxpayer revolution" which seemed to come to fruition in the late 1970s, had its origin in a reaction to the explosive growth in the size of the governmental sector of the economy, at all levels of government, that occurred in the late 1960s and throughout the decade of the 1970s. Constitutional tax and spending limits came to be discussed seriously as the public's faith in the capacity of ordinary legislative and electoral politics waned. In a real sense, the whole discussion of constitutional limits reflects an attempt on the part of the voter taxpaying-beneficiary public to regain control over its own fiscal affairs.

It is not possible to predict the effects of this movement in terms of formalized changes in state and/or federal constitutions. However, measured in terms of political signals conveyed to elected and potential office-holders, the "tax-revolt" of 1978 had a demonstrably important impact. Rates of increases in taxation and in governmental spending were lower in 1979 and 1980 than they would have been in the absence of the taxpayers' expression of concern.

part IV

Federal expenditures

T his part of the book discusses the expenditures of the federal government of the United States. To this point the discussion has been general, and it should be of some relevance and applicability for the public finance problems of any Western nation. In Part IV a more limited approach must be adopted. It is necessary to examine the budgetary institutions of the United States in some detail.

A complete survey of government expenditures in the American economy must include state and local units. These will not, however, be discussed in Part IV. Instead, Part VIII of the book will be exclusively devoted to an examination of the combined tax expenditure structures of the subordinate units of government.

17

The federal government budget

THE MEANING OF THE "BUDGET"

The word "budget" is used to mean many things. In household economics, a budget usually refers to an accounting record of expenditures made during a specified period. When they discuss macroeconomic policy, economists speak of manipulating the government "budget" in the carrying out of fiscal policy. In this context, the budget refers to the whole fiscal structure of the federal government, the combination of receipts and expenditures. In popular political discussion, the budget suggests a document that the President submits to the Congress for consideration at the beginning of each year.

In its forward-looking sense, the budget is best understood as a program or a plan for government activity over a designated fiscal period. It includes the various activities upon which public authorities propose to spend revenues, and, as a secondary part, it also includes a listing of the various tax sources from which revenues are to be secured during the period. By and large, however, in the United States the "budget" is considered as a plan or program for government expenditure, not for government revenue raising.

In a backward-looking or ex post sense, the budget provides a record of expenditures actually made and tax revenues actually collected. This ex post conception of the budget is useful in determining the impact of governmental activity on the economy, but it is only indirectly important in determining the program for governmental fiscal activity in the future. The forward-looking or ex ante interpretation of the budget is the more appropriate for policy-making purposes.

THE EXPENDITURE BUDGET AND THE EXECUTIVE

It has been traditional in Western democracies for the executive branch of the government to make the expenditure budget, at least initially. The legislative branch of government, the Parliament or the Congress, then approves or disapproves the budget submitted by the Executive. There is some distinction here between the U.S. system and the parliamentary systems of government. The U.S. Congress possesses much greater traditional power to modify and to expand budgeted activities than parliaments normally have possessed. Congress participates in budget making in the United States. Nevertheless, especially since the Budget and Accounting Act of 1921, under which the Bureau of the Budget was organized, the executive branch of the federal government has borne the major responsibility for determining the pattern of federal spending. However, in July 1970, by Executive Order, the Bureau of the Budget was changed to the Office of Management and Budget (OMB).

Once again we find an asymmetry between the spending and the tax sides of the fiscal account. The executive branch has never been considered to possess similar powers of determining the direction and the magnitude of the taxes to be imposed on the private economy, taxes which are necessary to finance the expenditures included in the budget. Powers of taxation are concentrated much more closely in the legislative bodies.

The asymmetry between the decision making on taxes and on public expenditures stems from the historical development of representative government and the struggle of legislative bodies to secure independence from the monarchies. The power to tax was the great oppressive weapon of the monarchy in earlier periods. The first stages of free societies were those during which this power was taken from the monarchies and granted to legislative assemblies.

Broadly speaking, the expenditure budget represents the financial embodiment of the administration's program for federal policy. In its essence, the expenditure budget reflects the prevailing political philosophy of the Executive. But, especially in the United States, the expenditure budget must also reflect some recognition of the realities to be faced on the revenue-raising side. Additional public expenditures can only be secured at additional cost during times of substantially full employment of the nation's resources, and a failure of the budget makers to incorporate some sort of weighing of costs and benefits would lead to a breakdown of the whole budgetary process. Faced with the fact that the legislative branch of government possesses somewhat more ultimate control over the levy of taxes, the budget makers in the executive branch must try to present a composition of public expenditures that falls within the desired relationship to the total tax revenues estimated to be forthcoming.

THE EXECUTIVE BUDGET

Decisions on federal expenditures are made during the course of a lengthy and complex process. Final decisions embody the interplay of individuals and groups trying to act in accordance with their own version of the public interest, trying to gain partisan political advantage, trying to construct or to maintain bureaucratic empires, and trying to advance the positions of particular pressure groups in the society. The budget-making process is such that no single individual, group, or agency possesses effective centralized power of choice. Congress ultimately bears the responsibility for decision, but the executive branch of the government is charged with the preparation and submission of the budget. The various departments, agencies, and bureaus, more expert in their own particular fields of responsibility, share with the OMB the duty of providing the detailed classification of broader budgetary items.

This process can best be discussed by tracing through the preparation of the federal budget for a specific fiscal year. We shall choose the budget for fiscal 1980 which was submitted to Congress by President Carter on January 22, 1979. Our story begins much earlier.

The federal budget can not be adequately understood as a "new" document or program of expenditures submitted to Congress each year. The budget submitted in 1979 depended to a very important degree on programs and plans that had gone before. Federal government expenditures normally are undertaken for projects that are of more than a year's duration and it is not characteristic of governments to relinquish particular types of public responsibility once these are started. Recognizing this, any complete history of the federal budget for fiscal 1980 would require us to trace out the origins of various budgetary items. The Social Security Program, for example, began in the late 1930s. Urban development programs date from 1949. The so-called "Great Society" programs, commenced under President Johnson's administration, committed federal revenues to many programs such as mass transit, education, and aid to the disadvantaged. In one sense, of course, decisions are made annually. But the differences between a decision to inaugurate a new program of public spending and the continuation of a program in being, along with its increase, is significant and important.

Even if we disregard the direct interdependence between the composition of the 1980 budget and those that have gone before, we shall have to return to early 1978 to begin consideration of this specific budgetary process. Sometime prior to April 1978, the individual bureaus and agencies within the larger federal departments and administrative units had substantially completed the initial planning for their own spending programs for fiscal 1980, which would begin some 18 months later. During the months of April and May 1978, the budget offices in the departments and independent agencies worked with smaller administrative units in formulating overall departmental and agency budgets. Sometime in mid-1978 the central administration, the Office of the President working through the Office of Management and Budget, outlined broad budgetary plans for the fiscal year that would begin 15 months later. These plans consisted of decisions to allow expansion in certain branches and agencies, to force contractions or to disallow expansion in others. These broad budgetary policy directives were made on the basis of a consideration of general administrative policy in the light of fiscal policy targets as constrained by revenue estimates. If necessary, ceilings were imposed on certain departmental requests.

During the summer months of 1978, departmental budget offices worked to revise the departmental budget estimates in accordance with the broad budgetary plans laid down by the President. Normally this process consists of cutting, trimming, and rearranging departmental estimates to reflect central policy planning. Finally, by the end of September, the departments and independent agencies were supposed to submit departmental budgetary requests to the OMB. Between this time and the middle of November, the professional staff of the OMB reviewed the departmental requests and conducted hearings. Upon completion of this stage, the director of the OMB reviewed the overall estimates and the federal budget as an organized document took form. In November and December, the President reviewed the programs as submitted to him by the director of the OMB, keeping in mind the broad policy objectives that he had previously outlined and bringing to bear any changes in this policy that seemed appropriate.

In February 1979 the budget was submitted to Congress as a document incorporating a rather detailed classification of expenditures and the revenues proposed for fiscal 1980. With the submission of this document, the President delivered an annual budget message to the Congress. This message outlined in broad detail the makeup of the budget, its composition, and its size. The message also discussed the budget in terms of its impact on the economy generally. This budget, as submitted, then became the basis for administration requests for new spending authorizations and appropriations.

THE CONGRESSIONAL BUDGETARY PROCESS

Between the time of the submission of the budget in January and the start of the fiscal year in October, Congressional action on the budget should be taken. There are two essential components of Congressional consideration of the budget. First is the traditional review and approval of specific spending programs. Second, as a result of the Congressional Budget Reform Act of 1974, the Congress must set overall spending and revenue limits. These two functions are obviously interrelated as total appropriations for individual programs must conform to aggregate spending limits.

Under the Budget Reform Act, which took full effect in 1976, budget committees in the House of Representatives and the Senate are charged with looking at overall expenditure and revenue targets. These committees prepare a budget resolution to be submitted to the whole Congress not later than April 15 of each year. This resolution designates overall spending and revenue targets. Spending targets are set for the major functional categories of the budget but not broken down into specific items. The Congress considers this proposed resolution, amends it as desired and, not later than May 15 of each year, a general set of Congressional budgetary targets is approved.

Although no appropriations legislation is voted upon by Congress until after approval of the May budget resolution, the process of reviewing the various specific spending items in the budget begins much earlier when the President's budget is initially submitted. Initially, the budget is taken up in its separate parts by the various subcommittees of the Appropriations Committee of the House of Representatives. Appropriation legislation normally is considered first in the House. These subcommittees are organized on the basis of broad functional classifications such as armed services, public works, education and labor, and atomic energy. After lengthy hearings, each subcommittee reports an appropriation bill to the full committee, which later reports its own action, through the established channels, to the full House of Representatives. Normally, between 10 and 15 major appropriation bills are handled in this way. After passage by the House, appropriation measures are taken up by the Senate, and there they follow a similar process of consideration by subcommittees, committees, and the full membership. Final passage of an appropriation measure takes place only upon compromises between the House and the Senate versions, after which the appropriation bill is forwarded to the President for his approval or veto.

Congress, after the action of the separate appropriations Committees and after passage of the standard appropriations bills, then must review the overall results in view of the overall budget targets set in the May resolution. If the targets have not been met, adjustments must be made either in appropriations levels and revenue receipts or, alternatively, the targets themselves may be altered. By no later than September 15, a second concurrent resolution on the budget must be passed which sets actual spending ceilings and revenue floors. Further action may then be necessary to reconcile actual appropriations and (if needed) taxes, to conform to the levels contained in this second resolution. This work should be completed prior to the start of the fiscal year in October 1.

The Budget Reform Act of 1974 was designed to correct a widely perceived deficiency in the Congressional budgetary process, specifically, the failure to examine the budget as a unit. Appropriation decisions were considered independently of tax legislation and, as a consequence, final decisions tended to lack any sense of weighing the burdens of additional taxes against the additional benefits of public expenditures. In addition, the Congress did not explicitly consider the macroeconomic effects of budget policy.

The fiscal 1980 budget was only the fourth budget to be considered under the new congressional budget procedures. A clear picture has not yet emerged about the effectiveness of these new procedures in meeting their objectives. Several more years experience will undoubtedly be required before any definitive evaluation of this reform can be made.

PROGRAM EVALUATION IN THE BUDGET PROCESS

The 1974 changes in the Congressional budget process were primarily designed to help the Congress exercise better control over budgetary aggregates. In addition, however, as the federal budget has grown in size and complexity, attempts have been made to improve procedures for evaluating the individual components of the budget. The record of success in this latter area has been rather mixed.

Perhaps the most ambitious attempt, to date, to improve program evaluation was the implementation of the Planning and Program Budgeting System (PPBS) during the 1960s. PPBS was first implemented at the federal government level in the Department of Defense and extended to all other agencies in 1965. The basic notion underlying PPBS was rather simple. Program objectives were to be specified and alternative ways of meeting these objectives were to be rigorously examined. Decision makers were to be provided with enough information to evaluate not only these alternatives but also ultimately the budgetary tradeoffs among objectives. The relative costs and benefits of various programs were to be examined.

Although simple in concept, PPBS proved extremely difficult in practice and was ultimately abandoned on a government-wide basis in 1971. Many reasons have been offered for its failure. First, the informational requirements were extremely large. In many cases, program evaluators were confronted with the task of quantifying essentially unquantifiable costs and benefits. Finally, there was a general failure to recognize the impossibility of specifying any objective criterion for evaluating budget tradeoffs at the highest levels of government decision making. To the extent that the PPBS approach was viewed as a means of introducing "scientific decision making" in federal budget process, its objectives were foredoomed to remain unsatisfied. There are no "right" or "wrong" budgetary allocations in

any objectively measurable sense and especially for the major break-
downs among large budgetary components.

Two new methods of attempting to improve both executive and
congressional control over individual spending programs were receiving considerable attention in the late 1970s. These were Zero-
Based Budgeting (ZBB) and sunset legislation.

President Carter had introduced ZBB into the Georgia state government when he was governor of that state and, upon his election to
the Presidency, began to implement it at the federal government
level. In essence, the ZBB procedure starts at the lowest level spending program and requires that all spending be justified starting from
a "zero-base." Bureaus are required to evaluate the consequences of
complete elimination of their programs and also of alternative funding levels which may be higher and lower than current levels.

In some respects, ZBB seems prone to the same sorts of difficulties
which beset PPBS—large information requirements, difficulties of
quantification, etc. At the same time it is somewhat more flexible in
considering the effects of alternative funding levels. PPBS started at
the top of the decision process with specifications of overall program
objectives. One objective of this was to systematically analyze the
tradeoffs among various programs perhaps funded in different agencies which had, nonetheless, similar objectives. It remains to be seen
whether the "up-from-the-bottom" approach of ZBB can deal effectively with these sorts of difficulties.

Sunset legislation was also receiving considerable attention in the
late 1970s although no actual legislation had been passed at the federal level. Under sunset provisions, spending programs are given an
automatic termination date. In order to continue in existence beyond
that date it would be necessary to convince the executive and congress that the program was meeting its objectives and that those objectives remained relevant. The primary objective of such legislation
would be, of course, to prevent agencies and programs from remaining
in existence long after they had ceased to serve any useful purpose.

THE UNIFIED BUDGET

Major reforms in presentation of the government's fiscal account
were introduced with the 1969 budget document. Prior to this time,
primary attention was devoted to the Administrative Budget. This
excluded both receipts into and outlays made from the federal trust

fund accounts. Due to the dramatic increases in the magnitude of these accounts, and especially during the 1960s, the Administrative Budget came to be less and less indicative of the impact of the federal government on the economy. Recognition of this led to the increasingly widespread usage of the Consolidated Cash Budget, which was separately presented prior to 1968. As a result of recommendations made by a special commission in 1967, a unified budget was adopted for fiscal 1969 and subsequent years. The most important change was the inclusion of the trust funds, but other changes involved the offsetting of certain proprietary receipts directly against outlays and a somewhat more straightforward distinction between new obligational authority for spending and existing authority.

THE BUDGET AS A COMBINED ACCOUNT

For many purposes, the budget is considered primarily as a program for the composition and size of federal expenditures. In its broader meaning, however, the federal budget incorporated both sides of the fiscal account; it includes estimated revenues as well as proposed spending.

For any orderly overall picture of government fiscal operations to be presented, the combined account form of the budget is required. Therefore, in the budget document each year both estimated revenues and estimated expenditures are included. Table 17–1 shows the proposed budget for fiscal 1980 in this combined account form.

BUDGETARY CLASSIFICATIONS OF FEDERAL EXPENDITURES

Functional classification

Federal expenditures may be classified in any of several ways. The most useful classification will vary with purpose. The most general is classification by major functions. This classification is also the one most often discussed in the public press. It represents an attempt to present the allocation of total federal expenditures, or proposed expenditures, among a limited number of functions performed. Each broad heading must, of course, include many subsidiary functions and the location of any particular subsidiary function is not at all clear in many instances.

TABLE 17–1
Proposed budget receipts and expenditures by function,
fiscal 1981

	In millions
Budget receipts	
Individual income taxes	$274,367
Corporation income taxes	71,574
Social insurance taxes	
and contributions	187,397
Excise taxes	40,209
Estate and gift taxes	5,938
Customs duties	8,403
Miscellaneous receipts	12,100
Total budget receipts	$599,988
Budget outlays by function	
National defense	$146,241
International Affairs	9,612
General science, space and technology	6,442
Energy	8,107
Natural resources and environment	12,819
Agriculture	2,802
Commerce and housing credit	712
Transportation	20,159
Community and regional development	8,820
Education, training, employment and	
social services	31,989
Health	62,449
Income security	219,982
Veterans benefits and services	21,731
Administration of justice	4,699
General government	4,931
General purpose fiscal assistance	9,617
Interest	67,197
Allowances	2,570
Undistributed offsetting receipts	−25,119
Total budget outlays	$615,761
Budget surplus or deficit	−15,773

Source: *The Budget of The United States Government,* Fiscal Year, 1981, p. 552.

Expenditures are broken down by function in the combined budget exhibited in Table 17–1. As can be seen, the functional classification employed in the federal budget document is as follows:

National defense
International affairs
Energy
Education, training, employment and social services
Health
Income security
Veterans' benefits and services
Administration of justice
Agriculture
Natural resources and environment
Commerce and housing credit
Transportation
Community and regional development
General purpose fiscal assistance
General government
General science, space and technology
Allowances
Interest

Controllability classification

As suggested earlier, many of the spending categories in the federal government's budget include outlays that result from programs enacted in earlier periods. In part due to increasing congressional and public pressure against the explosively rising budgetary totals, but also in part due to the simple effectiveness in presentation, the budgets in recent years have emphasized the controllability aspects. Table 17–2 indicates the breakdown between controllable and uncontrollable outlays projected for the 1980 fiscal year.

The proportion of the budget which is uncontrollable in the short run has been rising. In 1970, 64 percent of the expenditures made fell into the uncontrollable category. By 1980, as Table 17–2 indicates, this proportion had risen to 76 percent. Some primary reasons for

TABLE 17–2
Controllable and uncontrollable items in the budget for fiscal 1980

	In billions
Relatively uncontrollable..........................	404.1
Payments for individuals	(250.5)
Other open-ended programs and fixed costs.....	(65.7)
Outlays from prior year contracts and obligations	(87.9)
Relatively controllable outlays	132.9

Source: *The Budget of the United States,* Fiscal Year 1980, pp. 560–61.

this change include the fact that defense spending, a substantial portion of which is controllable, declined during the period relative to other budgetary components, and the fact that two important uncontrollable components, mandatory grants to state and local governments and benefit payments to individuals, have grown.

The relative sizes of the controllable and uncontrollable components of the budget indicate the difficulty that arises when attempts are made to cut down budgetary totals, regardless of the urgency of the need to do so or the will to do so. Responsible fiscal decision making, by either the Executive or the Congress, must be based on the recognition that program enactments involve budgetary commitments over extended periods.

Agency classification

Classification of spending items by functions to be performed is helpful in providing a broad understanding of the composition of federal expenditures. But it is not very helpful in accomplishing some of the other purposes that the budget document must serve. The budget is a composite result of a process of choosing an allocation of funds among the separate departments, agencies, and subsidiary units of the whole federal bureaucratic structure. The Air Force is relatively disinterested in the budgetary appropriation for national defense as shown in the functional classification. It is primarily interested in the expenditure authorization allocated to Air Force defense under the broader Department of Defense classification. The breakdown of total

TABLE 17–3
**Proposed federal budget expenditures, by agency,
fiscal 1981**

	In millions
Legislative branch	$ 1,318
The Judiciary	649
Executive Office of the President	105
Funds appropriated to the President	9,263
Agriculture	20,084
Commerce	3,416
Defense—Military	142,700
Defense—Civil	3,052
Education	13,479
Energy	8,689
Health and Human Services	219,333
Housing and Urban Development	11,776
Interior	4,242
Justice	2,672
Labor	31,795
State	2,171
Transportation	17,873
Treasury	80,348
Environmental Protection Agency	5,'97
National Aeronautics and Space Administration	5,437
Veterans Administration	21,697
Other independent agencies	33,012
Allowances	2,570
Undistributed offsetting receipts	−25,119
Total	$615,761

Source: *The Budget of The United States Government,* Fiscal
1981, p. 553.

expenditures by departments and agencies authorized to make the outlays is more useful than the broad functional classification in the day-to-day administrative implementation of the budget. And it should be recalled that it is through the desires, plans, programs, and purposes of the separate subsidiary units that the budget originally evolves as a combined program of spending. The classification of the budget by agency is presented in Table 17–3. The totals are those which were proposed to the Congress by the President in January 1980, for fiscal 1981.

18

Efficiency in federal spending

THE NOTION OF "EFFICIENCY"

Efficiency as a norm for fiscal organization has been discussed in Chapter 7. It was suggested that the "ideally efficient" or "ideally neutral" fiscal structure is that which makes individual choices for collective goods and services as closely analogous as is possible to such choices for private goods and services in a perfectly functioning market economy. The criterion of efficiency becomes the degree of correspondence between the individual benefits received from public services at the margin and the costs of these services imposed on the individual, again at the appropriately defined margin of provision. As was indicated, this broad conception of efficiency is of limited usefulness. Fiscal systems are organized, they develop, and they change in accordance with many conflicting goals and stresses. Efficiency in this broad sense is perhaps a relatively unimportant influence in many cases.

Nonetheless, efficiency remains the economist's stock-in-trade, and it can continue to be a useful norm if defined differently at a second-order level of consideration. But second-order efficiency can mean many different things. In Chapter 7, the principle of "least price distortion" was shown to be helpful in evaluating some fiscal institutions. This principle uses the criterion of efficiency in the production and use of private goods and does not involve the efficiency with which public goods are supplied or used. The fiscal structure that minimizes its impact on individual and group behavior, will, in this second best sense, maximize the productivity of resources devoted to private purposes.

In this chapter, quite a different conception of second-order efficiency will be introduced. If it is accepted that public or collective goods and services are to be provided through governmental processes, the notion of "efficiency" must also be applied to the allocation of public expenditures among the many collective purposes that are possible. This allocative approach, which is traditional in economists' discussions of public spending, somewhat arbitrarily divorces the expenditure process from the revenue-raising or taxing process. In a later section, some of the deficiencies in this respect will be noted, but at this juncture we shall accept provisionally the legitimacy of this approach.

We now assume that a decision has been made to devote a specific sum to public or governmental purposes. This initial assumption al lows us to separate the "size of government" decision from the "com position of government" decision. This converts the budgetary prob lem into one that is identical with that assumed to confront the individual consumer in elementary price theory. The consumer is as sumed to have a fixed total income that is to be spent on several goods and services. We make the budgetary process identical by postulating that a given revenue sum is available for public spending. As with the consumer, the problem becomes, in this way, one of *maximizing* the return from this limited or scarce resource, which is, in this instance, total revenue.

An "efficient" allocation of any scarce resource is defined as one that maximizes the useful return or output from any *given* total output.[1] This elementary definition is completely general, and it may be applied to an oil furnace, a gasoline engine, a nuclear power plant, a church organization, the operation of a firm, or the consumer's trip to the supermarket. In each of these cases, some meaning may be attached to the term "useful output," be this BTUs, horsepower deliv-

---

[1]Any allocation problem can be stated in either maximization or minimization terms. An efficient solution maximizes the return from a given output, or, conversely, minimizes the input necessary to produce a given output. Either the numerator or the denominator of the input-output ratio must be fixed. The maximization or the minimization of a ratio is not a meaningful criterion.

ered, kilowatt-hours, souls saved, the present value of a profits stream, or family utility.

THE CRITERION PROBLEM

The last sentence may be stated differently by saying that, in each of the cases mentioned as examples, a reasonably definite *criterion* exists by which alternative possible operations' processes, or allocations may be measured and evaluated. We may, for example, wish to compare two oil furnaces costing the same amount initially and burning the same amount of fuel. The primary consideration then would be the thermal units of heat produced. If we can ignore such factors as noise of operation, cleanliness, and so forth, it becomes relatively easy to decide which of the two furnaces is the more "efficient," that is, which one provides the more units of output per dollar of outlay. If needs be, in such instances we may employ consulting engineers or technicians to give us the correct answers. They would be able to do so because we are able to tell them precisely what we want; we define a criterion in advance.

The criterion problem becomes considerably more perplexing in the supermarket example. Here we assume a given resource; money to be spent. The consumer must maximize the return from limited outlay. But what *criterion* is to be used in this case? How can any one combination of supermarket products be ranked higher than another? The common denominator here can only be some subjective "satisfaction" or "utility." The money is spent efficiently when the maximum utility is secured. But this is a rather vague criterion. Whereas the aid of the consulting engineer is very helpful in choosing furnaces, the consulting "home economist" is of considerably less assistance in choice making. The individual consumer finds it difficult, often impossible, to specify precisely what "utility" means. To do so would amount to telling the observer just what the taste pattern is, and the individual may not really know until actually confronted with the alternatives from which choice must be made. A good share of modern advertising and sales promotion techniques is based on the assumption that consumer tastes are, in fact, determined only at the moment of decision. This amounts to saying that the objective definition of a criterion becomes extremely difficult in consumer choice. In spite of this, we may speak of "efficiency" in a meaningful way here. We may do so because the consumer can judge subjectively among "better" and "worse" allocations of expenditure; objective definition of a criterion is not necessary.

PUBLIC EXPENDITURE: HIGH-LEVEL EFFICIENCY

A whole new set of problems arise when we try to apply the notion of "efficiency" to the allocation of a given budget among the many possible public expenditure categories. Some criterion must be employed in evaluating alternative budgetary compositions. But what is the "thing" that public activity, the "government," is supposed to achieve? What is to be maximized by the allocation of limited funds among the various public sectors?

One answer to these questions is "social welfare" or "the public interest." But what do these terms mean? How can they be defined objectively? The terms mean different things to different people, and, this being the case, which people (or better, which one person or like-minded group) is to do the defining? As we have emphasized before, the "government," as such, is not an independent organism, and government decisions must be made by individuals. If, in fact, everyone could agree on an unambiguous definition of "social welfare," which would have to include a fixing of the appropriate trading ratios among all conflicting social goals, some discussion of "efficiency" in public spending could become possible. But since this required sort of agreement seems out of the question in a free society, "efficiency criteria" for high-level budgetary planning do not appear to exist.

RATIONALITY IN DECISION MAKING

Does the absence of efficiency criteria in the normal sense suggest that any one allocation of federal expenditures is as good as any other? And, if this should be the case, would not some random selection procedure be appropriate as a means of budget making? The answer is, of course, negative. Some budgetary allocations are better than others, *to me*. But the last two words in the sentence need emphasis. As with the consumer in the supermarket, no objectively determinate means of defining a criterion exists; but individual choice must be based on some subjective notion of efficiency.

The fundamental point to be made is that to the official in the government department or agency, to the fiscal expert in the Office of

Management and Budget, or to the legislator, some criterion of "efficiency" exists. If not, decisions would be wholly arbitrary. But the criterion differs from individual to individual, and there is no objective manner of assessing the relative worth of various individual evaluations. Representative Jones from Michigan may feel, with all honesty, that greater contribution to "social welfare" is to be made by federal spending of a million dollars on reforestation in Upper Michigan than by spending a million dollars for an irrigation project in Nevada. Representative Brown from Nevada may feel precisely the opposite. It is impossible for the analyst, the specialist, to determine which, if either of the two is "correct."

Just as with the consumer, however, federal spending decisions, by whomever made, can be more "rational" if decision makers are more fully informed. Therefore, for high-level decisions on the allocation of federal expenditures, the task of the analyst is to inform decision makers of alternative courses of action. Actual decision-making processes must be examined with a view toward determining whether or not full information concerning the consequences of alternative course of action is provided. "Rationality," defined in this way, must replace "efficiency" as something which can be objectively measured by the observer.

In this view there is no real meaning to be attached to the complaint that the federal government is not spending "enough" on domestic poverty relief programs and that it is spending "too much" on national defense. If the executive and legislative departments, as normally constituted, are fully informed of the consequences of action taken, the decision that emerges must be taken to be as good as any other. There is simply no basis, other than the purely subjective one, upon which the presumed "expert" can say that we need an extra $10 billion to spend on urban renewal.

LOW-LEVEL EFFICIENCY: COST-BENEFIT ANALYSIS

As we shift our attention to lower levels of decision-making, to the breakdown of the larger budget items into their component parts, "efficiency" in the accepted sense can assume a sharper form and it can, in certain cases, provide a basis for improved performance in budgetary allocation. The reason for this difference between high-level and low-level application of the efficiency concept is that, at lower levels of the budget, somewhat more definite criteria can be introduced.

Cost-benefit analysis represents an attempt to apply the criterion of economic efficiency at relatively low levels of the fiscal decision process. The conceptual basis of cost-benefit analysis is straightforward. Costs and benefits of a particular government project are estimated. If the benefits of the project are greater than its costs, the project is worthwhile. If costs exceed benefits, the project should be abandoned. In actual practice, cost benefit-analysis is usually a very complex procedure and the validity of the results is often subject to controversy. The main problem areas in this regard are the procedures for estimating costs and benefits, the choice of the appropriate discount rate, and the distributional consequences of alternative government projects.

Some of the earliest attempts at cost-benefit analysis involved the evaluation of federal spending for water resource development. For many years before the method was generally adopted, the Army Corps of Engineers and the Bureau of Reclamation used cost-benefit estimates in evaluating projects. Project evaluation in this area was reasonably amenable to the cost-benefit approach. Benefits from water resource projects accrue to specific population and occupational groups and take the form of increments to capital values. Careful analysis can quantify these in dollar terms. The same thing is true for the cost side. As the use of cost-benefit analysis was expanded to a larger number and variety of government projects, problems with quantifying benefits mounted. The benefits of many government projects are intangible and not easily subject to either measurement or valuation by an external analyst. An educational program, for example, may improve the productivity of its participants in terms of their eventual participation in the work force. This component of the program's benefits can be estimated in the form of the increased market value of work effort supplied by these individuals. However, other benefits, produced jointly with the increased productivity, are much more difficult to quantify. How can one assign a value to the improved citizenship of individuals who are more capable of making informed judgments of alternative public policies? By the same token, education may enhance the ability of individuals to enjoy such things as fine literature, music, and art. These may be benefits of a particular program, but they are not easily amenable to valuation by a disinterested analyst.

For many government projects, costs and benefits do not accrue immediately, but rather are spread over a considerable period of time. At the time of project evaluation, projected future costs and benefits must be converted into present values before any assessment of the project's worth can be made. The reason for this is that a dollar today and a dollar a year from today are not the same thing. Generally, today's equivalent or present value of a dollar payment to be made in one year is some amount less than a dollar. Future dollars of benefits or costs must be discounted to express present values. The choice of the appropriate discount rate is the source of some controversy among students of cost-benefit analysis.

From one point of view, the discount rate used in cost-benefit analysis should give an accurate conversion of future costs and benefits into present values to the representative taxpayer. How much is that individual willing to give up today in order to have X dollars of additional consumption at the relevant time in the future. An alternative view is that the discount rate should reflect the marginal productivity of private sector investment. Choosing the discount rate on this basis imposes the requirement that government investment projects be at least as productive of future consumption benefits as private investments of the same amount. In a perfectly functioning capital market, with appropriate adjustments for risk, these two discount rates would be the same. In the real world, however, this is not the case. The tax system, most notably the corporate income tax, drives a wedge between the marginal productivity of investment and the pure rate of time preference. Individuals invest as long as the net return exceeds their marginal willingness to trade present for future consumption. With an approximately 50 percent tax on investment income, a gross return of 10 percent is necessary to provide a net 5 percent return to the investor.

Additional controversies surrounding the choice of discount rate center on the appropriate assignment of risk to government versus private projects and the question of whether or not individuals tend to discount the future unduly in their private evaluation of the tradeoff between present and future consumption.

A third area of controversy in cost-benefit analysis surrounds its distributional implications. Implicit in the whole cost-benefit comparison, is the assumption that a dollar's cost or a dollar's benefit is "socially" equivalent to any other dollar's cost or benefit, no matter upon whom the cost is imposed and to whom the benefit is promised.

In other words, the whole methodology of cost-benefit analysis is distributionally indifferent. The landowner in California who secures the dollars' benefit from an irrigation project is equally important with the Maryland truck driver who pays additional tax to help finance the project. Once this distributional assumption is made clear, it seems obvious that many persons will not accept the direct and straightforward application of cost-benefit analysis as a means of selecting among alternative public expenditure projects. There may be many projects which fail the cost-benefit test but which are preferred by decision makers precisely because of the distribution of costs and benefits. Alternatively, projects which are highly rated by cost-benefit comparisons may be rejected because of undesired distributional consequences.

EFFICIENCY AND INTERDEPENDENCE

Federal spending looms so large relative to the total economy in the United States that continuing attempts to introduce greater "efficiency" can be expected. Systems analysis, operations research, and cost-benefit calculations are various terms used to define separate and related efforts to provide some scientific guidance in the decision-making process. But the context within which "efficiency" in public spending is discussed must ever be borne in mind. At best we speak of a second-order idea of efficiency. The best of efforts at suboptimization are likely to appear frustrated until and unless this is fully recognized.

The allocation of public expenditures is dependent on the structure of federal taxes. The initial assumption in the approach to efficiency in public spending is not appropriate. Governments do not have a specified revenue sum to allocate among the various uses. If they did, much greater objectivity could be introduced into the budgetary processes. The "efficiency" approach would be limited here only by the absence of a meaning of the term in high-level budgetary decisions. But the amount of revenues that Congress raises through federal taxation is tied quite closely to the allocation of federal expenditures among the separate uses. Broadly speaking, the decisions on expenditures and taxes must be considered to be made simultaneously, despite the institutional structure of Congress. This fact makes any independent achievement of "efficiency" in public spending rather meaningless, even at the lower decision-making levels. The best of cost-benefit estimates may, for example, indicate that federal spending on improvement of rivers and harbors be substantially cut. But congressional approval of the heavy tax burden implicit in a $500 billion federal budget may be dependent on a substantial appropriation for river and harbor improvement, with considerable geographic dispersion of the projects undertaken.

Quite similar processes apply at still another budgetary level. The point to be made is that the overall size of the budget cannot be separated from its composition. The two decisions are interdependent. This makes the approach to "efficiency" in the use of public expenditures somewhat elusive at best, and misleading at the worst.

BUREAUCRATIC LIMITS TO GOVERNMENTAL EFFICIENCY

Standard discussions of efficiency in public spending have largely neglected any examination of the limits that a bureaucratic structure places upon the carrying out of any assigned governmental task. Yet, as the discussion of Chapter 14 has indicated, this may be a problem of considerable importance and cannot be neglected in any complete approach to efficiency in government spending.

Bureaucratic inefficiencies can have an important impact on the effectiveness of the various optimization techniques discussed in this chapter. The costs of various projects are likely to be higher than necessary if those projects are managed by public bureaus. Reliance on cost-benefit ratios without simultaneously searching for the optimal arrangement, for example, could conceivably result in the rejection of many projects which might be worthwhile if managed efficiently.

In quite a different sense, bureaucratic structure imposes severe limits on the flexibility of the whole budgetary process. Economists are somewhat prone to assume implicitly that the budgetary allocation is made carte blanche at the beginning of each fiscal period, tempered, of course, with some recognition that existing program commitments embody continuing budgetary obligations. The complexity of the whole budgetary process tends to be overlooked, and the degree of rigidity in budgetary allocation is rarely appreciated. Recent studies have demonstrated empirically that surprisingly good predictions about future budgetary allocation can be made on the basis of quite simple and quite naïve projections, for the most part percentage increases in the appropriations made to various agencies. These results must give pause to all proposals for introducing greater efficiency in the budget process.

CONCLUSIONS

The notion of efficiency in the allocation of public expenditures must be recognized to be of a second-order sort since overall efficiency in fiscal organization would involve a simultaneous determination of the size and the composition of the budget. Nevertheless, some progress may be made by assuming at the outset that the government possesses a fixed revenue sum to be allocated among the many possible uses. This places the government in a role analogous to the consumer. But this immediately raises the question of the appropriate criterion by which various budgetary compositions may be evaluated. At the higher levels of decision making, say as concerns the decision between the amount of funds to be appropriated to national defense and to federal housing projects, the notion of efficiency itself seems misleading. All that can be done at this level is to assist decision makers in outlining the consequences of alternative courses of action to be taken or choices to be made.

Further down in the budgetary hierarchy, a more scientific approach to budgeting can be taken. Criteria can be more acceptably defined. The rapidly developing skills of the operations research or systems analysis specialist can be brought to bear to assist in the formulation of these low-level budgetary decisions. Aside from the application to the military budget, scientific approaches to decision making have been attempted primarily in the allocation of federal spending in the fields of resource development. Here the use of cost and benefit estimates have been introduced and employed as aids in the decision process. The application of these methods has raised many problems in the appropriate methods of evaluating benefits and in estimating costs.

Any attempts to push the notion of "efficiency" too far in the making of budgetary decisions runs afoul of the fundamental fact of interdependence between the composition of public expenditures and the size and composition of the federal revenue totals. Any realistic analysis of the federal spending process should start from a recognition of this interdependence.

And finally, the important limits that the bureaucratic structure itself can place on the carrying out of assigned spending tasks must be recognized. Bureaucratic structures must be analyzed as organizations of separate individuals, each acting within a special capacity, and each one of them possessing personal qualities that are best assumed to be average or ordinary in any careful analysis. Improvements in governmental efficiency can be secured through careful readjustments of rewards and punishments in the civil service.

SUPPLEMENTARY READING

This chapter owes much to the work of R. N. McKean. See his *Efficiency in Government through Systems Analysis* (New York: John Wiley & Sons, Inc., 1958), and, his *Public Spending* (New York: McGraw-Hill Book Co., 1968).

For some of the problems involved in cost-benefit estimates in particular, the student is referred to Samuel B. Chase, Jr. (ed.), *Problems in Public Expenditure Analysis* (Washington, D.C.: The Brookings Institution, 1968).

For a discussion of the limits imposed by bureaucratic hierarchies, see Gordon Tullock, *The Politics of Bureaucracy* (Washington, D.C.: Public Affairs Press, 1965).

The empirical results referred to in the text are reported in Otto A. Davis, M. A. H. Dempster, and Aaron Wildavsky, "On the Process of Budgeting: An Empirical Study of Congressional Appropriations," *Papers on Non-Market Decision Making*, vol. 1 (1966), pp. 63–132.

A former Director of the Bureau of the Budget provides an experienced view of the problems of securing efficiency in Charles L. Schultze, *The Politics and Economics of Public Spending* (Washington, D.C.: The Brookings Institution, 1969).

19

Federal expenditures

The fiscal 1980 budget of the United States government proposed total expenditures of almost $532 billion. Spending of such magnitude is almost impossible for the average person to comprehend given direct experience of budgeting personal expenditures denominated only in the thousands. Expressing federal spending in per capita terms may make it somewhat easier to gain some real appreciation of the size of the federal budget. Assuming a 1980 United States population of 220 million, proposed federal spending would average slightly over $2400 per capita.

Any detailed examination of the large and varied number of federal government programs is obviously beyond the scope of this text. Rather, this chapter is devoted to an overview of federal expenditures broken down into broadly defined functional categories. Some general analytical observations will be made about particular programs. Students interested in more in-depth analysis of specific programs and policies are encouraged to seek out the numerous published studies of specific policy issues.

NATIONAL DEFENSE

A critical issue in the national debate over the federal budget is the allocation of total spending between national defense and domestic programs. Such a broad categorization of spending obscures many important allocational decisions within each category. However, in the eyes of many, if not most citizens, the division of spending into these two areas is an important reflection of national priorities.

The fiscal 1980 budget proposed defense expenditures of approximately $126 billion which represented about 24 percent of proposed total spending. This proportion claimed by national defense was relatively stable during the latter half of the 1970s following a dramatic decline begun in the late sixties when domestic and social spending by the federal government began to increase dramatically. In 1965, for example, defense expenditures accounted for 40 percent of total federal expenditures.

When adjustments are made for inflation, defense spending proposed for 1980 was considerably lower in real terms than was the case both during the Vietnam War years of the late sixties and early seventies and also in the early sixties. Table 19–1 illustrates the pattern of real defense spending over the two decades from 1960–1980. The absolute and relative decline in the defense budget sparked an ongoing national debate between those who saw it as a much needed adjustment in national priorities, and others who perceived a significant weakening of United States power and influence abroad with potentially serious long-term consequences for national security.

Total defense spending is allocated among several categories or missions. These include the strategic forces, the primary mission of which is to deter nuclear attack on the United States, general purpose forces which perform more conventional military functions and research and development of new military technologies. Other categories are intelligence and communications, the national guard and reserve forces, supply and maintenance, training and other personnel activities, administration, airlift and sealift, and support of other nations. Table 19–2 provides a breakdown of these programs in the fiscal 1980 budget. It should be noted that the dollar amounts in this table are proposed obligational authority so the total will not correspond exactly to the previous total, which was proposed outlay.

The manner in which individuals are induced to serve in the armed forces is a topic of continuing concern and controversy. A decision was made in the early 1970s to shift from at least partial reliance on conscription to an all-volunteer armed force. After several years of experience with the voluntary system, some political pressure developed in the late seventies to return to the draft at least on a standby basis.

The controversy over an all-volunteer, as opposed to a conscripted,

TABLE 19–1
National defense expenditures in constant
(1972) dollars, selected years, 1960–1980

Year	Defense expenditures (in $ billions)
1960	73.8
1962	77.2
1964	77.0
1966	76.3
1968	101.4
1970	90.3
1972	76.6
1974	67.9
1976	65.6
1978	67.3
1980*	70.4

* Estimate.
Source: *The Budget of The United States Government*,
Fiscal Year, 1980, p. 578.

TABLE 19–2
Obligational authority for national defense by program fiscal 1980

Program	Obligational authority (in $ billions)
Strategic forces	10.8
General purpose forces	50.0
Intelligence and communications	9.1
Airlift and sealift	1.9
Guard and reserve	7.1
Research and development	11.8
Central supply and maintenance	13.3
Training, medical, and other general personnel activities	27.9
Administration and associated activities	2.6
Support of other programs	0.6
Total	135.0

Source: *The Budget of The United States Government*, Fiscal Year, 1980, p. 89.

military force is best analyzed from both a historic and an economic perspective. Prior to World War II, the United States did not maintain a standing army of any significant size. Forces larger than token size were recruited only during periods of active conflict and preparation for such conflict. The postwar period marked a sharp change in this longstanding tradition. For the first time it was considered necessary to maintain a large permanent military establishment. Conscription was retained as a means of maintaining the desired defense establishment.

During wartime, conscription has traditionally been the primary means of recruiting military personnel. However, coercive recruitment and maintenance of the armed forces tends to break down when only a relatively small proportion of the eligible age group is required. Unless the universality of obligation can be extended across all potentially eligible groups, any system of conscription will seem arbitrary and grossly inequitable. Recognition of this was the source of much unrest during the middle and late 1960s and increasing support was given to replacing the draft with a wholly volunteer supply of military personnel. Such a policy was adopted in 1972.

The primary criticism of the all-volunteer armed forces in the late 1970s was that insufficient numbers of qualified individuals were being attracted to enlist either in the regular or reserve forces. It was argued that military preparedness had been drastically reduced. However, it is important to put these claims in perspective. There is little logical reason why price incentives cannot be used in recruiting military personnel. Individuals can choose a career in the military service in much the same way as they choose a career in medicine, accounting, or any other occupation. Generally, reliance on conscription reflects a military pay and benefits schedule which provides insufficient rewards for individuals to voluntarily choose military service as an occupation. The increased pay and allowances which are required to attract individuals to voluntary enlistment reflect, not an actual increase in the true economic cost of maintaining the military establishment, but rather a shifting to the general taxpayer of costs previously borne exclusively by draftees. In fact, it is almost surely the case that the actual tax borne by those drafted exceeds the amount of money which would be required as an explicit additional outlay in order to attract volunteers. This is because, under the working of a price incentive scheme, those persons most willing to work in the military would be selected. By contrast, conscription entails no direct means of selecting those most willing to serve.

If an increase in the quantity and quality of military personnel were to be achieved, the preceding discussion suggests two possible methods. First, military pay and allowances could be increased to levels required to attract the desired personnel. This method would allocate the increased costs among the general taxpaying public. Alternatively, conscription could be restored with the resulting disproportionate increase in tax burden on those individuals actually drafted into the military.

INTERNATIONAL AFFAIRS

Federal expenditures in this category have been quantitatively important only since World War II. During the decade of the 1970s, expenditures range from $4.2 billion in 1970 to $5.9 billion in 1978. Proposed outlays for fiscal 1980 were $8.2 billion.

The bulk of expenditures in this area consists of various programs of economic aid to foreign countries. Of the proposed outlays for 1980, $5.5 billion was targeted for various programs of this type, in some of which the United States participates independently and in others on a multilateral basis with one or more additional donor countries. Both humanitarian aid and the encouragement of economic development in the Third World are stated objectives of U.S. foreign aid expenditures.

Conduct of foreign affairs is the second largest category of spending under International Affairs. Activities here would include, of course, the activities of the Department of State in representing the United States abroad. U.S. contributions to various international organizations were also included in the proposed 1980 expenditures here of $1.5 billion.

Other spending programs under international affairs (and proposed 1980 expenditures) include military assistance ($.5 billion), foreign information and exchange activities ($.5 billion) and international financial programs, the most important being the Export-Import Bank ($.3 billion).

GENERAL SCIENCE, SPACE, AND TECHNOLOGY

Federal expenditures in this area remained relatively stable during the 1970s. Outlays of $4.5 billion were made in 1970 and $4.7 billion in 1978. The 1980 budget proposed outlays of $5.5 billion. Given the inflation which occurred during the 1970s, these relatively stable money expenditures would imply a decline in real expenditures.

Expenditures in this area encompass government support of basic scientific research in both the physical and social sciences and in the space program. The government's role in financing basic research is especially interesting from an economics perspective. Basic research, as opposed to applied research, would seem to exhibit many of the characteristics of a genuine public good. Knowledge, once produced, is indivisible and, especially in the case of basic research, generally nonexcludable. The patent system provides a way for inventors and persons or firms active in applied research to establish marketable property rights over any scientific or technological discoveries emergent from their efforts. This marketability provides a financial incentive for such activity. Such an incentive is rather more difficult to provide the more basic is the research in question. Because of this, the market is likely to underproduce such research and therefore some justification for government action is present.

ENERGY

The federal government's involvement in the energy area increased dramatically during the 1970s. Direct expenditures increased more than eightfold, over the decade, from slightly under $1 billion in 1970 to a proposed level of almost $8 billion in the fiscal 1980 budget. Changing spending levels tell only part of the story, however. Probably the most significant facet of the federal government's changing role in this area was the increase in direct regulatory intervention in domestic energy markets which occurred in response to the challenge posed by the OPEC oil cartel. Many economists would argue that this regulatory response, which sought primarily to restrain domestic price increases, worked to benefit OPEC by discouraging competing domestic production. By the late 1970s this perception seemed to be spreading among politicians and their constituents also, with accompanying pressures to at least partially dismantle the regulatory apparatus. Legislation allowing the phased deregulation of natural gas prices was approved in 1978 and in 1979 President Carter began lifting the controls on domestic oil production.

The bulk of proposed 1980 expenditures for fiscal 1980, $4.4 billion, was directed toward increasing energy supply. These include funds directed toward development of new energy technologies and construction of new facilities to transmit energy produced from government operated facilities, primarily the Tennessee Valley Authority.

Another sizable component of total expenditures was targeted for continued development of the Strategic Petroleum Reserve.

NATURAL RESOURCES AND ENVIRONMENT

In the proposed budget for fiscal 1980, expenditures for natural resources and environment netted out at $11.5 billion. Gross anticipated expenditures were approximately $13.4 billion, however. The smaller figure which entered into the budget totals was obtained by subtracting from the expenditure anticipated receipts from such things as timber sales, grazing fees, and other direct user or buyer charges. Federal government expenditures in this area increased fairly steadily during the 1970s from $3.1 billion in 1970 to $10.9 billion in 1978. Spending under this heading tends to be controversial in many respects thus making it a category of considerable importance in discussion of overall federal policy.

The largest subcategory of expenditures in the natural resource area is that planned for pollution abatement and control. Outlays of $4.7 billion are projected here for fiscal 1980. The bulk of these expenditures, $3.6 billion, take the form of grants to subfederal governments for construction of waste treatment plants.

The federal government's role in setting pollution control standards has been a major source of controversy. A key issue is whether the same standards should be applied nationwide. This is presently the case with respect to federal air pollution standards. A result of this policy is that the same minimum level of air quality must be attained in Los Angeles as in Des Moines, despite the fact that attaining that minimum level is likely to be much more costly in the former city than it is in the latter. If the decision respecting air quality standards were left to state or local units of government, it is likely that such standards would vary widely among governmental units, depending both on the costs of achieving specific levels of pollution abatement and on different preferences of residents of different areas. There seems to be no compelling argument on grounds of either equity or efficiency to the effect that all regions of the country should be required to have the same minimum level of air quality.

Water resources and power comprise a second major category of expenditures in the natural resource area. The expenditures of $3.7 billion projected in this category for fiscal 1980 included outlays for flood control, improved navigation, electric power generation, irrigation projects, provision of water for recreational use, improvements in water supply to urban areas, and overall river valley developments.

Federal spending programs in this area receive a disproportionate amount of discussion for several reasons. The most important is that benefits from such programs are almost always concentrated in particular geographic areas. Hence the local pressure on individual members of Congress to secure appropriations of federal funds for such projects is immense. This category is widely recognized to be extremely sensitive in a political sense.

A major issue involved in the discussion of natural resource expenditures concerns the degree to which federal tax revenues, collected from all citizens of the nation, should be used to undertake projects whose benefits are geographically concentrated in specific areas of the country. Here we encounter, in a real case, the asymmetry between the tax and the expenditure sides of the fiscal account to which we have referred several times before. Geographically discriminatory federal taxation would be unconstitutional under existing interpretations of the law. But geographically discriminatory expenditure is not unconstitutional. The asymmetry prevents the federal government from imposing special benefit-type taxes on the residents of the areas directly affected by federal spending programs on natural resources. As a result, programs that are undertaken with federal funds represent a net transfer of income from taxpayers as a group to the particular residents of project areas. Historically, the individuals who have lived in the arid western states have especially benefited on this account at the expense of those citizens living in the eastern states. This net transfer has been redistributory in the direction of greater, not less, income inequality since the average level of incomes in the western states has been higher. Some modification of these results can be predicted as federal attention comes to be placed on poverty and on the rebuilding of urban slums.

A return of those spending functions that involve concentration of benefits to the state units of government might seem to provide an appropriate solution here. In many cases, however, this organizational change is prevented by the nature of the projects, even if not by other factors. River valley development normally involves several states in a region, and, for this reason, independent state action is not likely to be fully effective. In the absence of regional authorities, the federal government has stepped in to handle, and to finance, the genuinely interstate resource projects. Some solution might be sought through the expanded usage of interstate compact arrangements, but no effective start has been made in this direction. Continued federal financing of such projects may be surely predicted, accompanied by strong pressure for expansion on the part of the beneficiary regions and by strong, but less concentrated, opposition on the part of federal taxpayers generally who will object to the net income transfers that are accomplished through the projects.

AGRICULTURE

Proposed spending on agriculture in the fiscal 1980 budget was $3.7 billion. This is a relatively small proportion of the federal budget, less than one percent of total spending. However, under existing programs this amount is not subject to a great deal of government control. This is because the bulk of government spending on agriculture ($2.7 billion in 1980) is used to subsidize the income of farmers. The specific objective of the farm subsidy program is to guarantee a minimum return on agricultural land devoted to the production of certain products. Thus the costs of the program are tied to the prices which farmers can receive in the marketplace, and are highly dependent on the vagaries of not only U.S. but also international demand and supply of agricultural products.

An important issue to address is why the federal government should single out agriculture as an industry for major subsidization from tax revenues. The industry has been declining in relative importance fairly consistently during the 20th century. Since about 1910, agricultural employment has been falling, but output has continued to rise, largely because of revolutionary changes in production techniques. National income has also risen rapidly and population has expanded. However, income increases do not generate proportionate increases in demands for agricultural products and, therefore, secular increases in demand tend to be tied rather closely to the rate of population expansion. As a result of these forces, the supply of agricultural products has increased more rapidly than demand over the past 70 years.

If the industry had been allowed to respond to these forces of secular change in a normal manner, prices and farm incomes would have fallen rapidly relative to income elsewhere in the economy. This would have accelerated the shift of persons and resources out of agriculture and into nonagricultural employments. This pattern of change did not occur with full effectiveness, however, because of federal government policies attempting to shore up the industry by preventing the declines in prices and farm incomes that the forces of demand and supply would dictate.

Present farm policy had its origin in the Great Depression of the 1930s. Once the federal government began programs of assistance to manufacturing industries and to the unemployed during that period, farm bloc supporters argued, with some legitimacy, that the same sort of support should be granted to the agricultural industry by supporting farm prices and incomes. The agricultural policy of the Roosevelt New Deal involved two approaches to the farm problem. The first was an attempt to destroy existing and to reduce future surpluses, while the second instituted government purchases in order to keep prices above market equilibrium levels. Only the second policy was found to be effective.

The federal government became committed to supporting farm prices at "parity" or some high percentage thereof, parity being defined as some ratio that would provide farmers with "terms of trade" with the nonfarm sector comparable with that which they enjoyed in the 1900–14 period. The policy was continued in years following World War II and as production increased rapidly, the federal government found itself purchasing huge quantities of agricultural commodities in order to prevent farm prices from falling below congressionally determined levels in response to normal demand and supply considerations.

The price support program, of course, created a major problem of effective disposition of surplus agricultural commodities acquired by the Commodity Credit Corporation. Some of these surpluses were given away in the form of domestic relief, some were tied into foreign aid, either directly or under such rubrics as "Food for Peace." Some of the surpluses were sold at below market prices to foreigners, that is "dumped" on foreign markets. Numerous international complications were created as a result of attempts to dispose of such surpluses.

A significant change in the nature of agricultural subsidies took place in the early 1970s. Government purchases of agricultural surpluses in order to maintain prices at parity were eliminated. Direct price supports were retained but at much lower levels. On top of these price supports, "target prices" were set for major crops with the provision that if actual market prices should fall below the target prices, the federal government would pay farmers the difference between actual revenue and revenue which would have been earned if crops had been sold at the "target prices." A maximum limit of $20,000 was set on payments of this kind to any farmer. Provisions were also included in the act to automatically adjust the "target prices" upward or downward if production costs should rise or fall and to adjust them in accordance with productivity changes; that is, in accordance with changes in average crop yield per acre. Both of these provisions have the effect of maintaining at a constant level a minimum profit per acre of land used in production, which the government, in essence, guarantees to American farmers.

Under the new policy, the federal government is no longer required to accumulate large stocks of agricultural commodities for storage and eventual disposal. Nor is government geared to maintaining high market prices for such commodities. Minimum prices are still guaranteed to farmers but these are set to roughly correspond to normal market levels. However, it should be noted that only the nature, and not the fact, of subsidization of agricultural producers by the taxpayer has been altered. The present farm program retains the characteristic of guaranteeing, from federal tax revenues, if necessary, a minimum income to American farmers. To the extent that "target prices" exceed normal market prices, overproduction of agricultural products is also encouraged.

COMMERCE AND HOUSING CREDIT

Proposed net expenditures in this functional category for fiscal 1980 were $3.4 billion. Total planned spending was larger than this because some activities in this category generated income which was offset against spending. In fact, three agencies which were expected to generate operating surpluses were the Federal Deposit Insurance Corporation, the Federal Home Loan Bank Board, and the National Credit Union Administration.

Spending in this area is allocated among three general functions. The first of these encompasses the federal government's involvement in the housing mortgage market and with the regulation of thrift institutions—banks, savings and loan organizations and credit unions. Generally the federal government provides some type of mortgage insurance or mortgage interest subsidies for various types of housing including low-income housing in both urban and rural areas, and middle-income housing in economically depressed urban areas. The federal government's activities in chartering and regulating savings and loan institutions and insuring deposits in those institutions and commercial banks are also included here.

The second major category of spending under the Commerce and Housing Credit classification is a direct subsidy of $1.7 billion proposed for the U.S. Postal Service.

Other proposed spending in this area includes funds for guaranteed small business loans administered by the Small Business Administration, the collection of data, and the dissemination of economic and demographic statistics.

TRANSPORTATION

Federal government expenditures of $17.6 billion were proposed for ground, air and water transportation during fiscal 1980. These expenditures encompassed subsidies to the various modes of transportation and regulatory activities.

The largest single spending item in this area was approximately $6 billion targeted for highway construction and improvement. These funds are allocated to the states on a matching grant basis with the federal government bearing a 90 percent share of interstate highway construction and 75 percent of the costs for noninterstate federal highways. The bulk of these expenditures are made from the highway trust fund for which certain revenues from federal excise taxes on gasoline and tires and other highway user taxes are earmarked.

Remaining transportation expenditures are primarily subsidies to certain modes of transportation. The federal government has been involved in subsidizing urban mass transit since the late 1960s. In the fiscal 1980 budget $2.5 billion was targeted for this purpose. Railroad transportation also receives federal subsidies for both passenger and freight services. Federal subsidy programs for air and sea transportation were also contained in the 1980 budget.

COMMUNITY AND REGIONAL DEVELOPMENT

Federal spending in this category provides development assistance to both urban and rural areas. Of the $17.3 billion proposed expenditure in the 1980 budget, the largest single spending program was for community development. The major portion of the $4.3 billion funds in this latter area was to be allocated to local communities in block grant form. Recipient communities could use these funds for several purposes including provision of social service, construction of public facilities and rehabilitation of buildings.

For spending on area and regional development, $2.5 billion was proposed, while slightly over $.5 billion was planned for disaster relief and insurance.

EDUCATION, TRAINING, EMPLOYMENT, AND SOCIAL SERVICES

Total outlays of $30.2 billion was proposed for this functional category in the fiscal 1980 budget. Proposed education spending of $13.3 billion was the largest of the three major components, followed closely by proposed spending of $11.5 billion in training and employment services. Planned social services outlays of $5.4 million were primarily in the form of grants to the states to provide special services to such groups as the disabled, the elderly, low income families and abused or orphaned children.

Prior to the 1960s, education was considered to be a public function normally reserved for state and local governments. During that decade, however, major new federal educational programs were developed. At the elementary and secondary levels of education primary federal involvement is in aiding special groups of students such as the handicapped and the disadvantaged. In the area of higher education, emphasis is on direct financial assistance to students in the form of grants, loans, and subsidized employment through the work-study program.

Training and employment programs have the primary objective of increasing the employability of the unskilled. Various types of vocational training and on-the-job training programs are included under this rubric.

HEALTH

The federal government's involvement in the provision of health care and other health related services has increased dramatically since the mid-1960s. Less than $2 billion was spent in this category in 1965. By 1975 expenditures had risen to almost $28 billion and the fiscal 1980 budget proposed total outlays of $53.4 billion.

The bulk of the federal government's outlays in the health area are for the direct provision of health services. Spending of $48.5 billion was proposed here for fiscal 1980, with most funds being spent through the Medicare and Medicaid programs which finance health services for the aged and low-income individuals respectively.

The federal government's experience with the Medicaid and Medicare programs is illustrative of the type of difficulties which can arise from substantial subsidization of any good or service. Both of these programs significantly lowered the costs of health care services borne directly by qualified beneficiaries. The response was increased demands by these individuals for both quantity and quality of health care. These demand pressures tended to increase the cost of health care services rather dramatically. In an attempt to limit the federal government's expenditures in health services, the Carter administration proposed that direct cost controls be imposed on hospitals. To the extent that such controls were effective, the likely outcome was a reduction in the quality of health care and also shortages in the health care market.

INCOME SECURITY

This is the largest single component of the federal budget. Outlays of $179 billion were proposed for fiscal 1980, approximately 34 percent of total federal spending. The bulk of these funds ($115 billion) was projected on outlays under the Old Age, Survivors and Disability Insurance Program, more commonly known as Social Security. Because of the importance of Social Security in the total federal budget, a separate chapter, Chapter 20, will be devoted to description and analysis of this program.

Expenditures of $31 billion were proposed for public assistance and income supplement programs. Four programs accounted for the bulk of federal expenditures here. They were the Supplemental Security Income Program ($6.3 billion), Aid to Families with Dependent Children ($6.7 billion), the Food Stamp Program ($6.9 billion), and various types of low-income housing subsidies ($5.3 billion). Other major expenditures under the income security category are for unemployment compensation ($12 billion) and the federal employees' retirement and disability insurance program ($14 billion).

Welfare reform is a topic of considerable current interest. Two key issues are the relative allocation among federal, state and local governments of responsibility for financing and administration of public assistance or welfare, and the extent to which public assistance programs should take the form of flat cash grants to recipients, as opposed to some form of income-in-kind transfer.

A strong argument can be made for complete federalization of the welfare function as a means of insuring uniformity in benefit payments in different areas of the country. The current program of Aid to Families with Dependent Children (AFDC) can illustrate some of the difficulties here. Federal support of AFDC is in the form of matching grants to states. The states have substantial administrative responsibility and set benefit levels. There are significant disparities among the separate states and therefore some concern that these may generate migration of recipients from low-payment to high-payment states.

The Supplemental Security Income Program (SSI) which began in 1974 provides a useful contrast to AFDC. Its basic impact was to establish a uniform, federally guaranteed, minimum income for the aged, the blind, and the disabled. Although provisions are contained in the program to allow the states to supplement the federal payments if their citizens should desire to do so, and some cost-sharing between the federal government and the states for providing certain direct services to these groups was retained, the bulk of responsibility, both financial and administrative, for public assistance to these groups is located at the federal level.

Both AFDC and SSI provide unrestricted cash transfers to their beneficiaries. Other public assistance programs, most notably food stamps and low-income housing subsidies subsidize particular items consumed by the poor. These latter income-in-kind transfers probably provide less satisfaction to recipients than if the tax monies used to finance them were instead transferred directly to the recipients without being tied to consumption of particular items. However, it is important to consider that there are two sides to this issue. Tax money transferred to the poor in the form of food subsidy is likely to increase food consumption by a greater amount than is the same money, were it used to provide an unrestricted income transfer. Although welfare recipients might prefer the cash transfer, net tax contributors to the program may well be especially interested in increasing food consumption. From the point of view of this latter group, the food subsidy will be the preferable program.

VETERANS' BENEFITS AND SERVICES

Federal expenditures for veterans' benefits and services was budgeted at $20.5 billion dollars in fiscal 1980. Somewhat more than one half of these expenditures represent compensations and pensions and they do not, therefore, exert as substantial an effect on the private economy as direct federal outlays on goods and services. These payments are part of a fiscal transfer process that takes funds from taxpayers and shifts them to those who qualify for service-connected or nonservice-connected pensions. Experience amply indicates that veterans make up a group that society chooses to subsidize through direct income transfers. A net income redistribution from taxpayers to veterans is socially sanctioned. While there is probably some net equalization of incomes accomplished as a by-product, this is not the main purpose of the process which is, instead, simply to aid veterans, as such.

Why should a democratic society choose to single out veterans as a group to be especially subsidized? Military conscription directly affected a rather small proportion of the total population, and veterans' benefits provide a means through which the whole society "pays back" those who have been subjected to conscription in past wars. For injured veterans, the case for a transfer payment is clear. These individuals may have lost a substantial share of earning power, a loss that was not compensated for at the time of injury. Veterans' compensation represents payment for this loss. Experience indicates, however, that the appropriate levels of compensation are extremely difficult to determine.

Although there are reasons why society should choose to redistribute income toward veterans through the fiscal process, the actual composition and magnitude of the transfer may not appear to reflect rational considerations. Perhaps to a greater extent than any other major category of federal spending, veterans' services and benefits are highly sensitive in a political way. Benefits are provided that are readily measurable and easily individualized. Veterans' organizations are large, and they maintain staffs equipped to promote the maintenance and expansion of federal spending. Members of Congress, and the Executive, are reluctant to suggest reductions even where these might be possible. In one way of looking at the federal budget, veterans' expenditures may be considered as part of a larger "social compromise" that the budget must reflect when it is finally adopted each year. A coldly rational decision maker bent on economizing and possessing adequate decision-making power might greatly reduce federal outlay on veterans. But decisions on federal spending are made by no such decision maker; there are many participants in the final choices. And, when viewed realistically, federal expenditures on veterans may be "efficient" in that only by allowing these expenditures to remain relatively large, can the remaining, and to some eyes, more important, federal services secure adequate appropriations.

ADMINISTRATION OF JUSTICE

Outlays of $4.4 billion were proposed for this functional category in the fiscal 1980 budget. These funds were to be allocated among the law enforcement activities of the federal government, litigative and judicial activities, and the operation of the federal corrections system. In addition, programs of federal aid to state and local criminal justice systems were to be continued.

GENERAL GOVERNMENT

This category includes the costs of Congressional operations and also financing for the Executive Office of the President. The costs of running the Internal Revenue Service and also the General Services Administration, which manages federal properties and serves as a central procurement agent, fall under the general government category as well. Total outlays in the fiscal 1980 budget were $4.4 billion.

GENERAL PURPOSE FISCAL ASSISTANCE

Outlays in this category take the form of grants to state and local governments. There are no major restrictions on use of the funds and matching funds are not required. Grants made under the general revenue-sharing program comprise the bulk of proposed total outlays of $8.8 billion. Proposed grants under revenue sharing were $6.7 billion.

Revenue sharing began in 1972 and was initially authorized for an experimental five-year period. In 1976, authorization and funding were extended through 1980. Under the program, funds are allocated among the states using formulas which took into account both measures of relative "need" and of tax effort. Within each state, one third of the funds is given to the state government and the remaining two thirds to local governments. The President made no recommendation in the 1980 budget as to whether the revenue sharing program should be extended after expiration of current authorization through fiscal 1980.

INTEREST

Interest payments on the national debt amounted to $65.7 billion in fiscal 1980. Certain interest receipts of the government are offset against interest payments in this functional category, leaving net interest payments of $57 billion. Problems found in financing and managing the national debt will be discussed in a separate part of this book.

CONCLUSIONS

The brief survey of nondefense federal spending that this chapter has included should provide some appreciation of the varied projects that are financed through revenues drawn from the federal taxpayer. An interesting challenge to the student would be to attempt to classify all of the public services that the federal government finances into the three categories discussed in Chapter 4. Recall that these three categories are: collective goods, quasi-collective goods, and private goods publicly provided. It is clear that some of the goods and services financed by the federal government fall under each of these three classifications. For example, expenditures on foreign aid must be classified, in intent at least, as providing genuinely collective benefits to the nation. Federal expenditures that provide quasi-collective services involve things such as public housing, aid to hospitals, and irrigation projects. Postal services, highways, and goods of this nature are primarily private, but are provided publicly. In addition to this classification scheme, which applies to the so-called productive outlay of government, we must add those expenditures that consist of transfer payments from one group to another. Such items as veterans' benefits and public assistance programs may be classified under this heading.

Strong and effective arguments can, of course, be made for a continuation and an expansion of each of the programs discussed in this chapter and for many new ones not even as yet proposed. But also, at least for most of such programs, strong and effective counterarguments can be made that the programs should be reduced in scope, eliminated, or not commenced. The costs of publicly provided services can only be measured in terms of alternatives that are sacrificed. For a dollar's worth of a specific federal program, one less dollar's worth of resource is available for either some other public program or for some private good or service. In assessing the whole federal operation, the observer, including the ordinary taxpayer-voter, must try to weigh costs against benefits, as best he or she can. For some subsectors of the budget, analytical and scientific aids may be applied with some effectiveness, and here the so-called experts can assist ultimate decision makers in their choices. For other, and major parts of the federal budget, the resort to the scientific approach is of little or no assistance. And the observer, the decision maker, must remain aware at all times of the necessary interdependence of the whole expenditure pattern. The federal spending program as outlined in the budget, even if limited to nondefense items alone, is too complex for the single decision maker to comprehend adequately. The actual decision process on federal spending must be fragmented and decentralized, with only some semblance of coordination through the budget bureau and the budget document.

20

Social security

The U.S. social security program provides a substantial component of retirement income for elderly retirees and their spouses. Benefits are also provided to disabled workers and their dependents and to dependent survivors of deceased workers. The Medicare program provides health care services to the aged. As was noted in the preceding chapter, outlays for income security comprise the largest single functional component of the federal government's budget and social security outlays, in turn, account for the bulk of these expenditures. In fact, if the proposed social security outlays of $115 billion in the fiscal 1980 budget were considered as a separate category, they would rank second only to national defense in terms of total spending.

Social security began during the depression years of the 1930s. Then, as now, the program was financed by revenues from an earmarked payroll tax with the tax burden nominally divided on an equal basis between employees and employers. In 1935, a tax of 2 percent was levied on the first $3,000 of annual earned income. In 1979, the tax rate was 12.26 percent with a maximum tax base of $22,900. This increase in tax burden is obviously a significant one. However, benefits have, in the past, more than kept pace with social security taxes. Individuals currently receiving social security retirement benefits, for example, are receiving a very favorable return on social security tax payments made during their working careers. This is undoubtedly the primary explanation for the almost unprece-

237

dented political popularity which the social security program has enjoyed for many years.

In recent years, however, the social security program has become a source of controversy. The future financial viability of the program has been called into question and certain features of the benefit structure, most notably the treatment of working women, have been criticized as inequitable. There is, in addition, some controversy about whether the social security program has significantly retarded capital formation and economic growth in the economy. Because of these problems and because of the importance of social security in the overall federal budgetary picture, it seems worthwhile to devote a separate chapter to examination of this program. Emphasis will be in the retirement benefits provided by social security, although the student should bear in mind that social security provides other benefits as well.

ALTERNATIVE CONCEPTIONS OF SOCIAL SECURITY

From the start of the social security system there has been a continuing debate over opposing philosophies or approaches to governmental provision of old-age security. This debate has not been squarely resolved in favor of any one of these approaches. Instead, the existing social security program reflects elements of several different ideas.

The first view is that the system should be independent in a financial sense from the general federal budget and that, as an independent accounting unit, the system should be self-supporting on an actuarially sound basis. The dominance of this first view in the original legislation is indicated by the establishment of the Old-Age and Survivors Trust Fund outside the administrative budget and by the earmarking of employment tax revenues for, and the outpayments of benefits from this trust fund account. Implicit in this conception of the system is the idea that a central objective of its operation should be financial soundness in accordance with criteria that would guide the operations of a private rather than a public pension plan. That is to say, sufficient funds should be collected from employment taxes during any one period to equal the discounted value of the benefit obligations, to be paid in future periods, which are incurred in that period. In equilibrium, the system should operate so that, on the average, the contributions of each individual worker, along with those paid by the employer, should accumulate a fund over that employee's working life sufficient to finance his or her own retirement. Consistent with this conception of the system, it should have been expected that, during the early years of operation, a large reserve should be built up against future benefit obligations. The experience of the American system during the initial years reflects this view to the extent that funds collected from employment taxes exceeded benefit payments for more than 20 years, until 1958. Since 1958, social security benefit payments have slightly exceeded employment tax receipts, which means, of course, some depletion in reserves. In its first 20 years of operation, the trust fund account accumulated more than $20 billion, never sufficiently large on an actuarial basis. Any attempts to accumulate reserves, as such, were finally abandoned. Employment taxes have not been sufficiently high to maintain full actuarial soundness in the system, given the rate of outpayments. If the current system should be, in fact, a private pension plan, it would not be adjudged financially sound by competent auditors who looked at its accounts. At existing and projected rates of tax, on both employers and employees, and with existing or projected benefit obligations, the system involves an implicit federal debt of major proportions, almost three quarters of a trillion dollars (precise estimates are extremely difficult to make here). That is to say, the present value of benefit obligations exceeds the present value of future tax collections by roughly this total. This debt is not, of course, included in the standard computations for public debt.

Under the strict, private insurance, actuarial concept of the social security system, bankruptcy would have long since been declared. However, under a second, and more sophisticated, concept the existing system can be, and has been, strongly defended. For purposes of discussion, we may label this the *intergeneration-transfer* concept. In this approach, the worker is subjected to the payroll tax, funds from which are then used to finance pensions to those persons already retired. The contributing worker is, however, still paying for his own retirement benefits in that he is making an implicit "exchange" with the government. He is, in effect, agreeing to finance the retirement pensions for those aged persons already retired in "exchange" for a commitment that the government will impose taxes on future generations of workers to finance his own retirement pension. In a certain sense, the "insurance" aspect of the system is retained under this concept, and the earmarking of tax revenues and the separation of the trust fund account from federal general funds can be justified. Proponents of this concept can claim that it has advantages over the strictly actuarial concept, involving a direct analogy with a private insurance scheme. No reserves need be accumulated under the *intergeneration-transfer* concept; hence, the actual operations of the current system in matching tax revenues roughly with benefit payments can be defended. In addition, and more important, the worker who contributes can secure a return on his or her tax payments that are roughly equivalent to the growth rate in the national economy. In effect, this concept views the workers as investing in their own retirement at a rate of return equal to the rate of growth in the economy. By contrast with this, the rate at which actual funds could be invested in a reserve accumulation scheme may be less than the rate of growth in the national economy. The rate on private investment, or on a public fund accumulation, may not fully reflect the rate of growth in population and, especially, may not embody inflationary growth.

Both the private insurance and the intergeneration-transfer concepts of social security embody the fiscal isolation of the system from the general federal budget. A third concept of social security, the *tax transfer* concept, abandons this isolation. The independence of the trust fund account is held to have no special merit, and the financing of benefits is held to be justified on precisely the same basis as the financing of other federal spending programs. Under this view, which would, if implemented, embody major institutional departures from the existing system, taxes to finance social security benefits should be levied on the same bases as all other federal taxes. Hence, under this view, the levy of taxes on employment, on payrolls, would find little or not justification on ordinary principles of equity. Proponents of this approach stress the regressivity of these taxes which is insured by the maximum limits on wage-salaries subjected to tax. On the benefits side, those who take this overall view are not concerned with relating benefit payments to the level of contributions made, and they are quite willing to add beneficiaries to the system who have not contributed at all. In this concept, general or universal standards of eligibility should determine benefit payments, standards which are divorced from payments made into the system under the payroll tax. And, in fact, the payment of a tax over the years of work experience does not, under this view, provide the individual with any claim at all to benefit payments. As is clear from this brief description, if this concept were fully effective, there would be no "insurance" aspects to the social security system, and the whole system would be equivalent to other federal welfare programs.

As it has actually developed, the American system embodies elements of all three of these approaches or philosophies of social "insurance." In the early discussions of the system the private insurance concept seemed predominant. But political determination of tax and benefit levels prevented accumulation of adequate trust fund reserves. In one sense, the more sophisticated intergenerational-transfer concept emerged as an apologia for what was in existence. If actual operation of the social security system is to continue to embody the central features of an intergenerational transfer, it must, first of all, continue to be self-financing. That is to say, total outlays must be covered by tax revenues collected; resort to financing from general tax revenues would represent a distinct shift toward the third, simple tax-transfer concept. The intergenerational-transfer concept also requires "responsible" modifications in tax rates and in benefit payments to assure that the worker does, in fact, participate in the implicit exchange involved. Also, it is inconsistent with this concept of social security for noncontributors to become eligible for benefits or for benefit payments to be divorced from rates of contribution.

To the extent that social security is allowed to become an engine of income redistribution rather than retirement security, the system is necessarily shifted in the direction of the third, tax-transfer, approach. Certain elements of the current benefit structure do, in fact, reflect this idea. The benefit structure, for example, is progressively related to preretirement earnings. The greater were covered earnings and payroll tax payments during the working years, the higher will be the retirement benefit paid under social security. Benefits increase less than proportionately with earnings, however. The spouse and survivor benefits provided by social security also mark a departure from a pure insurance concept of social security in the direction of the tax transfer idea.

THE FINANCIAL VIABILITY OF SOCIAL SECURITY

Social security is financed on a pay-as-you-go basis. This means that current payroll tax receipts and current benefit outlays are maintained in rough balance with the relatively small trust fund serving primarily as a buffer against those periods when receipts and outlays are temporarily out of balance. As has already been discussed, this financing scheme is consistent with the intergenerational-transfer concept of social security. For a long time social security revenues grew more rapidly than beneficiaries, enabling substantial growth in real average benefits. Several factors contributed to this growth. Most important was growth in the payroll tax base as a result both of a growing labor force and of growth in real wages and salaries. In addition, the increases in tax rates and maximum taxable earnings which have occurred since the program's inception have already been noted. Some of these increases were used to finance new types of benefits. Disability coverage, for example, was added to social security in the 1950s. A considerable portion, however, was diverted toward improving the old-age benefits under the program.

Social security is facing some long-term financial difficulties in the sense that it is going to be much more difficult to provide the same real benefits to future retirees as are being provided to current retirees with continued financing on a pay-as-you-go basis. The reason for this is the sharply changing age profile of the American population. With a growing population, the number of workers per retiree will increase over time. Even without any growth in average earnings or in the payroll tax rate, this would enable an increase in average retirement benefits over time. The growth in the U.S. population and the workforce made possible by the so-called post-war baby boom had a lot to do with the real benefit increases enjoyed by social security retirees. The baby boom, however, peaked in the late 1950s and, by the late 1960s and early 1970s, the birth rate had fallen to levels barely consistent with a zero population growth. The consequent demographic bulge has serious consequences for future social security financing. Currently there are about 30 retirees for every 100 workers. Early in the 21st century, when the baby boom babies start to reach retirement age, that ratio will rise, under current projections to about 45 retirees per 100 workers. Even with the anticipated continuing growth in real wages, significant increases in the payroll tax rate will be required if benefits are to be maintained at current real levels.

The intergenerational-transfer concept of social security relies on the government's power to tax. In a democracy, however, taxes must be politically feasible. The size of future social security benefits thus depends very much on what tax rates the future voting population will be willing to impose. In this respect, it is important to realize that the future voting population will include retirees and those about to retire. Generally, the older a voter is, the higher is his perceived rate of return on the social security tax payments which he or she will make during the remaining years before retirement. A person one year away from retirement, for example, might be willing to support rather sizable increases in the payroll tax. The higher tax burden will only have to be borne for one year and a sizable increase in retirement benefits procured. Someone just entering the workforce, on the other hand, would get the same increase in anticipated future retirement benefits but will have to pay the higher taxes for many more years. By the 21st century, the median age of the voting population will be greater than it is currently, which suggests the possibility that, other things equal, the median voter will be willing to support a higher payroll tax rate than the current median voter would find desirable. However, a word of caution is in order here. Other things may not be equal in 30 years. One of the difficulties with making predictions about social security is, of course, that the future is uncertain.

PROTECTING SOCIAL SECURITY BENEFITS AGAINST INFLATION

When an inflation occurs, any benefits which are fixed in money terms will decline in terms of real purchasing power. Inflation has been a fairly persistent phenomenon in the United States in the years since the end of World War II, but it became increasingly severe in the late 1960s and the 1970s. Between 1968 and 1978, for example, the general price level almost doubled. Prior to 1972, inflation caused reductions in the real value of social security benefits were dealt with by periodic legislated increases in money benefits. In 1972, however, the social security law was amended to provide for automatic adjustments in money benefits in response to increases in the price level.

The idea of adjusting retirement benefits in order to prevent their real value from being eroded by inflation is not a controversial one. It seems an essential component of an equitable program. However, the choice of indexing procedures is, as we shall see, an important one. The indexing procedure adopted in 1972 had a very serious technical flaw. Benefits of future retirees were, in essence, double-indexed and, as a result, real future benefits were made very sensitive to the inflation rate. The method was changed in 1977. Had the change not been made, continued relatively moderate (in terms of recent experience) inflation would have resulted in skyrocketing real social security benefits. It literally would have been possible for some future retirees to qualify for annual social security benefits in excess of their annual earnings just prior to retirement.

A new indexing procedure was adopted in 1977 which corrected the very serious problem outlined above. In making this correction, the Congress had to choose between two indexing procedures, one of which preserved the existing relationship between real preretirement earnings and real retirement benefits and a second which built into the system a graduate increase in real benefits relative to real earnings. The latter procedure was the one chosen.

In order to understand the new indexing procedure, it is necessary to understand how social security benefits are initially computed for a new retiree. The basic social security benefit is based on a measure of the average earnings of the retiree in covered employment in the years since 1951 or, beginning in 1991, the retiree's 22d birthday. Five years of lowest earnings are excluded and no earnings in any year in excess of the amount subject to payroll taxation in that year, may be counted. Prior to 1972, a straightforward arithmetic average of monthly earnings was computed. Average monthly earnings were then divided into fixed brackets and the monthly social security benefit was derived by taking a declining percentage of each bracket.

Under present law, the benefits of individuals, once they have retired, are indexed to the price level. In addition, the monthly earnings histories of new retirees and the brackets into which average indexed monthly earnings are divided for benefit computation purposes are also indexed. It was the choice of indexing procedure used here which had the aforementioned effect of building a gradual growth in real benefits into the system. Congress chose to index brackets and earnings to average changes in money wages rather than to changes in price. Because money wages tend to grow more rapidly than prices due to productivity increases, wage indexing of past earnings provides a larger average indexed monthly wage than would price indexing.

Proponents of the wage indexing procedure argue that it is only fair that the retired should enjoy some of the benefits of productivity increases in the economy. Supporters of the more conservative price indexing scheme, on the other hand, were primarily concerned with limiting the future growth of real benefits levels in the face of the future financing problems already confronting the system because of the demographic bulge caused by the end of the baby boom.

SOCIAL SECURITY AND CAPITAL ACCUMULATION

The desire to accumulate financial resources for retirement is undoubtedly an important motive for individual saving. It seems likely that one effect of the social security program has been to weaken this motive. Some empirical work has indicated that personal saving in the economy has been reduced significantly. Because personal savings provide funds for private investment, a reduction in the savings rate implies a reduction in private capital formation.

Two features of the social security program tend to discourage private saving for retirement. First, a rather heavy tax is levied on individuals during their working years. Simultaneously, individuals are promised a retirement annuity. A third feature of the program works in the opposite direction. Social security encourages individuals to retire at an earlier age than they otherwise would. Between the ages of 62, when benefits may begin, and 70, any labor earnings of a beneficiary in excess of $5,000 result in a fifty-cent reduction in benefits for every dollar of wage or salary. When individuals retire at a younger age, any personal savings which they may have accumulated must be spread over a greater number of years to be spent in retirement. Because of this individuals might want to increase their savings somewhat. However, empirical evidence suggests that this latter effect is not sufficient to offset the reduction in personal savings brought about by the first two factors mentioned.

Social security would not reduce total saving and capital formation in the economy if the government were to save and invest a sufficient amount from payroll tax revenues to offset the reduction in private sector saving. If, for example, social security were run on the same principles as a private pension plan, the program would probably be neutral in terms of its effects on aggregate saving. However, pay-as-you-go financing of social security involves no government saving at all. Rather, the program transfers income from the current working to the current retired generation with the latter group obviously having little motivation to save out of their social security income.

THE CONTROVERSY OVER SPOUSE BENEFITS

Social security provides benefits not only to individual retired workers, but also to their spouses. A spouse is generally entitled to a separate monthly benefit equal to one half of that granted the retiree. (If the spouse begins to collect before age 65, the benefit amount is reduced slightly.) This benefit is granted regardless of whether the recipient has ever worked in covered employment subject to the payroll tax. If the retired worker should predecease his or her spouse, the latter's benefit is increased to the full amount previously received by the retiree.

The provision of a separate benefit to spouses is a significant departure from a pure insurance conception of social security. Benefits are divorced from prior tax payments in the sense that an unmarried retiree with the same history of earnings and payroll tax payments as a couple will receive, nonetheless, a smaller benefit. The justification commonly given for the separate spouse benefit is that it ties the total social security benefit received by a household to the "need" of that household. A couple needs more money than a single person to maintain the same material standard of living. In this sense, the spouse benefit is more closely aligned with the tax-transfer concept of social security than with the insurance concept.

The manner in which spouse benefits are computed is an especially controversial feature of the social security benefit structure. Spouses of retired workers, who have themselves also worked in employment covered by social security, cannot collect both a spouse benefit and a retired worker benefit. Instead they are granted whichever benefit is the larger. Working wives, who typically earn less than their husbands, are the spouses most commonly affected by this provision and they argue that the system discriminates against them in two ways. First, a wife may work and have her earnings subject to the payroll tax, but she may not receive a retirement benefit any greater than if she had never paid employment. In addition, it is possible for two couples with identical total preretirement earnings and payroll tax payments to qualify for different total benefits under social security, depending on whether one or both spouses had been active in the labor force. The single-earner couple can qualify for a larger benefit than the dual-earner couple.

It is important to appreciate the distributional implications of the present method of providing spouse benefits. With pay-as-you-go financing for social security, in essence, a fixed sum of money is available at any point in time to be allocated among the elderly population. The current law provides a relatively greater share of those funds to couples in which only one spouse had been an active labor force participant than to couples in which both spouses had significant preretirement earnings. In 1939, when the relevant features of the spouse benefit were first passed into law, the vast majority of couples were characterized by the husband being the primary wage earner and the wife being a full-time homemaker. From a public choice standpoint it is not surprising that a benefit structure favorable to the majority of households was adopted. By the same token, it is not surprising that these same provisions are very controversial today. One of the most dramatic changes to have occurred in American society during the past 40 years is the increase in labor force participation by married women. By the late 1970s, almost half of all married women were working outside the home at any point in time, and the vast majority of women were expected to spend enough time in the labor force to qualify for full retired worker benefits under social security. Of the many proposals to reform the spouse benefit provision, almost all involve a relative redistribution of benefits in favor of dual earner couples.

THE PAYROLL TAX

As has already been mentioned, social security is financed by a tax on wage and salary income. In 1979, individual earnings up to $22,900 were subject to this tax. There are two separate and equal taxes levied on the maximum wage base: one levied on the employee and the other on the employer. The combined employee-employer tax rate was 12.26 percent in 1979. The 1977 amendments to the social security law provided for some automatic future increases in payroll taxation. By 1987, the combined payroll tax rate was scheduled to rise to 14.3 percent on a maximum wage base of $42,600.

The coverage of the payroll tax is wide. Certain groups, such as some state and local employees, railroad employees covered by a special retirement plan, and some civil service employees, are exempted from coverage. But most members of the wage and salaried classes are covered under the system. Self-employed persons are also contributors to the system and at differentially favorable rates. The self-employed secures the credit for full coverage by paying a total tax only three fourths as large as the combined employer-employee total.

Incidence and economic effects

The wide coverage of the employment taxes suggests that there is no easy way for the employee to escape paying his portion. Only by shifting his activity to some form in which he does not earn income covered by the tax can the individual escape. And there are so few areas of employment not subject to the tax as to make shifting by this means almost impossible. For all practical purposes, the final incidence of the employee portion of the tax rests squarely on the employee and is equivalent, in effect, to a proportional income tax on basic wage or salary income up to the maximum limits of the taxable base.

The employer portion of the tax is more controversial and the analysis is not so straightforward. The tax is nominally levied on the employer, but there is nothing to prevent the shifting of the tax through modifications in behavior. Since the tax is imposed on wage and salary income, to the employer it represents an increase in the cost of the labor inputs. The effects on the employer's behavior should be, therefore, equivalent to the effects of a proportionate wage increase below certain specified limits of total earnings. Since labor must cooperate with capital in the productive process, and since high-income labor must cooperate with low-income labor and with capital, the employer will be motivated to substitute capital and high-income labor for low-income labor as a result of an increase in the tax. This will reduce the overall demand for labor below the maximum base limits. Wage rates will tend to be depressed, since there is no change in the overall supply of labor. The net result is that the employer portion of the tax is also shifted to the workers. If the wage level should not be lowered as a result of the tax, the unemployment rate will rise. In either case, it can be concluded that the employee pays both the employee and the employer portion of the tax. In effect, the distinction between these two parts serves largely to create an illusion that the employer pays, an illusion that is soon dispelled by elementary economic analysis.

SUPPLEMENTARY READINGS

A useful collection of papers dealing with the financing problems confronting social security and with the various indexing methods is presented in a volume edited by Colin D. Campbell entitled *Financing Social Security*

(Washington, D.C.: American Enterprise Institute for Public Policy Research, 1979).

A pertinent public choice analysis of the determination of social insurance tax and benefit levels in democratic political process, including the effect of the median age of the voting population, is provided by Professor Edgar Browning in a paper entitled "Why The Social Insurance Budget is Too Large in a Democracy," (*Economic Inquiry*, September, 1975).

Students interested in the treatment of women by the social security programs might consult *Women and Social Security: An Institutional Dilemma* by Marilyn R. Flowers (Washington, D.C.: American Enterprise Institute for Public Policy Research, 1977).

Professor Martin Feldstein has examined the effects of social security on capital accumulation in a paper entitled "Social Security, Individual Retirement and Aggregate Capital Accumulation." *Journal of Political Economy* (September/October, 1974).

part V

Federal taxation

*T**he power to tax*. The discussion in Part V, and in some of Part VII, is devoted to taxation. It is useful to discuss briefly the basic "power to tax" by way of Preface to a more detailed analysis of actual tax institutions.

Taxation involves governmental activity that imposes charges on persons or economic units that must be met by transfers of resources or claims to government, charges that are legally enforceable. Taxes may be levied only for some ultimate purpose of financing government spending, but there is no legally required connection between the two sides of the fiscal account.

In a genuine "fiscal exchange" model, as previously discussed, there would be no effective "power to tax," because all persons would ideally agree to the tax charges in exchange for the public-goods benefits received. But the reality that we observe is far from any fiscal exchange idealization, and historically governments have always been granted powers to tax. The importance of this basic grant of power has been recognized. The ascendancy of the English Parliament through its restrictions on the revenue-raising powers of the monarchy is a part of our political heritage. And, even in the 1980s, there remain legal-constitutional limits on government's taxing authority.

Attitudes toward the government's power to tax seemed to change in the late 1970s, as we have indicated in the discussion of Chapter 16. More and more taxpayers were asking whether or not the taxing authority might not have been extended beyond its proper bounds. The tax institutions of the United States, as discussed in the following chapters, may be subjected to increasing critical examination in the 1980s and beyond, examination that is quite different from the standard arguments treated in the chapters that follow.

21

The federal revenue structure: an overview

In the budget document submitted to the Congress for fiscal 1980, it was estimated that the federal government would, during fiscal 1980, collect from the public approximately $503 billion, or something more than 20 percent of the value of estimated GNP. Actual revenues collected in fiscal 1978 amounted to $402 billion. This compares with a total of $194 billion in fiscal 1970, $117 billion in fiscal 1965, and $80 billion in fiscal 1958. These data alone suggest the potential revenue growth that is built into the federal revenue structure. A portion of the more than twofold increase between fiscal 1970 and fiscal 1980 is explained by the rapid inflation that occurred over this period. The continual increase in federal government revenues stem, of course, from the growth in the tax base, roughly measured by GNP, which is computed in nominal monetary units.

Table 21-1 indicates the breakdown of federal receipts into the major revenue categories. Note that collections from the personal or individual income tax make up some 45 percent of total federal receipts. The corporation income tax collections amount to an additional 14 percent. And social security taxes on employees and employers have become increasingly important in the late 1960s and 1970s. These taxes now make up some 32 percent of total federal col-

TABLE 21–1
Federal receipts from the public, fiscal 1980

Description	Estimate for fiscal 1980 (billions)
Individual income taxes	$227.3
Corporation income taxes	71.0
Social insurance taxes and contributions ...	161.5
Excise taxes	18.5
Estate and gift taxes	6.0
Customs duties........................	8.4
Miscellaneous receipts	9.9
Total	$502.6

lections. All remaining federal tax sources account for less than 9 percent of federal revenues.

The characteristic feature of the federal revenue system lies in the importance that it places on personal income taxation as a revenue source. When it is recognized that employment taxes, certainly to the extent that these are paid directly by the employee, are also levied directly on the basis of personal incomes, almost 80 percent of federal receipts are drawn from direct personal taxation. The proper definition of direct and indirect taxation remains subject to controversy but, for many purposes, corporation income taxation is also treated as a direct tax. In this sense, the American federal revenue structure is heavily dependent on direct taxation. Taxes on consumption, on expenditure, and on production are relatively unimportant as federal revenue producers.

This feature of the overall American fiscal system becomes somewhat less pronounced when state-local revenue structures are combined with that of the federal government. State governments, especially, rely on sales and excise taxation, and local governments rely heavily on property taxation. Nevertheless, even when all subordinate units are included, the American fiscal structure, relative to most other countries of the world, is more dependent on direct tax sources. Only in the United Kingdom and in West Germany are individual income taxes more important than in the United States, when tax structures are compared in a sophisticated manner.[1]

This relatively greater reliance on direct taxes, especially in the federal revenue structure, led to arguments advanced in the early 1960s in favor of a broadly based value-added tax (VAT) at the federal level. The argument lost much of its force in the late 1960s, when equity considerations reassumed dominance in political discussion and the economic objective was given less emphasis.

Major changes in the federal revenue structure have not taken place in the postwar period, and despite the publicity of tax reform, such changes are not likely to occur. Federal revenues will, of course, increase substantially over time unless tax rate reductions explicitly offset the built-in revenue growth, especially if the rate of inflation continues at the 1968–78 rates. The bias in the decision-making structure will be toward using the revenue increment for expanding federal government outlays rather than toward tax rate reduction.

---

[1]For a sophisticated comparative analysis that reaches this conclusion, see Vita Tanzi, "Comparing International Tax Burdens: A Suggested Method," *Journal of Political Economy*, vol. 76 (September/October 1968), pp. 1078–84.

22

Personal income taxation: Conceptual problems

$\mathbf{B}$efore describing the personal income tax as it exists in the United States, it will be useful to discuss some of the problems and principles of personal income taxation considered more generally. This introductory discussion will provide a frame of reference for the descriptive discussion that follows, and some of the controversial issues in personal income taxation can be appreciated only in broader context.

THE DEFINITION OF INCOME

What is meant by the term "personal income tax"? At the elementary level of discussion, the term suggests a coercive levy by government on the individual, or person, with income as the criterion for determining tax liability. The individual is the subject of the tax, and income is the base. But serious problems arise if any attempt is made to define terms more precisely. What is "income"? The appropriate definition of income for tax purposes has continued to be one of the most perplexing problems in fiscal theory.

There are two ways of defining income for determining tax liability. The first conception is a *flow* or *product* conception, and the second is an accretion-of-wealth conception. In the former, income is considered to be the flow of services from a capital asset (or assets) during a specified period of time. Capital in the form of human capacities, so-called human capital, must, of course, be included in any measurement here. The income available to a person becomes, in this conception, a measure of the *annual value* of the size of the capital that he controls. This flow conception of income is the standard one used in economic theory and in accounting, and it must be used in determining the valuation of real assets and claims. In taxation, this conception of income represents a straightforward extension of the more general meaning of income in nontax uses.

In the second approach, income is defined as the maximum amount of real goods and services that may be consumed over a finite period of calendar time without reducing the value of real capital. In other terms, this represents the net accretion to capital if no consumption is undertaken. The distinction between this and the first definition is that, whereas the first measures income in terms of a flow of real services to the economic unit, the second measures income as the addition to the size of the wealth or stock of assets, which may or may not be converted into a flow. For many applications, the two definitions reduce to one and the same. For example, in a closed national economy, the net flow of goods and services received by all individuals must be equal to the total amount of consumption that could possibly be achieved without "eating up" real capital. The two definitions produce quite different results, however, when applied to the problems of determining personal tax liability under the income tax. The fundamental differences between the two lie in the treatment of the increased value of capital assets owned by individuals, in the treatment of income saved, and in the treatment of gifts and bequests.

Although these specific differences in treatment may be discussed later, we may illustrate here by reference to the treatment of capital gains. Are capital gains legitimately to be counted as personal income? Under the flow conception, increases in the capital values of real assets or claims are not included in personal incomes. This may be illustrated by a simple arithmetical example. Suppose initially that an individual owns a real asset that yields an annual income of $100 over and above full allowance for depreciation and maintenance. If the market rate of interest is 5 percent, this asset will have a present value of approximately $2,000. Now suppose further that something changes to cause the owner to expect that, instead of $100, the asset will begin to yield $150 per year. The capital value should immediately rise to $3,000. The owner will have enjoyed an unrealized capital gain of $1,000. Is this gain to be counted as personal income at the time that the expected future income increment is capitalized into a higher present value? Under the first or flow conception of income, no additional income has been received by the owner of the asset since the increased flow of real goods and services will only begin to take place in future periods. Under the contrasting accrual conception, the individual has received an addition of $1,000 income because he or she may now choose to sell one third of the asset for $1,000, convert this into real goods and services to be consumed currently, and still retain an asset with a capital value of $2,000, the same as before. The capital gain, even though it is unrealized, constitutes income under this conception, and it should be included in the tax base.

At this point, we shall not discuss further the relative merits of these two income conceptions. As we shall see in Chapter 23, the income tax, as actually administered in the United States, is not fully consistent with either conception. But the issue concerning the appropriate treatment of capital gains remains a highly controversial one, and this issue, along with others, will be explored more thoroughly in Chapter 24.

DEFINITION OF THE REPORTING UNIT

Who is to be considered a person, for income tax purposes? This is also the subject of much controversy, and many of the issues remain unresolved, even among the experts. Since 1948, the U.S. tax system has allowed married couples to split their incomes for tax purposes. In effect, this provides a married couple, even if there is only one income earner, to treat its joint income as if it were earned by two separate reporting units rather than by one family. The advantages that this proposal allows under a progressive rate structure are clear. Through income splitting, the rate bracket is shifted downward, and a lower total bill results. In a sense, income splitting places a differential tax premium on marriage. In Great Britain, by contrast, the income of a married couple is considered jointly, placing a premium there on remaining single. In France, income splitting is extended to the entire family, including children. The resolution of the issues here must remain largely arbitrary, and personal standards of equity will dictate whether or not the rules in existence seem broadly equitable.

There seems to be little current (1980) agitation for a return to the situation before 1948, when income splitting was not allowed. In the 1969 tax reform bill, the tax on single persons was substantially reduced.

BASIC PROBLEMS OF MEASUREMENT

Once an acceptable definition of income is agreed upon, more specific measurement problems begin to arise. How can personal income best be computed? If all income were received in the form of wages, salaries, dividends, royalties, or similar income shares, there would be little conceptual difficulty in measurement. But all income is not received in this way. Income may be received outside the ordinary monetary mechanism; instead of money income, which may readily be measured, the individual may receive income in kind. Income in kind is defined as the total of real goods and services received in some manner other than ordinary monetary units. Real goods and services directly received constitute income in kind. The most familiar example is provided by the farmer who grows his own vegetables. Since the consumption of these vegetables allows the farmer to reduce his spending on vegetables in the market, the value of the home-produced vegetables is clearly real income. But how can the total value of this income in kind be estimated properly?

The farmer's homegrown vegetables are the easiest of all sorts of income in kind to measure, however. What about the income produced by the services of housewives? There is no doubt but that these household services produce real income; the household would have to purchase some such services through the marketplace with money unless they were performed by the housewife at home. But how can any criteria for tax liability be adjusted so as to include some estimate of these elements of income? On the other hand, unless some such estimates are included in the calculation of the tax base, can real income be said to be the true base of taxation? Similar difficulties arise when we consider the real income produced by householders in performing all sorts of do-it-yourself activities.

The durable goods possessed by the individual family also yield real income in any given period of time. Should this income be included in the tax base? The estimated rental value of an owner-occupied house is subjected to the income tax in some countries, but not in the United States. But the exclusion tends to place a premium on home ownership relative to the rental of housing accommodations. Similarly, real income is surely yielded to the individual through the ownership of an automobile, a high-fidelity phonograph, and all of the other so-called consumer durables. The estimation of the real income yielded by these items would be extremely difficult in practice, but unless such income is included in some way, relatively too many resources tend to be devoted to the production of these goods.

Even more complex problems arise when a portion of the individual's compensation from his employer is received directly as income in kind. It is almost impossible to separate that part of such compensation that is real income to the individual and that part that is representative of necessary outlay to the employer. The most characteristic modern form of this is expense account compensation. The businessman who travels for his firm does so on an expense account. He is not obligated to pay personal income tax on this part of his total compensation, because, presumably, the expenses he undergoes constitute genuine costs of carrying out the duties of his position. But it is clear that some part of many business expenses is real income. Its exclusion from the tax base leads to the continuing increase in the use of this device as a means of escaping tax liability.

Perhaps the most difficult of all measurement problems lies in the impossibility of measuring real income in any "opportunity cost" sense, which, conceptually at least, should be the basis for computing tax liability. This point can best be illustrated by an example. A particular individual may desire to live in Florida rather than in New England, and in order to satisfy his desire he will accept a lower salary in Florida than he would in New England. Let us say that he will accept a Florida salary of $15,000 per year and a New England salary of $20,000. Presumably, in this example, the individual we are considering is no better off in New England at the $20,000 salary than he is in Florida at the $15,000 salary. Therefore, the $5,000 nonpecuniary differential should be counted as real income to the Florida resident. Otherwise, taxation based on money income alone will tend unduly to favor those occupations and those communities possessing net nonpecuniary advantages. Quite clearly this is a measurement difficulty that can never be surmounted satisfactorily in the actual organization of a personal income tax law. But the example does illustrate well the immense gap between the ideal conception of the personal income tax and its actual working out in practice.

NONINCOME BASES FOR TAX DISCRIMINATION

The personal income tax, as normally administered, is not based solely on income, even if definitional and measurement problems could be effectively solved. Some important criteria other than income always exist for the determination of tax liability. Each individual receiving the same income will not be subjected to an equal amount of tax; several nonincome differences among individuals are held to be relevant in determining the tax load. To subject all individuals receiving identical incomes to the same tax burden would be held to violate the principle of "equity" or "equal treatment for equals" that we have previously discussed.

One of the most significant of these nonincome differences is family size. There may be only one income receiver per family unit. The size of the tax liability placed on the head of the family will be inversely related to the number of dependents to be supported. Some specific allowance for dependents will, therefore, be found in all fiscal systems using the personal income tax as a revenue source. In many cases, dependents need not be members of the immediate family. One interesting, although limited, means of looking at the allowances for dependents is the following: If children are considered to be similar to consumption goods for the family, the introduction of dependents' allowances in the tax structure represents a subsidization of this form of personal income. Individuals are provided with a special incentive to take their personal income in the form of more children rather than in other forms.

Another characteristic that is sometimes introduced to distinguish among individuals for tax purposes is age. In the United States, persons over 65 years of age are given double personal exemptions. Similar treatment is given to persons who are blind.

A more widely employed distinction among persons, although it is not an important distinction for the U.S. tax structure, is that between income earned from work and income earned from the ownership of assets. This amounts to discrimination among individuals in accordance with the source as well as with the size of their incomes. This is one feature of the income tax in Great Britain. Income received from wages or salaries, so-called earned income, is given more favorable treatment than is income received as a return on capital assets, such as dividends, interest, and rentals. This distinction is justified in the following way. The owner of a capital asset is allowed to deduct full allowance for depreciation and maintenance of the asset before computing the net taxable income. Human beings, are, economically speaking, capital assets; in order to maintain and to replace the individual human being, some expenditure for consumption goods and services is essential; just as is the allowance for depreciation and maintenance for the nonhuman capital asset. However, it would be impossible for any actual tax system to distinguish between that portion of consumption that is necessary to account for the depreciation of the human being and that portion which represents real income more genuinely measured. Some compromise with the ideal must be accepted here. One such compromise is that of allowing some differentially favorable treatment to those persons earning income from work. The degree of differentiation must remain, in any case, somewhat arbitrary.

This argument is perhaps convincing, providing that the income from assets is not subjected to additional taxation somewhere in the system. However, if investment income, for example, should be subjected to a supplementary income tax as it is received by the corporation, there seems to be no reason for differential treatment against this sort of income at the personal level. This fact apparently has served to prevent any significant discrimination in favor of earned income to be generally introduced into the American tax structure.

DISCRIMINATION BY INCOME SIZE: PROGRESSIVE TAXATION

One of the characteristic features of the modern personal income tax is its discrimination among individual taxpayers in accordance with the size of income received. In other words, the simple use of income as a tax base would suggest a common rate of tax independent of income size. But modern tax systems almost invariably include tax rates that vary directly with income size. That is to say, modern income tax systems are normally *progressive,* rather than *proportional* or *regressive.* It is necessary to define these descriptive terms carefully at this point.

The proportional tax or tax structure is the easiest to define. A proportional tax is one for which the rate does not vary as the tax base varies. In terms of an income tax, proportionality would suggest that the individual is subjected to the same rate of tax on his adjusted income, as measured, whatever the size of this income happens to be.

For example, if the rate were 10 percent, an individual with an income of $1,000 would be obligated to pay $100, while the individual with an income of $10,000 would be obliged to pay a total tax of $1,000. Strictly speaking, proportionality as a characteristic relates the tax rate to the specific tax base. But some confusion is present when the attempt is made to relate the effective rates of one tax to some assumed ideal base. For example, most excise or sales taxes are proportional, strictly speaking. If the sales tax is 2 percent of sales, this is a proportional tax, since this rate does not vary. But it is sometimes said that the sales tax is regressive rather than proportional. This means that if income rather than sales is used as a base, the effective rate of tax on income may be regressive. Care must be taken to use these terms clearly and precisely.

A progressive tax is defined as one in which the rate increases as the tax base increases. A progressive income tax imposes a higher rate of tax on individuals with the higher incomes than on individuals with the lower incomes. For example, if the individual with a measured adjusted income of $1,000 is subjected to a 10 percent tax rate, the individual with an income of $10,000 might be subjected to a 20 percent rate, while the individual with $100,000 might be subjected to a 50 percent rate. Another way of defining progression in a tax rate structure is to say that the *average* rate of tax on income is lower than the *marginal* rate of tax. The average is calculated by dividing the total tax bill by the total income. The marginal rate is calculated by dividing the added tax on the last increment of income by the total size of the last increment of income.

A regressive tax is defined as one in which the tax rate decreases as the tax base increases; the rate of tax and the base are inversely related. Regression is not characteristic of the modern income tax, and in the strict sense, few regressive taxes are to be found. Some forms of tax that are nominally proportional in rates may, however, be classified as regressive if these taxes are related to income as the base. As suggested previously, it is in this way that many excise or sales taxes are held to be regressive.

Almost without exception, modern income taxation excludes the lowest level incomes from tax liability. Some exemption is included; if income falls below this minimum, no tax liability is imposed on the income recipient. This feature of modern income taxation is explained on both administrative and ethical grounds. It would be very difficult to administer an income tax that subjected all incomes to tax. And, ethically, the taxation of the lowest incomes has been ruled out on the argument that a certain existence minimum is necessary for human survival. The combination of an existence minimum and a proportional rate structure above this minimum will result in an overall tax that has some degree of progressivity. Such a tax is not usually classified as progressive; however, some writers have defined this as a degressive tax.

As suggested, almost all modern systems include an existence minimum that is wholly exempted from tax, and they include a structure of progressive rates above this minimum. Income taxes, as they actually exist, are highly progressive. As we shall see later, the fact that different levels of income are subjected to differing rates of tax creates many of the problems in income tax administration.

THE BASES FOR PROGRESSIVE TAXATION

It is important to understand the principle upon which modern income tax progression is based. One of the traditional principles for the distribution of total tax liability among individuals has been that of taxing in accordance with ability to pay. This principle was discussed briefly in Chapter 9. This principle or criterion has been widely accepted by the public and by policy makers in the United States and other Western democracies. One of the attractive features of this principle, from a political point of view, is its very ambiguity. It is almost impossible to define ability to pay in any meaningful and objective fashion. A few characteristic features of the tax structure do, however, seem to correspond to popular ideas about ability to pay. The first of these is the obvious one that the tax liability of any individual should vary directly with income, that is to say, income is one suitable measure of taxpaying ability. A proportional or even a regressive tax structure would also meet this first test. But ability to pay, as ordinarily understood, requires something more than this. The ability of an individual to pay taxes supposedly increases more than in proportion to his increase in income. Therefore, tax progression has come to be considered by a majority of the people as a desirable part of a fiscal system. This progression is explained or justified as being required by the application of the ability-to-pay principle.

Until the 1930s, isolated attempts were variously made to give meaning to the conception of ability to pay by concerning the tax rate structure with individual enjoyment of income. The utilitarian approach involved the assumption that the utility of income could be measured and compared among persons. Since the marginal utility of income presumably declines as more income is received, the principle of minimizing the sacrifice of utility for all persons taken together was held to require progressive tax rates. This approach has now been all but wholly abandoned. It is widely accepted that utility cannot be measured, and that, even if it could, the utility of income to one individual could hardly be compared with the utility of income to a different individual.

One basis for progressive taxation is the explicit avowal of greater equalization of incomes as a social objective, and the deliberate utilization of the tax structure to further this objective. A few scholars in fiscal theory have stated this basis openly, but the equalization argument is rarely encountered in political discussion of the tax structure. Net income redistribution is, of course, accomplished through the operations of the progressive income tax. But this is accomplished indirectly rather than directly, at least for the most part.

There exist bases for the adoption of progression in tax rates that involve neither the egalitarian objective nor the ambiguous ability-to-pay notion. If the tax is viewed as an institution having a quasi-permanent existence, once it is adopted, and if income expectations of individuals are highly uncertain, progression provides an efficient means of meeting the obligations for genuinely collective services. An individual who is confronted with an obligation to pay a share of the costs of government may prefer to meet a disproportionate share of the allocated costs in those years of relatively high income. Progression in a rate structure allows the bunching of tax obligations in high-income years.

As noted in Chapter 8, increasing attention in the early 1970s was turned to questions of distributive justice, and notably to the contractual bases for distributive norms. To the extent that this attention influences policy, the income tax, as the principle instrument, will be subject to modification.

NEGATIVE INCOME TAXATION

The most widely discussed issue in public finance in the late 1960s was the negative income tax, although interest waned somewhat in the early 1970s. Interest stemmed from the reemergence of concern with poverty relief as a governmental objective coupled with an increasing criticism of the hodgepodge of welfare schemes, many of which seemed to discourage personal effort and initiative. If the income tax is to be employed for the purpose of achieving redistributional objectives, a strong argument may be made for eliminating the arbitrary kink in the rate schedule at the zero-tax point and for extending the rate schedule to include negative values. If attention is limited to the tax side of the fiscal account alone, the person or family who earns less than the amount defining initial eligibility for income tax secures no benefits at all from the tax, no matter how progressive the schedule might be. Redistribution to persons at these very low incomes is limited to the expenditure side of the account under the restriction of income tax rates to positive values. Advocates of negative income taxation allege that extension of the tax rate schedule into the negative value range will allow some of the explicit spending programs aimed at poverty relief to be eliminated or reduced. Opponents of the negative income tax point to the difficulties of eliminating any governmental spending program once it has been in existence, and to the probable costs of a general program of income maintenance represented by the wholesale adoption of a negative income tax.

CONCLUSIONS

Before discussing the actual institutions of the personal income tax, it is useful to consider some of the conceptual problems involved in income taxation. The first of these is the appropriate definition of income itself for tax purposes. There are two basic conceptions or definitions of income, and these may differ quite sharply when applied to the determination of individual income for computing the appropriate tax base. The flow conception does not include as income accretions to capital values, whereas the accrual conception does count such accretions as income. A second group of major problems arises when the attempt is made to measure income. Money incomes are relatively easy to measure, but real income received in a nonmonetary way presents difficult problems.

Personal income taxes are rarely levied on the basis of income alone. Nonincome considerations introduce several other bases for discrimination based on the size of income itself. Modern tax structures involve progressive rate structures, as distinct from proportional or regressive rate structures.

23

Personal income taxation in the United States

T he personal income tax is the most important source of revenue for the federal government. In the 1977 fiscal year, this tax produced an estimated $157 billion, or approximately 44 percent of total federal government receipts.

This tax is only slightly more than a half-century old. It came into being after the adoption of the 16th Amendment to the U.S. Constitution in 1913. An income tax was imposed and legally upheld during the Civil War, but a later 1894 tax was declared unconstitutional on the grounds that discrimination among persons in accordance with income levels violated the constitutional requirements that all direct taxes be uniformly distributed among the states in proportion to population. The 16th Amendment specifically gave Congress the power to levy taxes on income without regard to the distribution of the population among the separate states. Since 1913, the personal income tax has undergone many changes in details of coverage, rates, and in administrative characteristics. Most importantly, perhaps, it has been transformed from a tax applying to a relatively small part of the population to one that is very broadly applicable.

As the economy grows in monetary terms, whether from inflation or from real growth, revenues from this tax, at any given rate structure, will increase so as to allow disproportionate expansion in the public sector, unless other taxes are reduced, or unless rates are cut.

Recognition of this built-in growth provided much of the argument for the nominal rate reductions enacted in 1969 and 1976, reductions which did little more than keep real rates from increasing.

DEFINITION OF THE TAX BASE

The word "personal" suggests that the tax is levied on persons, or individuals. A very large proportion of American adults are included in the coverage of the tax. The income tax is the most universal of all those in the fiscal system. More than 82 million income tax returns were filed in 1976 with the Internal Revenue Service.

The base of the tax is the income received during the calendar year by the reporting unit, individual, or family. As Chapter 22 discussed, many issues of definition arise. Almost any personal income tax system must include some quite arbitrary definitions as to what constitutes income for tax purposes. The U.S. system is no exception. However, the major sources of income included in the tax base present few difficulties. All money wages, salaries, bonuses, commissions, interest, dividends, rents, royalties, and other like payments are taxable as personal income. Relatively few items of income are specifically exempted from the tax base. These include such things as interest on state and local government securities, social security benefit payments, limited totals for scholarship and fellowship grants, gifts and inheritances, and compensation for sickness.

The important definitional measurement problems arise in connection with those receipts that do not constitute ordinary income but which yet retain certain characteristics of personal income. One of the most important of these is receipt of income in kind from the employer. If the individual receives income in kind as part of the wage or salary, this is taxable just as money income receipts. However, if the income in kind is received as a part of the employment itself, it is not normally taxable. The importance of this distinction has come to be more widely recognized in recent years as employers and employees have begun to incorporate more and more contractual arrangements that are, at least in part, designed to convert taxable income into nontaxable income. It is, of course, extremely difficult to separate those items of income in kind that constitute genuine payments to the employee from those that are necessary as a part of the employment itself. If, for example, a salesman is provided with a suite of rooms, at his firm's expense, in a New York hotel during the time that he is calling on city clients, the value of this suite is not taxable to him as personal income received. But his real income, considered in any meaningful way, may be substantially increased by the opportunity to enjoy the benefits of the suite during his annual trip to New York. Or the executive may take a winter trip to Florida to see Miami business associates. Should or should not the expenses of the Florida trip be included as a part of her taxable personal income, quite apart from the question of the allowable deductibility of these from the corporation tax base? It is clear from these examples, which could be multiplied, that many decisions of importance must be made by the tax administrators. If rules are to be laid down in advance, these rules must be quite arbitrary. And the complexity of the problems here increases with the development of institutions that have been designed with tax avoidance as a primary or subsidiary purpose.

A problem of a slightly different sort arises in the treatment of capital gains. As suggested in the preceding chapter, rigid adherence to the flow concept of income would exempt all capital gains from income taxation, whereas full acceptance of the accretion conception would take full account of both capital gains and capital losses in measuring income for tax purposes. The individual income tax, as administered in the United States, is not fully consistent with either of these definitions of income. Capital gains, to the extent that they are realized during the lifetime of the individual, are taxable but they are granted differentially favorable treatment. Gains from the sale of assets held less than one year are defined as "short-term gains" and are fully taxable as income to the individual. Gains from the sale of assets held for more than one year are defined as "long-term gains." Only 40 percent of long-term gains are included in the base as taxable income. Special provisions apply to the sale of owner-occupied homes. Capital gains are, however, subject to certain "minimum tax" provisions to be discussed later.

Capital losses are not accorded treatment that is fully symmetrical with gains. Capital losses, long and short term, are fully deductible from the tax base only to the extent that they are offset by capital gains plus some adjustments against ordinary income. If a capital loss is not fully offset in this way, there is a possibility of carrying such losses over to subsequent years and offsetting them against gains and the ordinary income offset for each year.

EXEMPTIONS AND DEDUCTIONS

Adjusted gross income, computed after the basic measure procedures have been completed, is not the actual base for determining the tax liability of the reporting unit. To arrive at taxable income from adjusted gross income, personal exemptions and deductions must be taken into account.

Through 1969 each person was allowed a personal exemption of $600 plus $600 for each allowable dependent. The exemption was increased to $750 in 1969 and $1,000 in 1978. (Individuals over 65 and individuals who are blind receive double exemptions.) A dependent is defined for tax purposes as anyone who receives more than one half of his or her financial support from the taxpayer and who meets other broad eligibility requirements.

Personal exemptions were maintained at the $600 level (with the exceptions noted) from 1948 to 1969. Children have been allowed exemptions equal to those of adults only since 1944. Over the half century of the income tax, personal exemption levels have fallen dramatically in real value to the individual, and this change, in itself, has done much to convert the income tax into its current status as a very general tax.

Some $159 billion were removed from the potential tax base in 1975 through the allowance of personal exemptions. That is to say, if the personal exemptions were to have been eliminated in 1975, this amount of additional taxable income would have come into being.

A second major adjustment in moving from adjusted gross income to taxable income is that for allowable personal deductions. These deductions are of two basic kinds. The taxpayer may choose to itemize deductions, or may choose to take a standard deduction, either in the form of a special low-income allowance or as a percentage of adjusted gross income. In 1975, an unmarried taxpayer was allowed to take as a standard deduction 16 percent of gross income up to a maximum of $2,300. This deduction is allowed without detailed reporting. For the taxpayer at a very low-income level there is a special low-income allowance; in 1975, this took the form of a minimum standard deduction of $1,600 for a single taxpayer.

Itemized deductions, those which require detailed reporting, are more likely to be used by persons in the higher income brackets. About 32 percent of all taxpayers utilize the itemized deduction. In 1975 this included approximately 70 percent of all taxpayers reporting more than $15,000 of gross income.

Quantitatively, personal deductions are important, and they have recently become somewhat more important than the personal exemptions, in reducing the size of the total tax base. In 1975, total deductions, standard and itemized, amounted to $223 billion. Of this total, $122 billion represented itemized deductions and $101 billion standard deductions.

Taxpayers choosing to itemize their deductions must carefully estimate and compute the various allowable items which they report on their income tax returns. It is with respect to the items that should or should not be allowed as personal deductions that much of the controversy and discussion concerning the gradual erosion of the personal income tax base has been found. It will be useful to discuss each category briefly.

CONTRIBUTIONS

The taxpayer is allowed to deduct contributions made to various religious, charitable, educational, scientific, or literary organizations, up to a maximum limit of 50 percent of adjusted gross income. To qualify for inclusion here, the contribution must be made to nonprofit institutions that meet rather loosely drawn requirements. Restrictions are placed on institutions presumably serving propagandistic purposes, and contributions to political parties have not been allowed. Carry-over provisions allow the taxpayer to "bunch" actual contributions in particular years without incurring excessive tax liability.

The deductibility of contributions must be based, in principle, on the notion that individuals will be encouraged, by the possibility of tax deduction, to undertake specific activities that will generate external economies, external benefits on others in society. To an extent, the private activity encouraged substitutes for alternative public activity. Charitable contributions best fit this description, and contributions to educational institutions presumably are justified on this ground. Contributions to religious institutions are somewhat different, in that privately encouraged support for churches cannot be considered a substitute for potential government financing. A logical extension of Supreme Court ruling on religion would be the prohibition of tax deductibility on constitutional grounds.

The incidence and economic effects of tax deductibility are not so evident as naive analysis might suggest. The latter would indicate that the person who takes advantage of the deduction receives a "bargain" at the expense of the general federal taxpayer. Once it is recognized, however, that the political decision-making mechanism will, over the long run, respond to the behavior of the taxpayers, persons who take advantage of the deduction may not be in any better position than they would be without the deduction. This point can perhaps be made most clearly in the case of a deduction for educational outlay, for the contribution made to a university or college. Insofar as this private expenditure of funds should make unnecessary a like amount of public funds, at the federal or state-local level, all taxpayers secure benefits from the activity of the person who makes the contribution.

More than $15 billion were allowed as personal deductions under this category in 1975. This is a less-important personal deduction, in aggregative tax base reduction, than either that allowed for interest or for state-local taxes, and, is only slightly more important than the medical expenses deduction.

INTEREST

The taxpayer is allowed to deduct from gross income all interest paid on personal debts. For example, if the individual owns a home that is mortgaged, that part of the payments which represents interest may be deducted. In fact, the data available indicate that the deduction of mortgage interest is the most important single use made of this opportunity to reduce taxable income. But interest payments on funds borrowed for almost any purpose are also deductible. In 1975, almost $39 billion were deducted as interest payments.

The interest deduction may be used to illustrate in a more practical manner the issues of definition and measurement raised in Chapter 22. We may introduce a simple example. Suppose that an individual borrows $1,000 at an interest rate of 5 percent. Interest payments amount, therefore, to $50 a year. Any one of several things may be done with this borrowed capital. First, let us say that it may be invested and earn a 5 percent return, or $50 per year. If the earnings equal the cost of interest, it is clear that the individual's net worth is not modified. Therefore, if the accretion or accrual definition of income is adopted, the taxpayer should not be subjected to a tax liability. Rather, the interest charges should be allowed as a deduction from the income receipts of $50 in computing tax liability. But now let us suppose that the same individual spends the $1,000 in purchasing stereo components. Presumably, at the time of the combined borrowing-purchase operation, the stereo equipment must be considered to yield a rate of return in real income at least equal to the 5 percent interest charge. In terms of tax liability, if the interest charge is allowed as a deduction, but no income from the stereo equipment is imputed to the individual as taxable, he or she is thus differentially favored over the one who borrows to invest in a direct money return. On the other hand, if the interest charge is not allowed as a deduction, the individual in the first instance who does receive a money return is taxed on income even though his or her net worth is not modified. In principle, the reforms needed here are clear, but, as in so many cases, such reforms are difficult to achieve in practice. Interest charges should be allowed as deductible only to the extent that income from borrowed funds is included in the tax base. The same thing could be accomplished, of course, by leaving the interest deduction unchanged but imputing to individuals income from owned assets that yield income in kind.

TAXES

The single most important category of deductions from adjusted gross income is that of taxes paid to state and local units of government. In 1975, more than $44 billion were allowed as personal deductions under this category. Taxpayers are allowed to deduct from gross income most of the taxes that they pay for general-purpose operations of state and local governments. They are allowed to deduct such taxes as state income and property taxes, local property taxes, state excise and sales taxes, and automobile license fees to the extent that these are based on the value of the vehicle. Taxes levied by state-local governments that are not deductible are sumptuary levies on tobacco and alcohol along with those in which the tax payment is related specifically to the benefits received, such as local assessment of city streets. In 1978, new tax legislation removed the deductibility of state and local motor fuel taxes except when the vehicle was used for business purposes.

This deduction has been present since the beginning of the income tax, but there is little logical reason for its continuation. In a real sense, state and local taxes are "prices" paid by the individual for the purchase of public services provided by the state-local governments. Viewed in this light, these taxes should not be deductible any more than ordinary personal expenditures for goods and services.

The deductibility feature serves to reduce the effective rate of allowed taxes on local taxpayers, and, in this way, the net effect is that of shifting at least some of the burden of the financing of state and local expenditures onto the shoulders of the general federal taxpayer.

MEDICAL EXPENSES

The fourth, and remaining, major deduction that the individual is allowed to take is that for medical expenses. If these expenses exceed 3 percent of adjusted gross income (with some limitation on the computations for expenses on drugs), the excess above 3 percent is deductible. In 1975, deductions of $11 billion were taken in this category.

A change was introduced, effective in 1967, which made this category of personal deductions more significant than previously. Individuals were allowed to treat health insurance premiums separately from other medical expenses, and they were allowed to deduct one half of such premiums up to a maximum of $150. This was not subjected to the 3 percent of gross income limits imposed on other medical expenses. As a result, many additional taxpayers began to take advantage of medical deductions.

The allowance for medical expense deductions is based on a different "principle" from the allowance of, say, the charitable deduction. The medical expense deduction is based on the recognition that income, as ordinarily measured, does not in certain cases, constitute a satisfactory criterion upon which to determine tax liability. The individual family, faced with unexpectedly heavy medical and hospital charges, is deemed less able to pay taxes than the family with a similar income that is less burdened with such charges. To this extent, the medical expense deduction seems well grounded in equity considerations. However, to the extent that outlay for medical services reflects voluntary purchase of "consumption" services, this deduction, like the others, surely produces undesirable distortions in the national economy. Viewed in this light, the changes which allow the general usage of this deduction by all persons who purchase health insurance do not seem efficient.

MISCELLANEOUS DEDUCTIONS

Several other miscellaneous deductions are allowed the individual taxpayer before computing taxable income. Quantitatively, this whole set of deductions amounted to slightly more than $12 billion in 1975. The Revenue Act of 1964 modified certain of these miscellaneous deductions. The allowable deductions for child care and for moving expenses were liberalized. The casualty loss deduction was tightened. Other miscellaneous deductions are for the most part particular expenses incurred in connection with the individual's employment, such as union dues.

SUMMARY OF PERSONAL DEDUCTIONS

No attempt has been made here to catalog in detail the various deductions that are allowed in the current administration of the personal income tax in the United States. Only a careful and current perusal of the Internal Revenue Code can provide currently relevant information in detail. This discussion has been aimed, instead, at providing a general survey of the major categories of deductions that are currently allowed. The fact that so few changes in these allowable deductions were made in the Revenue Act of 1964, or in 1969 or 1976, despite earnest efforts on the part of many fiscal experts and despite initial efforts on the part of the Treasury Department, suggests that the major categories of deductions have come to be institutionalized into the American tax pattern. Changes of import in these major categories do not seem likely to occur in the foreseeable future.

RATE STRUCTURE

After having estimated the adjusted gross income, the individual taxpayer must choose either to itemize deductions or to elect the standard deduction. After these deductions are made to adjust gross income, an estimate of taxable income is produced. This is the criterion for determining the total tax liability of the individual taxpayer. It is to this measure that the rate structure is applied, and from this application the taxpayer's obligation for any particular calendar year is computed.

The computation procedure for individual taxpayers who earn less than $20,000 adjusted gross income and who do not find it advantageous to itemize deductions is quite simple. They need not compute the optional standard deduction at all, since this is accounted for in the tax table which they are allowed to use in determining their tax liability. A shortened tax form is available to taxpayers electing this option. This procedure requires the taxpayer to compute his total tax by using only his income and the number of his personal exemptions.

Before discussing the rate structure of the income tax further, it is essential to clarify the two terms, *average rate of tax* and *marginal rate* of tax. The average rate of tax is computed by dividing the tax bill or tax liability by the tax base, either adjusted gross income, or taxable income. As suggested earlier, the characteristic feature of a progressive rate structure is the excess of the marginal rate of tax over the average rate. The marginal rate is computed by dividing the *change* in tax liability by the *change* in the tax base, over specified income changes. With specific reference to the tax table applying only to gross incomes below $20,000, and using 1978 schedules, the maximum marginal rate was 34 percent. For example, the single individual with no dependents who earned $19,950 in adjusted gross income and who chose to file the short form of return based on the tax tables was obligated to pay $3,982 (at 1978 rates). This same individual, by earning up to the $20,000 limit would pay $3,999. The ratio between the added tax liability ($17) and the added income ($50) is 34 percent. This is the individual's marginal rate of tax. The average rate, on the other hand, is the total liability of $3,999 divided by $20,000 or 20 percent. Only in a purely proportional tax structure without allowable exemptions or deductions would the average rate of tax on gross income be equal to the marginal rate.

For individuals who choose to use the longer methods of computing their tax liabilities, more information is required than the figures for adjusted gross income and for the number of exemptions. Allowable deductions must be itemized, and a figure for taxable income attained. After taxable income has been determined, tax liability is computed by reference to the applicable tax schedule.

One such schedule is given as Table 23–1. This is the 1978 schedule applicable to income earned in 1978, for a single taxpayer filing a

TABLE 23–1
Rate schedule for 1978 tax return—single taxpayers who do not qualify as head of households

If taxable income is:

Over*	But not over	Tax is:	Taxable income in excess of
$ 2,200	$ 2,700	14% of	$ 2,200
2,700	3,200	$ 70 plus 15%	2,700
3,200	3,700	145 plus 16%	3,200
3,700	4,200	225 plus 17%	3,700
4,200	6,200	310 plus 19%	4,200
6,200	8,200	690 plus 21%	6,200
8,200	10,200	1,110 plus 24%	8,200
10,200	12,200	1,590 plus 25%	10,200
12,200	14,200	2,090 plus 27%	12,200
14,200	16,200	2,630 plus 29%	14,200
16,200	18,200	3,210 plus 31%	16,200
18,200	20,200	3,830 plus 34%	18,200
20,200	22,200	4,510 plus 36%	20,200
22,200	24,200	5,230 plus 38%	22,200
24,200	28,200	5,990 plus 40%	24,200
28,200	34,200	7,590 plus 45%	28,200
34,200	40,200	10,290 plus 50%	34,200
40,200	46,200	13,290 plus 55%	40,200
46,200	52,200	16,590 plus 60%	46,200
52,200	62,200	20,190 plus 62%	52,200
62,200	72,200	26,390 plus 64%	62,200
72,200	82,200	32,790 plus 66%	72,200
82,200	92,200	39,390 plus 68%	82,200
92,200	102,200	46,190 plus 69%	92,200
102,200	....	53,090 plus 70%	102,200

*If not over $2,200 your tax is 0.

separate return. Separate schedules are provided for married tax-payers who file joint returns, and for single taxpayers who qualify as heads of households. Note that the first $2,200 income is exempt from taxation and that the initial marginal rate of tax on the first bracket above $2,200 is 14 percent. Note that the marginal rate of tax increases rapidly as taxable income increases, and attains a maximum of 70 percent for all incomes over $100,200. Prior to the 1964 changes, the maximum marginal rate, applicable to incomes over $200,000, was 91 percent.

It is important to emphasize that the marginal rates of tax shown in Table 23–1 apply to taxable income. For example, if the individual taxpayer reported between $34,200 and $40,200 in taxable income for the year 1978, the marginal rate of tax was 50 percent. Out of each additional dollar reported as income over this bracket range, additional tax liability of 50 cents was incurred; only 50 cents on the dollar remained as income after taxes.

Marginal rates of tax on adjusted gross income need not be nearly so high as those on taxable income. Exemptions and deductions intervene between these two income computations, and it is possible that the taxpayer may receive additional income without incurring the full marginal liability if a portion of this income can be converted into an allowable deduction. For example, suppose that the single taxpayer receives a salary increase from $32,000 to $33,000. With the added $1,000 let us suppose a contribution of $500 is made to a university or college, and that the full percent allowable in this category had not previously been exhausted. In this way, only one half of the additional income becomes taxable. On this half the taxpayer must pay a marginal tax rate of 50 percent, but the marginal rate on the adjusted gross income becomes only one half this, or 25 percent. The incentive for the individual to convert gross income into deductions increases as the marginal rate of tax increases. There is a purely economic reason why the rich provide more than their proportionate share of total philanthropy. Aside from contributions and taxes, however, the importance of exemptions and deductions in reducing the marginal tax rate on gross income becomes rather unimportant at the higher income levels. This is due to the ceiling placed on deductions for medical expenses, the uniform dollar value of personal exemptions, and the low probability that higher income taxpayers will have large interest obligations on borrowed funds.

There remains, however, one very important means through which higher income taxpayers may reduce their overall tax liability below that which simple glances at rate schedules might suggest. They may, in various ways, convert what would have been ordinary income into capital gains. In this way, they may reduce the marginal tax rate to a maximum of 28 percent. This may be achieved through investment in corporations that choose to retain earnings rather than to pay them out in dividends. For example, if these taxpayers invest their savings in a growing enterprise that reinvests their earnings, the capital value of equity shares will increase over time. If the taxpayers choose to convert some of this increased value into current purchasing power, they may sell off shares in the market. However, only 40 percent of the capital gain must be counted for tax purposes. This provision encourages corporate retention of earnings, and probably does enhance the rate of economic growth. Were it not for this position and the other means of avoiding high marginal rates of tax, the tax burden on the higher bracket income would be less acceptable.

Average tax rates on either taxable income or on adjusted gross income are, of course, considerably lower than marginal tax rates. Considering taxable income alone, a schedule of average tax rate, applicable for the single taxpayer and computed directly from Table 23–1, is shown in Table 23–2.

As suggested, the average rates of tax on adjusted gross income are considerably lower than average rates as shown on taxable income in Table 23–2. The total of exemptions and deductions is sufficiently

TABLE 23–2
Schedule of average rates of tax on the taxable income of a single taxpayer, 1978 return

Taxable income	Average rate of tax (percent)
Under $ 2,200	0
$ 2,200– 2,700	0–3
2,700– 3,200	3–5
3,200– 3,700	5–6
3,700– 4,200	6–7
4,200– 6,200	7–11
6,200– 8,200	11–14
8,200– 10,200	14–16
10,200– 12,200	16–17
12,200– 14,200	17–19
14,200– 16,200	19–20
16,200– 18,200	20–21
18,200– 20,200	21–22
20,200– 22,200	22–24
22,200– 24,200	24–25
24,200– 28,200	25–27
28,200– 34,200	27–30
34,200– 40,200	30–33
40,200– 46,200	33–36
46,200– 52,200	36–39
52,200– 62,200	39–42
62,200– 72,200	42–45
72,200– 82,200	45–48
82,200– 92,200	48–50
92,200– 102,200	50–52
102,200	52

large to make for a substantial difference in the level of average rates of tax. For example, in 1975, the total adjusted gross income was $948 billion, on which a tax of $125 billion was paid. The average rate for the whole set of taxpayers was, therefore, 13 percent. For the same year, 1975, taxable income was $590 billion, making for an average rate of taxable income of 21 percent.

Table 23–3 shows adjusted gross income by income classes, income tax paid by each class, and average rates of tax, by classes, for 1975. This table is helpful in suggesting the concentration of total income in the middle'and lower levels, below $25,000. Note that, in 1975, only about one third of total adjusted gross income was earned by those earning above $25,000.

And only about 9 percent of income was received by those in excess of $50,000. This suggests that adjustments in either direction in the rates of tax on the very high-income receivers can have relatively little effect on total tax yields. Basically, the personal income has come to depend, for its important revenue potential, on the middle and lower income classes.

TABLE 23–3
Individual income tax returns, 1975*

Adjusted gross income by income classes	Total no. of returns (millions)	Adjusted gross income (billions)	Tax (billions)	Average rate (percent)
Total	82.2	$947.8	$124.5	13.1
Under $ 5,000	24.9	53.4	1.2	2.3
$ 5,000– 10,000	19.9	146.5	10.7	7.3
10,000– 15,000	14.9	185.6	19.2	10.3
15,000– 20,000	10.3	179.0	21.2	11.8
20,000– 25,000	5.6	124.3	17.0	13.7
25,000– 50,000	5.5	174.8	29.6	16.9
50,000 and over	1.1	84.2	25.6	30.4

* Includes nontaxable returns.
Source: Statistics of Income, 1975: Individual Income Tax Returns.

MAXIMUM AND MINIMUM TAX PROVISIONS

Two other features of the current U.S. personal income tax structure are worthy of mention. These are provisions setting a maximum tax on earned income and a minimum tax on certain other items given preferential treatment in the personal income tax laws.

As was mentioned in Chapter 22, the U.S. personal income tax does not generally treat income from work and income from assets differently. There are some exceptions to this, however. Capital gains income receives preferential treatment. In addition, a maximum marginal tax of 50 percent is imposed on earned income which includes such things as wages, salaries, and fees, received in compensation for personal services rendered. In addition, income from pensions and certain other annuities received in compensation for work effort are also subject to this provision.

The minimum tax provisions, on the other hand, are designed to set a lower bound on the amount of tax liability which an individual can avoid as a result of receiving income from sources which are given preferential treatment under the tax code. Examples include such things as stock options and accelerated depreciation of real property. The limit on taxation of earned income is not included here and 1978 legislation removed capital gains and itemized deductions in excess of 60 percent of adjusted gross income from the basic minimum tax computation. However, an alternative minimum tax which includes these items is levied if it exceeds the sum of the taxpayer's standard tax and a minimum tax computation under the standard formula including these two items in the base.

To compute the standard minimum tax, the taxpayer must first total all tax preference items. This amount is then reduced by either $10,000 or one half of regular tax liability, whichever is the greater. A 15 percent tax is then levied on the balance.

THE EARNED INCOME CREDIT

In 1975, a limited version of the negative income tax, discussed briefly in Chapter 22, was incorporated into the federal personal income tax structure. Originally authorized on a temporary basis, the so-called "earned income credit" was made a permanent part of the tax law in 1978. It works in the following way. A credit against personal income tax liability is computed on the basis of the taxpayer's earned income. If the allowable credit exceeds tax liability computed in the standard way, the difference is paid directly to the taxpayer. Only households with at least one dependent child are eligible for this credit.

More specifically the credit is computed in the following manner.

The maximum credit allowed to any eligible taxpayer is 10 percent of the first $5,000 of earned income. Earned income is generally defined as compensation for personal services with such things as investment or rental income being excluded. A taxpayer with earned income of $4,500 could not receive a credit of more than $450, for example, and no taxpayer could receive a credit in excess of $500. The maximum credit is reduced if adjusted gross income (or earned income, whichever is larger) exceeds $6,000. The amount of credit allowed falls by $12.50 for every $100 of income in excess of $6,000 and thus the credit is phased out completely for taxpayers with incomes in excess of $10,000. For example, suppose an otherwise eligible taxpayer had earned income of $4,500 and rental income of $3,000 with the corresponding adjusted gross income of $7,500. This taxpayer would be eligible for an earned income credit of $262.50 which is $450 minus 12.5 percent of the $1,500 by which adjusted gross income exceeds $6,000.

COLLECTION AND ENFORCEMENT

Almost three fourths of the total revenues collected under the federal individual income tax is withheld by employers from wage and salary payments and is transmitted directly by employers to the Treasury Department. The employer in this way acts as the collector for the federal government. Individual taxpayers never really possess that part of their gross income that is paid in this manner. Their knowledge of this income is limited to their acquaintance with the figure for their before-tax income, and to the reminder given to him each year by their employer. At this time, they receive from their employer a piece of paper, a copy of which the employer forwards to the Internal Revenue Service, indicating the amount of total taxes withheld from each individual's income during the calendar year. This form is then used by the taxpayers in computing their tax liability for the year when they file their annual returns, which they must do on or before April 15, for income of the preceding year. If the employer withheld less than the computed tax liability, the taxpayers must supplement the previously withheld total by some additional payment. If the employer has withheld more than the computed liability, the taxpayers may claim a refund.

The amount of wage, or salary, to be withheld by any single employer will be calculated on the basis of information received from the taxpayer concerning the number of personal exemptions. This number allows the employer, or the company accountant, to determine the proper withholding rate by consulting a table prepared by the Internal Revenue Service. If the information provided to the employer concerning the number of exemptions is correct and the total of allowable deductions taken by the taxpayers is approximately average, the taxpayers should neither receive a refund nor be required to make any supplementary payment, provided that they have received all of their income as wages, or salaries, subject to withholding and provided that their total income in each case is in the low- or middle-income ranges.

If, however, the taxpayer receives more than $500 in income that is not subject to withholding, or if total income exceeds $20,000, he or she must file a Declaration of Estimated Tax along with a claim for a refund or a payment of a supplemental tax on April 15. This Declaration of Estimated Tax is an estimation of income to be received for the year in progress, and the individual taxpayer must schedule a payment of this estimated tax over the four quarters of the year. The purpose of this requirement is to enable the taxpayer who is not fully covered by withholding to pay the tax bills quarterly rather than in one lump sum at the end of the taxable year. If the estimated income is computed properly and the quarterly payments are made as provided, no unduly large adjustments should have to be made on the final return.

The withholding method of tax collection, which was introduced into the U.S. system during World War II, has an apparent advantage if the tax is viewed from the point of view of the individual taxpayer. The psychological burden of the tax payment is greatly reduced if the individual does not ever have full possession of the income in the first place. A whole private budgetary calculus may be worked out on some income-after-tax basis so there will not be any serious pressure to reduce private spending or savings at any particular time during the year. The withholding feature, along with the requirement of quarterly payments on income not withheld, does possess the virtue of convenience.

The withholding of taxes has a major disadvantage, however, when the broader problems of fiscal decision making are introduced. The failure of the individual taxpayers to have income in their possession tends to make them relatively indifferent as to the level of taxes levied, and, in this way, tends to make them support public expenditure measures that are perhaps not actually worth the real opportunity costs. That part of the income tax collected through withholding becomes similar to indirect taxation in this respect. The whole subject of tax consciousness has been studied very little, but it seems clear that withholding, as an institution, has the effect of reducing the cost consciousness of the taxpayer. Whether or not this effect is considered to be desirable or undesirable in the organization of the fiscal structure depends, perhaps, on the conception of political-fiscal order that the student accepts.

Although tempered considerably in the case of taxes withheld from wages and salaries, an essential characteristic of the federal income tax is the location of the primary responsibility for computing tax liability on the individual taxpayer. The tax depends on *self-reporting*. The individual is responsible for (1) making an annual return if earnings are above the minimum, (2) for reporting income properly, as measured, (3) for taking exemptions and deductions in accordance with stipulated regulations, (4) for computing individual tax liability, and (5) for making final adjustments in tax payments. The whole administration of the tax is based on the presumption that the individual will, in fact, carry out the separate stages of the income tax process. Each taxpayer is provided with a return to be filled out, and is given detailed instructions as to the rules to be followed in filing that return. But the responsibility for filing the correct return rests with the individual.

If the individual fails to file a return at the proper time, if a return is filed but all of the income received is not reported, if all income received is reported but more exemptions and deductions than are allowed are taken, or if the tax is improperly computed, the individual is subject to penalties or to criminal prosecution if the intent is shown to be fraudulent. The task of the Internal Revenue Service in trying to ensure enforcement is, of course, immense. Limited staff prevents the careful auditing of each and every tax return, although major changes in auditing procedures are being made through the widespread installation of data processing devices.

The most difficult problems of enforcement arise in the uncovering of deliberate attempts to avoid payment of taxes. Certain premiums are granted to informers who report delinquents, but there is no systematic means of policing the tax effectively. This is a problem that is inherent in the nature of the personal income tax, as this tax is organized in the United States and Great Britain. The effective administration of the tax depends upon a rather high degree of taxpayer morality. It works well only if the number of persons who seek deliberately to disobey the law remains relatively small. A high degree of taxpayer morality has characterized both the American and the British systems in the past. Evidence continues to mount, however, which suggests that the level of taxpayer morality is declining in both countries. There is coming to be an increasing recognition of the danger of widespread fiscal fraud, and public attitudes toward the avoidance of tax obligations are changing notably. Fiscal fraud is surely important in reducing the tax bill for persons in those professions and occupations where the bulk of income is not withheld. It is almost impossible, of course, for wage or salary earners to avoid payment of their proper share of taxes. But it is relatively easy for individuals who receive their income directly from the sale of services or products, especially if they can receive it in cash, to avoid at least a certain share of their tax.

If the problem of fraud should become more serious over time, the administration of the personal income tax may be modified in the direction of removing the primary responsibility from the individual taxpayer and placing more and more power in the hands of the tax authority. The French and Italian taxes are the characteristic form of this sort of income taxation. It comes to be widely accepted, under such institutions, that individuals are under no moral obligation to pay more in taxes than they must pay. The tax authority must try, in such circumstances, to set up certain rather arbitrary, but objectively measurable, rules for determining the tax liability of the individual. The manner in which people spend their incomes usually becomes one criterion for determining tax liability in such systems. This sort of income tax administration has never proven so productive of revenue as the self-reporting type practiced in the United States and Great Britain. It is, also, much more restrictive of individual freedom. But the necessary shifting of the American system in this direction must be faced.

The incentive for avoidance, evasion, and fraud is directly related to the level of income tax rates. One desirable effect of tax rate reductions is that of reducing somewhat the incentive for individuals to invest resources in evading tax.

CONCLUSIONS

The personal, or individual, income tax provides more than two fifths of the total revenues of the federal government. The importance of this revenue source does not seem likely to diminish, and especially in the face of continuing inflation.

The tax is levied on persons as heads of family units or as individuals. Certain problems arise in defining income, but, by and large, all ordinary income from the sale of personal or resource services is included in the tax base. The total amount of income received measures adjusted gross income. The taxpayer is allowed to subtract from this certain allowances for personal exemptions and allowable deductions. This step complete, taxable income is given, and it is on this that the actual tax liability is computed.

The rate structure is highly progressive. The lowest bracket rate on taxable income is 14 percent, and the marginal rate increases to a high of 70 percent in the high-income ranges. It is necessary to distinguish carefully between the marginal rate of tax and the average rate of tax, and also between the use of adjusted gross income and taxable income.

One of the important means through which the individual taxpayer may reduce overall tax liability is through the conversion of ordinary income into long-term capital gains. This conversion has the effect of reducing the rate of tax on this income or gain. The loophole here is of major significance for the higher income groups, and it does allow individual taxpayers in these groups to escape the unreasonably high rates that continue to apply nominally to these brackets. The existence of this possibility of conversion makes it advantageous for corporations to retain earnings rather than to pay them out as dividends, a policy that does serve perhaps to increase the overall rate of corporate investment.

The U.S. personal income tax is collected from the individual, and the individual retains the primary responsibility for filing the tax correctly. However, in the postwar years almost three fourths of the tax has been collected from employers who withhold estimated amounts of taxes from wage and salary payments made to employees. This sytem has a certain convenience for the individual taxpayer as well as for the tax administrators, but its long-run effects on the fiscal consciousness of the taxpayers seem to be questionable.

The level of taxpayer morality has, in the past, remained relatively high in the United States. This may be changing, however, as the income tax remains at high levels. Some shifting of tax administration in the direction of establishing more objectively determinate measures of individual taxpayer liability may prove necessary, and the federal power over the individual through the taxing mechanism seems surely to increase in future.

This chapter has discussed the major features of the personal income tax as it exists in the United States. It should be recognized that the complex institution represented by this major revenue source is subject to constant evolution as well as deliberate change. As the experience of both 1964 and 1969 indicated, however, few of the basic features of the tax seem likely to be modified despite continued clamors for "tax reform." Changes will take place in details of administration and structure. Particular loopholes may be opened or closed. But, on balance, the basic structure is unlikely to be dramatically revised. Progressiveness will remain a characteristic element.

SUPPLEMENTARY READING

The student can learn much about the personal income tax by securing a set of returns and instructions for preparing such returns, and illustrative preparation of returns will be helpful in indicating the general structure of the tax.

For more detailed factual material, the student should consult the Internal Revenue Code or one of the Tax Service publications that may be found in any library.

24

Personal income taxation: Economic effects

For a long time now, outstanding scholars in public finance have believed that the personal income tax provides the most suitable means of raising revenues for general-purpose public expenditures. It is therefore not surprising to find that this tax occupies such an important position in the fiscal systems of Western countries. The alleged superiority of the personal income tax over other revenue-raising devices arises out of a comparison of economic effects, along with other considerations of equity. In order to understand why students of fiscal systems have given such whole-hearted support to personal income taxation, it is necessary to analyze the economic effects of the tax carefully.

A caveat must be introduced here, however. Traditionally, the support for progressive income taxation, both in theory and in reality, has been based on the presumption that modern nations can maintain tolerable monetary stability. To the extent that worldwide inflation continues and possibly accelerates, the progressive features of this tax become increasingly undesirable unless adjustments are made. These problems will be examined in this chapter.

THE NOTION OF A GENERAL TAX

One of the long-accepted criteria for taxation states that, where possible, a tax should be *general* rather than specific. By a general tax is meant one that applies *generally*, that does not impose a differential burden on any particular individual or group. Among the set of potentially practicable taxes that yield sizable revenue, the personal income tax best meets this criterion.

Several subsidiary advantages are implied by the idea of generality. First of all, a tax that is completely general cannot exert any economic effects. If a tax applies to every individual in all circumstances, there is no way in which an individual can change his or her behavior with the purpose of escaping all or a portion of his or her tax liability. As a matter of fact, the absence of such changes in behavior as a result of the tax is the best way of determining whether or not a given tax is *general*. In other terms, a general tax cannot be shifted, since the only way in which individuals can shift a tax is through some modification of their own behavior. By contrast, a specific tax or a nongeneral tax may be shifted. For example, a tax on the sale of beer is actually paid by the selling firm. But the firm may shift the tax to the consumer by changing its behavior with respect to setting the sales price. It may pass the tax along, or shift it, to the final consumer, who may, in turn, escape tax liability by refraining from beer consumption. The income tax, on the other hand, will apply equally whether the individual chooses to drink beer or water. It is not easily shifted.

This generality of a tax also implies *directness*. A *direct tax* is defined as one which is borne by the individual upon whom it is levied. This is the same thing as saying that a general tax is a direct tax. It can be seen that, quite apart from economic effects, the direct tax has major advantages from the point of view of equity or fairness in the distribution of the overall tax burden. The final burden, or *incidence*, of a tax rests squarely upon the shoulders of the person or persons upon whom the tax is levied by the government. There is no necessity to examine all of the secondary repercussions of the tax in order to determine who actually pays for the cost of the government services financed.

The personal income tax comes closer to meeting the criterion of generality and directness than any other tax that could be used as a major revenue producer in a modern fiscal system. But *the personal income tax is not a general tax.* This point should be emphasized. If the tax were completely general it would generate no changes in individual behavior; it would, in a sense, have no economic effects, and the remainder of this chapter need not have been written.

Before we discuss the reasons why the personal income tax does not fully meet the requirement of generality, it will be useful to examine the "ideal" general tax, even though it should be recognized that such a tax could never be very important in practice.

The "ideal" tax, in the sense of generating no changes in behavior, is the *lump-sum tax.* By this we mean a tax that is imposed on the individual quite independently of wealth, income, occupation, consumption pattern, family status, age, work habits, or any other distinguishing characteristic. Only if the tax were completely unrelated to each of these characteristics would the individual find it impossible to escape some of the tax burden. The tax which meets these requirements is truly a lump-sum tax which the individual must pay. It is questionable whether such an "ideal" tax could ever be devised in practice. If all individuals should place the same relative evaluations on public services, the *poll* tax, or *capitation* tax, would meet the "ideal" standards. This tax levies a fixed sum on the individual without reference to any particular characteristic or criterion. Each must pay the tax, and in the same amount, regardless of economic status or position and regardless of individual behavior. Each would pay a fixed sum *per unit of public services provided by government.* This tax would be analogous to a price paid by the individual for a private good in the marketplace. In the market the price that an individual confronts, say, for a loaf of bread does not in any way change if the individual's economic position changes or if individual behavior changes. The total payment may change, depending on how many loaves are bought, just as the individual taxpayer's total bill may vary, even under a truly lump-sum tax, as the size of the public sector varies. If individuals place differing relative evaluations on public services, the ideal tax would, of course, have to be different from one individual to another. The simple head tax no longer meets the criterion. Since individual evaluations differ and since these evaluations cannot be determined independently, it is clear that the "ideal" general tax can never be actually utilized.

ANNOUNCEMENT EFFECTS OF AN INCOME TAX

Although it comes closer to meeting the generality requirement than any other tax that would be practically acceptable, the income tax does have important *announcement* effects. By announcement effects we mean those changes in behavior that may be produced as a result of the imposition of the tax.

Work versus leisure

First of all, the tax on income discriminates against the earning of income. To be at all practical, the tax must have some objectively measurable base, normally the money value of real income received by the individual. If, however, there is some direct relationship between the amount of the tax and the amount of measured real or money income, the individual may reduce tax liability by a change in behavior. The ultimate scarce resource for all individuals is, of course, time, and earning income is not the only way in which time may be used. The tax on income puts a differential premium on leisure as opposed to income earning.

It is questionable as to how important this premium on leisure really is. The importance will vary from one culture and from one individual to another. In primitive and underdeveloped societies, the earning of money income is not so significant as in a developed economy. Hence, attempts to raise revenues by taxing incomes in those societies may fail because individuals will respond by simply working less. On the other hand, in the more developed economies, the earning of income may be so important relative to the enjoyment of leisure that even quite heavy taxation of income will have little effect on human behavior. This result is reinforced by the existence of many institutional constraints which tend to fix some standard length of the work day, the work week, and the work year, even the work life, for many groups of the population. Some effects on behavior must be present, however, even if the quantitative significance is difficult to ascertain.

Income in kind

We have already discussed one important variant of this announcement effect of an income tax. If the actual tax base includes money income only, a very strong incentive is provided for individuals to shift their actions so that they will receive income in kind, or, in other words, income that is nontaxable. Many nonpecuniary equivalents of real income must be included in such a category.

American taxpayers have a strong economic motivation, because of the tax structure, to invest in the ownership of durable consumer assets: residences, appliances, and automobiles. Such assets yield real income that is not taxable. Taxpayers also have an economic motive to reorganize their affairs so that they get real income in the form of the various fringe benefits of employment, such as employer contribution to pension plans, rather than direct payments of money income. The results of the announcement effects are clearly those of producing some distortion in the pattern of individual purchases. They invest more in durables than their pretax preference pattern might dictate. And their own mobility among alternative employment opportunities tends to be reduced by the increasing importance of fringe benefits.

Various effects of the sort mentioned here are recognized to be of major importance in the American tax structure. And these become more and more significant as institutions emerge to represent adaptation to the conditions of a high-income tax world. There has been, and there will probably be a gradual erosion of the income tax base on account of such announcement effects, with more and more real income received in such a way as to allow individuals to avoid some ordinary tax liability.

Incentives to save

Any tax on measured income of the individual will also tend to reduce the incentive of the individual to save *relative* to a tax on that part of income that is spent. One of the oldest debates in tax theory has been concerned with the so-called double taxation of saving. If income is defined as a flow of real goods and services to the individual over time, that income which is saved and invested is subjected to double taxation under any income tax. The income is taxed as it is originally received, and then the yield on the investment is taxed when it accrues in future periods. This conception of the problem has led many students to argue persuasively that income taxation involves an inherent discrimination against saving and should be replaced by a tax on expenditure.

On the other side of the argument, if income is defined as an accretion in net worth of the individual, no double taxation of saving can take place. The individuals' net worth increases as they initially receive income. They are taxed on this accretion, not on any concrete "flow" of real goods and services to them. If they choose to save and invest a portion of this income received, their net worth will again increase over time, and they will be subject to new taxes on the new accretion to their wealth. No double taxation is involved at all. The difference between these two constructions of taxation depends on the difference in income definition, a difference that cannot be resolved analytically.

PROPORTIONAL AND PROGRESSIVE INCOME TAXATION

The announcement effects discussed in the preceding section occur under any tax levied on personal income as a base, quite independently of the rate structure of the tax itself. More specifically, the effects discussed would apply to a proportional income tax. But, as we have seen, income taxation in Western countries normally involves progression in the rate structure. That is to say, there is some discrimination among sizes of incomes received.

This additional discrimination can be expected to lead to an additional set of announcement effects which we must now discuss. The progressive income tax is less general than the proportional income tax; it generates more influence on individual behavior.

The decreasing "price" of leisure

The general discrimination against earning income and in favor of enjoying leisure is present under any income tax, as noted. But if the rate structure is progressive, the discrimination becomes increasingly pronounced as the individual moves up the income scale. With the marginal rate of tax increasing, the "price" of leisure decreases at higher income levels. Therefore, we should expect a more significant incentive effect among the higher income groups.

A simple arithmetical example can illustrate the point. Let us suppose that, by working 12 months rather than 10, a medical doctor (one of the new rich in modern America) can increase her annual taxable income from $100,000 to $120,000. With the maximum marginal tax rate on earned income at 50 percent, the "price" of two months' leisure in the Caribbean is only $10,000; she gives up only this amount by leaving her practice. By contrast, let us suppose that the assistant professor, through teaching two months in the summer school, can increase his taxable income from $10,000 to $12,000. Since the marginal tax rate for this range is 27 percent, the "price" of the two months' leisure is almost three-fourths the value of the marginal income. It follows that, given ordinary economic motivation, the physician in our example will be somewhat more likely to "purchase" the leisure than will the college professor.

The importance of this effect on those who receive high incomes is very difficult to assess. The limited number of studies that have been made indicate that the incentive effects on the activity of members of the high-income groups are easily overemphasized. Other considerations seem to be as influential, and possibly more so, in determining the behavior of individual members of the high-income groups. Such things as prestige, institutional patterns of behavior, and social status make the business executive, the corporation lawyer, the society doctor, and other like members of the richer classes pay less heed to the high-marginal rates of tax than might be expected, at least insofar as the incentive to work is concerned.

In recognition of the effects of progressive rates of tax on income-earning decisions, a maximum bracket rate of 50 percent was placed on "earned" as opposed to other forms of income receipts in the 1969 tax legislation.

Rational occupational choice

To a certain extent at least, individuals determine the pattern of their earnings over a lifetime by the occupational choice made quite early in their lives. This important decision is, in many cases, not entirely a free one. For many individuals, opportunities for entering many of the professions and occupations are closed, for many reasons, some necessary, some wholly unnecessary. Even where widespread opportunities exist, the important occupational or professional decision is often made on quite capricious and nonrational grounds. Despite all of these important qualifications, however, it must be recognized that individuals do, in some degree, *choose* the income stream that will come to them over time. For example, college students choosing to pursue academic careers may be doing so deliberately in the face of the knowledge that they are not going to maximize the present value of their expected money earnings stream in this way. They may be perfectly rational in this; they may consider the nonmonetary rewards of the academic career to be sufficient to more than offset the monetary differential. Such individuals may be contrasted with fellow students (who we shall assume have the same capacity for entering an academic career), who choose to enter business because in so doing they value the expected monetary reward more highly.

Insofar as the actual income differences among individuals result from such rational choices as ways of earning income, the progressive income tax can exert important influences on individual behavior. The tax clearly places a differential premium on those occupations and professions that promise nonmonetary advantages, and a differential discount against those occupations and professions, perhaps somewhat disagreeable in themselves, that promise the highest monetary returns. The effect is to cause a relatively smaller number of persons to choose the higher income, but "undesirable," professions and occupations.

Over a long period of time, this effect of the progressive income tax may well be more significant than that which operates directly on the incentives of individuals in choosing to modify hours, or days, or years of work once a profession has been chosen. With continuing high rates of progression in the income tax, young persons may come to be more and more attracted to the "safe" and "soft" professions, to those activities that lack adventure, that are not risky, that promise to yield a "quiet" life in modern middle-class suburbia, perhaps with employment in an increasingly large bureaucracy. Or, alternatively, young persons may "opt out" of the income-earning race, in part because the game does not seem worth the candle.

One particular point remains to be mentioned in this connection. The progressive income tax will have the effect of discriminating against ventures which involve high degrees of risk and uncertainty. Those occupations and professions which offer to the individual a small chance of making a great gain along with many chances of losses will tend to be abandoned. Those individuals who are fortunate will earn high incomes; if they are unlucky they earn no income and may go bankrupt. But with the progressive income tax, they pay the full amount if they are lucky; they get no subsidy for their efforts if they lose. These individuals will be quite reluctant, or at least more reluctant, to enter risky professions, or to undertake risky ventures within the ordinary work of any given profession. Risk taking is very much less than would be present under a proportional income tax.

Incentives to save

As noted previously, any tax on income does, in a certain sense, discriminate against saving and in favor of consumption spending. The particular impact of a progressive income tax on saving is quite different from this.

It is generally recognized that the proportion of income saved increases as income increases. In other words, individuals with higher incomes save proportionately more than individuals with lower incomes. This being true, it follows that a progressive income tax, which bears most heavily on higher incomes, will reduce saving more than a proportional income tax of comparable yield.

EFFECTS OF EXISTING INSTITUTIONS OF INCOME TAXATION

The effects already discussed are necessary results of progression in the income tax structure. Additional effects may be caused by the specific characteristics of a given tax system. It will be useful to discuss some of these effects that stem from the U.S. system of income tax administration.

Absence of averaging

Since income is a flow conception, some time dimension must, necessarily, be placed on the tax base. Income per year, per decade, or for a lifetime must be the basis for taxation, not some present value, a stock conception. But there is no need that income in any one calendar year should be the exclusive criterion of determining tax liability of an individual in that year.

Note that under the proportional income tax rather than the progressive tax, no problems would arise in this respect. The absence of averaging provisions exerts an economic effect only under a progressive rate structure. Also, if income should be received uniformly over time, no problems would arise, even with progression.

To illustrate, let us consider an example of two individuals who each received taxable income totaling $200,000 over the five year period ending in 1978. The taxable income of individual I was $40,000 in each of the five years. Individual II had taxable income of $100,000 in 1978 and $25,000 in each of the preceding four years. For simplicity, we will assume that the earned income component of II's 1978 income was not sufficiently high to be affected by the maximum tax provisions. We will also assume that each individual was a single taxpayer who was not a head of household.

Although the 1978 tax tables did not actually apply over the entire four year period preceding the year, they will be used for that period for purposes of our illustrative computations. Individual I, with taxable income of $40,000 in each of the sample five years, would have paid annual taxes of $13,190 for a total five year tax bill of $65,950. Individual II, on the other hand, would have paid taxes of $6,310 in each of the four years, 1974–1977, in which taxable income was $25,000. The ordinary tax on an income of $100,000 in 1978 would have been $51,572. Therefore, in the absence of any income averaging provisions in the tax law, II's total five year tax bill would have been $76,812, almost $11,000 more than I paid on the same total five year income.[1]

The averaging provisions in the 1978 tax code would have enabled individual II to substantially reduce tax liability in that year. To illustrate, it seems best to simply trace through the process of income averaging which II would have employed to compute 1978 tax liability. An individual may take advantage of income averaging if the difference between taxable income in the current year and 30 percent of total taxable income for the preceding four years is greater than $3,000. This difference is the taxpayer's *averageable income*, and, in the case of our sample individual, would have been $70,000. Tax liability would then be computed in two parts. First, one fifth of averageable income is added to 30 percent of total taxable income over four years preceding the current tax year. These two figures would be $14,000 and $30,000 respectively. Tax is then computed from the appropriate tax schedule on this amount, $44,000. This component of tax liability would have been $15,380. A second component of tax liability involves finding the difference between this tax and the tax on 30 percent of the preceding four year total. Tax on $30,000 would have been $8,400 so this difference would be $6,980. This difference is then multiplied by four to yield the second component of total tax

---

[1]In our simple numerical example, we neglect the problem of comparing present values of the separate income streams. The fact that both of the income streams total $200,000 over five years does not, of course, suggest that they are equivalent in present value terms. This comparison will depend on the rate of discount of future income held to be appropriate.

liability, $27,920. Total tax liability is thus $43,300, and $8,272 less than it would have been in the absence of averaging.

The introduction of income averaging in 1964 did much to remove the discrimination against certain types of occupations that the progressive tax structure had previously contained. Without the averaging option, individuals had incentives to steer clear of employments with widely fluctuating incomes. Ideally, of course, an averaging scheme would allow the taxpayer to compute income on the basis of an earnings stream over a whole lifetime and it would also allow full loss offsets for those years in which the individual earns negative income. However, the administrative problems involved in implementing such a scheme would be large, and the provisions now incorporated in the tax law do much to correct the problems presented by progressive taxation.

FAVORABLE TREATMENT OF CAPITAL GAINS

The American income tax is not based on an internally consistent definition or conception of income, as we have noted. If it were, capital gains would be wholly exempt from or fully subject to the tax.

If the flow conceptions of income is adopted, capital gains are simply not income. The British income tax largely embodies this view. The implication is that capital gains are quite distinctive from ordinary income and that conversion of ordinary income into capital gains and vice versa is not easy to accomplish.

A full acceptance of the accretion conception of income would require full taxation of capital gains and full deductibility of capital losses. Under this view any accretion in the individual's net worth is properly includable in the income tax base.

The American tax is closer to the accretion conception of income, but we have never been willing to accept full taxation of capital gains except during the early years of income tax administration. The tax that exists is a compromise on this point. Long term gains, those enjoyed on assets held for longer than one year, are taxed at especially favorable rates and then only when realized by sale of the asset. Only 40 percent of a long term gain, defined as the difference between the sale price and the original purchase price, must be included as taxable income. For a taxpayer in the 70 percent marginal tax bracket, the effective marginal tax on this capital gains income is thus reduced to 28 percent.

For a long time the tax code allowed some long-term capital gains to escape taxation altogether. If an individual did not realize a capital gain in the course of his or her lifetime, heirs were liable for capital gains tax only to the extent that the value of the asset increased further between the time of inheritance and the time of sale. Suppose, for example, an individual purchased an asset for $1,000 and held it for several years during which time it increased in value. The individual died and the asset, now valued at, say, $1,800, became the property of an heir. This individual, in turn, held the asset for a period of years and then sold it for $2,500. Prior to the Tax Reform Act of 1976 only $700 of capital gain would be subject to tax. The 1976 legislation, however, provided that beginning in 1980, capital gains on inherited assets would be computed with the original purchase price as the base, not the value at the time of inheritance.[2]

As a result of the favorable treatment of capital gains, the existing law does generate economic effects by causing individuals to convert ordinary income into long-term capital gains where this is possible. The individual who succeeds in accomplishing this reduces his or her tax liability considerably. There are several ways in which such conversions can be carried out. The ordinary receipt of income may be exchanged for an equity share in a firm, and as the equity share values rise over time, the income taken out of the business becomes taxable to the individual as a long-term capital gain when a share is sold.

This is facilitated by the practice of modern business corporations in retaining earnings and plowing them back into corporate investment. This activity increases the net worth of the corporation, and in so doing, the market value of equity shares. The equity owners of the corporation thus receive capital gains, and if they choose to take income out of the corporation they do so by selling shares on the market. The difference between the selling price and the original buying price is taxable as a long-term gain, provided only that the stock has been held longer than one year. In this way, it becomes advantageous for the individual to invest in a corporation which does follow this practice rather than paying out earnings as dividends to stockholders. The mere establishment of corporations that are designed for tax avoidance is not legal.

---

[2]This carryover provision in the capital gains law was politically controversial and, in late 1979, efforts were being made in Congress for its repeal.

Should future tax reform proposals be aimed at eliminating all favorable treatment for capital gains and requiring taxpayers to report all such gains as ordinary income? There are three possible reasons why this step should not be taken unilaterally.

First of all, capital gains tend to be "bunched" in time, especially if taxed only when realized, and any move toward full taxation of gains as ordinary income would have to extend the averaging provisions. In effect, the favorable treatment accorded long-term gains can be considered as a crude method of allowing averaging for this source of income.

Second, any proposal to include all long-term gains as ordinary income in the tax base would have to include more adequate treatment of long-term capital losses. Full-loss offsets would necessarily have to be provided in order to prevent the full taxation of gains from seriously hampering risky and uncertain ventures.

The third, and perhaps the most important, reason why the inclusion of long-term gains in fully taxable income has not been more strongly supported is found in the high marginal rates of tax imposed on upper bracket incomes. The capital gains loophole allows a large number of individuals at the upper end of the income scale to lower the effective rates of taxes paid. In a very real sense, the favorable treatment of gains allows the high marginal rates to be a smoke screen which satisfies divergent political demands.

INFLATION AND PROGRESSIVE TAXATION

The most important threat to the continued viability of the progressive tax on personal incomes as a major element in the U.S. revenue structure lies in the incompatibility between this tax and long-continued inflation. This emerged as a relatively new problem in the 1960s and 1970s because of the apparent lack of policy success in keeping inflation within reasonable bounds. The income tax, as it has been traditionally discussed and administered, involves the application of a progressive rate structure with successively higher percentage rates imposed on successively higher brackets that are specified in nominal money incomes. With general inflation, prices and incomes defined in purely monetary terms shift upward, but these shifts need not be accompanied by any corresponding changes in real values. An income tax will, therefore, obligate a person to meet a higher tax bill solely because of monetary inflation, and independently of any change in real purchasing power.

The bias toward increased budgetary sizes created by inflation is clear. Inflation becomes a means of reducing the disposable incomes of individuals defined in real terms, and increasing the disposable income of the government *without* any explicit change in the rate structure itself. Inflation is essentially a hidden or concealed way of increasing the rate of personal income tax, quite apart from the different tax on the holders and users of money that inflation represents.

Let us consider the example of the single person who has a taxable income of $10,000 in 1978. At the rates of tax shown in Table 23–1, this individual would have paid a tax of $1,542 or an average rate of 15.4 percent. Suppose that general inflation of 50 percent occurs between 1978 and 1983 and that the individual's money income just keeps pace with the rate of inflation; real income does not change over the period. If taxable income rises to $15,000 in 1983 and if the rate structure remains unchanged, the individual's tax bill would be $2,862. The average rate of tax has increased from 15.4 to 19 percent. Disposable income which was $8,458 in 1978 rises to $12,138 in 1983, but note that this rise is *less* than the 50 percent which would be required to maintain real purchasing power. In real terms, disposable income has been reduced. The individual is paying a larger share of real income to the government in income tax in 1983 than was paid in 1978 solely because of being shifted by inflation into a higher marginal rate bracket in the progressive schedule.

From the government's side of the picture, the opposing results hold. Strictly due to the inflation, in 1983, government would collect more than enough to finance the same bundle of real goods and services as was being provided in 1978. Real disposable revenue available to government increases as the real disposable income to the individual falls. The effects of inflation are identical to those of a specific increase in the real rate of tax on personal income. There is, however, a major political difference. With inflation, the increase in real rates of tax occur without explicit political decision. Congressmen do not have to face constituents who oppose tax increases. Inflation allows government's share in the economy to be increased with a progressive income tax in such a way that elected politicians can escape their tax setting responsibility. The proclivity of elected politicians to enact new and expanded programs for public expenditures ensures that inflation will be a popular financing device. Indirectly, it increases the rate of income tax, quite apart from the direct financing of spending that inflation itself allows to take place.

An additional feature of the inflation-induced increase in the real rates of a progressive income tax should be noted. The increases so generated will remain as permanent parts of the structure, until and unless explicit political action is taken to modify the rate structure. Consider our same example. Let us now suppose that, after 1983, through some new magic, the government should succeed in eliminating inflation. From 1983 onward, prices and incomes would be stabilized, and incomes would go up only with real growth in the national economy. But this monetary stabilization would do nothing toward reversing the changes that would have been made over the inflationary period. Real rates of income tax would remain permanently higher than they were before the onset of inflation. Even a temporary inflation will, therefore, exert a long-run effect on the rate structure of the progressive income tax, an effect that will not readily be corrected.

Our example of the increasing real rate of tax that inflation produces ignored another important impact of inflation which makes real tax rates even more sensitive to inflation. Any aspects of the progressive rate structure that involve designations of liabilities, exemption limits, deduction levels or capital gains bases in monetary units are also affected in real terms by inflation. Consider the $1,000 personal exemption that was in effect in 1978. If a 50 percent inflation in the general price level were to occur between 1978 and 1983, the purchasing power of $1,000 will have gone down. To maintain this level of exemption in real terms the personal exemption would have to be increased to $1,500. Capital gains taxation presents another interesting example. Suppose an individual purchased an asset in 1978 at a price of $500 and in 1983, after a 50 percent increase in the price level, sold the asset for $750. No real capital gain would have occurred but the individual would, nonetheless, incur a tax liability on the purely nominal gain of $250. In order to eliminate this effect, the original purchase price would have to be indexed to the price level and thus measured in current dollars at the time of sale rather than of original acquisition. It should, perhaps be noted, that these effects would be present even if the rate structure itself were proportional rather than progressive.

It must, of course, be recognized that inflation does not shift all incomes upward equally; some persons and groups gain in relative terms while others lose. These distributional gains and losses from inflation should not, however, be allowed to obscure the central point that we have attempted to emphasize in this section. This is that even if all incomes should shift upward equally during an inflation, there would still be produced an increase in the real rates of tax under progression. Even under this extreme set of conditions, the government gains and the taxpayer loses.

Ad hoc adjustments in rate structure

It should be clear that long-continued inflation will seriously distort the assignment of liabilities under a progressive income tax with an unchanging rate structure, including exemption levels and deduction limits, and also will modify the place of this particular tax within a more inclusive revenue structure. Over a sustained period of significant monetary inflation, the structure of real rates would lose all connection with what might have been the initial intent of those who supported the tax legislation in the first instance. Tax rates will have been increased, and more persons will be brought under the tax, without any explicit approval of such changes by orderly political process.

This result could scarcely be defended on any plausible grounds. Yet this effect of progression has not normally been discussed at length in the standard treatments of income tax. Why? Perhaps the primary reason is that long-continued inflation of the sort experienced in the United States and elsewhere in the Western world is a relatively new phenomenon. For example, between 1955 and 1965, the implicit price deflator for GNP increased less than 20 percent over the whole decade. Serious inflation was not really considered to be a major problem for economic policy until the mid-1960s.

Some recognition of the increases in real tax rates that inflation produces have, of course, been present in the various proposals for income tax reform. Changes instituted in 1969 and also in 1976 were, to an extent, motivated by this recognition. In nominal terms, legislation in these years involved rate reductions including increases in exemption levels and deduction limits. In real terms, these changes tend to restore effective real tax rates. The marginal tax brackets were also widened in 1978 in an attempt to reduce the impact of future inflation.

Reliance on *ad hoc* or piecemeal adjustments to correct for the rate-increasing effects of general inflation does not seem to be sound economic policy. There would seem to be little reason to open up the Pandora's box of the rate structure of income taxation anew each and every time an adjustment for inflation-induced rate increases is indicated. To the maximum extent that is possible, adjustments for inflation should be made automatically.

Built-in or automatic adjustment for inflation

In order to isolate the progressive income tax rate structure from the effects of monetary inflation, it is necessary to define this structure independently of nominal monetary income, exemption, and deduction units and to replace these by real values. This requires that some adjustment be introduced which will allow a translation to be made between nominal monetary values and real values, an adjustment for the declining purchasing power of a monetary unit, a dollar, during periods of inflation.

Such an adjustment can be readily incorporated into the progressive income tax. Specifically designated monetary values appear in the income brackets subject to tax, in the personal exemption levels, in the limits to percentage standard deduction, in the basis for computing capital gains, and elsewhere in the tax structure. The rate structure can be made inflation-proof by adjusting each of these values, as it appears in the schedule or tax form, upward by some price-level index which measures the degree of inflation.

For purposes of illustration, let us suppose that the rate structure in existence in 1978 is that which is desired to be maintained in real terms over the inflation period of 1978–83. If the 1978 rate structure is to be maintained, in real terms, all monetary values must be adjusted by a price index. There is some slight difference as among different indices here; but these differences are relatively insignificant in the large. Let us suppose that the consumer price index is adopted as the adjusting device. . . . Consider the rate brackets in Table 24–1 which were taken directly from Table 23–1 and which applied to money income received by a single person during 1978. Suppose that, using 1978 as a base, the consumer price index increased by 10 percent between 1978 and 1979. For that portion of the tax table shown, the rate brackets should have been adjusted upward as indicated in Table 24–2.

For individuals in the income ranges shown, this adjustment would ensure that real rates of tax remained unchanged despite the inflation. Similar adjustment would, of course, have been made for all brackets, for exemption levels and deduction limits, and for bases of

TABLE 24–1

Taxable income		Tax is	Taxable income
Over	But not over		in excess of
$ 6,200	$ 8,200	......$ 690 plus 21% of	$ 6,200
8,200	10,200	...... 1,110 plus 24%	8,200
10,200	12,200	...... 1,590 plus 25%	10,200

TABLE 24–2

Taxable income		Tax is	Taxable income
Over	But not over		in excess of
$ 6,820	$ 9,020	......$ 759 plus 21% of	$ 6,820
9,020	11,220	...... 1,221 plus 24%	9,020
11,220	13,420	...... 1,749 plus 25%	11,220

capital gains. The personal exemption of $1,000 would have been automatically increased by $100 to $1,100 and the maximum limit on the percentage standard deduction from $2,300 to $2,530.

So long as rates of inflation remained within "reasonable" limits, say, those prevailing before 1965, the additional costs involved in administering the automatic adjustment might have been sufficient to warrant neglect of this reform. Under the adjustment, the Internal Revenue Service would, of course, be required to print new forms each year, with different brackets, based on deflation by some price index as of a specified date, perhaps on January 1 of each year. *Ad hoc* adjustments of the rate structure might have, under these conditions, seemed preferable to automatic adjustment. When, however, annual inflation rates in excess of 5 percent are experienced, and especially as these continue over a series of years, the costs of the automatic adjustment seem relatively minor relative to the benefits that the change would produce. Automatic adjustment for inflation would allow the political decision makers to determine the real rate structure of the progressive tax independently of worries and concerns about rates of inflation. This would surely ensure greater fiscal rationality in public decisions. Perhaps more importantly, the change would remove one of the most severe biases toward continued expansions in the size of the public sector.

Experience in other countries

The possibility of action on these proposals in the United States was enhanced by the introduction of adjustments in several Western countries during the late 1960s and early 1970s. Denmark introduced such an automatic adjustment in 1969; Holland introduced such a reform in 1971; and, most importantly, Canada enacted such legislation in 1973. Automatic adjustments have also been used in Latin American countries, which have experienced extremely high rates of inflation, but these countries have never relied on the personal income tax to the extent comparable with the United States.

CONCLUSIONS

No tax that would be acceptable and at the same time practically workable can be completely general in the sense that it exerts no economic or announcement effects. Of the major revenue producers currently employed in Western countries, the personal income tax meets the generality criterion better than any other tax. But the tax does exert major influences on individual behavior.

Any income tax must, to some extent, affect the decisions to earn income itself, and it also affects decisions concerning the type and the timing of income that is earned. The progressive income tax exerts more pronounced effects on behavior than the proportional income tax, which is, by definition, a more general tax. The progressive tax tends to discriminate more against risk taking and against saving.

Inflation causes some special problems with a progressive income tax. There is a basic incompatibility between long-continued inflation and the progressive rate structure of income tax, an incompatibility created by the practice of designating brackets, exemption levels, and other features in nominal monetary units. Inflation has the effect of increasing real rates of income tax by shifting persons to higher monetary brackets even without increases in real incomes. To prevent this unintended increase in real tax rates, some adjustment for the effects of inflation is suggested.

SUPPLEMENTARY READING

The book by Richard Goode, *The Individual Income Tax* (Washington, D.C.: The Brookings Institution, 1964) provides a comprehensive treatment of the economic effects of the tax, in particular application to existing federal institutions in the United States.

More particular studies dealing with important aspects of the tax are: Harold Groves, *Tax Treatment of the Family* (Washington, D.C.: The Brookings Institution, 1964), and Harry Kahn, *Personal Deductions in the Federal Income Tax* (New York: National Bureau of Economic Research, 1960).

For a general treatment of federal tax policy which concentrates heavily on the personal income tax, see Joseph A. Pechman, *Federal Tax Policy* (Washington, D.C.: The Brookings Institution, 1966).

25

The corporation income tax

The corporation income tax is a major revenue producer for the federal government. As was revealed in Table 21–1, in fiscal 1980 the tax on corporate income provided roughly 14 percent of all federal receipts. A total of about $71 billion was collected from this source.

The relative importance of the personal income tax compared to the corporate income tax is a post–World War II phenomenon. Up until 1944, the tax on corporate income was a more productive revenue source than the tax on individuals. Relative to the personal income tax, the corporation tax has continued to decline in importance in the postwar period.

THE TAX BASE

The corporation income tax, as it is applied in the U.S. federal revenue system, treats the business enterprise, or corporation, as a legal person. The income of this enterprise is subjected to taxation in much the same manner as individual income. In fact, the Internal Revenue Code includes both the tax on individuals and the tax on corporations under the same major heading, *Income Tax,* and many provisions of the Code apply equally to both taxes.

All receipts of the corporation over and above actual expenses are taxable, after appropriate deductions for depreciation and for interest paid out on loans. Of course, no personal exemptions are allowed a corporation, and there is a rather limited set of special deductions. In addition to state and local taxes paid, a corporation may take a deduction up to 5 percent of income for contributions to nonprofit organizations.

Capital gains are treated in roughly the same way under both taxes. Long-term gains for corporations are taxed at rates lower than those imposed on ordinary income. In 1979, the maximum rate was 28 percent. Capital losses are deductible to the extent that they offset capital gains, although there is a certain loss carry-over here as with the individual tax.

TAX ADMINISTRATION

One of the most difficult problems in administering the corporate income tax is that of placing appropriate guidelines on the degree of flexibility to be allowed firms in taking depreciation of assets. Complete freedom to depreciate assets at the time of the firm's choosing has never been allowed in the American system. Unless this is done, however, the tax authorities are obliged to lay down rules concerning what schemes are and are not acceptable. Until 1962, the authorities tended to follow rather rigid and conservative accounting precepts in this respect. As it came to be widely recognized that depreciation guidelines exert major influence on corporate investment policy, tax authorities, in 1962, substantially liberalized depreciation schedules. Acceptable asset lives were dramatically shortened in many instances, which means that corporations can now write off, in depreciation, the original or cost values of assets in a smaller number of years than was possible before 1962. This provides the corporation with an incentive to replace obsolete equipment more quickly.

In the Revenue Act of 1964, the rate on corporation income was reduced, but the timing of payments was modified so as to bring corporate payments more on a current basis. Corporations now pay the tax on a current basis, in quarterly remissions.

RATE STRUCTURE

There is some progression in the corporate rate structure with a maximum marginal rate of 46 percent imposed on corporate taxable income in excess of $100,000. Corporate taxes were reduced in 1978.

Prior to that reduction a maximum marginal rate of 48 percent was levied on taxable income in excess of $50,000. The corporate tax schedule contained in the 1978 legislation is given in Table 25–1.

TABLE 25–1
Corporation income tax schedule

Income bracket	Tax rate on income in the bracket
$ 0–$ 25,000	17%
25,000– 50,000	20
50,000– 75,000	30
75,000– 100,000	40
over $100,000	46

Averaging provisions have been included in the corporation income tax for some time. Clearly, the need for allowing corporations some adjustment for losses incurred in bad years makes the need for averaging provisions even more acute here than under the personal income tax. These provisions were liberalized in 1976 when the time period over which losses may be carried forward was extended from five to seven years. Corporations may also carry back losses over a three-year period. These provisions are reasonably sufficient for all corporations except those which incur losses over an extended period.

RATIONALE OF THE TAX

As suggested previously, the corporation is treated as a legal person for purposes of taxation. This treatment follows directly from the legal practice of considering the corporation in this way for many purposes, but it should be obvious that the corporate entity is, in no meaningful sense, something separate and apart from the living persons who own the entity. The tax on corporation income must be finally paid by some individual. In other words, the tax must result in the income of some individual or set of individuals being lower than it would be without the existence of the tax. Viewed in this light, there would seem little justification for taxing persons through the fiction of the corporation, as it were. A much more straightforward manner of taxing individual persons would seem to be to assess the full burden on them directly through the income tax on individual income receipts.

Attempts have been made from time to time, however, to provide some rationale for the levy of taxes on the corporation as distinct from the person. While the ultimate impact of the tax on some persons cannot be denied, it may be argued that the privilege of doing business in the corporate form is a privilege sanctioned by government, and that this privilege, in itself, is sufficiently valuable to those who invest in this form of business organization to warrant the levy of a special tax. This argument would carry considerably more weight if the advantages of conducting business under the corporate form were not quite so great. Actually, the major share of business activity in the United States is conducted by corporations. This general usage of the corporation reduces the argument for the separate tax on corporate income, for, if most investment takes this form, there is no real differential advantage provided by government to any special group of investors.

The attempts to justify the imposition of a tax on corporate income are, for the most part, made after the tax has been in existence for some time. It is far easier to explain the origin and the continuation of the tax than it is to provide a justification for it. The explanation is very simple. The political decision makers find it very easy to impose a tax on corporate income and very difficult to impose a tax on individual income. This is in large part due to the fact that the corporation is, in fact, a legal entity. Private people treat the corporation as something apart from its owners, and the real incidence of the tax, as we shall see later, is difficult to locate with any precision. Legislative bodies encounter relatively little opposition to taxes on corporate incomes. This becomes doubly true when the political climate is unfavorable to business.

CYCLICAL INSTABILITY OF REVENUES

The tax is based on the net incomes or profits of corporations. This includes both pure economic profit and the yield on equity capital. Both of these income shares tend to be residual. That is to say, contractual obligations of the corporation to pay for materials, to pay wages and salaries to workers, and to meet interest on bonded indebtedness represent the primary claims against the gross income. Only after these primary claims have been met does net income appear. This almost guarantees that in any situation where there is any degree of market fluctuation over time, the tax base will fluctuate rather widely from year to year. For this reason we find the revenues collected under the corporation income tax to be the most unstable federal revenue source.

THE DOUBLE TAXATION OF CORPORATE INCOME

Judged from the point of view of fairness or equity in the distribution of the overall tax burden among persons, the corporation income tax comes off very poorly in comparison with other taxes, and especially in comparison with the personal income tax. The levy of the tax on the income of the corporation, without regard to the personal ownership of the corporation leads to a situation where the actual rate of tax (assuming that owners do pay the tax) imposed on any individual is entirely capricious and almost unpredictable. If individual income is accepted as the most appropriate criterion for determining personal tax liability, the tax levied on corporate income is inequitable regardless of the incidence. If the tax falls on the equity shareholders of the corporation, the individual bearing the tax may be in a high-income or a low-income group. There is no necessary connection between the amount of common stock owned and the place in the income scale, but all individuals are subjected to the same rate of tax in this part of the fiscal system. If, on the other hand, the tax is passed along to consumers, it is equally unfair. While overall consumption may be a justifiable basis of taxation in some cases, little argument can be made for a discriminatory tax on those consumers who enjoy the products and services of the most profitable corporations.

The equity argument against the corporation income tax has often been put in terms of the double taxation aspects. If the flow conception of income is adopted, and if the tax is supposed to rest, in whole or in part, on the equity shareholders, the income of the corporation is subjected to double taxation, once as it is received as gross receipts of the corporation, and second, as it is received by the individual in dividend payments. As suggested earlier, the owner may escape a portion of the second tax by allowing the corporation to plow back earnings into expansion; but even here, if the capital gains are to be realized, the individual must pay gains tax.

If the accrual or accretion conception of income is adopted, there can be no double taxation. The whole question reduces to determining the most suitable criterion for placing a tax on individuals, for everyone must accept the fact that individuals, as such, ultimately pay all taxes. Thus, whereas the advocate of the flow conception of income would emphasize the double taxation, the advocate of the accretion conception would stress the inequitable treatment of the particular individuals who happen to be equity shareholders. There is little difference in the two positions. In either case, the special discrimination against corporate income receivers is not clearly justified.

An argument in favor of some discrimination may arise from the idea that in this country's individual income tax no special advantage is provided for the receipt of so-called earned income, that is, income received for the sale of labor services. There is some justification for treating labor incomes more favorably than nonlabor incomes. This is because a tax system cannot easily allow a deduction for depreciation of human capital. Yet it must be acknowledged that a part of all labor income is necessary to keep the "asset" of the human being alive and maintained. This distinction between labor income and nonlabor income, the income from assets and claims, suggests the appropriateness of some adjustment in rates, as the British tax does. This argument has been weakened somewhat due to the imposition of a maximum tax on earned income in the U.S. personal income tax system.

Proposals to reduce or eliminate the double taxation of corporate income generally involve some form of corporate tax integration. Sample proposals would be allowing the corporations to deduct dividend payments for tax purposes or, alternatively, allowing dividend recipients some credit against their personal tax liability based on corporate tax paid on the income from which dividends were distributed. The treatment of retained earnings is a somewhat more complex problem in terms of a complete integration of corporate income taxation. These earnings do not flow directly from the corporation to its stockholders but rather provide income to stockholders through the indirect route of capital gains. Computing any sort of credit to the stockholder for corporate taxes paid on capital gains income is obviously more complicated than that involved with dividend income. On the other hand, it might be argued that because capital gains already receive preferential treatment in the personal income tax structure, the whole problem of double taxation is less severe with respect to retained earnings than it is with respect to dividend income.

DIRECT ECONOMIC EFFECTS

Debt and equity financing

In traditional discussions of the effects of income tax on the behavior of corporations, the incentive offered to corporations to finance investment through borrowing rather than through the issue of equity capital has been stressed.

The tax is imposed on the net income of the corporation, sometimes called net profit, and this profit or income is defined in the way that accountants define profits. Actual expenses are deducted from gross receipts, and allowance is made for interest paid out on loans and for depreciation of capital equipment. But no allowance is made for dividends on equity capital invested in the corporation, even to the extent of some "normal" rate of return. Because the tax does not allow for some deduction of an average yield on equity, it actually is imposed on a part of what the economist, as opposed to the accountant, would call opportunity cost rather than profit.

In many cases, the corporation will face some choice between the two methods of financing an expansion from external sources. It may expand its equity through selling common stock or it may sell bonds. Since the tax allows the interest payments to be deducted from gross income before computing tax liability and does not allow any deduction for a return to equity, the traditional argument stated that there is a tax-induced premium put on debt financing. Hence, so the argument goes, the corporate income tax causes the corporate financial structure to be distorted toward debt and away from equity financing.

Taken in isolation, the argument is correct. But when the corporate income tax is put alongside the personal income tax in the overall revenue structure, the effects are not necessarily those which the isolated analysis would predict. As we noted earlier when discussing the personal income tax, there is a premium put on converting ordinary income receipts into capital gains distributions to the maximum extent that is possible. One of the most important means through which individuals may do this is to invest in corporate equity shares which shift upward in value as growth takes place. This effect, in independence from the corporation income tax, would place a premium on equity issues. When both taxes are considered, there is no necessary direction of effect on the corporate financial structure. The incentive toward debt financing under the corporate tax may be more than offset by the premium placed on equity financing by the capital gains provisions of the personal income tax.[1]

Expenditure to secure nontaxable income

The high marginal rate of tax on corporate income, 46 percent, must make many decisions of corporate managers different from what they would be in the absence of the tax. In a very real sense, when the corporation spends one additional dollar in a way that can be counted as an additional cost, it is bearing only one half of this cost. The remaining half is being shifted effectively to the shoulders of federal taxpayers in general. For each additional dollar that is spent by a corporation that is classified as a cost, there is a net reduction of roughly $0.50 in federal government revenues. The results of this tax seem clear; corporation managers will be less careful in making corporate outlays than they would be should the full outlay represent real costs to the corporation or its shareholders.

Care must be taken, however, not to press this apparent point too far. Insofar as an additional dollar's worth of outlay is intended to produce an additional dollar's worth or more of ordinary corporate income, the tax need not affect the decisions of management a great deal. While it remains true that the corporation will be giving up only about one half for each additional dollar of cost outlay, it will also earn only $0.50 on each additional dollar of income that the outlay generates. The marginal decision as to whether or not to undertake the production of additional output, to add a new line of product, or to introduce some innovation, for example, should not be greatly affected by the existence of the high marginal tax on income.

Certain outlays exist which will add to cost but will not directly add to taxable income. These cost outlays will provide a nontaxable return, and the incentive provided by the tax for the expansion of this sort of outlay is evident. For example, the effects of an increased outlay in institutional advertising may serve to increase the prestige and

---

[1]This analysis is treated in detail in Joseph E. Stiglitz, "Taxation, Corporate Financial Policy, and the Cost of Capital," *Public Economics*, vol. 2 (February 1973), pp. 1–34.

goodwill of the corporation without adding measurably to short-run taxable profits. Corporate philanthropy, which has been growing, may have the same effect. There seems little doubt but that corporations will be encouraged to spend more on such ventures, which are essentially productive of generalized long-range benefits that are not directly, or currently, subject to tax. Another familiar example that is often discussed has to do with corporation resistance to wage demands of unionized employees. If a corporation management feels that the granting of a general wage increase will lead to a more tranquil period of labor relations, this is one way that management, even if not the shareholders, can secure a higher nontaxable real income. Salary scales for executives may be similarly boosted upward through this factor.

Sluggishness in resource response to profit opportunities

A market economy is a profit and loss economy, and the function of profits and losses is that of serving as signaling devices which prompt the flow of resources into and out of various employments. At any one moment of time, there will be a wide divergence between rates of return in separate industries, and the economic structure will be in the process of adjusting to this fact. Resources will be observed moving into those industries where profit opportunities are relatively high and moving out of those industries where losses are being realized, and where they are expected to persist.

The corporate tax acts to reduce the relative spread between the profitable and unprofitable employments of resources. The signals for shifts of resources are, in a sense, "dimmed" by the tax, and it seems clear that this serves to slow down the time rate at which resources flow from one employment to another. The effect of the tax seems clearly to be that of introducing an unnecessary sluggishness into the response of the economy to dynamic changes.

INCIDENCE OF THE CORPORATION INCOME TAX

The most important direct economic effects of the corporation tax have been discussed above. More complex and indirect effects are also present, and the discussion of these introduces the whole question of incidence. This is a question that has been the subject of much discussion among businessmen, politicians, and economists for decades, without any satisfactory resolution, even among the experts. In the 1960s, several important studies were devoted to this topic, with the result that the average student has become perhaps more confused than ever.

Who does pay the corporation income tax? This is a very important question in itself since over $70 billion are collected annually from this source, a total that will rise as the economy develops unless rates are reduced. The answer to this question depends on the announcement effects that the tax is assumed to exert, and these effects will, in turn, depend on the appropriately chosen model for analyzing the behavior of corporations.

Neoclassical model: No short-run shifting, some long-run shifting

It will be useful to discuss several models. First, assume that the tax were levied (which it is not) on the "pure" economic profits of a corporation. In this case, an allowance would be made for some "normal" return on equity capital invested in the corporation, and this return would be deducted from gross receipts, along with explicit costs, before computing the tax base. In this case, economic analysis would lead to the prediction that the tax could not be shifted to consumers in either the short run or the long run. If it is imposed on pure profit, and if it takes the form of a percentage rate of such profit, there would be no rational motivation for the corporation to modify its behavior. Profit is maximized when marginal revenue equals marginal cost, and a tax on pure profits cannot directly affect either marginal revenue, which depends on buyers' evaluation of the product or service, or marginal cost, which depends on the production function. If the corporation is maximizing its pure profit in the absence of the tax, it cannot improve its behavior by reacting to the tax. Output will remain unchanged, and the prices of final products and services will remain unchanged. The tax reduces the net income accruing as a residual to owners of the equity shares in firms that secure differentially high profits. To be at all symmetrical, such a tax on pure profits would have to allow rebates for losses, or, in other words, to contain provision for full loss offsets. Whether or not such a tax would or would not generate any revenue, in the net, would depend on the extent to which pure profits exceed losses.

No long-run changes could be predicted to occur since the average or normal rate of return on capital would not be modified by the tax. The only important effect in this case would be the sluggishness element discussed briefly above.

This "hypothetical profits tax" provides a good beginning of analysis, but an important emendation must be introduced to make the model at all realistic. The corporation income tax, as it is actually imposed, does not employ pure profit as its base. No allowance is made for the genuine opportunity cost of owner-invested capital. The failure of the tax, as it exists, to exclude from the tax base some normal, or average, return on equity capital introduces the possibility that individual investors may escape some of their tax liability, even in the neoclassical model, by shifting their investments to other assets than corporate stock. This sort of shifting will, of course, be of the "long-run" variety, to use economist's jargon. There seems little doubt but that shifting of this sort does, in fact, occur, to a degree. Individuals invest smaller amounts in equity shares of corporations relative to other forms of business enterprise—individually owned proprietorships and partnerships. The great advantages that are present from business operations under the corporate form serve to reduce the magnitude of this shift, however, and the overall impact may be of rather limited importance.

A second effect will be the shifting of some funds away from direct investment in the operation of business enterprise. Individuals may try to escape the tax by investing in fixed yield claims and real assets (bonds and real property). This shift will drive the price of such assets down until an equilibrium is reestablished after the imposition of the tax. In balance, the total investment in fixed yield claims and income-yielding real assets is probably larger than it would be in the absence of the corporation income tax.

A third effect will operate through shifting funds into investments in human as opposed to nonhuman capital. Faced with comparable alternatives, the individual will be motivated to invest capital in his own income-earning potential rather than in corporate assets.

The changes discussed above are essentially allocative, and such changes could possibly occur even if the total supply of saving in the economy remains unchanged. However, the most important effect of the corporation income tax may be that of reducing the marginal return on all income-earning assets, the marginal productivity of investment throughout the economy. This reduction in yield may affect the incentive of individuals to save, and through this, real capital formation in the economy may be modified. Effects of this nature cannot be predicted with certainty, but some reduction in the overall rate of capital formation seems more probable than its opposite.

The foregoing effects—the shift from corporate to other forms of business organization, the shift of investment from equity shares to real assets and claims, the shift of some investment to human capital, and the possible reduction in saving and real capital formation—combine to make total investment in enterprises organized as corporations less than it would be without the tax, other elements in the analysis being equal. From this it follows that output in the corporate sector is somewhat lower than it would be without the tax. This implies, in turn, that prices of products and services produced in the corporate sector may be somewhat higher than would otherwise be the case. If this is true, then one of the effects of the tax, if not its incidence in narrow terms, tends to harm consumers of products of the corporate sector.

It should be noted, however, that the shifting of the tax that takes place in this model occurs over the long run, after full allowance is made for a shifting of investment from the corporate sector. A temporary or short-run shifting of the tax cannot readily take place, even when it is recognized that, as it is imposed, the tax is really not limited to pure profit. The modified analysis does not substantially affect the conclusions reached with the more simple model. The primary incidence of the tax rests with the investor, and any significant reduction in the rate of tax could not be expected to lead to sizable short-run reductions in the prices of goods and services.

General equilibrium model: A tax on capital

In a major theoretical paper published in 1962, Professor Arnold Harberger analyzed the corporate income tax as a levy on the return to capital invested in corporate enterprises. Employing a general equilibrium model, he was able to attain definitive conclusions as to the incidence of the tax which both reinforce and modify, to an extent, the conclusions of the neoclassical analysis discussed above.

Since the return to investment must be equalized in all employments, and since the tax is restricted to capital invested in corporations, it follows that pretax rates of return in the corporate sector must be higher than rates of return in the noncorporate sector. The equalization of post-tax returns between the corporate and the noncorporate sectors of the economy is accomplished, after the necessary long-run adjustments, by a shift of resources out of the corporate sector and into the noncorporate sector. This tends to reduce, generally, the rate of return on all invested capital. Prices of products and services produced in the corporate sector rise relative to the prices of products and services produced in the noncorporate sector.

Since the equalization of rates of return on investment is accomplished only through the shift of resources, differing assumptions as to the factor proportions between the different sectors can lead to changes in the structure of factor prices. And, in some of the models, an effect of the tax is a lowering of the return to labor as well as capital.

If this general equilibrium model is extended slightly to include the equalization of output prices as between the corporate and noncorporate sectors, which seems relevant since these sectors are not distinguishable in terms of product categories, then the differential price effects vanish. The final result is that the differentially large share of resources invested in nonincorporate employments implies a net inefficiency in resource use in the economy, in other words an excess burden of the corporation income tax.

Harberger developed his model based on the assumption that aggregate supplies of capital and labor were fixed in the economy. If we acknowledge that the stock of capital relative to the labor supply is the result of decisions by individual economic units to save and invest, a somewhat different approach to tax incidence may be required. The corporate tax lowers the return received by investors. One possible consequence is a lowering of the rate of saving and investment and, consequently, over the long run, a lowering of the capital stock relative to labor. This would allow a relatively greater share of corporate tax burden to be shifted to labor due to lowering of the marginal product of labor and hence, the real wage rate. This problem will be explained in greater detail in Chapter 28.

Market-power model: Short-run shifting

Businesspeople and politicians, as well as many economists, have not accepted either of the above models of corporate tax incidence. Much of the discussion of this tax suggests that there is an underlying prediction of short-run shifting. It seems to be presumed that the tax tends to be shifted forward to consumers of corporate products and services as soon as it is levied, and without the necessary allocative shifts in resources in the economy or the final effects of personal saving behavior.

Upon what theory of business behavior can such a prediction of short-run shifting be based? Quite clearly, assumptions about the nature of the pricing process different from those present in the neoclassical and general equilibrium models must be introduced here. If the corporation is not assumed to behave so as to maximize the present value of its expected profits stream but is instead assumed to price its products and services on some cost-plus or "satisfactory" profit basis, the tax may be shifted immediately to the consumer once it is levied. In this case, corporate tax rate reduction should also redound to the short-run benefit of the individual consumer.

The point at issue here concerns the appropriate model for analyzing the operation of the whole business sector of the economy. If the economy is strongly competitive, the very pressure of competitive survival will force business enterprises to follow a profit-maximizing policy. The firms that fail to act so as to maximize profits, which may also be minimizing losses, will be left out of the race. In strongly competitive sectors, therefore, no effective short-run shifting of the corporate income tax is possible. On the other hand, in the monopolized sectors of the economy the firm is not placed under the same pressure to be efficient in its operation and pricing policy; the competitive necessity that it follow a profit maximization rule is not so immediate here. The firm that posseses a substantial degree of monopoly power can decide to follow a policy of pricing its goods at some level that will yield "satisfactory" profits, provided, of course, that monopoly power implies positive profits, which need not be the case at all. Such a policy of "satisficing" rather than "maximizing" may be advantageous in that potential rivals may be discouraged from entering into close competition. Under some such assumptions as these, an increase in the corporate tax rate should lead the firm to increase the selling price of its product sufficiently to ensure that it receives the same profit after the rate increases as before. The tax is effectively shifted forward to consumers. And a substantial reduction in the rate leads to the opposite conclusions.

On balance, firms that are both willing to forego profit opportunities and able to forego them over the long term seem relatively scarce. If this conclusion is accepted, the market power model should have little predictive value. The corporate tax will be shifted to consumers in the short run only to a relatively limited extent.

EFFECT ON COLLECTIVE CHOICE

The corporation income tax may be criticized on many grounds, but one of its most serious implications is often overlooked by students of fiscal theory. Precisely because of the uncertainty concerning its real incidence and economic effects, the tax is convenient for politicians to impose on the general public. This is clearly evidenced by the continuing importance of the tax in the revenue structure despite the absence of any substantial support from economists. Yet no one would propose that the real costs of public services are lower because they are financed by the tax on corporations. The costs tend to be concealed from the ultimate taxpayer, whoever that may be. If this is the case, the decisions that must be made in balancing off the benefits of additional public services against the costs involved in an additional increment of taxes will not be based on a fully informed comparison of alternatives.

This point can be made obvious in terms of a simple example. Suppose that a new federal spending program, estimated to cost $5 billion annually, is proposed, and that this program is to be differentially financed with a higher rate of corporate income tax. Suppose, further, that you are given the task of writing to advise your member of Congress on the decision that must be made for or against the two proposals. Presumably you could, after a fashion, make some rough estimate of the benefits of the spending program. But how could you make even a rough estimate of the costs that the increase in the corporation tax rate would impose on you, personally? Yet if you could not do this, neither you nor the member of Congress can make a well-informed decision about the proposals presented.

SPECIAL FEATURES OF CORPORATE INCOME TAXATION

The discussion to this point has been devoted to an examination of the tax and its effects considered in general terms. There are several other important special features of the tax, as administered in the United States, and these features exert economic effects of some interest. It will be useful to discuss some of these briefly.

Loss carry-over and carry-back and corporate mergers

The element of progression in the corporate tax structure generates some need for income averaging in the treatment of fluctuating income, although the wide income brackets and the relatively low income level at which the maximum marginal rate is attained probably lessen the severity of this problem per se. A serious additional need for averaging under the corporate tax is based on the recognition that corporate profits are almost as likely to be negative as they are to be positive. And if the tax should be levied on positive profits alone without adjustment for years during which a corporation incurs losses, the tax would have a major effect in reducing investment in risky and uncertain enterprises. The rate of innovation in the economy might be substantially reduced.

The need for some adjustment for losses has, to some extent, been recognized in the administration of the corporation income tax. Loss carry-overs and carry-backs are allowed. If a corporation reports a net operating loss (negative profit) during a particular year, this loss may be carried back over the three preceding years and a tax refund claimed against taxes paid in those years. Or, alternatively, the corporation may carry this net operating loss forward over the next seven years, during which it will be allowed as a deduction against income, thus reducing corporate tax liability. These provisions allow a corporation to average out its income over a ten-year period in computing final tax liability.

With the exception of new corporations that experience losses from the start of their operation and, therefore, never earn income against which to offset the losses, these provisions do allow for substantially equivalent tax treatment of gains and losses.

The carry-over provisions have one important economic effect that may not be desirable. Insofar as the competitive economy is accepted as the norm for public policy, an institution that tends, on balance, to reduce the overall competitiveness of the system must be viewed with suspicion. The carry-over of losses makes the merging of corporate structures quite profitable under many circumstances, quite independently of any underlying or "real" benefits from the mergers. For example, let us suppose that a relatively inefficient corporation has accumulated a large operating loss carry-over. This corporation, given its current management, might never expect to have sufficient net taxable income to offset the operating loss carry-over. On the other hand, suppose that, at the same time, an efficient and successful corporation is making a larger current profit, all of which is fully taxable. It becomes advantageous, purely for tax reasons, for the successful and the unsuccessful corporations to merge, retaining the shell of the unsuccessful one, in order to utilize to the full measure the accumulated operating loss carry-overs. Each dollar of operating loss deduction "purchased" is worth 46 cents to the profitable management. It will not have to value the assets of the inefficient corporate shell very highly in order for a mutually advantageous merger to be effected, even if actual lines of production are quite different.

For any particular merger of this sort there need be little, if any, reduction in the overall competitiveness of the economy. But the cumulative effects of this provision for carry-overs in encouraging mergers will tend to cause an increasing concentration in the economy as a whole. In addition, there will be the evident tendency to include under the same corporate shell wholly distinct and unrelated production processes, making full ranges of specialization in management more difficult to achieve.

This effect on mergers does not suggest that operating loss carry-overs should be disallowed as a feature of the tax. It would be a relatively simple matter to reduce the incentive for mergers provided by the use of the carry-over provisions. The most severe would be that of disallowing any loss carry-over to a reorganized corporate structure. This would perhaps be overly severe, however, and might prevent the carrying forward of genuinely efficient mergers. Something should be worked out which allows those mergers that are genuinely "economic" to proceed without undue tax interference while at the same time preventing the purely tax-induced mergers from taking place.

Depletion allowances

Perhaps the most widely criticized provisions in the corporate income tax law for many years were those which allowed firms in certain extractive industries to deduct an allowance for depletion before computing taxable income. The rationale of depletion allowance was that ordinary depreciation charges against original costs of capital assets were not sufficient in extractive industries because the operation of the firms allowed depletion of assets, the reserves of the particular resource being extracted, which were of unknown value. The allowance was held to be necessary to encourage an "adequate" amount of development and exploration.

Depletion allowances are computed as a percentage of the gross income of the firm. Through 1974, the maximum allowance was 22 percent. Firms entitled to this maximum allowance could deduct, in other words, 22 percent of gross income before computing the tax base. This was, of course, over and above the deduction for ordinary depreciation for capital equipment and could be taken annually.

The economic effects of the depletion allowances were relatively easy to predict, and these were agreed on by most economic analysts. Insofar as the depletion allowances were excessive, and most experts agreed that they were, there was a clear tendency for additional capital investment to shift into favored areas of employment. Relative to the remaining investment opportunities, there would be overinvestment in the extractive industries that qualify for the depletion allowance. The rate of return net of tax would be equalized, but this would imply that the rate of return, gross of tax, would be lower in the extractive industries. The effect of the allowance was that of introducing a distortion into the resource allocation process, of generating an element of "inefficiency" in the nation's allocation of investment among competing opportunities.

In 1975, the depletion allowances granted to the oil and natural gas industries were eliminated with some minor exceptions. Allowances of other extractive industries were reduced.

INFLATION AND THE CORPORATE INCOME TAX

Several features of the corporate income tax structure have the effect of making real rates of taxation sensitive to inflation. First, the element of progression in the tax structure introduces the same types of effects as were discussed with respect to the progressive personal income tax in Chapter 24. Corporations which experience a purely nominal increase in taxable income which moves them into a higher marginal tax bracket will end up paying a larger real tax as a result. In addition, failure to appropriately adjust depreciation and inventory expenses for inflation also works to increase corporate tax burden in the face of inflation. The deductibility of interest expenses tends to work in the opposite direction in the sense that, if inflation is anticipated, a nominal inflation premium will be added to the real rate of interest. This factor combined with inflation-caused depreciation of the real value of the corporation's monetary debt works to offset the other effects increasing total real tax burden, although empirical study suggests that the offset is not complete. These problems will be discussed in greater detail in Chapter 27.

CONCLUSIONS

The tax on corporate income has been, and will continue to be, an important source of revenue for the federal government. This is true despite the fact that few arguments based on either economic or ethical grounds can be advanced in its favor. The tax is grossly unfair as to the distribution of burden among persons, and its economic effects, while unpredictable in large part, can scarcely be consistent with equity, efficiency, or growth objectives. The importance of the tax is explained largely by its popularity with the public and with the politician. Since its true effects and its real incidence remain obscure, the tax is accepted much more readily than the personal income tax. Among economists and tax experts, there remains widespread sentiment that the tax "should" be reduced and, ideally, eliminated. But to the political decision makers, the corporate tax does, in fact, provide a means of generating federal revenues without imposing charges directly on individual voters. Business firms do not vote, and from this simple fact it can be predicted that the tax will remain important.

SUPPLEMENTARY READING

For many years the standard treatment of the corporate income tax has been Richard Goode, *The Corporation Income Tax* (New York: John Wiley & Sons, Inc., 1951).

Important recent contributions to the discussion of corporate tax incidence are: A. C. Harberger, "The Incidence of the Corporate Income Tax," *Journal of Political Economy*, vol. 70 (June 1962), pp. 251–40; M. Krzyzaniak and R. A. Musgrave, *The Shifting of the Corporation Income Tax* (Baltimore: The Johns Hopkins Press, 1963); and Challis Hall, "Direct Shifting and Taxation of Corporate Profits in Manufacturing 1919–1959," *American Economic Review*, vol. 54 (May 1964), pp. 258–71.

Several separate contributions are included in *Effects of Corporation Income Tax*, ed. by M. Krzyzaniak (Detroit: Wayne State Press, 1966); and R. J. Gordon, "Incidence of Corporation Income Tax," *American Economic Review*, vol. 57 (September 1967), pp. 731–58.

26

Federal transfer taxation

The general revenues for the federal government are raised primarily from the income tax that is imposed on individuals and on corporations. Employment taxes are becoming increasingly important but the revenues produced from these are earmarked for the financing of the social security system. For the financing of general federal functions, aside from income taxes, there exist only the transfer and excise taxes, both relatively minor sources of revenue. For completeness, however, this brief chapter examines federal transfer taxation, and Chapter 27 examines federal excise taxation, but in the more general context of the use of taxation to restrict demand.

ESTATE AND GIFT TAXES

Taxes imposed on transfers of wealth—estate and gift taxes—produce for the federal government at current (1980) rates about $6 billion annually. This total is relatively unimportant with reference to total federal receipts. The distinct features of these taxes are such that it seems worthwhile to discuss them in somewhat greater detail than they warrant when considered purely in terms of their quantitative importance.

Tax legislation in 1976 substituted a single unified rate schedule and tax credit for the federal estate and gift taxes replacing the previous separate rate schedules and specific exemptions under the two taxes. The unified tax is progressive with marginal rates ranging from 18 percent on the first $10,000 of taxable transfers to 70 percent on transfers in excess of $5,000,000. The general tax credit, $42,500 in 1980 and $47,000 for the years thereafter, adds to this progressivity. The credit replaces a previous tax exemption for estates under $60,000 and a lifetime gift tax exemption of $30,000.

Federal estate tax˙

The base of this tax is the estate of the decedent at some estimated market value. Because of the general tax credit mentioned above, estates smaller than $175,000 are generally exempt from taxation after 1981. Sizable deductions are allowed under this tax for property passing to a surviving spouse. The maximum marital deduction is the greater of $250,000 or one half of the estate transferred to the spouse. In addition to the general tax credit, additional tax credits are allowed for state or foreign estate taxes and federal gift taxes. This credit provision against state taxes was originally introduced in order to encourage the states to enact estate tax legislation and to prevent interstate competition for the aged rich. With the credit it becomes highly advantageous for a state to impose a tax at least up to the limit of the federal credit since, if it does not, the taxpayer will have to pay the full amount of the federal tax anyway. Most state taxes are considerably in excess of the federal credit allowed.

The first distinctive feature to be noted about the federal estate tax is that it is levied on the *estate* of the decedent and not upon the *inheritance* of the recipient. Also, the rate progression is defined in terms of the gross estate. For example, assume that an estate is valued at $1 million, excluding exemptions and deductions, but including allowable credit against state taxes. The estate tax on this transfer will be the same regardless of whether or not it is received by one legatee or ten. An inheritance tax, by contrast, would be based on the amount of the transfer *received* by each legatee, and the gross tax on a $1 million estate would be larger if it were to be transferred to only one legatee than to ten, assuming that the rate structures were at all progressive.

The distinction between the estate tax and the inheritance tax introduces the second interesting feature of all taxes on transfers. By the nature of the transfer itself, two persons are involved in the determination of the tax liability. In discussing both the equity of the tax and the incidence and economic effects, the position and behavior of both parties to the transfer must be taken into account. The estate tax concentrates almost exclusively on the testator, the person who plans to bequeath the estate to others. Implicitly, this person is considered to be the one who finally pays the tax, since progression in the rate structure is determined by the size of the gross estate. Inheritance taxation, on the other hand, concentrates attention on the person who receives the bequest.

The incidence of the estate tax is not so evident as it might at first appear. The final burden of the tax would seem, at first glance, to rest with the recipients, since they will receive less as a result of the tax. But if the right of disposition over an estate is considered to provide some satisfaction to the testator, the reduction of this right through estate taxation clearly reduces this satisfaction, and he or she may be said to bear a portion of the final incidence. In any case, it is the behavior of the testator rather than that of the recipients that is likely to be modified as a result of the tax. The announcement or economic effects that do occur will be the result of this change in behavior.

These effects may take several forms. First of all, the testator will try, through all legal means, to evade the necessity of paying the tax through the planning of the estate in such a way that a portion of it will escape taxation. Various devices are possible through which this can be accomplished to a certain extent. These take the form of special trust fund devices, transfers through gifts before death, and many other devices in the domain of the professional estate planner. The actual economic effects must involve some change in the supply of labor services or in capital accumulation. The rich person, knowing that the estate will be heavily taxed, may be encouraged to retire earlier, to devote less energy to earning income, and to take longer vacations. The overall importance of this sort of reaction does not seem likely to be large, although it is, of course, very difficult to determine empirically.

A second possible effect is some reduction in the overall rate of saving, and through this, real capital formation. Individuals may not be deterred from earning incomes during their lifetimes by the knowledge that the estate tax will prevent their free disposition over all of the accumulated wealth, but they may be led to spend a somewhat greater proportion of earned income on current consumption than they would in the absence of the tax.

In a more practical way, the estate tax does have some effect on reducing the rate of real capital formation. The tax is sufficiently high on large estates to make necessary, in some cases, some breaking up of the ownership pattern in order to pay the tax. The assets of the estate must be placed on the market in order that sufficient funds to pay the tax can be secured. Insofar as this procedure disperses the ownership of the assets of the estate, some reduction in the concentration of wealth is accomplished and, with this, perhaps some reduction in the rate of capital formation. Rather than subject the estate to the tax, the individual may choose in such cases to bequeath the estate, in whole or in part, to a charitable or educational foundation. Through such a bequest the estate effectively escapes the tax, and, in one sense, the tax is shifted to the general federal taxpayer by such action.

The equitable basis for the imposition of high taxes on either estates or inheritances is well established and commands widespread acceptance. Inherent in the political philosophy of the free society is the idea that individuals should, insofar as is possible, be guaranteed some equality of opportunity. Despite the many ambiguities that this concept introduces, the unlimited right of individual persons to pass along accumulated wealth to heirs would seem to violate this equality of opportunity objective, as this is understood by most people. The taxation of transfers of wealth provides one means through which the government can ensure some greater equality of opportunity without, at the same time, causing major disincentive effects. In past discussions on this point, however, too much has perhaps been claimed for the tax on transfers of wealth on these grounds. If individuals' opportunities in life should depend solely on the pecuniary assets that they are able to inherit from their families, significantly greater equality might be achieved merely through a wise use of the estate and inheritance taxes. But it must be recognized that the opportunities of these individuals depend equally on the environment in which they have been reared and the families to which they have been born. These advantages and disadvantages, as the case may be, could never be equalized by a tax on the transfer of wealth in any measurable sense. Equality of opportunity must remain a desirable social objective, but one which can scarcely be attained. Estate and inheritance taxes should be recognized as one means of moving toward an accomplishment of the objective, but their inherent limitations must be fully acknowledged.

The federal gift tax

An individual is allowed to transfer as gifts up to $3,000 per year per recipient without being subject to any gift tax at all. This provision encourages dispersion of gifts among persons and the spreading of these gifts over time. There is no limit on the number of persons to whom gifts can be made and no limit on the number of years over which this exemption applies. Gifts to individuals in excess of $3,000 each become cumulative to the giver and these become the tax base of the gift tax. As noted, tax legislation in 1976 substituted a tax credit for the previous lifetime exemption of $30,000 on taxable gifts. Prior to 1976, gift tax rates were significantly below estate tax rates which encouraged transfer of wealth through gifts. Deliberate transfers through gifts in anticipation of death are not allowed and the general legal presumption is that gifts made within three years of death are of this nature and then become subject to estate taxation, unless it can be satisfactorily shown that estate tax avoidance was not the purpose of the gift. An estate tax credit for gift taxes serves to offset double taxation under these circumstances.

As with the estate tax, the donor is considered the party to the transfer that is subject to the tax. The recipient of the gift is not subjected to tax, even as ordinary income, since gifts are specifically exempted from the personal income tax. If the accretion conception of income were thoroughly adopted in tax administration, both inheritances and gifts would be subject to full taxation as personal incomes. The absence of effective averaging provisions in the latter tax would, however, make this inclusion of inheritances and gifts somewhat unfair to recipients relative to other income receivers. If inheritances and gifts were included in the individual income tax base, there would be much less reason for levying special estate and gift taxes on transfers. In one sense, therefore, the present special taxes on estates and gifts represent a substitute for including these accretions of wealth in the individual income tax base.

The real rate of tax on *inter vivos* gifts is increased with inflation because of the decreasing value of the annual and lifetime exemption. A $3,000 gift in 1980 is no greater in real terms, in purchasing power, than a gift of $1,500 in 1968. In order to isolate the effects of inflation from the rates of taxation, an inflation adjustment might be applied to both the estate and gift tax, as to the personal income tax.

SUPPLEMENTARY READING

Two Brookings Institution studies may be consulted for further treatment of federal transfer taxes. These are: Carl S. Shoup, *Federal Estate and Gift Taxes* (Washington, D.C.: The Brookings Institution, 1966); and Gerald J. Jantscher, *Trusts and Estate Taxation* (Washington, D.C.: The Brookings Institution, 1967). For a more recent study, see Richard E. Wagner, *Death and Taxes* (Washington, D.C.: American Enterprise Institute, 1973).

27

Federal excise taxes, and demand-restricting taxes generally considered: Sumptuary levies, pollution-control charges, and energy taxes

Federal excise taxes are discussed in this chapter, along with a more general discussion of taxation that is designed for nonrevenue purposes.

FEDERAL EXCISE TAXATION

Federal excise taxes were projected to generate more than $18 billion in revenues in fiscal 1980. In absolute terms, this is a significant total, but, relative to other general revenues of the federal government, it is unimportant. Of this total, approximately one half is earmarked for special trust funds, almost exclusively for the highway trust fund. Until 1974, this insured that outlay would be used on the nation's roads and streets, but new legislation now allows some diversion of highway trust fund revenues to support mass transit systems in urban areas. Aside from the taxes levied on items related to highway usage, which are, in one sense, indirect user charges, federal excise taxation is largely limited to the major sumptuary levies on tobacco and alcohol. For fiscal 1980, federal alcohol taxes were expected to produce $5.6 billion in revenues, while the federal taxes on tobacco produced roughly $2.5 billion.

Aside from the possible imposition of special demand-restricting taxes, to be discussed below, it seems desirable that federal reliance on excise taxation should be decreasing in importance. Excise and sales taxation provides a more efficient source of revenue for state governments in the overall U.S. fiscal structure. If the federal political structure—that is, an effective division of power between the central and the state governments—is to remain viable, with the states retaining some semblance of independent fiscal authority, a rough separation of tax sources seems highly desirable.

As we shall see in a later chapter, states do rely quite heavily on excise and sales taxation. For this reason, and since the analysis is the same regardless of the government imposing the tax, we shall not discuss here the economic effects of excise taxation. These will be discussed when we consider taxes at the state level.

TAXES TO RESTRICT DEMAND

The purpose of taxation is normally conceived to be the raising of revenues for financing the provision of goods and services provided by the government. This traditional purpose of taxation has been supplemented, since the 1930s, by a fiscal policy or macroeconomic norm. In orthodox Keynesian prescription, taxation provides an appropriate instrument to restrict aggregate monetary demand during periods of excessive inflation, quite apart from any budgetary financing that it facilitates. This prescription has been more widely accepted in textbook and classroom discussion than in the practical precepts of politicians. Legislatures have proven to be extremely reluctant to increase taxes except when overriding revenue needs are present, needs defined in the traditional sense.

We shall examine here another demand-restriction purpose of taxation, this time in the micro rather than the macro setting. We examine the possible use of selective and nongeneral taxation to cut back the final consumption of particular goods and services, with this restriction, as such, providing the purpose of the action.

Sumptuary taxes

Tax systems at all levels and throughout history have incorporated this demand-restricting purpose, but with varying importance. *Sumptuary* taxes have rarely been absent from tax structures. By definition, a sumptuary tax is one that is levied on the production, sale, or consumption of a commodity or service with the expressed intent of reducing its final consumption relative to other goods and services in the economy. The familiar levies on alcohol, tobacco, lottery tickets, horse and dog racing, playing cards, pool tables, and numerous other goods find their origins in this purpose, at least to some degree. The commodities or services in question here are those which are deemed "undesirable" as final consumption items by at least a significant proportion of the electorate, but for which there is acknowledged to exist a sizable demand which makes outright prohibition less feasible than taxation as a policy alternative. The paternalist puritan who frowns on others' consumption of such items is enabled, through selective taxation, to make the transgressors pay, thereby securing general budgetary revenues as a by-product. The public-choice approach to political decision making is helpful in understanding the persistence of sumptuary taxes in modern fiscal systems, despite economists' warnings that all such taxes violate both efficiency and equity precepts for taxation. Such taxes are best viewed as means, or instruments, through which the conflicting desires of the citizenry are reconciled, desires regarding the appropriate limits on individual freedom of choice in consumption.

We shall not discuss sumptuary taxes further in this chapter, except insofar as the same basic analysis applies over all cases of selective taxation. Instead we shall discuss different, but closely related, objectives of taxation, objectives that have become increasingly relevant in the policy discussion of the late 1970s. We shall discuss the possible use of selective commodity taxation to reduce the consumption of goods and services that do not fall within the familiar set defined by the paternalists' criteria. Specifically, we examine two types of tax, those which have been advanced as instruments for the control of pollution, or, more generally, for improving environmental quality, and those that have been proposed to reduce final consumption of energy in the face of unanticipated demand and supply shifts, notably in the markets for fuel oils and gasoline.

TAXATION AND POLLUTION CONTROLS[1]

Public and political recognition of the importance of environmental quality came only in the 1960s. Cleaning up the air and water, or at least the maintaining of defined quality standards, became significant national policy objectives. With relatively few exceptions, economists proposed the use of selective taxes or charges as the most suitable control instruments. They suggested that properly set effluent taxes be imposed on potential polluters, individuals, firms, or governmental agencies, whose ordinary economic behavior generates spillover effects that cause environmental quality to deteriorate. In more technical terms, units generating external diseconomies were to be subjected to penalty taxes measured by the extent of the spillover costs on all members of the community. Through a system of effluent charges or taxes, decision makers would be led to produce the efficient or optimal levels of pollution.

This textbook-type analysis sketched is simple and straightforward. Consider Figure 27–1, where D represents the demand curve for a single commodity; S represents the supply curve, with equilibrium price at P. Suppose that it is now recognized that the production or use of this good involves a social or spillover cost that has been previously unknown, which is measured in per unit terms by T. The policy implication is clear. If a tax per unit of T is levied, price will rise to P'; quantity demanded will fall to Q', and the economy will again attain efficient results because full social cost will be incorporated into price.

The use of taxes to control pollution appeals to economists because it allows the ultimate objective, better environmental quality, to be secured indirectly. If the tax is accurately set, producers and consumers will be led, by their own profit-seeking and utility-maximizing behavior, to generate results that are socially efficient. There will be no need for direct governmental or bureaucratic regulation.

The economists' argument for penalty taxes or pollution charges as

---

[1]The analysis of this section is treated in more detail in the paper, James M. Buchanan and Gordon Tullock, "Polluters' Profits and Political Response," *American Economic Reveiw* (March, 1975).

FIGURE 27–1
Pollution taxes

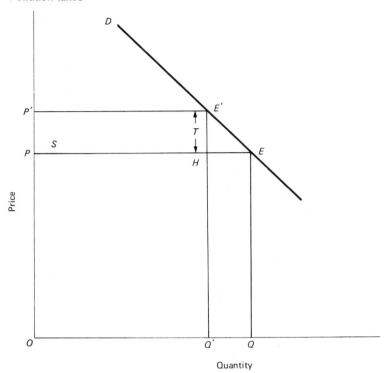

Quantity

instruments to reduce market demand is indeed a strong one. None-theless, actual usage of these instruments seems to be exceptional. Politicians seem to prefer direct regulation in the form of explicit prohibitions or restrictions on specific actions. How can this procliv-ity be explained? Why are taxes widely employed as demand-restricting devices for sumptuary items and shunned for similar ap-plications in pollution control?

The public choice approach to political decision making offers an understanding of the differences in the two cases. As noted, in the case of sumptuary levies, large numbers of citizens desire that the final consumption of certain items be sharply restricted or even eliminated, while other citizens desire freedom of purchase and use with respect to these items. Sumptuary taxes offer a means of com-promising these basic value conflicts in the community. By contrast with this, all, or nearly all, citizens in the community may be the final consumers, or users, of the commodities or services which, in either the production or the consumption process or both, generate pollution. For example, almost everyone uses electricity, yet its generation and distribution may affect environmental quality. Despite the universality or near universality of consumption of such commodities, however, all persons, or substantially all, may recognize the effects on environmental quality and they may acknowledge the need to restrict final demand.

Under these conditions, we may consider the penalty tax and the direct regulation alternatives. Suppose that the commodity is produced under conditions of constant long-run cost and that the industry is organized competitively. This is the situation depicted in Figure 27–1. Suppose that an accurately measured tax is imposed on producing firms. In the long-run, price will rise to P', quantity produced will fall to Q', and the socially efficient results will be achieved. Suppose now that, instead of the penalty tax, producers in the industry are directly regulated as to output. They are directed to reduce total industry output to Q'. In this case, price will again rise to P'.

At an elementary level of comparison, consumers will be placed in identical positions under these policy alternatives. But producing firms, and those persons who are employed by these firms, will clearly prefer the direct regulation, even if the industry is competitively organized. In effect, the direct regulation has the effect of enforcing a cartel-like restriction of output on the industry, to the benefit of producing firms, and their owners and employees. The restrictions on output will, of course, push market price above long-run costs. This will, in its turn, offer strong incentives for existing firms to expand rates of output and for new producing firms to enter the industry. Through either or both of these effects, the profit opportunities that the direct regulations generate may be dissipated over the long run. But short-term profits will be made in any case, whereas firms can only anticipate short-term losses under the imposition of the penalty tax. The producers' pressures put on politicians for the enactment of direct regulatory measures, rather than penalty taxes, may be too strong to resist.

At a more sophisticated level of comparison, these pressures may, or should be, somewhat offset by consumers' preference for the penalty tax alternative. The tax, if levied, produces revenues, and revenues finance public goods and services which are presumably valued positively by beneficiaries. To the extent that this benefit side of the fiscal account is recognized to be directly related to the levy of the tax, prospective beneficiaries among consumers of the commodity taxes should clearly prefer this to direct regulation. Under the latter, as noted, the differential between price and cost at the restricted output accrues to producers. Under the tax, this differential accrues to government and, ultimately, to public goods beneficiaries, at least in part. If, however, pollution-generating production or consumption activity involves a good or service that is relatively unimportant in the average consumer's total budget, the political pressures from consumers, as a group, are likely to be insignificant relative to those of producer groups.

THE TAXATION OF ENERGY

Neither the use of resources in producing energy nor the final consumption of energy itself need reduce the quality of the environment, although specific ways of producing and/or using energy resources have been the focus of much attention in the pollution-control discussions of the 1960s and 1970s. The generalized production and consumption of energy may, however, give rise to problems of social control that are similar to those that arise in attempts to improve environmental quality. Recognition that the natural resource base is finite, and, thereby, potentially exhaustible, leads directly to conservationist arguments which are fully analogous to pollution-control arguments. In both cases, there may be widespread agreement to the effect that the demands placed on resources should be somehow constrained, or restricted, over and above the restrictions that a freely functioning system of market pricing would necessarily ensure. Price adjustments, even if these should be allowed freely to operate, may not be considered to embody sufficiently the potential exhaustibility of the resource base. (We need not examine the economic validity of this argument here. For our purposes, it is enough to note that many persons accept such an argument, and that proposals for restricting energy usage generally were widely advanced in the mid-1970s.)

We may analyze the effects of imposing a general tax on energy in the same manner as that applied to a specific excise levy. With energy usage generally, however, we cannot assume (as we did in the construction of Figure 27–1) that long-run per unit costs are constant. In Figure 27–2 therefore, we have drawn an upsloping long-run industry supply curve. The effect of a unit tax on all energy production, say, on

BTUs, would be to drive a wedge between market price after tax, P_a in Figure 27-2 and the price received by producing firms, P_b, while reducing the quantity of energy used from Q to Q'. To consumers, the introduction of the tax is equivalent in effect to a shift leftward in the supply schedule; to producers, the introduction of the tax is the same as a shift downward in the demand schedule. Ignoring the benefits or expenditure side of the fiscal account, both groups will tend to oppose the tax.

But if energy usage, overall, is to be curtailed, what is the alternative to the general tax? What direct regulation alternatives may be considered that would accomplish roughly the same aggregate results? The government may impose quantitative restrictions on the output of firms, ensuring that overall production is reduced to Q'. In this case, however, consumers will find that market prices will be the same as those emerging under the tax alternative, and that quantities demanded will, of course, be identical in the two cases. Under such direct regulation, producing firms, and the owners and employees of such firms rather than the government, will secure the differential rents or profits that are created by the wedge between market price and cost price. As noted earlier, to the extent that producer interests dominate the political choice-making process, we should predict that the direct regulation alternative would be selected rather than the energy tax.

Under normal and piecemeal implementation of economic policy, producer interests will tend to be overrepresented relative to those of consumers. This is because of the concentration of costs and benefits, which make investment in political activity profitable to producing groups and unprofitable to consuming groups. The generalized interests of all consumers may be important in the large, but no person or small group may find it sufficiently important to attempt to influence collective outcomes. Under such configurations, political decisions tend to be biased toward the support of producer interests.

With a generalized and very important commodity or service such as energy, however, this bias may not be present. For a sufficiently important item in the consumer budget, the interests of consumers may offer ample opportunity for political entrepreneurship. This has become especially true after the rise of various consumerism movements in the 1960s. Consumers' interest may lie in restricting overall demands on energy in such a manner that neither producing firms nor the government capture the rents generated by the wedge in-

FIGURE 27–2

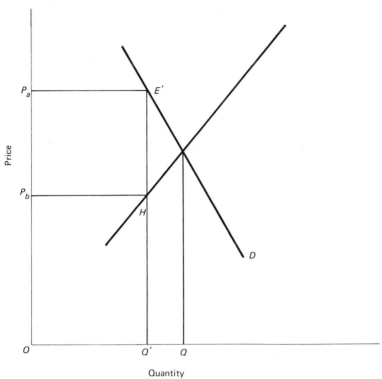

Quantity

serted between market price and cost price at the desired overall quantity levels.

Such a result may be accomplished by controlling market price, by holding it at P_b in the construction of Figure 27–2, while restricting quantities demanded to the available supply, Q'. At this solution, producing firms will remain in equilibrium at H; the solution lies on the industry (and firms') supply schedule. Consumers are forced out of equilibrium; at price P_b, they would prefer to purchase a larger quantity than that which is made available to them. Nonprice rationing of some sort must emerge to allocate the artificially created shortfall among potential demanders, whether this is formal coupon-type rationing or informal waiting-line, favoritism schemes. Institutional means of subverting the price control limits may, of course, be predicted to arise over time. But, for our purposes, note that consumers, as a group, will think themselves better off at the disequilibrium position, H, than they would be at the market equilibrium position, E', which reflects the market-clearing solution for the restricted quantity Q'. To the extent that consumers think in this fashion, and act accordingly through their pressure groups and political representatives, strong pressures may emerge for the price control-rationing package, as opposed either to the simple quantity restrictions or to the levy of a general energy tax designed to allow governmental collection of the differential rents.

The analysis suggests that, in democratic political or public choice settings, regardless of whether producer or consumer interests dominate, the demand-restricting tax does not rank highly as a control instrument. Politicians are, predictably, reluctant to listen to the advice of economists and to impose such taxes.

SUPPLY SHORTFALLS

The discussion of the generalized energy tax is helpful in understanding the political reaction to the so-called "energy crisis" which was one of the dominant policy issues during the 1970s and which seemed likely to continue as an important source of controversy well into the 1980s. The Arab oil embargo in late 1973 and early 1974 resulted in a significant reduction in crude oil supplies to the United States. The market was not allowed to freely adjust so as to bring reduced supplies into balance with demand at market clearing prices. Instead, price controls were maintained, necessarily creating artificial shortages in the relevant energy markets. Economists were very critical of political decision makers during this whole period, most notably because of their apparent failure to recognize this most elementary of economic principles.

The public choice approach to political process, which has been applied to both pollution control and energy taxation earlier in this chapter, allows the behavior of political leaders to be explained readily. Given the existence of nominal price controls which had been in effect since 1971, the unanticipated shortfall in oil supplies created an initial market disequilibrium. At the prevailing controlled prices, quantities demanded exceeded available non-Arab supplies. In order to eliminate the shortages and at the same time to forestall any need for nonprice rationing, controls could have been removed and prices allowed to rise to market-clearing levels. This action would have resulted in windfall profits to oil producing firms, domestic and non-

Arab foreign, which continued to supply the U.S. market. Consumers would have been confronted with higher prices, although there would have been no shortages as such.

As the construction on Figure 27–2 indicates, consumers, as a group, would have remained better off, at least in the short run, had prices been held at the artificially controlled level, P_b, and had non-price rationing of available supplies been introduced. Under this arrangement, the differential rents which might otherwise have gone to producing firms could instead, have been retained by consumers.

The price controls on domestic crude oil supplies and refined products were retained through the late 1970s. The end of the oil embargo eased market shortages considerably, both because of the renewed flow of petroleum from the Middle East and because price increases on foreign oil supplies dictated by the Organization of Petroleum Exporting Countries (OPEC) were under existing regulations passed on, in part, to consumers. However, periodic shortages, most notably of winter heating oil, also characterized this period. In 1979, following the Iranian revolution, during which exports of crude oil to the United States were sharply curtailed, shortages of heating oil and also of gasoline and diesel fuel again threatened to become severe. Political debate over the desirability of retaining existing price controls was heated. President Carter began lifting these controls in mid-1979, in accordance with authority granted by existing legislation which provided for complete removal of controls by 1981. However, political resistance on the part of consumers to this move was very similar to that which had led to original imposition of the controls.

EXCESS PROFIT TAXES

Partly in an attempt to appease consumer interests, the Carter Administration proposed to accompany decontrol of domestic oil supplies with an "excess profits" tax on the domestic oil industry. Price controls involve a cost through discouragement of supply increases over the long run. If price is retained at P_b in Figure 27–2, suppliers have no incentive to move upward along the supply curve whereas if price is allowed to move toward P_a, strong profit incentives are brought into play for increasing supplies of oil. However, the receipt of excess profits by producing firms which this latter policy would embody was not fully acceptable in the political climate of the late

1970s. This combination of circumstances prompted proposals for excess profits taxes on oil-producing firms.

The practical difficulties in levying and administering excess profits taxes are significant. These difficulties stem largely from the problems that arise in defining just what share of reported profits are "excess," along with problems of ensuring adequate supply-increasing response by producers while simultaneously capturing for the government some share of windfalls.

part VI

Inflation, capital formation, and government policy

28

Inflation, taxes, and resource allocation

The general level of prices, as measured by the consumer price index, almost doubled in the United States during the decade between 1968 and 1978. Although inflation had been a fairly persistent problem in the American economy in the years since World War II, this was the worst of those three decades in terms of sustained, rapid increases in money prices. During the *two* decades preceding 1968, for example, the overall increase in the price level was only in the neighborhood of 40 percent. By the late 1970s, inflation had become a problem of significant social and political concern and the seeming impotence of government policy in alleviating this problem suggested a continuation of this concern into the 1980s.

What causes inflation and what are its consequences? These are relevant issues to address in a public finance course because both are directly related to government policy. Recall that, in Chapter 4, monetary stability was listed as one of several collective goods for which the public sector might be assigned responsibility. As noted above, this responsibility is not one which has been satisfactorily fulfilled in recent years. The primary reason for this failure would seem to be that inflation is a type of disguised tax which democratic politicians, under pressure from their constituents to increase public sector benefits but not taxes, have found to be an attractive levy.

INFLATION AS A TAX

Throughout much of recorded history, governments have financed a portion of their public expenditures through deliberate deprecia-tion of the monetary unit. Early in the development of the market economy, the prince secured control over the "coin of the realm." This was secured even before the right to levy taxes, and the prince soon found that this right to coin money offered an opportunity to finance the purchase of services without the knowledge of his sub-jects. He could tax them without their being aware of it by clipping off the edges of all coins that passed through the royal treasury. In this way he could accumulate a surplus of precious metal which he could then melt down and reissue in the form of new coins. With these newly issued coins he could pay for the goods and services de-sired by the "government." This deliberate increase in the supply of circulating monetary units without, at the same time, any corre-sponding increase in the supply of real goods and services resulted in an increase in the level of product prices; that is, in inflation.

In this very simple conjectural model, which does, in its fundamen-tals, describe what went on during certain historical periods, the tax-ation implicit in this sort of inflationary process is clear. The "prince" depreciated the currency as a means of financing "public" services; this was an alternative to the more conventional methods of taxation. The tax was popular with the "prince" because he could conceal its effects, at least in part, from the citizens.

Since the process produced real goods and services for the "prince," someone must have suffered a real income reduction in the operation. Some individuals or groups must have borne the final in-cidence of the tax. Who really paid for the expanded "public" services enjoyed by the "prince" and his court? Those individuals and groups who held assets in the form of cash were the final bearers of the tax. Since the value of the monetary unit was reduced, the real goods and services that were commanded by a given stock of cash were reduced. The inflation had effects equivalent to a special tax imposed on all holders of cash and claims to cash.

INFLATION IN A MODERN ECONOMY

Minting arose as a means of preventing the medieval prince from devaluing the currency. But history also teaches that governments of modern national states finance expenditures in the same way, although the actual practice is much more sophisticated than that adopted earlier. Unless a commodity standard of money is in existence, and there are no such standards at the present time, national governments possess the power to regulate the value of the monetary unit through their control over the supply of money. This power of controlling the supply of money gives governmental authorities an almost irresistible temptation and opportunity to finance public services through currency depreciation; that is, through inflation, rather than through orthodox means of taxation.

How do modern governments generate inflation? In popular discussion, inflation is related to the failure of the federal government to keep spending within the limits of revenues, to the generation of budgetary deficits. This relationship between deficit financing and inflation in popular and political discussion is basically correct, but the precise institutional instruments should be examined more carefully. To the extent that the government creates a deficit, public spending must be financed by resort to some means other than explicitly imposed taxes. The two basic alternatives are debt issue and money creation. If, when a deficit is created, government should be forced to borrow, to issue bonds, there need be no inflation. The funds to finance the deficit would be drawn directly from private consumption or from private investment, assuming a fully employed economy. The power to regulate the supply of money in the economy rests with the Federal Reserve Board, and this power is exercised through the Board's control over banks and bank reserves. If the Board so chooses, it can ensure that government deficits generate no inflationary pressures at all. However, if the Board assists the Treasury by keeping interest rates down when a deficit is funded, there is a direct relationship between an increase in the deficit and an increase in the supply of money. This relationship emerges even more clearly when the Treasury is allowed to "borrow" from the banking system, which is the modern equivalent of simply running the printing presses. To the extent that this is allowed to take place, the costs of the deficit show up, not in increased interest rates and lowered private investment and consumption, but in the increase in the supply of money and its consequences.

The precise relationship between government deficits and inflation depends, therefore, on the behavior of the Federal Reserve Board. Furthermore, the effects of inflation on the economy depend on the underlying conditions. If the economy should be in recession, with major unemployment, financing deficits with outright creation of money may well be desirable. The effects may be to increase employment without undue upward pressures on the level of prices. In this setting, inflation cannot be treated as a tax. On the other hand, when resources are fully employed, or, even if they are not, when there exist major rigidities in the system, inflation will tend to drive up prices. This amounts to the levy of a tax on the holders and users of monetary assets.

INFLATION AND REAL RATES OF PERSONAL AND CORPORATE INCOME TAXATION

Money creation adds to real public sector revenue not only through the pure inflation tax as described above, but also as a result of inflation-induced increases in real rates of personal and corporate income taxation. Like the inflation levy per se, these latter tax increases are unlegislated in the sense that no formal action by the Congress is required to bring them about. They occur because the tax structure was not designed for an economy characterized by persistent inflation.

The impact of inflation on the progressive personal income tax has already been discussed in some detail in Chapter 24 and need only be reviewed briefly here. Recall that it is primarily the progressive rate structure which makes real rates of personal income taxation sensitive to inflation. When an inflation is occurring, money prices and money incomes tend to rise more or less together. (Actually, money incomes tend to rise somewhat more rapidly than the price level. This reflects the growth in real per capita income which tends to occur over time, irrespective of inflation, and which can be safely ignored here.) If the general price level rises by, say, 10 percent and an individual's money income also rises by 10 percent, real gross income is unchanged. If the personal income tax were a proportional tax, nominal tax burden would also rise by 10 percent, leaving real tax burden and hence real disposable income unchanged.

With a progressive income tax levied on a nominal base, however, an increase of 10 percent in money income will result in a more than 10 percent increase in nominal tax burden and thus an increase in real tax burden. Even though the gross income of the household has not changed in terms of real purchasing power, real after-tax income has fallen reflecting the increased real transfer to the public sector.

This effect is magnified when such items as personal exemptions and deductions are stated in dollar terms which decline in real value with the inflation. This latter effect, it should be noted, would also occur if the tax structure were not progressive.

As was noted in Chapter 25, there is some progression in the rate structure of the federal corporate income tax. As a consequence, this tax is also sensitive to the same type of inflation-induced increases in real tax rates as occur with the progressive personal income tax. However, the maximum marginal tax rate of 46 percent is attained when corporate taxable income reaches the level of $100,000. This constrains the amount of extra revenue which can be obtained from inflation in the standard way. However, three important features in the definition of taxable income are significantly affected by inflation and play an important role in making real tax rates sensitive to inflation. These are the treatment of depreciation, of inventory expenses, and of debt-financed capital.

The real value of depreciation expenses which can be deducted from gross corporate income for tax purposes is reduced by inflation. This is because depreciation is computed on a historic cost rather than a replacement cost basis. Suppose, for example, that a new machine cost the corporation $10,000. There are several ways under current tax law in which the corporation can spread depreciation expenses over time for tax purposes, but regardless of the method chosen, the maximum total depreciation expense which can be taken as a deduction on the machine is $10,000. If an inflation takes place during the depreciation period, the real value of the deduction is obviously reduced. Suppose, for example, that the corporation opted for straight line depreciation which would involve simply deducting $1,000 during each year of the presumed ten year life of the machine. With an increasing price level, the real value of this deduction will fall every year. Hence, assuming other factors constant in real terms, the real tax liability of the corporation will increase each year, whereas it would be unchanged if the price level were stable.

Inventory expenses are affected in much the same way. When the firm uses items from its inventory, it deducts as the cost of the item the original acquisition cost, not the replacement cost. The latter is the more correct measure of true opportunity cost. If the price level were stable, the difference in accounting treatment of inventory costs would be relatively insignificant. With a rising price level, however, current methods of measuring this component of costs will under-state the true value.

When an inflation occurs, outstanding debt liabilities of the corpo-ration fall in real terms. In addition, if the inflation is anticipated, the nominal interest rate will include an inflation premium. Under the corporate tax, the gain to the corporation from the reduction in its real debt is not subject to taxation. In addition, nominal interest payments are deductible for tax purposes. These two factors, consid-ered together, work to reduce corporate tax liability when inflation increases. However, empirical work by Professor Martin Feldstein and Lawrence Summers[1] suggests that the favorable treatment of corporate debt in the face of inflation does not completely offset the unfavorable treatment of depreciation and inventory expenses. In 1977, for example, when the inflation rate was almost 7 percent, in-creased taxes paid by corporations because of the understating of real depreciation and inventory expenses amounted to approximately $26 billion dollars. The reduction in tax liability due to the treatment of debt was only about $15 billion leaving a net inflation-induced in-crease in corporate tax liability of $11 billion.

In order to completely measure the impact of inflation on the total real tax burden borne by capital income in the corporate sector, it is important to look not only at the effect on real rates of taxation under the corporate income tax, but also to consider the effect on taxation of this income under the personal income tax. Inflation tends to in-crease this component of tax burden.

For example, the inflation-induced reduction in the real value of the corporation's monetary liabilities, described earlier, is an addi-tion to real corporate income. It is, however, the result of a pure in-come transfer to the corporation from its monetary creditors. No real increase in income produced in the corporate sector is involved. The gain to the corporation is not subject to tax under current corporate income tax laws. This point was discussed above. At the same time, the income loss of creditors is not included in the measure of income subject to personal income taxation. Considering this effect alone, real corporate income is understated for tax purposes and real per-sonal income overstated. The total effect on tax burden borne by cor-

---

[1]Martin Feldstein and Lawrence Summers, "Inflation and Taxation of Capital In-come in the Corporate Sector," NBER Working Paper, 1978.

porate income depends on the relative rates of corporate and personal income tax. If the average corporate rate exceeds the average personal rate, a net reduction in total tax liability results and vice versa. Empirical evidence by Feldstein and Summers suggests that these two effects are almost precisely offsetting under the U.S. tax system.

Corporate earnings net of tax accrue to the shareholders and can either be paid out as dividends or reinvested by the corporation. In the former case, dividend income received by corporate shareholders is subject to personal income taxation at normal rates. Retained earnings, on the other hand, generally increase the market value of the shares of corporate stock. This increase will be taxed as a capital gain if and when the stock is sold.

To the extent that inflation increases real corporate tax burden, which seems to be the case in the United States, income available for retained earnings or for dividend payments is reduced. The reduction in dividends tends to partially offset the inflation-caused increase in taxation at the corporate level. This is because no personal income tax is paid on that portion of corporate income used to meet corporate tax liabilities. The tax treatment of capital gains is more complicated, however. Under current tax laws capital gains are measured in nominal terms. A capital gain is defined as the difference between selling price and original purchase price. If the price level has increased during the period for which the capital gain is computed, an increase in the nominal selling price of a share of stock over its original purchase price may reflect no increase in real value. Nevertheless, under current tax laws, the seller would incur a capital gains liability. Thus, even though greater corporate tax liability results from the inflation and hence reinvested retained earnings are smaller than if no inflation had occurred, shareholders are subjected to increased capital gains tax liability because of the increase in the nominal value of their stock holdings.

The Feldstein-Summers study estimated that real personal income tax payments were approximately $21 billion higher in 1977 due to the effects of inflation on personal income originating in the corporate sector. Adding the estimated $11 billion increase in corporate tax liabilities, the total tax paid on corporate income during that year was $32 billion higher than would have been the case if the price level had been stable.

ECONOMIC EFFECTS OF INFLATION

In this setting it is useful to trace the economic effects of inflation in the same way that these may be traced for other taxes. What will be the effect of inflation on individual behavior patterns? What action will persons try to take to avoid the tax that inflation represents? Upon whom does the final incidence of the tax rest, even after account is taken of possible shifting?

The first point to be noted is that inflation, as an announced policy, will have different effects from inflation that is unexpected. If inflation is explicitly adopted as a policy, thus making it fully analogous with orthodox taxation, individuals and groups can take whatever action is available to escape the tax, to shift it to others. On the other hand, if inflation is unexpected there can be no announcement effect. The incidence must rest on those "caught," so to speak, when the action takes place.

If an inflationary fiscal policy continues for any length of time, the announcement effects will begin to be important. Governments will almost never announce inflation as a deliberate goal of policy, but repeated resort to the printing press or its modern equivalent ensures that these announcement effects will take place. Over the long run, the results will be almost equivalent to a policy of announced inflation.

When individuals expect inflation to occur, they will take action to prevent being subjected to the tax if possible. They will attempt to convert their asset holdings from money form into goods. If we recognize that various assets represent varying degrees of "moneyness" (liquidity), we can say that individuals, expecting inflation, will try to shift as far away from money as is possible. They will purchase those assets and claims that represent real values, the money values of which are expected to rise as the inflation proceeds. Prices of things such as land, real property of all sorts, and equity shares of debtor firms will tend to rise. The value of claims to fixed amounts of money, for example, bonds, will fall sharply as the demand falls off and the supply increases. Yield rates on such claims will rise. Wage contracts will not be renewed in the absence of escalator clauses adjusting wage payments to increases in the price level. The demand for real money balances will be reduced, and the interest rate on money will rise to include an adjustment for the expected rate of inflation. The velocity of circulation of money will rise rapidly.

In this situation, after the adjustment to an equilibrium path of inflation that is fully anticipated, the tax will be paid by those who must use money. This may be illustrated by reference to the case of complete avoidance of the tax. If, for example, individuals could dispense with the use of money altogether, the government could not collect this tax. The case is exactly the same as the tax on liquor which individuals may completely escape by consuming a zero amount. If individuals were willing, in fact, to "consume" a zero amount of monetary services, the government could not impose any tax by inflating the currency. No one would be willing to give up real resources for money in such circumstances.

It is clear that the modern economy requires money for its operation. Transactions must be made, goods and services must be exchanged, through a medium of money. Therefore, despite all attempts to escape the tax, and despite the undesirability of cash as an asset during periods of expected inflation, cash will be used. This will allow the government to continue to collect the tax through currency creation, and this taxation must be borne by those members of the group who must, by the nature of their economic activity, hold cash over time. The cash that is utilized must be held at all times by someone in the group, and these holders of cash will be subjected to the tax in proportion to the amounts held and the length of time held. Claims to fixed amounts of cash will completely disappear in the fully adjusted inflationary economy.

The expected or anticipated inflation will involve some wastage of resources in the use of substitutes for cash. Payments will be made more quickly, and various costly devices of barter will be arranged. These are costly in terms of economic resources. These may be said to constitute the excess burden of the tax.

There are other consequences of inflation in addition to those described above. Recall, for example, the earlier discussion of the impact of inflation on the total real tax rate levied on capital income originating in the corporate sector. To the extent that inflation-induced changes in the real rate of tax levied on capital income are more or less permanent and not eliminated through periodic adjustments in the nominal rate structure, the real net rate of return on investment, and consequently the rate of capital formation and economic growth, are made sensitive to the inflation rate.

Professor Axel Leijonhufvud[2] has argued that there are other con-

---

[2]Axel Leijonhufvud, "Costs and Consequences of Inflation," in G. C. Harcourt, *The Microeconomic Foundations of Macroeconomics* (London: Macmillan and Co., 1977).

sequences of inflation which arise because of the inability of individuals to predict the future inflation rate with certainty. Although individuals may expect inflation, based on past experience, it is difficult for them to know precisely how much inflation will occur. Future inflation is affected by government policy which is itself unpredictable. In addition, inflation does not work its way smoothly through the economy. Prices in some industries are likely to respond much more rapidly to inflationary pressures than in others. Because of these effects, individuals are confronted with increased uncertainty in terms of negotiating any long-term contracts or obligations. In addition, because inflation affects some prices more rapidly than others, it is difficult for individuals to sort out real relative price changes from nominal changes caused by leads and lags in the inflationary process. As a consequence, more "mistakes" in resource allocation are likely to be made as individuals and firms respond to incorrect price signals.

Even if real personal income is unchanged on average because of inflation, the increased uncertainty experienced by individuals concerning their own future incomes is, in and of itself, undesirable. Leijonhufvud argues that there will be two types of response to this uncertainty. First, increased resources will be diverted from production of goods and services into attempts to more accurately forecast inflation. Second, if inflation is severe and prolonged, individuals will seek government action to protect themselves against the uncertainty which the inflation causes. There will be more political pressure for direct regulation of economic activity and also, possibly, for government action to generate a more equal distribution of income.

INFLATION AND THE DISTRIBUTION OF INCOME

Inflation which is unanticipated can have an effect on the distribution of income in a society. Suppose the government finds expenditure needs running in advance of tax revenues and that it finances these through resort to the modern version of the printing press. People do not expect the inflation to occur. As the newly created money enters the economy, some initial increase in real income and employment may take place. However, it seems clear that prices of both final products and productive services will rise along with the increase in aggregate demand. But prices are unlikely to rise uniformly. Some will rise more rapidly, some more slowly, and others not at all during the short-run. Individuals in favorable positions to take advantage of more rapid price rises for their products and services will be able to increase their own real income positions at the expense of those marketing products and services characterized by more slowly rising prices. Debtors, those who are obligated to pay others fixed monetary sums, will find their real wealth position improved. Creditors who hold fixed monetary claims will find their real wealth reduced.

To the extent that inflation can be anticipated by individuals these types of real wealth redistributions will cease to occur. At the time that contracts which involve future monetary payments are negotiated, contractors will perceive the changes in the purchasing power of money which will occur over the life of the contract and make necessary adjustments, primarily by incorporating an inflation premium into the interest rate. To the extent that future inflation rates are never perfectly anticipated, however, some redistribution among creditors and debtors continues to occur. Debtors gain if the actual inflation rate exceeds what they expected and lose if actual inflation falls below anticipation. The situation is reversed for monetary creditors.

CONCLUSIONS

Throughout the ages, governments have resorted to the creation of currency in some form to finance a portion of their expenditures. Modern governments are no different in this respect. Government "borrowing" from the banking system is, in many cases, equivalent in effect to printing money. Prior to the "Keynesian revolution," Western democracies were constrained in their ability to finance government expenditures through money creation by widespread belief among the voters that the government's budget should be balanced. This balanced budget norm was destroyed by the general acceptance of the Keynesian norm that federal budget policy was a tool to be employed for macroeconomic stabilization purposes. As was discussed in some detail in Chapter 15, the Keynesian prescription that the budget need not always be balanced seems to have had the practical effect that the budget is almost never balanced. Democratic politicians find it relatively easy to accept deficit financing during periods of recession but the alternative of a budget surplus during periods of inflation seems relatively unpalatable.

Insofar as money creation does not cause inflation, there can be no real objection to this method of financing expenditures. In such cases, perhaps characteristic of very deep depressions, the government can secure resources without imposing any real cost on indiviudals. In more normal circumstances, any creation of money will drive prices upward, which will amount to a reduction in the real incomes of some individuals and groups in the economy. The effects are similar to those of a tax imposed directly on the holders of cash and claims to cash. A full understanding of inflation requires that the process be treated explicitly as a means of taxation.

There is no inherent reason why the holders of cash should not be subjected to a tax, anymore than the consumers of beer, meat, or playing cards. In this respect the inflation tax is no different from any other indirect tax and the excess burden of this tax, that is to say, the costs imposed on taxpayers over and above the real resource transfer to the public sector, must be compared with that of other taxes in assessing the relative desirability of their particular levy.

From a public choice perspective, a possible problem with the inflation levy is that it does seem to a large degree to be a disguised tax. Even after individuals learn to expect inflation, they seem to not fully appreciate its cause. Although they may more or less correctly perceive the costs of inflation, these are not seen as costs of public services. From this standpoint, fiscal illusion is present and taxpayers underestimate the costs of public services.

29

Government policy and capital formation

In the United States, capital as an asset or the income which it produces is subject to taxation not only under personal income taxes at all levels of government, but also under corporate income and property taxes. We will be examining the economic effects of this taxation in this chapter. The effects of public debt issue will also be examined.

Almost all taxes save the pure lump-sum tax have some effect on the disposition of the taxpayer's after-tax income. For example, a tax on beer will result in less beer being consumed. The effects of capital taxation are especially interesting for several reasons. First, by lowering the net return on saving and investment, capital taxation tends to bias individual choices in favor of current over future consumption. Given the long term financial problems confronting the U.S. Social Security Program, any provisions in the tax structure which tend to discourage individuals from making provisions to supplement social security benefits from private savings are worthy of careful examination. In addition, capital taxation may lower aggregate net saving and capital formation in the economy. Both theory and empirical evidence are somewhat ambiguous on this point. However, to the extent that there is an effect here, the results are potentially very significant in terms not only of the level of national income, but also of its distribution.

It is worth reiterating that capital taxation is not unique in terms of distorting individual economic choices. Again, almost all taxes have some adverse effects and, in this context, the merits and demerits of altering the degree of reliance on capital taxation in the tax structure will clearly be affected by the effects of alternative taxes. However, a first step in this analysis is to understand clearly what the consequences of capital taxation are. A better understanding of these consequences is the primary objective of this chapter.

SAVING, THE RATE OF INTEREST, AND CAPITAL FORMATION

Individuals save in order to increase future income and consumption. The price of an increase in future consumption is measured in terms of foregone current consumption and is inversely related to the market interest rate. For example, if the interest rate were 4 percent, an individual could "buy" a one dollar increase in consumption next year by giving up 96 cents in current consumption. With an interest rate of 8 percent, the price of a one dollar increase in consumption next year would only be 93 cents of current consumption foregone.

The existence of capital makes it possible for society as a whole to be a net saver. This is because when individuals save or consume less than current income, resources which might otherwise have been employed to produce goods and services for current consumption can instead be channeled into the production of capital which in turn increases the future productive capacity of the economy. In this way, aggregate future consumption can be increased by a reduction in current consumption.

It is important to have a clear understanding of the terms being employed. At any point in time, the productive capacity of the economy is determined by the available stock of land, labor and capital resources and by the existing state of technology. Capital depreciates over time. Therefore, net capital formation involves the creation of new capital in excess of that needed to replace normal deterioration in the existing capital stock. Income can be defined as the maximum amount of current consumption which can be produced by the economy if there is to be no net change in the size of the capital stock. This is, of course, analogous at the aggregate level to the accretion of wealth conception of individual income introduced in Chapter 22. Saving occurs if current consumption falls below current income. Positive growth in the capital stock which can only occur if there is net saving is a critical component of real economic growth.

In a well-functioning capital market without taxes, the interest rate received by savers will correspond to the marginal productivity of investment. If a one dollar capital investment will add ten cents annually to the future real income stream, then the market rate of interest will also be 10 percent. A capital tax, however, drives a wedge between the real rate of return on investment and the net return received by investors. If, for example, capital income is subject to a 50 percent tax, a 10 percent real return on investment will generate only a 5 percent net return to investors. An important issue in analyzing the effects of capital taxation is whether this tax-induced lowering of the net return on investment has an effect on aggregate saving and capital formation in the economy.

It is important to distinguish between the effect of capital taxation on private sector saving and investment and the effect on aggregate saving and investment. Even if capital taxation were to reduce saving and capital formation in the private sector, aggregate capital formation need not be affected if government investment out of tax revenue replaces the depleted private investment. If, however, the marginal propensity to save out of government income is less than that of the private sector, any tax-induced reduction in private investment will not be replaced in the public sector.

The relationship between private sector saving and the interest rate is theoretically ambiguous. When the interest rate falls, the price of future consumption rises. Although individuals can be expected to demand less future consumption given the higher price, saving, which represents total expenditure on future consumption need not necessarily decrease. Future consumption will be reduced even if saving remains unchanged.

Empirical evidence on the relationship between private sector saving and the rate of interest is mixed. Several studies have indicated that saving is not very responsive to changes in the interest rate. More recently, some evidence has indicated a significant positive correlation between saving and the rate of return. Further empirical work will undoubtedly be required before any consensus is found on this important issue.

Even if private saving is not responsive to changes in the interest rate, taxation of interest income will still generate an excess burden. This is because the interest rate is an important determinant of individual choice with respect to intertemporal resource allocation. With such taxation equilibrium in the capital market is characterized by the marginal evaluation of future consumption exceeding the cost of producing additional future consumption.

DEFICIT FINANCE AND CAPITAL FORMATION

Do government deficits financed by real debt creation have any effect on private investment and capital formation in the economy? This is an issue which has long been a source of controversy among economists. Early economists, notably David Ricardo, argued that there could be no difference between financing an increment in government spending through an increase in taxes or through the sale of government bonds to the public. The reason was that government bonds simply represented future tax obligations (to amortize the debt) which were precisely equal in discounted present value to the alternative current tax payments for which they were being substituted. Because of this fundamental equivalence between bonds and taxes, there could be no differential effects on taxpayer behavior as a result of a decision to substitute debt finance for tax finance or vice versa.

This Ricardian "equivalence theorem" is obviously inconsistent with elementary Keynesian macroeconomic theory in which an increase in the government deficit stimulates aggregate demand. Suppose, for example, that government spending were held constant and taxes were reduced with the sale of government bonds used to replace lost tax revenue. In the Ricardian framework, all of the money returned to the taxpayers by the tax cut would be used to buy up the new government bonds. There would be no change in current consumption spending or in real saving and capital formation in the economy. This is because taxpayers would perceive no change in their real wealth consequent on the increase in current disposable income. The current increase would be just offset by the future reduction in disposable income when taxes would have to be increased to amortize the debt. The increased supply in the bond market would be matched by an increase in demand as taxpayers seek to acquire additional future income claims to meet new future tax obligations.

The Keynesian analysis of this change in government finance would be very different. In this framework, the tax reduction and issue of new bonds would be perceived by taxpayers in general as a net increment to wealth. It is consistent with both the Ricardian and the Keynesian frameworks for current consumption to be a function of perceived wealth. In the Keynesian model, the issue of government bonds stimulates current consumption demand by increasing wealth. In other words, instead of simply buying up government bonds with the increase in current disposable income brought about by the tax cut, individuals would seek to use some of the money to increase consumption. In a fully employed economy, current consumption can be increased only by a reduction in current investment. (Remember, our example has been constructed with a constant level of government spending.) Because taxpayers are not willing to buy all of the government bonds at the prevailing interest rate, that interest rate will be bid up. This will, in turn, discourage some private investment. Projects which were marginally profitable when the interest rate was 6 percent will cease to be profitable when the interest rate rises to 7 percent, for example. Thus in a fully employed economy, a marginal shift from tax to debt finance will result in reduced private investment and capital formation.

Which model is correct? The answer to this question is obviously important to an understanding of the effect of government policy on capital formation and economic growth. At first glance, there would appear to be a serious flaw in the Ricardian analysis. Even if public debt creation is accompanied by simultaneous creation of a future tax obligation,[1] many taxpayers who are alive when the government debt is issued will not be living when the requisite taxes must be collected to make interest payments and amortize that debt. Because taxpayers' lives are finite, real debt creation might be viewed as a means of effectively shifting the burden associated with the coercive levy of taxes onto the next generation. Only if current taxpayers weigh the well-being of the next generation in precisely the same way as they weigh their own or, alternatively, if they view the future tax obligation as a reduction in the bequest which they plan to leave their

---

[1]If the rate of growth in the economy were to exceed the interest rate, the government could continually borrow to service the debt with no increase in the debt relative to gross national product. Public debt would not necessarily involve any future tax obligation in this case. However, this does not seem to be a currently relevant scenario and will be ignored here.

heirs,[2] does it seem plausible that a substitution of tax for deficit finance could be neutral with respect to real capital formation.

In an empirical sense, it does not appear that taxation and government borrowing are equivalent means of financing public expenditures. The persistent federal government deficits over the past two decades, at least some of which were financed by real debt creation, would seem to sugget that democratic politicians are not indifferent between the two sources of revenue. Recall, also, the discussion in Chapter 20 regarding the impact of the social security program on private saving and capital·formation. Empirical evidence suggests that social security has significantly reduced personal savings. Promised future social security benefits represent a significant implicit public debt. A corresponding reduction in private saving is inconsistent with the Ricardian view of public debt.

CAPITAL TAXATION AND THE DISTRIBUTION OF INCOME

If capital taxation and real public debt creation do, in fact, cause a reduction in saving and capital formation in the economy, the consequences extend not only to the size of national income but also to its distribution. The effect on total national income is obvious. The capital stock is lower today than it otherwise would have been. Hence, the productive capacity of the economy is smaller. Because current saving is also retarded by current capital taxation, national income will be smaller in the future than would otherwise be the case.

The effect on the distribution of income is somewhat more complicated. If factor markets are competitive, factor earnings will reflect marginal productivity. If the capital stock is lower relative to the labor force than would be the case in the absence of capital taxation, two factors combine to raise the marginal product of capital and hence the interest rate relative to the marginal product of labor or real wage rate. First, the law of Diminishing Returns states that the marginal product of a particular factor, in this case capital, will be

---

[2]Professor Robert Barro has argued that if individuals perceive that future tax obligations beyond their expected lifetimes involve a corresponding reduction in the value of any bequests which they plan to leave their heirs, individuals will regard debt and tax finance as identical means of raising public revenue for all practical purposes. See Robert Barro, "Are Government Bonds Net Wealth?" *Journal of Political Economy* (November/December 1974).

lower the greater is the amount of that factor employed with fixed quantities of other factors of production. In other words, the smaller is the capital stock combined with existing quantities of land and labor the higher is the real interest rate. In addition, it is generally assumed that labor and capital are complements in the production process. This means that the marginal product of labor is positively correlated with the amount of capital. A smaller capital stock thus implies a lower marginal product of labor and hence a lower real wage.

CONCLUSIONS

In recent years, some concern has developed that the rate of economic growth in the American economy is too low. This has spurred renewed interest in the effects of government policy on saving and investment. In this chapter, we have explored two methods of financing public expenditures which have the potential of slowing the rate of capital formation and economic growth. These are capital taxation and the creation of public debt. To the extent that the capital stock has been reduced as a consequence of such financing methods, per capita income has been lowered. The smaller capital stock also has distributional implications. The real wage rate is lower relative to the real rental rate on capital as a consequence of the lower capital-labor ratio in the economy.

Both theoretically and empirically the effect of capital taxation on saving and investment is ambiguous. However, even if capital formation has not been affected by existing capital taxation, the tax-induced wedge between the gross rate of return on investment has the effect of biasing individual choices in favor of current over future consumption.

What are the alternatives to capital taxation? This is, of course, the relevant policy issue. One alternative which has been receiving some increased attention, at least in academic discussions, is the substitution of a tax on consumption for a tax on income. The advantage of this tax is its neutrality with respect to the choice between current and future consumption. The consumption tax is often criticized on equity grounds as a regressive tax because the proportion of income consumed falls as income rises. This can be overcome, to some extent by making the rate structure progressive. With a consumption tax, two individuals with identical current incomes might pay different taxes because each chose a different level of current consumption. However, to the extent that the two were identical in terms of lifetime income and left comparable bequests, a consumption tax would tax them equally over their lifetimes despite differences in tax payments at particular points in time.

SUPPLEMENTARY READING

For a recent empirical study of the relationship between capital taxation and net saving see Michael Boskin, "Taxation, Saving and the Rate of Interest," *Journal of Political Economy* (April 1978).

Professor Martin Feldstein has examined the welfare implications of capital taxation in "The Welfare Cost of Capital Income Taxation," *Journal of Political Economy* (April 1978).

For a discussion of the effects of public debt creation see Robert J. Barro, "Are Government Bonds Net Wealth," *Journal of Political Economy* (November/December 1974). See also comments on Barro's work by Martin Feldstein and James Buchanan and a reply by Barro in *The Journal of Political Economy* (April 1976).

part VII

The national debt

30

The principles of
public debt

TAXATION
VERSUS BORROWING

Taxation can be considered as the normal way in which a government secures the revenues that it needs to finance public services. If we look on the fiscal process as an "exchange," taxes are the "prices" that individuals pay for the benefits of public activity. Individuals, acting through the political process (through elected representatives), subject themselves to reductions in real income of one kind (private goods and services) in order to be able to secure real income of another kind (public goods and services). The fact that taxation inherently implies coercion or compulsion does not modify this basic nature of the fiscal process. The fundamental characteristic of all taxation is the compulsory reduction in real income or wealth imposed on the individual in order that the government may finance the purchase of resource services which, in turn, yield some addition to individual real income or wealth through public service benefits.

For governments, as for private individuals, borrowing is essentially an alternative means of raising revenues to cover expenditures. Borrowing, that is, the creation of public debt, is a means through which governments may finance public services without reducing the real wealth of private individuals during the period when the funds are acquired. Insofar as resource services are used up in the provision of public services, some reduction in resource use privately must, of course, take place when the expenditure is made. But the essence of the borrowing process, as opposed to taxation, is that the government secures the revenues to finance its purchases on a voluntary exchange basis. Private individuals *purchase* government securities, not as a result of compulsion imposed upon them by the political structure, or even in the sense of exchanging current income for public service benefits, but in *exchange* for a government promise or obligation to provide them with future income. Thus, we see that government borrowing and taxation are contrasting methods of financing public services. In the one case—taxation—individual real wealth is currently reduced in "exchange" for goods and services directly provided by government, the terms of the "exchange," in this case, being dictated by the political decision process. In the other case, that of borrowing, individuals give up no real resource services to secure the current benefits of public services; they secure these through the government's contracting of an obligation to pay some income in future time periods to certain creditors, whether these be citizens or foreigners.

THE BURDEN OF PUBLIC DEBT

Viewed in terms of the contrast with taxation, it seems clear that the financing of public services through the issue of debt instruments— securities—does not impose any real burden or cost on citizens, generally, at the time that the public spending is actually undertaken. What do we mean by burden here? The only relevant meaning is that sacrifice of private goods and services made necessary by the fact of government spending. In other words, who really pays for the benefits of the public services that are financed through debt issue? Who bears the real cost?

Resources are, of course, drawn from the private sector during the period when the public expenditure is undertaken. But do the persons who give up resources really "pay for" the benefits secured? It seems clear that they do not, since they give up current purchasing power, not in any political "exchange" for public service benefits, but instead in a wholly voluntary exchange for the debt instruments which embody some obligation on the part of the government to make a return income payment to holders of such instruments in future periods.

From this conception, it follows that the real burden of the debt-financed public spending must rest with taxpayers during the future periods when the previously issued debt requires servicing and amortization. As contrasted with taxation, which must impose some current real cost on individuals, debt creation provides one way of financing public services without current cost. It provides a means whereby taxpayers in any given period may *shift or postpone* the real payment for public services until future periods. Only to the extent to which taxpayers anticipate these future payments and capitalize these into a currently valued reduction in wealth can a "burden" be located at the point of debt issue.

This elementary analysis concludes that the real cost of public debt, or rather of debt-financed expenditures, must be shouldered by those individuals and groups who must pay taxes to service and to amortize the debt obligations. The logic of the analysis seems irrefutable within the limits of the model discussed, and this seems to be the only fully appropriate model for the purpose at hand. Nevertheless, this conclusion has not been widely accepted, at least until quite recently. The claim has been repeatedly made by competent economists that the burden of debt cannot be postponed or shifted to future periods. Although this argument seems, at base, fallacious, it is worth careful consideration. The argument is based on the idea that it is impossible to transfer a real cost forward in time when the resources providing the public services are actually used up during the initial time period. The steel, copper, and oil, for instance, that were actually used up in producing war materials in 1944, were used up in 1944, not in some later year. The real cost, the sacrificed alternatives, of these resources could only have been shouldered in 1944, and by individuals who lived in 1944, who were somehow forced to sacrifice current consumption during that time. This argument seems initially plausible until it is recalled that, insofar as genuine debt was issued to finance these purchases, private individuals were not "forced" to give up anything; they were not compelled to give up either private consumption or investment opportunities. They gave up purchasing power voluntarily in exchange for government's promise to pay to them a somewhat larger real income in the future. When this point is accepted, debt issue cannot be claimed to impose a real cost on anyone during the period of resource use, despite the reduction in the amount of resource services left available for private disposition.

The argument here does not, of course, apply to public debt that is issued compulsorily; that is, to "forced loans." Nor does the argument apply at all to the issue of nominal "debt" as a means of generating inflation. In either of these two cases, no real debt is issued at all, and these methods are simply particular forms of taxing.

THE TRANSFER ARGUMENT

How can the whole group be subjected to net burden or cost in periods after that in which resources are actually used up for public purposes? One reason for continued adherence to the essentially fallacious view of debt burden is the concentration on the *transfer* aspects of debt service operations. If a government sells a bond to an individual living within its borders, the payment of interest on this bond represents a transfer of purchasing power from the taxpayers to the bondholder, in many cases the same persons. In this transfer process, the real income of the taxpayer is reduced; the real income of the bondholder is increased. But how can the whole group, taken in the aggregate, be said to shoulder any burden, any reduction in utility, as a result of servicing previously issued debt? This is the most persuasive part of the widely accepted argument concerning the location of the debt burden, and the effective refutation of this part requires a careful examination of the underlying logical assumptions.

We must return to the period of debt issue itself, and ask the question: What would happen if the public debt were not to be issued? The individual who purchases the government bond would, instead, purchase a private security, some other income-earning asset, or he would spend the funds on current consumption. In either case, the discounted value of the alternative purchases would be approximately equal to that of the government bond. There would be only some slight differential between the purchase of the government bond and its substitutes. Now let us consider the position of this individual in later periods, assuming still that he did not purchase the government bond. The analysis is simpler if we assume that he purchases a private bond instead of the government bond, although this is not a necessary assumption. The private bond will yield a return approximately equal to that of the government bond. Hence we must conclude that, differentially, the individual would have been in approximately the same position with or without the government bond. The existence of public debt, as such, does not provide the bondholders with differential benefits.

The situation of the taxpayer in these later periods is wholly different. With the public debt in existence, he is subjected to a coercive levy in order to finance the interest payments on the debt. This is the real cost of the debt-financed public spending, since the taxpayer in this situation is the only person who must suffer a net reduction in utility in "payment" for the public spending that has been previously undertaken. On the other hand, if the expenditure had not been made, if the debt had not been issued, the taxpayer, as such, would be under no charge in later periods, and would clearly be differentially much better off without the debt than with it.

If this analysis is accepted, it seems clear that it is erroneous to look on the payment of interest on an internal or domestic public debt as a "transfer" in any real sense of the word. Bondholders receive the interest as a part of a contract; taxpayers lose purchasing power through the imposition of a compulsory levy. To call these two sides canceling overlooks the fundamental difference between taxation and borrowing as means of financing public expenditures.

If the debt-financed expenditure turns out to be productive the taxpayer in later periods may, of course, be better off, even with the necessity of paying the interest charge, than he would be without the debt having been issued. But this is irrelevant to the problem of locating the real cost of the expenditures, the debt burden. This problem is precisely that of locating the individual or group which does "pay for" the benefits secured from the public outlay, quite independently of whether or not the outlay itself is productive or unproductive. Debt issue tends to shift this burden of payment onto the taxpayer in periods subsequent to the debt issue — expenditure operation. Taxation, by contrast, tends to place the burden on individuals in the period when the expenditure is undertaken. This is the basic difference between the two methods of financing public expenditure, and failure to recognize this point can only lead to confusion.

THE ANALOGY WITH PRIVATE DEBT

One of the points that is often made in the discussion of public debt is that it is fallacious to draw analogies between the debts of governments and the debts of individuals, that is, between public and private debt. The emphasis on this point stems from an acceptance of the argument that has been examined critically above. In many particular respects, public debt must be different from private, and any analogy between the two must be used with great care, as is the case with all analogies. But this does not suggest that the underlying similarity between the individual and public economy as regards debt issue can be overlooked. In the most essential respects, debt issue for the individual and debt issue for the government (which, in its turn, can best be considered as individuals acting politically) are analogous.

In each instance, borrowing (debt issue) constitutes an alternative to the more normally accepted means of raising revenues. Borrowing in either case is a means of securing additional current purchasing power without undergoing supplementary current cost. The costs of spending are effectively shifted to future time periods. In such periods, creditors hold a primary claim against the revenue or the income of either the individual or the government.

It may, of course, be fully rational for either the individual or the government to borrow instead of raising the funds in a more normal way. As we shall see later, the desirability of borrowing depends on the expected productivity of the spending and the time pattern of the expected yield. Here it is noted only that there is no fundamental difference between the individual and the government economy as regards the essential aspects of debt versus current financing of expenditure.

EXTERNAL AND INTERNAL PUBLIC DEBT

Still another result of accepting what has been labeled here as a fallacious conception of public debt has been the sharp distinction made between an internal and an external or foreign debt. A government borrows internally or domestically when it sells securities to its own citizens. In purchasing the bonds, the individuals voluntarily give up command over current usage of resources in exchange for the government's promise to pay a return in future periods. The government uses this purchasing power to acquire resources and services from the private economy. The citizens of the private economy have a smaller total of real goods and services available for private disposition than before the sale of public debt, but they hold debt instruments in the place of the differential amount of private goods, that is, claims against the government which are at least equal to the private goods in value. No person in this initial period in which the public borrowing and the public expenditure take place suffers any loss in utility as a result of the operation. It is important to emphasize that this conclusion holds even if the public expenditures are completely wasteful.

Let us now compare this with the process of external borrowing. Here the government sells securities to citizens of foreign countries who give up units of their own purchasing power in exchange. The government uses this purchasing power to acquire goods and services abroad, or to exchange with citizens who desire to acquire goods and services abroad. The total amount of resources available for disposition in the private economy is not changed. As with domestic or internal public debt creation, no one suffers any reduction in utility during the initial period of debt issue and expenditure, and if the project is at all beneficial, some individuals find their utility increased. Since there is no reduction in the amount of goods available privately, there are no claims to wealth, no debt instruments, held by citizens. Therefore it must be concluded that, at least in the initial period, there is no basic difference between the external and the internal public debt.

Similar results hold if we consider comparable situations in a period subsequent to that in which the government borrows and spends. For an internal or domestic debt, sufficient taxes will have to be levied to finance the interest charges. These payments will be made to bondholders who, in this case, are citizens living in the domestic economy. If, instead, the debt is externally held, the tax payments must be made to foreign citizens. On this level of comparison, the external debt seems clearly to be more burdensome than the internal debt, since there is no offsetting receipt of interest by local bondholders. The interest payments represent a net drainage of funds out of the domestic economy.

This is the source of much confusion. If a correct and careful analysis is made, the conclusion that the external debt is more burdensome can be shown to be erroneous. The previous simple comparison overlooks the fact that the total national income must always be larger in the external debt case. The reason is clear. Resources are not drawn away from the private economy when the debt is originally issued; instead, resources are drawn from abroad. Consequently, the private income in any subsequent period must be higher than it would be if internal rather than external debt is issued. The fact that income is higher in a situation with external debt allows for the necessary drainage of interest payments out of the economy.

There is no real distinction in the two cases, as long as the comparisons are properly made.

All of this should not suggest that there are no important distinctions between the internal and external national debt. The sale of securities to foreigners will introduce many supplementary problems that are not present when securities are sold to citizens. These relate to such factors as possible changes in exchange rates and transfer difficulties. There is no denying that such problems may arise, and given the fact that the international payments mechanism may work somewhat less smoothly than the domestic payments mechanism, the servicing of an external debt may be more difficult for a government than the servicing of an equally large domestic debt. The point here is that the important differences lie in such institutional arrangements as these mentioned, not in the fact that the two debt forms are intrinsically different.

REAL PUBLIC DEBT AND DISGUISED MONEY CREATION

In the previous discussion, the act of borrowing on the part of the government has been analyzed as an alternative to taxation as a means of financing public expenditures. In the full employment economy, these two methods exhaust the possibilities since the direct creation of currency (inflation) produces results that are equivalent to a form of taxation. If government expenditures are financed out of newly created purchasing power, it is clear that no real exchange of present for future income takes place; that is to say, no *real* debt is created. Real borrowing, or real debt creation, takes place only if some individuals or groups in the economy deliberately exchange current purchasing power for a governmental obligation to provide an income return in future periods.

It is essential that this basic meaning of real public debt be kept in mind because of the extremely loose usage of the words "debt" and "borrowing" that has come to be incorporated in the descriptions of fiscal practices. Whenever a national government deficit is created, that is, when the rate of spending exceeds the rate of tax collections, this deficit is financed by what is called debt issue. The nominal size of the public debt is always increased with the occurrence of a budget deficit. No distinction is made in ordinary public and political discussion between *real debt*, as defined above, and that which may somewhat legitimately be called "fake debt" or "disguised money creation." Failure to make this distinction has been the source of much confusion. Since the two methods of financing public expenditures have sharply differing effects, the lumping of the two under a single name tends to conceal the contrast between taxation and real debt issue that has been emphasized here. This failure also explains, in part, the reason why the substantially correct analogy between public and private debt has been rejected. Quite obviously, private debtors do not have recourse to money creation, in any form. Therefore, any borrowing must be real borrowing, in the sense used here. National governments, on the other hand, do have recourse to this means of financing public expenditures. It follows that if this process is to be called "debt issue," the analogy between public debt and private debt is wholly false.

The problem arises here because governments, or politicians, will rarely admit openly that public expenditures are financed through currency creation. The modern version of the money creation process is for the government to finance deficits by an operation that is called "borrowing" from the central bank and with its support, from the commercial banks. There is a certain spurious legitimacy in using the words "borrowing" and "public debt" to refer to this operation, because a nominal interest is paid on the obligations that these institutions of the banking system hold. But in real terms, no "borrowing" takes place at all since no individual or institution gives up any purchasing power or liquidity in exchange for the obligations of government. The purchasing power transferred to the government in exchange for these so-called debt instruments is created in the process. The banking system is provided with an interest income, not in exchange for any sacrifice of purchasing power or liquidity, but instead for creating additional currency, for carrying out the operation that is specifically within the constitutional power of the national government. In this sense, therefore, the interest payment on the "debt" created in this way is largely unnecessary, and does not serve at all the same purpose or function as interest payment on real debt.

The national debt outstanding at any given moment of time is made up of both of these components. A significant part of the debt is not the result of any real borrowing operation at all; instead it is the institutional "veil" which serves to conceal, not very successfully, an expansion of the money supply. Only that part of the nominal public debt which represents the results of real borrowing in past periods can legitimately be called real public debt. It is extremely unfortunate that the same words have come to be used to refer to fundamentally different things in these two cases.

The preceding sections have analyzed the effects of real government borrowing. In order to complete the analysis of "public debt," as this term is used in popular discussion, we must now analyze briefly the effects of "fake" debt issues; i.e., the effects of money creation that is disguised as public debt issue.

Here it is necessary first to distinguish between the economy characterized by high employment and the economy with substantial unemployment and excess capacity. In the high employment economy, any creation of additional purchasing power must be inflationary, must cause the price level to increase. The results are equivalent to a tax on the holders of cash balances. The burden of paying for the government expenditures financed in this way falls on those who hold such balances. Insofar as the "debt" issued in the process carries nominal interest, this burden of interest payment falls on taxpayers in future periods. The interest burden is, in this case, "excess" or "unnecessary" and represents the payment of a subsidy to the money-creating agencies, the banking system. In this model, the burden of interest payments cannot be considered to be the burden of paying for the expenditures, as such.

The situation in an economy with excess capacity and large unemployment may be different. Here, currency creation may be positively desirable under certain conditions. Unless bottlenecks and rigidities are present to make prices rise before some acceptable level of employment is attained, an increase in the supply of money should increase real income and employment without inflation. As suggested, insofar as this situation prevails, government expenditures can be, and should be, financed at zero or very low real cost. In such cases, neither taxation nor real borrowing should be undertaken. Direct money creation becomes an effective alternative means of financing public expenditures in situations like this, and this is the financing method that should be adopted. The obvious way to create money is to do so directly. But if the institutional veil of "borrowing from the banking system" is considered to be necessary, the nominal interest paid on the "debt" created in the process may be a small price to pay for the substantial benefits that may be secured from the fiscal operation.

In situations where substantial excess capacity and unemployment exist but where, also, a general increase in aggregate demand will lead to some inflation, money creation will, of course, take on some elements of taxation.

WHEN SHOULD GOVERNMENTS BORROW?

The important normative question to be answered is: When should governments borrow? The preceding analysis of public debt principles should provide a basis for answering this question correctly. But in order to do so, we must distinguish carefully between the full employment and the unemployment economy and between real borrowing and disguised money creation.

The answer is simpler in the case of unemployment, and this may be dealt with first. Suppose that the economy is characterized by substantial excess capacity and unemployment. We assume that an increase in total demand will have little or no effect on the level of prices but will serve to increase production and employment. As has been suggested several times, the government should create money in such a situation. Government deficits should be financed by an increase in the supply of money. *No taxation and no real borrowing should take place.* Either of these methods of raising revenues must serve to reduce somewhat current demand for goods and services, an effect that can only be undesirable in the under-employed economy.

The great advantages that direct money creation has over "fake" borrowing lie in the absence of interest cost. Currency pays no interest return to its holders, and the government, when it issues currency, does not place a burden on future taxpayers. "Debt" instruments as such, even if sold to banks, do carry some interest return and, because of this, involve some real cost shift to future taxpayers. If, despite the clear advantages of the more direct form, money creation should be created by the disguised issue of "debt" to the banking system, the interest payments should be, and can be, very low.

Essentially the same conclusions hold when the economy is characterized by both underemployment and pressure on prices. Here there may be a basic conflict between the two policy objectives, full employment and monetary stability. If the decision is made to promote the employment objective, the budgetary deficits should be financed by direct money creation or its closest equivalent. It is not appropriate here to finance deficits with real borrowing which will serve to reduce current purchasing power that the deficits are designed initially to increase. Hence, if the purpose of the whole fiscal operation is that of increasing total demand in the economy, regardless of the setting, this purpose cannot be served optimally by issuing real debt.

The question as to when governments should borrow becomes more complex when the full employment case is considered or when, in the above situation, a decision is made to maintain monetary stability, even at the expense of some unemployment. Under either of these conditions, money creation beyond that normally desired to maintain price-level stability should not take place unless the holders of cash balances are chosen as the group to be taxed. In the more normal setting, government borrowing, if it is undertaken, should be real borrowing.

We may, therefore, reduce the alternatives here to taxation and to real borrowing. What criteria should determine the government's choice between these two financing devices? These criteria must be drawn from the characteristics of the government expenditure to be financed. The major distinction between the two methods lies in the location of the real cost or burden in time, with the tax method concentrating this cost in the current or initial period and the borrowing method postponing this cost until some later periods. This basic difference allows some reasonably definite rules to be laid down concerning the choice. For those public expenditures or outlays that are expected to yield up all or a major portion of public service benefits in a reasonably short period of time, taxation should be employed. Clearly, resort to borrowing to finance spending of this nature will simply exploit future taxpayers for the benefit of current public beneficiaries. The admissibility of public borrowing here might open up a veritable Pandora's box of irresponsible spending proposals. If legislative assemblies can finance expenditures that yield current benefits without imposing current taxes, few restraints will be placed on the limits to such spending.

Real borrowing, as a method of financing public services, should, therefore, be limited to the financing of public expenditure projects that are expected to yield benefits over a long period of time, that is, those that are expected to be of a permanent nature. Here the analogy with the private economy is quite close. Business enterprises normally borrow, that is, sell bonds, to finance capital expansion programs. Borrowing is accepted as an appropriate method of financing outlays that are bunched in time and are devoted to the purchase of equipment which will last over a long period. The principle of amortizing the debt over the period of the useful life of the project is accepted in business, and this principle is also applicable to government units.

The appropriate rules for choosing between taxation and real borrowing have, to some extent, been incorporated in traditional fiscal practices. Borrowing is limited to the financing of extraordinary expenditures and to the financing of "capital" projects, and it is this distinction that lies behind much of the argument for separating the current and capital expenditure budgets of government.

The most important origin of national debt is war expenditure. Even here, however, the general rules can be applied. In one sense, the extraordinary spending necessitated by war takes the form of capital investment in the whole social structure, the benefits of which can be expected to endure permanently if the war is won.

In the peacetime economy, a few practical illustrations of the appropriate uses of taxation and borrowing may be cited. Taxation should normally be employed for the financing of current government operating costs, of all transfer payments, of subsidies such as those to agriculture, and of foreign aid. Resort to real borrowing is justified only for such expenditures as long-term highway construction, irrigation projects, river valley developments, and urban renewal programs.

There are possible dangers, however, in following these generally valid rules for choice between taxation and real borrowing too rigidly. When taxation is used there is some guarantee, however rough this might be, that the advantages or benefits of the expenditure outweigh the costs, at least to a majority in the legislative assembly. Taxation forces some sort of comparison between the benefits and the costs of public programs. Any resort to borrowing in lieu of taxation tends to weaken this necessary connection between real costs and real benefits. Even if borrowing is restricted to long-term projects, no real comparison may be involved in the decision to undertake the project, since both the benefits and the costs take place in future periods. Desired projects may be adopted without consideration of the tax burden. It seems essential, in this respect, that legislative assemblies should consider simultaneously the imposition of the future taxes necessary to service and amortize the debt over the useful life of the project.

A second ever-present danger in the modern economy is that attempted real borrowing will turn out to be disguised money creation. This applies only for national governments with the money-creating power. Care must be taken to distinguish as sharply as is possible between genuine debt issue and money creation, especially because of the unnecessary confusion that has been introduced by the loose usage of words during the past quarter century.

SHOULD PUBLIC DEBT BE RETIRED?

A second important normative question follows directly from the analysis of the first. Given an existing public debt, when should it be retired? If public debt is created only in those situations indicated above, that is, only to finance long-term public investment projects, the answer to this question has already been given. The debt should be amortized over the useful life of the investment project, and a schedule of taxes providing for such amortization or retirement should ideally be adopted at the same time that the debt is initially issued and the expenditure made. This principle of debt retirement is essential to the proposals made for separating capital expenditures from current expenditures; that is, for the use of capital budgeting by the government.

The more important question concerns another matter. A large national debt exists in the United States. This debt is in part the result of real borrowing and in part the result of disguised money creation. Even for that portion of the $780 billion (early 1978) that represents real debt, no permanent capital assets owned by the federal government exist which specifically represent the results of debt-financed outlay.

To what extent should the federal government take steps to retire this outstanding public debt? This is the central question of debt retirement. The interest payments on this national debt were almost $44 billion in 1978. Should deliberate policy steps be taken to retire this national debt? We shall discuss this question apart from the macroeconomic aspects; these will be introduced in the next section.

Debt retirement can take place only as a result of budget surpluses. Tax revenues in excess of current public expenditures will produce a surplus of funds that may be devoted to the retirement of existing debt, either by paying off issues of debt as they mature or by purchasing outstanding issues of debt in the open market. These additional tax revenues must be collected from individuals and institutions in the economy. The real cost of debt retirement must fall squarely on the current taxpayer. On the other hand, the real benefits accrue largely to taxpayers of later periods. Just as debt issue postpones the real cost, debt retirement concentrates these costs. Future taxpayers will be relieved of the interest burden on that part of the public debt that is retired. They will have a larger share of total income available for private or public disposition. A debt retirement operation, therefore, represents a net shift of disposable income from the current taxpayer to the future taxpayer.

Given the nature of the national debt that now exists, it is not at all clear that a positive policy of debt retirement should be followed, even when we ignore the macroeconomic aspects of this issue. The current generation of taxpayers bears little of the responsibility for creating the debt in the first place, and there seems to be no particular reason why these taxpayers should subsidize those of future periods. No generally applicable economic reasons for a debt retirement policy appear evident. In certain periods, a debt retirement policy may prove desirable; in other periods, the proper management of the national debt may consist in keeping the nominal size at some reasonable constant level.

Actually, political forces will probably prevent any substantial retirement of the existing national debt in any explicitly intended sense. The retirement which is possible may take place because of temporary and unanticipated budget surpluses and because of the opportunities for legitimate debt monetization over time. These will be discussed below.

One additional point should be made here. Treasury Department action may reduce the "real" size of the national debt without changing the nominal size. If the Treasury Department succeeds in reducing the overall interest cost of the debt, the "real" debt is reduced in the sense that a lower interest charge necessarily involves a lower carrying burden. To the extent that interest costs can be reduced without conflict with other macroeconomic objectives, it should, of course, be attempted. But here the temptation is great to resort to a simple substitution of disguised money creation for real debt instruments, with the resultant danger of inflation.

MACROECONOMIC POLICY ASPECTS
OF PUBLIC DEBT

In applying the analysis of public debt to answering the two questions, when should governments borrow and when should governments retire debt, we have not specifically considered the use of public debt issue or retirement for the purpose of expanding or contracting economic activity. It was suggested, as a part of the analysis, that genuine or real borrowing should never be employed as a means of increasing aggregate demand, the more efficient means being money creation.

Real borrowing acts to reduce purchasing power in the private economy. It follows, therefore, that if this operation is to be used for the promotion of macroeconomic policy aims, it must be employed in situations where some overall reduction in aggregate demand is needed. If underlying economic forces are such as to make general inflation threaten, the sale of real debt is one means of reducing excessive purchasing power. To be effective, the funds secured from the sale of debt instruments must not be employed to finance either direct public expenditures or debt retirement. Real borrowing, coupled with a policy of neutralizing the funds, can be a very effective anti-inflationary weapon. Since a sizable portion of the national debt is held by the Federal Reserve banks, a means of neutralization is present. By selling government bonds to the public at large and by using the funds acquired to "pay off" or "retire" government securities held in the Federal Reserve accounts, the government can prevent inflation. Any other usage of the funds would return purchasing power to the economy and would tend to offset, to some extent, the impact of borrowing from the public in the first place.

This anti-inflationary usage of public debt issue must be compared with taxation designed to accomplish the same purpose. As suggested, both taxation and real borrowing reduce the purchasing power available for private disposition in the economy. Aggregate demand is cut back in either case. The difference between the two cases is that while taxation reduces purchasing power through a compulsory levy on the incomes of private persons, debt issue reduces purchasing power through an exchange of debt instruments that embody a promise to pay a future income return to holders. In one sense, therefore, we can say that the issue of public debt to stop inflation will accomplish the purpose without imposing any real cost currently on individuals. Taxation, by contrast, will place the real cost squarely on current taxpayers. Viewed in this light, taxation seems to be recommended as the sounder policy. Debt issue as an anti-inflationary device seems to amount to shifting the real burden of the anti-inflationary measure to the future. There seems to be no more justification for this than there is for financing current expenditures through real borrowing.

We may now consider some of the macroeconomic policy aspects of debt retirement. This introduces explicitly some of the problems of debt monetization over time as a means of accomplishing some reduction in the annual interest burden. As the economy grows, additional money is required if the average level of product prices is to be maintained. There are several ways in which the required additional money may be introduced into the economy. The government could run budget deficits and finance these with direct money creation. But a more desirable policy might well be that of keeping tax revenues and public expenditures in balance and introducing new money through the retirement of real public debt. This may be accomplished quite readily by allowing the central bank to purchase debt instruments held by the nonbanking public. As the operation proceeds, the central bank, the Federal Reserve, would acquire more and more of the debt. While the nominal size of the public debt would not be reduced due to the peculiar usage of words, the real size of the national debt would be gradually reduced and the interest payments correspondingly lowered. Central Bank accumulation of public debt amounts to converting outstanding debt into money. This conversion is clearly undesirable except insofar as monetization may take place to advantage, provided that the government budget remains roughly in balance.

If serious recession threatens, such monetization can proceed more rapidly. If, for example, a depression the model of the 1930s should be imminent, a substantial share of the outstanding public debt might be monetized. While it seems reasonably certain that such a threat will not occur in the foreseeable future, the economy will surely grow over time. Debt monetization offers, therefore, the most substantial hope for genuine reduction in the annual burden of the national debt.

NATIONAL VERSUS LOCAL GOVERNMENT DEBT

The discussion in this chapter has been devoted to the general principles of public debt without reference to the particular governmental unit, although references have been confined to the national debt. The discussion of what we have called real or genuine public borrowing is applicable for any governmental unit, national, state, or local. The discussion which relates to debt as disguised money creation and to debt monetization applies only to the national government since it alone possesses inherent money-creating powers. State and local governments must issue real debt, and they do not have the opportunity to monetize outstanding debt.

CONCLUSIONS

Genuine public borrowing is an alternative to taxation as a means of financing public expenditure. The essential difference between these two financing methods lies in the nature of the operation through which the revenues are secured. Taxation is imposed on individuals compulsorily, supposedly in some sort of politically determined exchange for the government's direct provision of public service benefits from the expenditure. Borrowing, by contrast, represents a voluntary exchange for the government's promise to return income to them in future periods. Taxation, therefore, imposes a burden of payment for the public services directly on the individuals who are present during the time that the expenditure is carried out. Public borrowing, on the other hand, postpones this burden of payment until later periods. The issue of public debt shifts the cost of public expenditure to "future generations" of taxpayers.

This theory of public debt was not widely accepted during the 1940s and 1950s especially. A good part of the reason for the confusion over debt theory has been the failure to distinguish what is real borrowing from government operations that are called borrowing but are really disguised money creation. If the government borrows from central banks, the result is equivalent to the issue of new money, and the effects are wholly different from those of issuing real debt. This confusion led to the contrasting theory of public debt which states that no burden is shifted to future taxpayers, that there is no analogy between public and private debts, and that external public debt differs sharply from internal or domestic public debt.

Governments should borrow only in situations characterized by substantially full employment. Borrowing should be limited to the financing of genuinely long-term public projects, and some provision should be made for the servicing and the amortization of the debt over the useful life of the project. Public debts that have been created in the past should not necessarily be retired since debt retirement amounts to a subsidization of future taxpayers at the cost of current taxpayers.

Debt issue is one means of reducing inflationary pressures in the economy provided that the funds secured are effectively neutralized. Taxation seems to be preferred, however, as a general anti-inflationary weapon.

The primary prospect for reducing the annual interest burden on the national debt lies in the opportunity for gradual debt monetization as the economy grows. Practically, the proclivities of modern politicians to create governmental deficits, even in times of high employment, probably insure that the public debt of the federal government will continue to rise.

SUPPLEMENTARY READING

The material developed in this chapter follows closely that presented in James M. Buchanan, *Public Principles of Public Debt* (Homewood, Ill.: Richard D. Irwin, 1958).© by Richard D. Irwin, Inc. 1958.

Critical contributions to debt theory are included in James M. Ferguson (ed.), *The Public Debt and Future Generations* (Chapel Hill, N.C.: University of North Carolina Press, 1964).

31

Existing public debts

The general principles of public debt have been discussed primarily with the view of determining the appropriate conditions under which debt should be created and retired. These principles are applicable to all governmental units and for all time periods. The essential characteristics of the U.S. national debt, as it now exists, must be examined. Finally, data on local government debt in the United States will be presented.

THE ORIGIN OF THE U.S. NATIONAL DEBT

As of February 1979, the federal government debt of the United States amounted to approximately $792 billion, measured in terms of the principal, or maturity value, of the debt instruments outstanding. Table 31–1 traces the history of this national debt for selected years over the past half century.

A glance at Table 31–1 reveals that the great bulk of the existing national debt is the result of war expenditures, because both in World War I and World War II the national debt increased manyfold above prewar levels. Note that a serious attempt was made during the decade of the 1920s to retire a substantial portion of the debt created during World War I. The total was reduced from a high of more than $25 billion to a low of slightly more than $16 billion in 1930. The first half of the 1930s was characterized by government deficits produced by the onset of the Great Depression. These deficits were largely unintentional and were looked upon by almost all parties as undesirable.

TABLE 31-1
Principal of the national debt (selected years, 1915-1980)

Year	Total gross debt (in billions)	Year	Total gross debt (in billions)
1915	$ 1.2	1950	$256.1
1918	12.4	1954	270.0
1919	25.5	1958	276.0
1925	20.5	1962	295.4
1930	16.2	1966	316.1
1933	22.5	1970	370.1
1936	33.8	1972	426.4
1939	40.4	1974	474.2
1942	72.4	1976	620.4
1943	136.7	1977	698.8
1944	201.0	1978	771.5
1945	258.7	1979	839.2 (est.)
1946	269.4	1980	899.0 (est.)

Source: Figures for 1915-1976 are from the *Statistical Appendix to the Annual Report of the Secretary of the Treasury*, Fiscal Year, 1977; 1977 and 1978 Figures are taken from the *Treasury Bulletin*, April 1979; Estimates for 1979 and 1980 are from the *Budget of the United States Government*, Fiscal 1980.

In the second half of the 1930s, the federal government continued to practice deficit financing, with the consequent increase in the size of the total national debt. But, by the second half of this decade, the so-called "Keynesian revolution" in economic thinking had begun to occur, and the deficits were no longer viewed with such dire forebodings.

This period of depressed economic activity, the 1930s, merged into the period of rearmament and war in the 1940s. As is normal, the extraordinary expenditures made necessary by war generated huge government deficits. The national debt increased from $40 billion in 1939 to $269 billion in 1946.

The experience over the 1950s, 1960s, and 1970s would seem to indicate that the national debt, in terms of size, tends to move only in one direction. From 1966 through 1977, the national debt more than doubled, increasing by $380 billion. Even making adjustments for inflation, the real value of the principle of the debt increased by 18 percent.

If the size of the debt in comparison to gross national product is examined, however, the relatively small increases that have to this point occurred in the years since World War II need not be cause for great alarm. In 1946, the national debt reached a high point of 123 percent of GNP; in 1964, this percentage was approximately 51. As the postwar growth in GNP has taken place, the national debt has increased proportionately less. In 1978, the ratio of national debt to GNP was somewhat less than 40 percent.

THE COMPOSITION OF THE NATIONAL DEBT

What, specifically, is included in the national debt, as this term is commonly used? Officially, the debt is defined to include all interest-bearing obligations of the federal government, along with certain noninterest obligations that are of minor importance. The issue of currency by the federal government is not included in the figures for the national debt.

Interest-bearing federal debt may be classified on the basis of the type of security issued, which, in turn, reflects largely the maturity of the obligation. The important categories are bonds, notes, certificates, and bills. We shall discuss each of these categories separately.

Government bonds

Bonds are issued by the federal government for periods of longer than five years. The most familiar to the public, although not quantitatively the most important, are the Series E Savings Bonds. These are sold directly to individuals and are not *marketable*. An interest return is guaranteed on these bonds if they are held to maturity, or beyond, by the individual purchaser. If the purchaser desires to convert a savings bond into cash prior to the maturity date, a fixed redemption schedule is provided. Since the only loss in cashing such securities prior to maturity is a portion of the interest return, these bonds serve as close substitutes for cash in the asset holdings of individuals. They may be classified, for this reason, as "near monies." The individual holder is fully protected against any monetary capital loss. He may, of course, be subjected to loss in real terms during periods of inflation.

The marketable issues of long-term government bonds are more important in an aggregative sense than savings bonds. These marketable Treasury bonds are sold directly to individuals, to nonfinancial institutions, to financial institutions, and to commercial banks. By saying these bonds are marketable, we mean that the individual owner may convert one of these securities into cash at any time by selling it on the established market. A glance at the financial page of the daily newspaper reveals that an organized market does exist for such bonds, with prices quoted. The government provides for no redemption of such bonds before maturity, and it does not guarantee that any particular price will be supported on the open market. As compared with the savings bonds, the marketable issues are not so liquid, due to this greater price risk; hence, they do not serve the same functions of "moneyness" as do the savings bonds. The individual investor must take some risk of capital loss if he chooses to convert his bond into cash prior to its maturity date. In periods of rising interest rates, the holders of such long-term Treasury bonds may suffer sizable capital losses.

Treasury notes

Treasury notes are securities carrying maturity dates between one and five years. They are almost all marketable. Sice short-term interest rates are normally lower than long-term rates, these notes can be issued at somewhat lower cost to government than can bonds. The length and the terms of the issues can be more or less "tailored" to meet the special needs of investor groups. The legal ceiling on long-term bonds does not apply to short-term issues.

Treasury bills

The other important form of short-term debt takes the form of Treasury bills. These represent the so-called "short end" of the national debt structure. Treasury bills are issued for periods of 90 to 180 days. They are normally marketed at a discount, with the yield rate being determined by the rate at which a fixed maturity value is discounted. This feature is in contrast with most other government securities which carry fixed coupon rates of interest. Bills are quite clearly "near monies"; the purchasers are individuals and institutions, both financial and nonfinancial, that possess cash balances which are temporarily idle. Due to the high liquidity features inherent in the short maturities, these bills normally sell at lower rates of interest than longer-term securities. However, peculiarities in the supply-demand situations in the separate markets for government securities may, on occasion, drive the short-term rate above the long-term rate. A heavy Treasury refinancing that takes place largely in the sale of bills may drive the price of bills down and the rate of yield up beyond the rate on long-term bonds.

Table 31–2 shows the composition of the national debt as December 1978, both as to type of security and as to marketability.

Note from Table 31–2 that the government account series comprises a sizable share of the national debt. These special issues are sold directly to the various governmental agencies and trust funds, which are required by law to invest reserves in government securities. This type of public debt is usually called intragovernmental debt. Marketable issues make up slightly more than three fifths of the total national debt.

TABLE 31–2
Composition of the interest-bearing federal debt, December 1978
($ millions)

Type of security	Marketable	Nonmarketable
Bonds		
Treasury bond	$ 60,007	$ —
U.S. savings bonds	—	80,546
Foreign government series	—	29,539
Government account series	—	157,522
Other bonds	—	27,164
Notes	265,791	—
Bills	161,747	—
Totals	$487,546	$294,825
Total national debt		782,371

Source: *Economic Report of the President*, 1979.

THE OWNERSHIP OF THE NATIONAL DEBT

Public debt instruments are held by individuals, by business corporations, by financial institutions such as insurance companies, by commercial banks, by the Federal Reserve banks, by state and local governments, and by special governmental agencies and trust funds. Table 31–3 shows the distribution of ownership among these classes of investors as of February 1979.

The single most important distinction in the ownership pattern of the debt is that between bank-held debt and debt held outside the banking system. Commerical bank holdings of federal securities rep-

TABLE 31–3
**Distribution of ownership of interest-bearing federal debt,
February 1979**

Class of investors	Debt held ($ billions)
Banks	
Federal reserve banks	$103.5
Commercial banks	94.0
U.S. government investment accounts	170.1
Individuals	111.4
Insurance companies	15.1
Mutual savings banks	5.2
Corporations	23.5
State and local governments	68.6
Foreign and international	137.0
Other miscellaneous investors	63.8
Total	$792.2

Source: *Federal Reserve Bulletin*, January 1979.

resent potential reserves for a possible multiple expansion in the money supply. The banking system, based as it is on fractional reserves, can generate an expansion in the supply of bank credit which is some multiple of the net expansion in reserves. If the demand is present, a commercial bank can convert each dollar's worth of federal securities into reserves.

The Federal Reserve ownership of securities varies, of course, with the extent and the direction of its open-market operations. If inflation is threatened, the system will enter the market and sell holdings of government securities. This will reduce bank reserves and tighten up on the expansion of credit. Hence, a reduction in Federal Reserve ownership implies a policy of "tight money." On the other hand, in a recession, the Federal Reserve will enter the market and purchase government securities. Through this action, commercial bank reserves are increased and credit expansion made possible.

DEBT LIMITATION

As we suggested, national debt is created only when federal expenditures are in excess of federal revenue collections. Federal spending programs and federal taxes alike require the approval of both the

executive and the legislative branches of the government. Nevertheless, since 1917 Congress has imposed a ceiling on the amount of national debt outstanding. While this debt limit has almost always been
adjusted upward when Treasury operations have required, this limit
has served to impose certain supplementary restrictions on federal
fiscal activity. The existence of such a limit has caused some federal
operations to be financed in such a way that the debt issued would
not be subject to the legal ceiling. In terms of a logical structure of
decision, little can be said in support of a debt ceiling. However,
given the manner in which fiscal decisions actually are made, those
who desire effective limitation on spending can argue that the limit
does serve some purpose independently of direct congressional approval of spending programs. On the other hand, to those who desire
fewer effective limitations on spending by executive agencies, the
debt limit is clearly an undesirable restricting device.

In 1979, the "permanent" debt ceiling was set at $830 billion, with
some provision for temporary increases above this limit. As the national debt moves upward, adjustments in the permanent ceiling or
in temporary increases over this ceiling will be made.

"IMPLICIT" FEDERAL DEBT

The discussion in this chapter has been restricted to "official" public debts. We have not included discussion of "implicit" public debt,
created when a government commits itself to make payments in future
periods and does not, at the same time make provision for financing
such payments. For future-period taxpayers, the existence of such obligations to make payments, or commitments, is equivalent to public
debt. This "implicit debt" is important for the federal government,
and notably in the social security system, which involves obligations
to make benefit payments many billions of dollars over and above
those that may be financed by projected taxes.

STATE AND LOCAL DEBT

To this point, national debt issued by the federal government has
been discussed almost exclusively. To complete the public debt picture in the United States, mention must be made of state and local
government debt. In 1971, combined state and local government debt
amounted to approximately $257 billion, slightly over one third the

total for national government debt. This total has increased rapidly over the postwar years, having approximately doubled in the decade of the 1950s. Two thirds of this total represented obligations of local governmental units (counties, municipalities, townships, school districts, other special districts), while the remainder was issued directly by state governments.

A large percent of the debt outstanding was originally issued to finance educational facilities, indicating the importance of this item in capital outlays for states and localities. Other types of facilities financed by debt were streets and highways and the various local utility services.

The basic difference between state and local government debt and national debt has already been noted in Chapter 30. States and localities do not possess residual money-creating powers, as does the federal government. Hence they resort to debt only in case they desire to issue what has been called real debt. It is impossible for local units to disguise money creation under the name of public debt, the operation that has been the source of so much linguistic and analytical confusion in the case of national debt.

CONCLUSIONS

In the United States, the national debt remains largely the heritage of World War II, although the continued increases for the 1960s and 1970s suggest that national debt can no longer be treated as a war phenomenon. The size of the debt relative to GNP has diminished over the postwar period as the economy has grown, and in 1978, it was measured at less than 40 percent of the GNP.

The U.S. government debt may be classified by type of issue. Long-term issues, bonds, including those held by governmental agencies and trust funds, make up less than one half of the total. The short-term, nonfunded or "floating" debt is made up of Treasury notes, certificates, and bills.

The ownership of the debt is widely distributed. The sensitive part of the national debt is that part held by the commercial banks, since this carries with it inflationary potential. Federal Reserve operations by themselves can, of course, either encourage or discourage commercial banks from using their holdings of national debt to expand credit.

Public debt issues by subordinate units of government have increased dramatically in the postwar years and now total about one third that of the national government.

SUPPLEMENTARY READING

For current factual information concerning the composition of the national debt, the ownership of the debt, maturity schedules, and so on, the student should consult the monthly *Treasury Bulletin.* For more detailed accounting, including more historical data, the *Annual Report of the Secretary of the Treasury* may be consulted.

For a very helpful handbook, the student may also consult *Securities of the United States Government,* biennially published by The First Boston Corporation.

part VIII

State and local fiscal systems

32

State-local
expenditure patterns

Discussion and study of the public finances is too often concentrated on institutions and problems at the federal or central level of government, especially in the United States. The political structure of the United States is that of federalism, with sovereignty legally and constitutionally divided between the federal government and the states. Despite the increasing importance that the federal government has assumed in the past quarter century, any consideration of the public finances, or the public economy, would be seriously incomplete without some consideration of the fiscal systems of the state and local units of government.

It is important to note that the relative dominance of the federal government in the national fiscal scene has prevailed only over the years since World War II. A brief reference to Table 5–1 (Chapter 5) reveals that combined state-local expenditures in all years (other than war periods) were larger than federal expenditures up until the late 1930s. In the last half of the 1930s, the two shares were roughly in balance. Since World War II, however, federal expenditure totals have tended to predominate in relative importance. But even in these postwar years, state-local expenditures have been important, in both relative and absolute terms. Roughly speaking, the combined state-local spending totals add up to more than one half of federal totals or more than one third of total public spending.

Perhaps a more significant comparison lies in the relation of total state-local expenditures to GNP. Combined state-local expenditures amounted to approximately 14 percent of GNP in the late 1970s. This is a significant proportion, and it is sufficiently indicative of the importance of state-local systems. In absolute terms, the states and the local units of government were spending almost $250 billion annually in 1978. As Table 5–1 also shows, this total has been growing somewhat more rapidly than federal spending over the whole period since the Korean War. Urgent demands have been placed upon, and continue to be placed upon, states and localities, notably the municipalities. By the 1980s, state-local spending totals will exceed $300 billion annually, measured in current dollars. If inflation continues at the pace of the 1970s, this estimate will have to be adjusted upward.

The discussion in earlier chapters of federal expenditures by major functional categories indicated to some extent the division of fiscal responsibility between the federal government and the states. A major item of federal spending is national defense, a function that clearly belongs under central government control. Related items such as foreign aid, aid to veterans, and interest on the national debt are also clearly federal responsibilities. In addition, spending for generalized subsidy programs, such as that for agriculture, must be centrally financed. Hence a proportionally large share of the federal expenditure budget is devoted to items that fall appropriately within federal government responsibility. Relatively few federal programs are devoted to providing benefits that could be financed and administered efficiently by states and local units of government. These programs are, however, important and, because of the alternative possibilities for financing, are highly controversial. These include portions of the natural resources, commerce and transportation, housing and community development, health, labor and welfare, and education items in the federal budget. Perhaps the most characteristic feature of the changes introduced in the federal budget account in the 1960s, during the years of the "New Frontier" and the "Great Society" was the rapid expansion of federal spending categories in these areas.

State and local units provide public services that are more closely tied to the individual beneficiary, services which affect individual recipients more directly. Table 32–1 includes a generalized breakdown of state-local spending into broad functional categories that are roughly comparable with those employed in the discussion of the federal government budget. Note that, as a general rule, state and local governments provide services that fall within the category of quasi-collective services, which were discussed in Chapter 4. That is to say, few services provided by states and local units are purely collective in the sense that, say, national defense is collective. By and large, there is some aspect of private divisible benefit to be secured from public services performed by the subordinate units of government. The best example is, of course, education, which makes up the largest single item of state-local spending. Although the provision of education clearly has certain collective aspects, it also has certain privately divisible benefits which accrue directly to the individuals and families securing the services. Health and welfare services are quite similar in this respect.

TABLE 32–1
State-local direct general expenditures, in billions of dollars by major functional category for fiscal 1977 (including expenditures from grants-in-aid)

Education	$103
Highways	23
Public welfare	35
Health and hospitals	23
Other services	27
Interest	11
Miscellaneous	51
Total	$273

Source: Census Bureau, *Governmental Finances in 1976–77.*

DIVISION OF RESPONSIBILITY BETWEEN STATES AND LOCAL UNITS OF GOVERNMENT

The essential division of responsibility in a federal political structure is that drawn between the powers of the federal or central government and those of the state governments. This division of responsibility is presumably protected by constitutional provisions. Within each state there is also a second division of fiscal responsibility between the powers of the state and those of the local units—the counties, municipalities, school districts, and so on. This division of fiscal responsibility is more administrative and legislative than constitutional. All local units of government are creations of the states, which hold the residual power to destroy all units created. There is not, therefore, the same meaning of the separation of fiscal responsibility between the states and the local units as there is between the central government and the states.

The actual division of fiscal authority between the states and their subordinate units varies from state to state, and the administrative devices for coordinating state and local expenditure and tax systems are varied and diverse. Broadly speaking, the grounds for the division of fiscal responsibility here are similar to those that divide federal and state-local responsibility. The more divisible and the more concentrated are the benefits from the public services provided, the greater is the advantage in having the services performed by the small units of government. The benefits from a city sewage system, for example, accrue largely to the citizens of the city itself. Whether or not a particular city provides for a magnificent sewage system or one just adequate to its needs is normally left to the responsibility of the individual city. Residents of other subdivisions in the state are concerned relatively little by a particular city's decision on such questions. By contrast, if the individual city, county, or school district should decide to close its schools, this is a matter for concern of the whole surrounding area. Such decisions as the latter have decisive "spillover" effects. Hence we find that states have, without exception, assumed a considerable portion of the final fiscal responsibility for financing education. Educational expenses are shared between the state and the local units, with the state normally assuming the role of ensuring that certain "minimum" standards of service are satisfied in all local units.

For any particular public service there is, of course, a single most "efficient" size of governmental unit. And the more or less accidental political structure that has developed does little to guarantee that existing units are of the "optimum" size, considered solely in the cost sense. Some steps have been made in recent years toward improvements in this direction, but significant further improvements seem possible. Of course, noneconomic considerations may in many cases dictate that the "optimum" size governmental unit should not be organized.

STATE-LOCAL EXPENDITURES FOR EDUCATION

It will be useful to discuss each major item of state-local spending separately. Education is the most important category of the group by a considerable margin. In 1977, a total of approximately $103 billion out of a combined state-local outlay (including expenditures for federal grants-in-aid) of about $273 billion was devoted to the financing of education, or approximately 38 percent of all state-local general spending. Of this total, about 26 percent, or something over $27 billion, was spent directly by state governments, while the remaining 74 percent was spent through local governments. Education is financed and controlled locally by counties, cities, municipalities, townships, school districts, and perhaps other organizational units. The primary distinction among such systems is that between the independent school district, which is specifically organized to collect revenues and to finance education, and the more inclusive government unit, which normally has several other public service functions to perform. The school district is, however, the predominantly important unit.

One of the most striking of the postwar phenomena was the rapid increase in population. Birthrates were expected to increase during the war years, but demographers predicted an early slacking off in the rate of population increase in the immediate postwar period. Such a predicted decrease did not occur. Consequently, one of the most important changes in postwar America was the dramatic increase in the output of children. Only in the late 1950s and the early 1960s did the birthrate fall as had been predicted. The increase in children placed tremendous new burdens on the educational facilities of the nation, and the picture of the overcrowded classroom and the overworked and underpaid teacher became an American stereotype in the 1950s. While some aspects of this popular image resulted perhaps from shrewd propaganda on the part of certain professional associations, there is no denying that the pressure on the states and the local units to expand educational expenditures was very great.

The degree of response by governments to the educational needs of the postwar period was phenomenal. Table 32–2 traces total expenditures for education in selected years and examination of these figures indicates the dramatic increase in education expenditures which occurred in the two decades following World War II.

TABLE 32–2
State and local expenditures for public education
(selected years 1939–1977, $ billions)

Year	Amount	Year	Amount
1939	$ 2.4	1964	$ 27.3
1946	3.6	1966	34.8
1948	5.1	1968	41.1
1950	6.5	1970	52.7
1952	8.4	1972	64.9
1954	10.0	1973	69.7
1956	12.5	1974	75.8
1958	15.9	1975	87.9
1960	18.7	1976	97.2
1962	22.5	1977	102.8

Source: For years through 1957, data is taken from U.S. Department of Health, Education, and Welfare, *Financing Public School Facilities, 1959*. Data from 1957 on taken from U.S. Bureau of the Census, *Summary of Governmental Finances–1967*. Data from 1968–1975 are taken from Tax Foundation, Inc., "Facts and Figures on Government Finance," 1973, 1977 editions. 1976 and 1977 figures are from Census Bureau, *Governmental Finances in 1976–77*.

As the data show, educational spending increased more than tenfold between 1946 and 1968. This compares with an approximate sixfold increase in remaining items of state-local spending over the same period. Perhaps a more significant measure of the relative increase in educational outlay in the postwar period lies in some comparison with the growth in national output. In 1946, education expenditure at all levels of government amounted to only 1.7 percent of GNP; in 1975, this share had increased to 8 percent.

The pressures on schools arising from sheer numbers of children began to ease in the 1970s. Lowered birthrates during the sixties led to a decline in school age population in the mid-1970s. Growth in real education expenditure began to taper off also. If adjustments for price level changes are made, real education expenditures by state and local governments only increased by 43 percent between 1968 and 1977, compared to a real increase of over 100 percent during the preceding decade.

Economic rationale of educational spending

Education belongs in the category called quasi-collective services introduced in the discussion of Chapter 4. That is to say, there are direct beneficiaries from any outlay on education; these are the children who are educated and the family units of which these children form a part. In this respect, educational services are divisible and are similar to ordinary services produced in the market economy. Educational services are, in this respect, similar to automobile mechanics' services or symphony orchestra services. If this were all there was to it, educational services might be financed exclusively by private market organization and there might be no need for government financing or for government operation.

In addition to the divisible private benefits from education, however, there are important "social" benefits. That is to say, all members of the social group, at least a large number of them, secure indirect advantages from having the children in the community well educated. These benefits spill over from the family group to the other members of the society. If the full responsibility for "purchasing" educational services were left to the private families directly, there would probably be too little expenditure on education. This is because the private family would spend money only to the point that its own expected benefits equaled or exceeded the private costs. The private family directly benefited could not be expected to take into account in its own decisions the spillover benefits or advantages that accrue to society in general. In more technical terms, education provides an example where under normal institutional circumstances the "social marginal productivity" or expenditure will exceed the "private marginal productivity" unless some collective or organized effort is undertaken. This fact justifies the inclusion of education among those services that should be collectively financed, at least in part. Education becomes a quasi-collective service.

Economic effects of public financing of educational services

The fiscal process exerts important effects on the benefits or spending side of the budget as well as on the tax side. A thorough analysis requires that the economic effects of the separate types of public spending be examined. The first point to be made concerns the inherent difficulty that any governmental unit must surmount when it tries to "give away," that is, to provide publicly, any services that are divisible among persons, or even partially so. If a service is purely collective in the sense defined in Chapter 4, no problems arise. But if the service has both "public" and "private" elements, certain conditions must be met before governmental provision can be carried out at all efficiently.

If a service is financed through the taxing process, the benefits are normally divorced from the "prices" paid for the services in taxation. The individual who enjoys the benefits does not take into account, in his own marginal decisions concerning consumption of the service, the added taxation that may be required to finance additional increments. This suggests that for those services which do, in part, provide divisible benefits to particular individuals and groups, "free" public provision could lead to a gross overinvestment of public resources under certain conditions. If those benefited should be able to expand their consumption substantially as a result of the fact that the service is freely available to them, large amounts of resources would have to be devoted to supply the demands. The necessary condition that must be satisfied for a service of this nature to be provided publicly without undue problems is that the elasticity of demand for the service must be near zero over the range between a positive user price level and a zero price. Governmental units cannot efficiently provide "free" services, the demand for which is relatively elastic over such ranges, unless, of course, supplementary rationing devices are to be introduced.

Education fits the inelastic demand case reasonably well; therefore, it can be financed as a quasi-collective service from tax revenues without the necessity of supplementary private pricing. This point can be clarified by looking at the nature of the demand for education. Cultural and institutional patterns of behavior in society dictate that all children between roughly the ages of 6 and 18 attend schools. A family with three children will consume 36 years of educational services. If these are provided freely through public support, there will be no consumption beyond the 36 years. If services can be somehow standardized in terms of quality, the government can provide these freely without great wastage of economic resources.

This case may be contrasted with government attempts to provide, say, water without charge to residents of a municipality. If water is provided free, many individuals will use additional water to the point where the incremental return reaches zero. The result will be a great wastage of water, which is, in most places, a scarce resource costing taxpayers something. An overinvestment in water supply will take place unless private consumption is directly restricted by a user price placed on its usage or by some other rationing device. The demand for water is reasonably elastic, while that for education is reasonably inelastic over the relevant price range.

The sharp dichotomy drawn here should not, however, be pushed to extremes. The demand for educational services surely has some elasticity, and the provision of "free" public schools exerts an effect toward causing some families to consume more resources than they would consume if some price were to be charged. On the other hand, some other families might actually spend more for educating their own children if they were not provided with the "free" public alternative. On balance, it is difficult to say whether or not private full-cost pricing for education would reduce total or aggregate spending on education. What can be said is that some families would, under such a scheme, spend too little, and some children would surely be educated less than the amount that is socially optimal. The availability of the public system does, however, generate added demands for extra capacity, for higher quality instruction, for more varied offerings, and so on. Since the improvement of quality is not associated with the payment of a higher price through taxation, such demands as these can be predicted in connection with any similar public services.

To an extent at least, local political units repond to the demands of those desiring better quality education, and in some cases, social wastage of resources may occur. Public opinion, as well as most expert opinion, seems inclined to the opposing view, however. It is commonly argued that inadequate investment has been made in education by governmental units. Social waste is held to occur because of too little investment in education, not too much. It is difficult to develop suitable means of measuring or testing the validity of these or the opposing arguments. To do so one must examine the extent to which political processes, as they are currently organized, respond to the demands of citizens for increased public services on the one hand and for lower taxes on the other.

The view that there has been, and is, underinvestment in the provision of educational services stems, at least in part, from conceiving of education as a form of investment, rather than as a form of consumption. Education clearly represents investment in the human being as an asset; the person who becomes educated becomes a more productive member of the social group whether productivity is measured purely in an economic sense or in some more general way. This increased productivity resulting from educational investment will be partially enjoyed by the individual who is himself educated, but partially it will spill over to others in the community. This point has been discussed above. But when the investment approach is taken to education, a supplementary reason for public financing appears. Even if the spillover or external effects of educational investment are neglected, private persons might not invest a sufficient amount in education if left wholly to their own devices. This is because the individuals who stand to gain the most privately from the increased productivity that education ensures do not themselves make the decisions. These are made for them by their families, at least for the early years of education. Second, even if the individuals who are educated make their own decisions, as they presumably do for higher education, they may not have access to adequate markets for loan capital with which investment might be financed.

This point can perhaps best be illustrated by a brief analysis of higher education. The divergence between the private marginal productivity and the social marginal productivity of investment in education decreases as the stage of education is advanced. For education beyond the high school level, there is some question as to the extent of this divergence, especially since it can be assumed that decisions with respect to higher levels of education are made by the individuals themselves, in large part. For present purposes, let us assume that benefits from higher education accrue largely to the individuals who are educated, not to society as a whole. The argument for public support that was discussed previously would not hold under these conditions. If the benefits accrue solely to individuals, that is to say, if the benefits are wholly divisible, the private market economy might be expected to organize higher education effectively. But this result might not be produced under current institutional arrangements. The individual student may recognize that his or her future earnings stream may be increased by additional educational investment, and this increase may be more than sufficient to cover the current cost. But the student, or prospective student, may not have the funds needed to make a proper investment decision. Normally, in analogous situations in the market economy, the capital market can be resorted to as a source of loan funds. The prospective student may not, however, be able to borrow despite the long-range productivity of such investment. The real difficulty is only in part the result of imperfections in the capital market as such; the trouble lies in the fact that individual persons cannot legitimately consider themselves (their own persons), as capital assets for purposes of providing collateral for loans. The prospective lender of funds cannot secure a wholly valid legal claim against the person of the student in exchange for lending the required investment funds. This makes the whole problem of investing in education somewhat different from that of ordinary investment in physical plant. It may make necessary particular governmental action in the direction of opening up sources of loan funds to prospective student borrowers, either directly or indirectly.

The argument here applies more specifically to graduate and professional education than to ordinary college education. For the latter, there remain spillover or external benefits that warrant, to an extent at least, general public subsidization, quite apart from facilitating loan arrangements. For the purely professional education,however, there is no economic argument, as such, for public support of financing, although arguments can be advanced for public action to facilitate loan arrangements. This distinction has not been recognized sufficiently in the popular discussion concerning public financing of higher education.

STATE-LOCAL EXPENDITURES FOR HIGHWAYS

State and local governments spent approximately $23 billion on roads and highways during fiscal 1977. This included slightly over $6 billion in grants from the federal government. Highways claimed about 8 percent of total state-local expenditures during that year. This represented a decline from the early 1970s when highway spending accounted for about 15 percent of state and local spending total.

Highways—public utilities or public goods?

The provision of road and street service has been considered to be an appropriate public or governmental function at least since the days of the Roman Empire. Roads have traditionally been conceived to be genuinely collective goods because a road, once constructed, appeared to be equally available to all potential users. As long as congestion did not become serious, the road usage of one person did not reduce the services that were available for others. Roads provided general access to property and provided a means for general communication among cities, towns, and villages. The "public" financing of public roads out of revenues collected from generally imposed taxes seemed fully acceptable to the citizen of almost any governmental unit prior to World War I.

The traditional view of the appropriateness of the "free" public road changed with the automotive revolution that has occurred during the 20th century, particularly in the years since World War I. The United States has literally become a nation on wheels, and this dramatic change in the American transportation pattern has decisively modified the traditional conception of the highway function of governments. The road or street no longer serves primarily as a means of providing access to property and as a means of general communication among localities. Highway services constitute a major input into the production and distribution of an important share of national real income.

Highways in modern times can more appropriately be classified as public utilities. Although their development will undoubtedly continue to be the direct responsibility of governments units, it seems clear that some method of pricing these services directly to users can be employed. Certain specific individuals exist who secure primary and direct benefits from having road and street services available and individual usage of these services can be measured directly without difficulty.

Highway taxes as user prices

The "public utility" conception of the highway function has not been fully accepted. However, the fiscal demands which the automotive revolution has placed on hard-pressed governments has forced a de facto recognition of this modified view of the highway. All states impose some taxes directly on owners and operators of motor vehicles and in many states the revenues raised from these taxes are earmarked for expenditure only on road construction and maintenance. These taxes include excise taxes on gasoline, motor vehicle registration fees, and third-structure taxes on gross receipts, ton-miles, axle-miles, and so on, which are imposed on commercial highway users. Such taxes are essentially user prices in that they represent an attempt on the part of the government concerned to impose differentially heavy taxes on the direct beneficiaries of the public services provided.

The direct user price is employed for toll highways, tunnels, and bridges. Prior to development of the federally financed interstate highway system, the toll road was gaining increasing popularity in the United States. However, the interstate highway program has replaced the need for additional toll facilities at least for an interim period.

The choice between direct pricing through tolls and indirect pricing that is represented by highway user taxes can be illustrated with reference to the interstate highway system. The federal government finances 90 percent of the costs of construction of this system of limited access roads, designed to connect the major population centers in the country. The principle of charging highway users directly with the full costs of the system was embodied in the original revenue legislation enacted in 1956. The federal share is financed through revenues collected from the federal highway user taxes. In this way, highway users will pay for the interstate system. But a more efficient method of payment would seem to be that of removing the federal user taxes and replacing these with a system of tolls to be charged on the completed system. Since design standards require that all roads in the system be of limited access, there would be no administrative reason why tolls could not be established. Certainly, the direct-pricing method would result in a more efficient usage. With indirect financing through user taxes, all motorists, whether or not they use interstate roads, will pay for the system. With the direct method of pricing, only those motorists who use the new facilities would be charged. The fact that the toll method of financing was never seriously proposed for the interstate highway system suggests that the traditional conception of the "free" public road has not been fully replaced by the public utility conception, although public opinion is willing to accept a de facto recognition of this more appropriate view through the levy of user taxes.

Criteria for highway investment and expenditure

What is the correct amount of spending on highways, roads, and streets? Should more be spent for this important function? Or are the states and the federal government currently spending too large a share of the nation's scarce economic resources in creating an ever-expanding network of concrete and asphalt? What criteria may be introduced to assist governmental units in making decisions such as these?

Insofar as user taxes are specifically tied to the direct benefits from highway consumption, some version of the profitability criterion seems to be indicated. The simplest rule would be one which limits highway expenditure to revenues collected from earmarked taxes. If these revenues prove more than sufficient to maintain an existing road network and to amortize the debt that may have been issued at the time of construction, a surplus will be generated which can be plowed back into new construction, improvement, and expansion of the system. If revenues are just sufficient to cover full maintenance and amortization charges, this indicates that neither expansion nor contraction of the highway network is needed. Finally, if revenues are not large enough to cover the necessary maintenance and amortization charges, the highway system should be reduced in scale.

This simple profitability rule works well only if certain conditions are present. The most important of these is that user prices must be set in a manner analogous to the competitive market price. The price charged to users of the facility must be sufficiently high to eliminate all excess demand if the facility is too small, and sufficiently low to eliminate all excess supply if the facility is too large. If expansion of the system is to be internally financed without debt issue, the user price must exceed the long-run average cost of supplying services. If user price is set equal to long-run average cost, excess demand will exist if the facility is too small, but no excess revenues will be accumulated for internal investment in expansion. Instead of "prcfits" being accumulated, a "shortage" of services will occur; unsatisfied demanders will be present.

The highway investment problem is made especially difficult for several reasons. In the first place, although user taxes do represent genuine user prices to a large extent, governments have never seen fit to set these taxes in accordance with accepted public utility pricing principles. At best, user taxes tend to be established at average cost levels regardless of the scale of operation to which the highway network has been constructed. Since, by the standard criteria, it seems almost certain that this network has remained too small during most of the period of the last 40 years, revenues from user taxes have not been sufficient to finance internally the expansion that has been needed.

One aspect of the difficulty arises from the peculiar nature of highway services. When roads are "underpriced," no "shortage" appears in the sense that would occur if water or electricity were underpriced. Roads do not "run out"; they are not "used up" in consumption. Instead, the quality of services enjoyed by each road user is diminished if the point is reached where excess demand is present. There are external diseconomies in road usage beyond a certain point, and these take the form of congestion, the characteristic phenomenon of modern urban America.

If, in fact, highway services are "underpriced," an increase in the general level of user taxes can accomplish two results at the same time. First, and most important, the increases can provide a source for accumulating funds with which road system expansion can be financed without resort to debt issue. Second, the increases, through the rationing inherent in any price structure, can reduce somewhat the usage of existing highway network; congestion can to some extent be relieved during the period of highway expansion that the elimination of congestion itself finances. A rudimentary examination of the highway system in the United States suggests that a general increase in highway user prices would be desirable for both of these reasons.

If highway user taxes are not increased, there are two alternative prospects. The first is simply that the congestion itself will establish some sort of equilibrium. Motorists will pay a major share of the costs of highway usage in the form of congestion. It should be emphasized that congestion costs involve an investment of economic resources just as much as does the construction of a highway network.

The second prospect is that projected traffic at current levels of user taxes be estimated along with the revenues that existing taxes will produce. If these future revenues can be accurately estimated, then a policy of debt financing for the required expansion in the road network may be undertaken. As shown in Chapter 30, the issue of public debt is justified where the benefits from investment are expected to accrue over long periods of time. A needed short-run construction program can be facilitated by resort to careful debt financing. A major difficulty with this approach lies in the fact that better highway facilities will themselves generate more traffic. Therefore, the issue of debt instruments to finance a planned once-and-for-all expansion in a highway network may not really resolve the dilemma. When the network is constructed, revenues produced may all be required to service the debt issue. No excess funds will be available to construct an expansion of service that the unanticipated demands on the network have created.

In the postwar period, states have followed all three routes toward solving the "highway problem." First of all, it is evident to all motorists that congestion has been allowed to develop. Second, highway user tax rates have been generally increased, and there seems to be no likelihood that these increases will cease in the near future. Highway construction costs have gone up rapidly so that some increases in tax rates would have been required even to maintain existing networks. Finally, states have issued bonds to finance road expansion. The federal government, in its important highway legislation of 1956, chose to finance its predominant share of the construction costs of the interstate highway system through increases in user taxes. After a heated and lengthy discussion and debate, those who advocated a pay-as-we-go federal program carried the day. The opposing group, who had proposed an issue of special federal highway bonds to finance the major part of the outlay on the interstate system, was defeated.

STATE AND LOCAL EXPENDITURES FOR PUBLIC WELFARE

In fiscal 1977, state and local governments spent almost $35 billion on public welfare. Over half of this, $19.5 billion, was financed by grants from the federal government.

A major change occurred with respect to state responsibility for public assistance when the federal Supplemental Security Income program was instituted in January 1974. This program has already been discussed in some detail in Chapter 19. Basically, the program provides a federally guaranteed minimum income for the needy aged, blind, or disabled. While states can supplement federal payments and, in fact, are required to do so if payments to their citizens prior to the SSI program exceeded the new minimum federal payment, the bulk of responsibility for aiding these groups has been taken over by the federal government.

Aid to Families with Dependent Children (AFDC) was unchanged by the 1974 SSI program. This program remains one of federal grants to the states on a matching formula basis. State governments have substantial administrative responsibility and determine the actual levels of benefits payments. In addition to federally subsidized assistance programs, most states and localities also finance general assistance programs from their own revenue sources.

Substantially all expenditures included under the various public assistance programs are transfer expenditures. That is to say, no public services, as such, are provided. Payments are made directly in money to eligible recipients. As previously discussed, transfer expenditures exert somewhat less-extensive economic effects than so-called productive expenditures that involve direct governmental purchases of either resources or final goods and services. Individuals' choices are modified to a lesser degree with direct payments of money than with free provision of particular goods and services.

Public assistance programs do not fit neatly into the classification of collective goods, quasi-collective goods, and private goods publicly provided that was set up in Chapter 4. Public assistance payments clearly benefit individuals directly, as private individuals. These benefits are wholly divisible, and individual shares can be readily calculated. The collective aspects of these payments stem from the external effects on citizens as a group arising from the relief of poverty and misery in the whole community or society. The relief of poverty is a genuine "social" or "collective" objective that can be met, in part at least, through the transfer process facilitated by the fiscal system. Through the fiscal process, individuals as taxpayers can transfer funds impersonally to individuals as eligible recipients. This transfer process becomes supplementary to the set of private transfers which is implemented through private philanthropic means. To a degree, private charities are also facilitated by the fiscal process. The deductibility of contributions to charitable organizations for federal (and some state) income tax computations provides a strong fiscal incentive for the furtherance of private relief of poverty.

Public assistance programs are deliberately aimed at modifying the distributive results that the market economy, in its modern institutional form, produces, even the results that emerge after the imposition of the tax system which, of course, accomplishes its own net redistribution. These public assistance payments embody a social recognition that those who are not able to contribute sufficiently to national production so as to earn privately what society might consider to be a "minimum" living requirement should be directly aided. These payments are almost purely redistributive in effect.

If substantial economic growth can be sustained in the American economy, if the nation can become progressively more affluent, the need for the relief of poverty should be reduced, provided that the income gains are general throughout all sectors of the population. Poverty is, of course, always a relative, not an absolute, condition, and the adage "the poor are always with us" remains true regardless of the average level of income. There will always remain the lowest one third or one fifth of income receivers. And social values will tend to support measures aimed at some improvement in the relative position of the "poor." In addition, if the gains are not evenly distributed throughout the whole social structure, economic growth may be accompanied by "pockets of poverty." The intensive campaign reflected in the "war on poverty" publicized in 1964 was based on both of these elements, plus a liberal dosage of partisan politics. Perhaps surprisingly, the "war on poverty" seemed to catch fire politically, and it provided the basis for the many and various programs commenced under the Johnson spending explosion between 1965 and 1968. Throughout the late 1960s, the redistributive objective remained an important element in American liberal politics. Dissatisfaction with the results of existing welfare and assistance programs caused more emphasis to be placed on reforms centered around the concept of general income maintenance, with the negative income tax prominently featured in the discussion.

The economic effects of public assistance programs are relatively easy to trace. Insofar as individuals receive direct income subsidies from government, there will be some net reduction in their incentives to earn incomes in the private economy and to put aside incomes for the provision of retirement support. The direction of such effects cannot be denied, although it is extremely difficult to estimate the extent to which behavior is actually modified. Public assistance payments to those individuals who are wholly incapable of earning incomes in the private economy do not have this effect, of course. But the "pre-welfare state" means of treating such individuals was some provision from family resources. In one sense, the governmental unit has replaced the family in its acceptance of responsibility for the indigent. Family responsibility and solidarity has been weakened by this change, along with many other changes, in the 20th century. Whether this is viewed as good or bad depends on individual value judgments.

HEALTH AND HOSPITALS

In 1977, more than $22 billion were spent by states and local units of government for public health services including construction, operation and maintenance of public hospital facilities. Expenditures were divided in roughly equal proportions between states and localities.

Expenditures for hospital operation may be contrasted with those for public assistance in that the former involve the direct provision of a service rather than a transfer payment. The object of the public provision of hospital care is not, therefore, simply that of relieving poverty. The object is that of ensuring that a specific service, adequate medical and hospital care, is made available to all citizens. In other words, the "free" provision of hospital care to those individuals who cannot afford private facilities produces spillover benefits to the community at large; the services provided are essentially quasi-collective in terms of our earlier classification.

Public hospital services may also be contrasted with public educational services in a different way. Whereas the experience of the United States has included the provision of "free" public education to most children of the nation, with privately financed education being the exception rather than the rule, this has not been true as regards to medical care and hospital services. In the latter case, at least until the late 1960s, privately financed medical care and privately financed and privately supplied hospital services have been the normal order of affairs. Before Medicare, public or collective provision of these was normally extended only to those who were considered unable financially to bear the full costs of treatment. Thus public education in the United States has never been primarily considered to be redistributional in effect, while the "free" public provision of medical care, clinics, and hospitals has been included directly as a part of the overall "social services" with strongly redistributionist overtones. In Great Britian since 1948, medical and hospital care has been provided at "zero" prices through the National Health Service, financed from general tax revenues. Great Britain has chosen to define medical care as a quasi-collective service to the fullest extent.

In the United States, provision of this service has traditionally been left to the market economy, although its quasi-collective nature has been acknowledged by provision of care to those unable to purchase this service in the market.

The financing of medical and hospital care underwent major changes with the adoption of the Medicaid and Medicare programs in the late 1960s. Medicaid provides health care services to the poor with financing shared by federal and state governments on a matching grant basis. Under Medicare, the major share of medical services required by the aged are financed by federal funds collected from the proceeds of an increment to the employment tax and earmarked for the social security trust fund. These programs resulted in substantial additions to the total demand for medical services with predicted economic effects. The price of health care services at all levels rose dramatically during the late 1960s and the 1970s. The rise in hospital costs was particularly dramatic, and by the late 1970s, there were increasing public demands for direct public controls of this component of health care costs. If such controls materialize in the 1980s and if proposals for more widespread government subsidization of health care purchases are adopted in the form of some national health insurance scheme, the impact on state and local government-run hospitals will be significant. Hospital administrators are likely to be confronted on the one hand with further substantial increases in demand for both quantity and quality of service and, on the other hand, with stringent controls on the extent to which higher costs can be incurred to meet these demands.

OTHER SERVICES

The main categories of other services provided at state and local government levels in the United States include such things as police and fire protection, sewage and sanitation services and parks and other recreational facilities and services. In fiscal 1977, expenditures for these other services were $27 billion, 10 percent of total direct expenditures.

The services in this category fall in two distinct classifications. First of all, there are those services that are genuinely collective in the sense described in Chapter 4, but which are collective only to the limited geographic area. The indivisibility of benefits extends only to the proximate boundaries of the local unit of government. Second, there are many services which are primarily private in terms of benefit classification. These are really private goods and services that are publicly supplied. Almost every one of such services will have some collective aspects, but the reason for public provision, as such is to be found elsewhere. They are really "public utilities" in the traditional usage of this term. Such services as water supply, sewage disposal, transit facilities, electric and gas distribution systems, and even roads and streets can be included under the public utility classification.

Among the local services that are genuinely collective, but which are limited in geographic coverage, police and fire protection are the clearest cases. The location of the firehouse and fire company within the ward of the city benefits citizens who are residents of the ward indivisibly. That is to say, the protection of one house does not reduce the protection available for another house within its same vicinity. Individual or private protection against fire is, of course, possible, but, due to this indivisibility in usage, collective organization to provide fire protection is far more efficient than private organization. This collective organization could, of course, be voluntarily introduced, as witness the many volunteer fire departments in small villages and towns. But, as a general rule, collective action implies action through the fiscal process of the local government unit.

Parks and recreational facilities are further examples of this type of good or service. There are clearly divisible benefits from many such facilities, however, and the demand for their services may be quite elastic. Therefore, the public financing of recreational facilities may have to be supplemented by some direct pricing of the services to prevent undue congestion and overcrowding, especially in highly populated areas.

DEBT SERVICE

The principles of debt issue for states and local units of government are the same as those discussed in Chapter 30. The only difference between state-local debt and national debt is that state-local units do not have access to money creation; they must, therefore, issue real or genuine public debt. They have no opportunity to issue currency disguised as "debt."

The total state-local debt outstanding in 1977 was approximately $257 billion. For rough comparative purposes, this total was only slightly less than the annual rate of state-local expenditures, including debt service and amortization.

Tax exemption of interest on state-local securities

The one feature of state-local debt issue that seems worthy of note is the fact that the receipt of interest on state-local securities is specifically exempted from federal income taxation. This places a differential premium on the ownership of state-local debt instruments, especially for higher income groups, and this allows states and localities to market securities at highly favorable rates. As a result, yields on reasonably secure state and local bonds normally fall below yields on federal bonds, the interest from which is fully taxable.

This exemption feature periodically comes under criticism as an unwarranted loophole in federal income taxation. Because of the progressive rate structure of the federal personal income tax, wealthy taxpayers tend to predominate as recipients of state and local bond interest payments. However, some care should be exercised in interpreting this result. Because of the exemption, the market interest rate is lower on state and local bonds. Therefore, an individual investing in state and local bonds must make a larger investment than would be required to secure the same interest income from private sector bond issues. At some marginal tax bracket, investors are just indifferent between investing in state and local bonds paying taxfree interest and investing in private bonds, on which the interest payments are taxable. For individuals whose total income puts them in lower marginal tax brackets, private bond purchases provide the greatest net return. Individuals in high brackets have a positive incentive to invest in state and local bonds.

CONCLUSIONS

State-local fiscal systems are an important part of the overall pattern of public finance in the United States. Up until World War II, the combined impact of state-local systems on the economy was larger than that of the federal system, and even in the late 1960s, the state-local expenditure totals were almost as large as federal spending totals if national defense outlays were excluded from the latter. State-local spending declined in relative terms after the later 1960s partly as a result of increasing federal involvement in traditionally state-local functions. In absolute terms, however, state-local spending remains large.

The division of fiscal responsibility between the federal goverment and the subordinate units is reasonably clear cut. States and local units provide services that are more concentrated geographically and that are closer to the economy of the private citizen. A significant number of services provided by states and local governments, especially the latter, are of a quasi-collective nature. They provide certain divisible individual or private benefits in addition to the collective benefits accruing to the whole social group.

Expenditures for education are the most important single category for states and localities. These are followed by spending for highways, for public assistance, for public hospitals, and for community facilities generally. Almost any one of the separate items included in state-local expenditure programs raises many problems of interesting and important economic content. In many cases, the extent of collective interest is highly debatable, and this is subject to no fully acceptable measurement.

The expenditures made by states and local units have increased rapidly over the past decade and may be expected to continue to increase over the next one. The demand for collective services that are generated by the expansion in population and its concentration in urban areas confronts initially the local community. Because of this demand and because of the relatively rigid revenue structures characteristic of local units, an increasing clamor for federal government financial aid in support of essentially localized functions can be predicted.

SUPPLEMENTARY READING

For a book devoted exclusively to educational financing, see Jesse Burkhead, *Public School Finance* (Syracuse, N.Y.: Syracuse University Press, 1964).

For a treatment of the relationship between education and poverty, see Thomas I. Ribich, *Education and Poverty* (Washington, D.C.: The Brookings Institution, 1968).

For a discussion of negative income taxes, see Christopher Green, *Negative Taxes and the Poverty Problem* (Washington, D.C.: The Brookings Institution, 1967).

For a sophisticated treatment of the highway issues dicussed in this chapter, see A. A. Walters, *The Economics of Road User Charges,* International Bank for Reconstruction and Development (Baltimore: The Johns Hopkins Press, 1968).

33

State-local general revenue sources: Income taxation, specific excise taxation

T he states and local governments finance public services from revenues drawn from a wide variety of sources. An important part of local government activity is devoted to providing services which fall within a general category called public utilities. To a large extent, these services are financed from charges levied directly on users of the services. These revenues cannot legitimately be classified as "taxes." As was discussed in Chapter 31, in a broad sense, the maintenance of the highway and street systems is a "public utility," and this system is financed almost wholly from charges placed on highway users.

A second revenue source for states and local governments which may be discussed briefly at this point is the unemployment compensation tax. This tax in the several states is levied on employers, and the proceeds are earmarked for a trust fund account maintained by the state. Expenditures from this trust fund account are devoted exclusively to financing unemployment compensation payments to qualified workers during periods when they are unemployed and meet the required conditions of eligibility. The federal government, through a system of grants-in-aid, finances the administration of the unemployment compensation program.

In its broad outlines and in its economic effects, the unemployment compensation program is similar to the social security program. It is questionable whether the program should be discussed as a state or as a federal program, since federal government encouragement and support is so closely involved in the whole organization.

GENERAL REVENUE

User charges and employment taxes have been mentioned briefly with a view of eliminating them from further discussion in this chapter. The subsequent discussion will include only tax sources that produce general fund revenues for states and local units of government. Table 33–1 provides some rough indication of the importance of the various tax sources, including motor fuel and motor vehicle and operators' taxes, which are not properly general fund revenue producers. Other revenues available to states and local units, especially, are left out of account in Table 33–1, notably public utility revenues, unemployment compensation taxes, and intergovernmental transfers.

Property taxes are the predominant single source of general revenues for the combined state-local systems, and this source is used primarily by localities. Chapter 36 will be devoted exclusively to a

TABLE 33–1
Sources of tax revenue—state-local fiscal systems (fiscal 1977)

Type of tax	Amount ($ millions)	Percentage
Property	$ 62,535	35.6
Excise, sales and gross revenue	51,431	29.2
Motor fuel	9,164	5.2
Individual income	29,245	16.6
Motor vehicle and operator's license	4,941	2.8
Corporation income	9,174	5.2
Other	9,389	5.4
Total	$175,879	100.0

Source: U.S. Bureau of the Census, *Governmental Finances in 1976–77.*

consideration of some of the problems arising with the taxation of real property.

The most important source of general revenues for state governments is the taxation of general sales. This source will be discussed fully in Chapter 34.

In the present chapter, two of the most important remaining sources of general revenues will be discussed briefly — income taxation and specific excise taxation. The latter is exemplified by the taxation of liquor or tobacco products.

STATE AND LOCAL INCOME TAXATION

Income taxation is the primary source of revenues for the federal government, but this institution is much less important for states and localities. Note from Table 33-1, that individual income taxation produces about 17 percent of state-local tax revenues, while corporation income taxation produces an additional 5 percent.

Income taxation is understandably a much more suitable revenue source for the federal government than for the states, and, for the same reason, it is more suitable for states than for local units of government. Adam Smith said that the division of labor is limited by the extent of the market. This may be amended slightly here. The appropriateness of income taxation for a unit of government is directly dependent on the extent to which its boundaries are coincident with the extent of the market.

In 1978 44 states levied taxes on individual incomes. Forty-six states imposed taxes on corporation income. Rates under both state personal income taxes and state corporation income taxes tend to be lower than rates under the federal tax, for obvious reasons. Rate structures for the personal income tax tend to be progressive. Maximum marginal rates of tax vary from 2 percent to a high of 19.8 percent. Rate brackets vary widely among states, as do exemptions and deductions, although pressures are being brought upon state fiscal authorities to bring state structures more into line with federal procedures. Only Nebraska, Rhode Island, and Vermont, among all the states, compute liability for state personal income tax as a stipulated percentage of the federal tax liability.

Corporation income tax rates tend to be proportional, with 6 percent being the modal value. Minnesota levies the highest rate of 12 percent.

States tend to be limited in their usage of either personal or corporate income taxes by the fact that the national economy is an integrated market. The freedom of migration across state boundaries, for both human and nonhuman resources, tends to ensure that state governments will impose relatively low rates on incomes. Any attempt by a single state or by a single group of states to impose differentially high rates would cause some outmigration of resources to low-tax states. If a state cannot, or does not, impose an income tax, or imposes one at low rates, other taxes must, of course, be introduced. The income tax is, however, the most direct of all taxes, and individual resource owners are more likely to respond to income tax differentials than they are to differential indirect tax rates.

As of September 1976, some county and municipal governments in ten states[1] were imposing their own taxes on incomes. These taxes are normally proportional and are levied at very low rates, for the most part at 1 percent and in most cases not higher than 2 percent. New York City has a progressive income tax with rates ranging between 0.9 and 4.3 percent. In Philadelphia, the tax rate is approximately 4.3 percent. These municipal taxes tend to be based on gross incomes rather than net incomes.

Perhaps the most important problem in the administration of state income taxation (and even more acutely in that of local income taxation) lies in the inherent conflict between taxation on the basis of residence, or domicile, of the taxpayer and taxation on the basis of situs or place where the income is earned. An individual may be a resident of one state or local unit, and may earn all or a part of his or her income in another state or local unit. To which unit should the wage earner be liable for an income tax, the state of domicile or the state where income is earned? This problem has never been satisfactorily resolved, and it becomes progressively more acute as mobility increases. It is especially important in the large metropolitan areas where urban commuting patterns allow individuals to live in jurisdictions sometimes far removed from those in which they earn incomes. If either the earning pattern or the residential pattern were roughly equivalent among the various states and jurisdictions, consistent adherence to either conception of tax base would produce reasonably good results. However, such patterns are not uniform; some jurisdictions tend to be "dormitories" for others. Only through the

---

[1]Alabama, Delaware, Indiana, Kentucky, Maryland, Michigan, Missouri, New York, Ohio, and Pennsylvania.

introduction of reciprocal arrangements among the jurisdictions involved, such as that in effect between New York and New Jersey, can this problem be met.

The administration of the corporation income tax is even more difficult in this respect. Many corporations are, of course, organized to conduct business in many states. It becomes very difficult to separate the net income earned in one state from that earned in another. Given the difference in state laws determining the allocability of income earned, the corporation may be subjected to double taxation in some cases and may escape liability altogether on certain parts of income in other cases. The solution must at best be found through the use of rather arbitrary conventions.

As suggested above, the fundamental deficiency in state and local taxation of income lies in the fact that incomes are earned in the whole economy. The geographic limitation of fiscal authority imposed on the states gives rise to both the interstate competition for resources and to the conflict between domicile and situs bases for taxation. Partly for these reasons, and partly for the more general desirability of maintaining some separation of tax sources in a genuinely federal fiscal structure, many students of fiscal theory and practice argue that the taxation of income, both personal and corporate, should be left primarily to the federal or central government. States and local units should not utilize this revenue source to any great extent but should instead rely more heavily on indirect taxes and taxes on real property. This argument has much to commend it, especially when the overall fiscal system of both the central and state-local units is examined. The argument in support of more extensive use of income taxation by states and local units seems less convincing. This argument is normally based on the presumed regressive nature of indirect taxes and on the greater revenue productivity of income taxes.

SPECIFIC EXCISE TAX: SUMPTUARY AND REGULATORY

Taxes that are imposed on the act of producing, distributing, selling, or consuming particular products and services are important revenue producers for states and local government despite the fact that these taxes have been overshadowed in recent decades by taxes imposed more generally on all or a large number of goods and services.

Income taxes, property taxes, and general sales taxes are widely accepted as belonging to the category of taxes appropriate to the financing of general-purpose expenditures; these taxes are "general" in intent if not in effect. By contrast, the most important feature of the specific excise tax is its very lack of generality. It is justified precisely because of the fact that it is discriminatory. Hence, something other than the mere needs of government for revenue must be employed in support of singling out particular products or services for specific taxation. Why should the producers, processors, or consumers of this or that good or service be discriminated against by the fiscal system?

Specific excise taxes are interesting primarily because they do represent attempts made by governments to employ the fiscal process for purposes other than mere revenue raising. The very attempts here suggest that there exists some theory of the results or effects of the taxes. As we shall see, these taxes present a certain image to the public at large which, correct or incorrect, is widely accepted. These specific excise taxes are not normally designed solely for nonrevenue purposes, however; in certain instances, revenue-producing aspects loom as very important, notably when attempts are made to remove or reduce the levies. On the other hand, taxes such as these could rarely, if ever, be approved initially were it not for the nonrevenue aspects. Governments cannot readily impose a discriminatory tax without some cause and some justification.

Broadly speaking, there seem to be two general reasons why governments single out particular commodities and services for the purpose of levying specific taxes. A tax may be imposed for *sumptuary* or for *regulatory* reasons, although this separation between these two is not entirely distinct. A sumptuary tax is defined as a tax the effects of which are held to be desirable on moral or ethical grounds. As suggested previously, the support of a tax for this reason must assume that these effects are roughly predictable. In the sumptuary tax, a majority of a legislative assembly expresses its belief that the consumption of certain products or services should be discouraged. Thus, the implied assumption in all sumptuary taxes is that the imposition of a tax will, in fact, discourage the consumption of the product or the use of the service.

The obvious examples of sumptuary taxation are the levies placed on the production, sale, or consumption of tobacco products and alcoholic beverages by the federal government, the states, and the localities. These taxes are important revenue producers for the state-local systems. To these most familiar examples must be added those taxes on such things as playing cards, billiard tables, soft drinks, cartridges, cabaret admissions, and many other products and services which are to be found in one or more of the state revenue systems.

The citizens of a governmental unit, acting collectively through the legislative process, may try to prohibit or discourage the consumption of a particular product or service in two separate ways. First, they may approve legal regulations that prohibit the sale and use of the product directly. Thus we find various laws, state and local, that prohibit the sale of narcotics, the sale of alcohol to minors, the sale of fireworks, and so on. Laws such as these will normally be used only when the predominant majority of the citizens consider the consumption of the item in question undesirable.

The second method of sumptuary regulation is that of utilizing the taxing process as a supplement to the ordinary market process. Rather than impose a direct prohibition on the sale of fireworks, for example, a city government may levy such a high tax on the sale of fireworks that the end result is achieved. No revenue would be produced by a fully effective sumptuary tax such as this, but the regulatory purpose would be accomplished. Normally, however, the taxing device is employed only where no overwhelming consensus exists in support of direct prohibition of consumption. Certain groups in the society may desire to see consumption outlawed, but their numbers are not sufficient to superimpose their own desires on other citizens who desire no restriction on the consumption of the product in question. It is in situations such as this that the tax offers a satisfactory means of reaching what may genuinely be called a social compromise. The tax can be imposed in such a way as to discourage consumption without eliminating it. The voluntary purchase of the commodity can be allowed to continue on the assurance that those individuals who do consume will be forced to pay a differentially high price for this privilege. In a very general sense, this seems to offer an explanation of the relative stability in social attitudes toward liquor consumption in the United States during the past quarter century. Direct prohibition was tried and failed because there was not sufficient public support for the restriction on individual choice that the prohibition embodied. Prohibition was repealed, but in its stead voluntary consumption was allowed only after very high federal and state taxes were imposed.

Gambling provides an interesting example of an activity that is treated in different ways by the different states. In many states, all forms of gambling activity are legally prohibited; the taxing process is not utilized. In other states, gambling activity is legalized in certain specific forms, but heavy taxes are imposed on the consumption of risk by individual citizens. The pari-mutuel horse and dog tracks are the obvious illustrations of this approach. Nevada offers an example of a state which has widened the range of legalized gambling to include many other forms, and with this extension has come the increasing productivity of this sumptuary revenue source.

The second nonrevenue purpose of specific excise taxation may be regulatory rather than sumptuary. Sumptuary taxation is desired because it is regulatory, but the converse need not hold true. There are taxes which have as a direct purpose some reduction of consumption of particular goods but which do not imply any moral or ethical condemnation of the consumption activity. The best single example of this sort of tax is that imposed on the sale of oleomargarine in several states. Taxes levied on chain store sales provide a second good illustration.

Taxes such as these are likely to be imposed as a means of protecting state and local industries against the competition of products imported from other states in the national economy. This is obviously true of oleomargarine taxes; the taxes were introduced because of the political influence of dairy interests. Any state or local tax designed to serve primarily as a regulatory device to protect domestic industry is on the margin of constitutionality. This fact serves to explain why such protective taxes have not been more prevalent in state-local systems. The Constitution of the United States prevents states and local units of government from interfering directly with the freedom of commerce across state boundaries in the nation. One of the reasons for the rapid growth and the high-level productivity of the American economy lies in the extent of the free-trade area encompassed by the several states. If the separate states and localities were to be allowed to accomplish through taxation what they could not accomplish directly this great advantage would be lost. For the most part, such protective taxes are undesirable, not only for the whole nation, but for the interest of the states themselves. The attempts to impose protective taxation as a substitute for protective tariffs tend to be motivated by narrowly partisan interests. State fair-trade laws, state unfair-practices acts, and many state and local licensing arrangements and regulations are undesirable for the same reasons, and these are perhaps considerably more serious barriers to interstate and interregional freedom of trade than are state and local protective taxes.

SPECIFIC EXCISE TAXATION: ECONOMIC EFFECTS

The taxation of the sale or consumption of a single commodity or service provides the fiscal theorist with his best opportunity to apply the partial equilibrium approach to economic theory, an approach that was developed by Alfred Marshall. As Marshall himself suggested, almost all of the important principles of economics can be illustrated through the use of the tax device. As suggested earlier, much of the support for specific excise taxation is based on a presumed knowledge of its effects. Careful analysis tends to provide some verification of this popular image in a single case, although this is perhaps the most important of the several cases that will be discussed.

Competitive conditions—constant cost industry

We shall first examine carefully the one case in which the popular image of the tax is verified. This is where the tax is imposed on the product of a competitive industry that is small in relation to the total economy and employs no permanently specialized resources. After all adjustments to the tax have been made, the price to the consumer will rise by the full amount of the tax. The final incidence of the tax will rest exclusively with the consumers of the product, and the quantity consumed will be reduced to the extent caused by the tax-induced price increase.

To understand fully the process through which these conclusions are reached, an analytical model must be introduced and the effects must be traced out step by step. Let us assume initially that the industry under consideration is fully competitive and is in a position of long-run equilibrium before the imposition of the tax. This assumption implies that several conditions must be satisfied. First, there are sufficient firms in the industry to ensure that no single firm has any appreciable influence over the market price of the product. Second, each firm in the industry is producing at its most efficient scale of operations, and each firm is making normal returns on its capital investment. There is no incentive for capital investment in the industry to be either reduced or increased. Third, the price to the consumer is equal to the average cost of production, including in this cost the normal rate of return on investment. Fourth, the price to the consumer is also equal to the marginal cost of production for all firms.

For purposes of simplifying the analysis, we assume that each firm sells its product directly to consumers and that the products are sold immediately after they are produced.

We now impose a tax on the sale of the commodity produced by this industry. The tax is defined as a fixed amount per unit of product; the results would be identical if we assume that the tax is levied in terms of a fixed percentage of market price. The total tax must be paid to the tax collector by the producing firms.

The initial impact of this tax on the firm will be identical with an increase in both marginal and average cost. In order to produce and sell a unit of the commodity, the firm will now incur a cost equal to that previously incurred *plus* the tax which is due the revenue collector. The price received by the firm from the consumer will no longer be equal to the marginal cost of production, which must now include the tax. The firm will find it advantageous to cut back on production and sales immediately; it can improve its profit position by so doing. The firm will lay off workers and reduce its rate of purchase of other variable inputs. As the separate firms reduce output, the total industry output will fall. This reduction in supply will cause the market price paid by the consumer to rise. The extent of the price increase will depend on the responsiveness of demanders to the price increase. In the short run, the price to the consumer will not increase by the full amount of the tax. Some of the tax will be borne by the owners of resources which are relatively permanent in the industry. Over the long run, however, resources not making an average or normal return in the taxed industry will not be maintained and replaced; the effect will be a shifting of resources to nontaxed employments. This will gradually reduce the size of the industry; firms will shut down as plants are worn out. Finally, price will rise by the full amount of the tax and the industry will once more reach a position of long-run equilibrium. The price received by firms, net of tax, will be the same as before the tax. The price paid by consumers will be above the pre-tax price by the full amount of the tax. Fewer firms will be in the industry, and total industry output will be reduced, the extent of the reduction again being dependent on the responsiveness of quantity demanded to price increases.

This case is illustrated in Figure 33–1. The diagram is the familiar one of industry supply and demand. The price and quantity before the tax are shown as P_1 and Q_1 the price and quantity after tax as P_2 and Q_2. The tax is in the amount of P_2—P_1 per unit. As this figure shows, the tax is fully shifted to the consumers because, under the conditions postulated, supply is highly responsive to price changes over the long run. Resources are assumed to be able to shift to non-taxed industries without difficulty, given sufficient time for adjustment. On the other hand, consumers of the commodity taxed are assumed to be unable to substitute nontaxed commodities in consumption except insofar as is shown by the demand relationship.

The popular model is not so extreme as it might initially appear. When we consider that specific taxes are levied by single states within a national economy, the total share of the economy's resources affected is likely to be small. And if these resources are not highly specialized to the industry, the postulated adjustments on the supply side may take place with relatively little difficulty. If, for example, a state should place a tax on the product of an industry not located within the state and selling its output on the national market, the

FIGURE 33–1

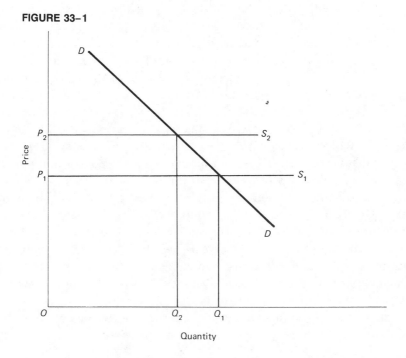

final results shown would take place immediately. The firms involved would simply refuse to market their products in a single state unless the price net of tax were as high as in other states. For example, a single state tax on billiard tables would almost certainly be paid exclusively by the individuals who play billiards and the owners of billiard parlors, both consumers of the product "billiard tables." The manufacturers of the tables would not sell their products in a single state at a lower net price than in other states.

This model of the specific excise tax becomes less applicable, however, when we consider either federal excise levies or those state taxes which are employed by many of the states. In these cases, the industries affected may be of significant size and may employ specialized resources. This requires that additional, and contrasting, models of tax shifting be examined.

Competitive conditions—constant demand price

We may now examine briefly the case which is the opposite extreme of the one just discussed. Although it is difficult to think of real-world examples, this case is useful as an analytical model. We can easily conceive of a specific tax being levied on the sale of a commodity that is produced with relatively specialized resources and the demand for which is highly responsive to changes in price. The case is characterized by a very high degree of substitutability between the taxed product and nontaxed products on the part of consumers and a lower degree of substitutability on the part of supplies of resource owners. In this case the full burden of the tax will rest, not with consumers, but with the owners of resources permanently employed by the industry. The tax will reduce the economic rents of these resources. Quantity consumed will be reduced only insofar as the suppliers are led by the reduction in return to reduce inputs of resources.

This case is illustrated in Figure 33–2. The notation is the same as that for Figure 33–1, but an important difference should be noted. In Figure 33–2, the price to the consumer stays fixed at P_1. The "wedge" imposed by the tax in this case pushes the price to the supplying firm down to P_1-T. In Figure 33–1 the tax wedge was inserted by pushing the consumer price upward while the supplier's net price remains the same in the long run. In this opposite case, the price to the consumer stays fixed in the long run while the price received by the supplier is pushed downward.

The first model is sometimes called that of *complete forward shifting;* this second model is that of *complete backward shifting* of the tax.

Competitive conditions—increasing cost industry, decreasing demand price

The preceding two cases are useful in setting certain limits to the process of excise tax shifting and incidence. In the real world, most cases will fall somewhere between the two extremes, perhaps somewhat more closely approximating the conditions postulated in the first model than in the second. We shall continue to assume that competitive conditions prevail, but we shall not introduce a more realistic third model in which both quantity demanded and quantity supplied are responsive to price changes, but in which perfect substitutability is not present on either side of the market.

If we start, as before, with an industry in long-run competitive equilibrium, the tax will be borne by both consumers of the product and by the owners of the specialized resources in reduced rents. The price will not rise by the full amount of the tax.

FIGURE 33–2

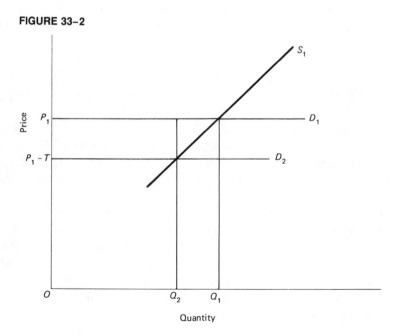

This third case is illustrated in Figure 33–3. Note that the tax wedge is now inserted by pushing the consumer price upward and the suppliers' price downward. The extent to which the tax will be shifted forward to consumers and backward to resource owners depends upon the relative slopes of the demand curve and the supply curve. If the supply curve is flatter than the demand curve, the greater share of the tax will be borne finally by the consumer. If, on the other hand, the demand curve is flatter than the supply curve, the greater share of the tax will be borne by the resource owner.

FIGURE 33–3

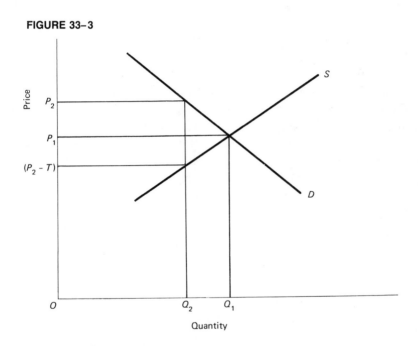

Competitive conditions—prohibitive tax

A fourth model of excise tax shifting may be briefly discussed. There may be many commodities which, if taxed, would disappear from the market altogether. The tax wedge cannot be inserted between demanders' price and suppliers' price at any level of production. If it is possible for resources to shift easily out of the industry and if consumers can easily shift to alternative products, the tax need not be large to be prohibitive. And a sufficiently high tax rate can always result in the industry's being eliminated.

This case is illustrated in Figure 33–4. The tax per unit is shown as the distance T_1T_2. There is no point where the vertical distance between the demand curve and the supply curve is as great as the tax per unit. Therefore the tax will cause the industry to disappear in the long run. Consumers are not willing to pay the tax, resource owners are not willing to pay the tax, and there is no way in which the tax may be shared between the two groups.

This case is useful in illustrating the dilemma faced by very small local units of government in their attempts to impose excise taxes. Suppose that a city tries to tax the sale of cigarettes. Immediately, consumers will start driving out to the borders of the city to purchase cigarettes by the carton. Supplying firms within the city will not be willing to absorb the tax. As a result, the sale of cigarettes in the city proper will almost disappear. Results such as these become even more dramatic if the small local government tries to tax commodities and services which command higher prices. For example, a small city would find it impossible to impose an excise tax of any significant amount on the sale of television sets. Both the long-run demand curve and the long-run supply curve for television sets *within a single city* will normally be relatively flat due to the existence of both buying and selling alternatives outside local boundaries.

FIGURE 33–4

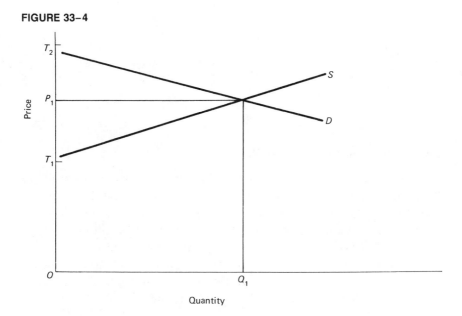

Monopoly conditions—constant costs

The cases examined to this point have all been based on the assumption that the product or service to be taxed is marketed under conditions of competition. While the competitive assumption seems the best single one that can be made for the consideration of many real-world problems, the analysis of the economic effects of excise taxation would be seriously incomplete if this assumption were not relaxed. It is necessary to examine how the conclusions reached under the assumption of the competitive model are modified when monopoly is explicitly assumed.

In monopoly analysis, we no longer can examine the behavior of an industry. The analysis must be at the level of the individual firm. By definition, a monopoly firm is one that can exert some control over the selling price of its product varying its rate of sales. In more technical economic terms, a monopoly firm is faced with a down-sloping demand curve for its output. In competition, the single firm, having no control over selling price, is faced with a horizontal demand curve at the ruling competitive price.

In equilibrium, the monopolist will tend to equate marginal revenue with marginal cost in order to maximize profits. By the nature of the demand or average revenue function, marginal revenue at any given rate of sales must be less than average revenue or selling price. Therefore, when the monopolist equates marginal revenue with marginal cost, average revenue or price must be greater than marginal cost. This is recognized as the major trouble with monopoly. The price to the consumer is greater than the supply or cost price of resources entering into the product purchased. Price is greater than marginal cost, and marginal cost accurately reflects the value of opportunities foregone elsewhere in the economy. The consumer evaluation for the monopolist's product, price, exceeds the evaluation that the consumer places on alternative productive opportunities for the resource, marginal cost. The overall efficiency of the economy can be improved by a shifting of resources to the monopolized industries and a relative expansion of this sector of production. By restricting output below competitive levels, the monopolist is successful in inserting a "monopoly wedge" between selling price and marginal cost.

As we did when we examined the competitive model, we shall assume that a monopoly firm is in equilibrium before the tax is imposed, and we shall initially assume that marginal costs of production are constant. We now assume that a fixed tax per unit of sales is levied, and that this tax must be paid by the monopolist. This tax will have the same effect as an increase in marginal and average cost. The monopolist will find it advantageous to reduce production and to increase selling price. But price will not rise by the full amount of the tax under normal conditions, even in this constant cost case. The reason for this is that some part of the tax will be paid out of the monopoly profits previously being earned in the industry. Monopoly profts are, in one sense, quite similar to rents, as our previous analysis has shown. The extent to which the price to the consumer will rise will depend on the slope of the demand curve, the responsiveness of consumer demand to price changes.

FIGURE 33–5

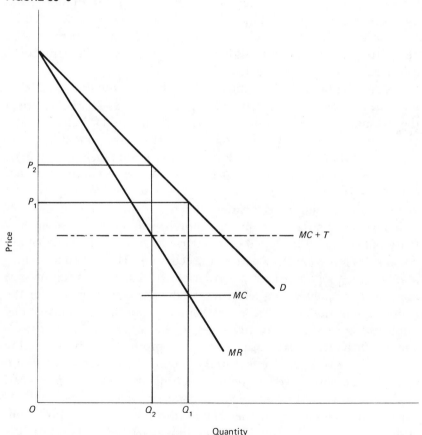

Figure 33–5 illustrates this case. The tax serves to shift the marginal cost curve upward. The firm finds it profitable to cut back production to Q_2 and to increase selling price to P_2. These are assumed here to be long-run adjustments. Insofar as the monopoly firm has fixed inputs geared for the larger output, the price will tend to be increased less in the short run than over time.

Monopoly conditions—increasing costs

If the monopolist produces under conditions of increasing rather than constant long-run marginal costs, which would be the case if there are resources specialized to the industry, some share of the tax burden will be shifted backward to resource owners. In this case, consumers, resource owners, and the monopolist will all share the final incidence of the tax. Figure 33–6 illustrates this case. Consumers are required to pay a higher price, shown at P_2. Resource owners are required to accept a lower average rate of payment, shown by C_2 in comparison with C_1, and monopoly profits are reduced.

These two monopoly models are sufficient to show how the conclusions may be modified from those reached with competitive assumptions. From the models discussed, it should be possible to predict with reasonable accuracy the effects of any single excise tax. For example, the tax on tobacco products, say, cigarettes, tends to be shifted forward to consumers, to reduce profits in the industry (which is characterized by certain elements of monopoly), and to reduce the rents of tobacco farmers. The taxes on whiskey tend to be shifted forward to consumers in higher prices and to reduce certain elements of profit in an industry not fully competitive. The West Virginia tax on soft drinks tends to be passed along to the consumers in higher prices and to reduce somewhat the profits of local bottlers, who seem to have elements of location monopoly in soft drink sales. In almost all cases, the consumer will bear at least some part of the burden of the tax. This tends to make the popular image of the tax, which assumes that the full burden is shifted to consumers, reasonably accurate. But the best evidence that producers bear the burden of the taxes also, either in reduced rents or in reduced monopoly gains, is indicated by the industry pressures exerted to prevent enactment of new taxes and to secure repeal of old taxes.

FIGURE 33–6

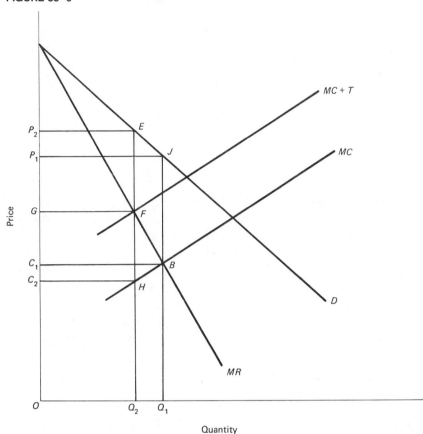

The excess burden of partial excise taxes

Fiscal theorists have commonly claimed that the imposition of an excise tax on a single commodity or service places an excess burden on the consumer. The consumer is led, due to the price distortion caused by the tax, to shift his purchase or consumption pattern away from that which he previously has considered to be desirable or optimal. Therefore, the argument has proceeded, the tax exerts a burden over and above that which would be exerted if a similar tax were levied on income or wealth in such a way that the consumption pattern is not changed. The discussion of this excess burden has occupied a great deal of space in the learned journals during the past 20 years. This book is not the appropriate place to cover the argument in detail. It is perhaps sufficient to point out that recent advances have made the excess burden argument less valid that it seemed at one time.

Choice through time—a case for specific excise taxation?

Orthodox or traditional fiscal analysis has rarely approached the fiscal structure from the vantage point of the individual taxpayer. Taking this approach offers interesting insights in certain cases. Will taxpayers ever be in a position such that they might actually *prefer* to pay a fixed obligation by means of a tax imposed on one specific item of their own consumption? If this question is asked, we can see that such positions may arise when, first of all, the taxpayers know that their consumption of particular items will take place only during periods of time when their basic needs are low relative to their incomes. The taxpayers may prefer to accept the payment of a specific excise tax on an item of luxury consumption, say, mink capes, if, through accepting this tax, they can reduce their tax liability during those years when their residual income will be devoted to spending on education and not on mink capes. This approach, which assumes that tax institutions remain in being over several time periods and also that both incomes and basic consumption needs fluctuate through time, has not been fully developed.[2]

The limitations on the partial equilibrium models

The analysis of partial excise taxes has been developed solely in partial equilibrium terms. That is to say, we have considered only one particular product and one particular industry. Conclusions reached in this way are likely to be of limited validity when extended to apply to the whole economy. For example, when we say that resources are shifted out of the production of the taxed product this implies that these resources are shifted into the nontaxed industries, and the increase in supply will reduce the prices of nontaxed goods. Just as the consumers of the taxed goods are harmed as a result of the

---

[2]This approach was presented in a paper. See James M. Buchanan and Francesco Forte, "Fiscal Choice through Time," *National Tax Journal*, vol. 17 (June 1964), pp. 144–57. See also, James M. Buchanan, *Public Finance in Democratic Process* (Chapel Hill, N.C.: University of North Carolina Press, 1967).

tax, the consumers of nontaxed goods find themselves in improved positions as a result of the tax. These and other like effects would all have to be fully traced before a complete analysis of a single tax could be said to be complete.

The usefulness of the partial equilibrium model in making real-world predictions depends in large part on the importance of the tax considered. If the tax is a relatively small one levied on a relatively unimportant product, these secondary effects will tend to be diffused throughout the economy, and they may be neglected for all practical purposes. On the other hand, if we are considering a high-rate tax to be placed on an impórtant product or on a range of products, the neglect of secondary effects can lead to serious error. As will be pointed out in the following chapter, a common error has been the extension of the analysis of a single excise tax to apply to the tax which is imposed on general sales, that is, on all commodities. An error that is almost equally dangerous is to extend the analysis of a single tax to apply to the whole host of single taxes taken as a group. In these cases, as with general sales taxes, the partial equilibrium models are of little value.

TAXATION AND CHARACTERISTICS OF THE TAXED COMMODITY

The standard analysis of commodity taxation, as described in the preceding sections, has tended to concentrate on adjustments in the market equilibrium quantity of the taxed commodity and the accompanying adjustments in product price and factor earnings. With respect to some commodities, at least, it seems likely that there will be an additional market response to imposition of a tax. Actual characteristics of the taxed commodity may be changed if the statutory definition of the commodity to be taxed is not a complete description. An example can best illustrate how this response might occur. Suppose that two different types of gasoline are technically feasible to produce. Type A gasoline yields 12 miles per gallon in the typical automobile; type B yields 20 miles per gallon. Each gasoline is produced under constant cost conditions. The marginal and average cost of producing type A is 80 cents per gallon. Type B costs $1.40 per gallon.

In the absence of any tax on gasoline, which type is the most efficient to produce? The answer is obvious. The implicit "good" being purchased by consumers of gasoline is "miles driven." Type A delivers any given number of miles driven at a lower cost than type B. Gasoline costs for driving 120 miles, for example, are $8 if type A gasoline is used and $8.40 if type B gasoline is used. In the absence of any tax on gasoline, profit-maximizing producers will produce type A gasoline. If the market is competitive, the price of a gallon of gasoline will be equated to its marginal cost of 80 cents.

Now suppose that a specific excise tax of 15 cents per gallon is imposed on gasoline. The tax statute defines the product to be taxed as a gallon of gasoline and makes no specification regarding mileage. The market will respond to this tax by shifting to production of type B gasoline. When tax costs are included, type B gasoline becomes the cheapest way of producing any given number of miles driven. Gasoline cost of driving 120 miles is now $9.50 with type A gasoline and only $9.30 with type B. Note that a new component has been added to the excess burden of the tax. The good, "miles driven," is now being produced in an inefficient way. The tax payment itself is a simple transfer from taxpayers to the fisc. Type A gasoline remains the least-cost way of producing miles driven in terms of the opportunity cost of resources used in the production process. At the same time, the more traditional component of excess burden resulting from reduced consumption of the taxed commodity is lowered. The reason is, of course, that the switch to type B gasoline lessens the final increase in the price of a mile driven which results from imposition of the tax. On the other hand, if the taxing authority adjusts the tax so as to yield some targeted amount of revenue, the switch to type B gasoline will generate, in turn, a higher tax per gallon and a further reduction in miles driven.

A final point can be made. In the standard analysis, there is no difference between a specific excise tax, in which the tax is some fixed amount per unit of the commodity, and an *ad valorem* tax in which the tax is some percentage of the selling price. If set so as to generate identical tax revenue yields, both taxes will cause the same reduction in quantity consumed and identical changes in price to consumers and in factor earnings. If commodity characteristics can be adjusted in response to taxation, however, this identity between specific and *ad valorem* taxation may no longer hold. If, in our example, the tax had been set at 20 percent of selling price, no shift to type B gasoline would have occurred because the relative costs of producing miles driven would not have been changed.[3]

CONCLUSIONS

This chapter has examined two sources of state-local revenues in some detail; taxation of personal and corporate income, and taxation of the production, sale, or consumption of specific goods or services. The limitation of local fiscal authority within the national economy makes the administration of state-local income taxation difficult and explains, in part, the relative unimportance of this basic tax in state-local systems. Income taxation is employed by a majority of the states, but maximum marginal rates are not high, relative to federal rates. Municipalities, sorely pressed for revenues in recent years, have in a few cases imposed gross income taxes at flat rates, usually 1 percent.

Discriminatory excise taxes are normally justified, at least in part, by nonrevenue considerations, both sumptuary and regulatory in content. The specific excise tax allows the economist to utilize the tools of partial equilibrium analysis, but care must be taken to incorporate relevant general aspects in any real-world analysis. The popular image that such taxes are passed forward to consumers has considerable validity, especially in certain models, but the possibility that a portion of excise taxes is finally paid by resource owners and investors must be kept in mind.

SUPPLEMENTARY READING

If the student desires to consult a single current source on state-local tax structures, he may see the volume *State Tax Guide,* issued and maintained in loose-leaf form by Commerce Clearing House, Inc.

For a general discussion of state and local taxation, see James A. Maxwell, and J. Richard Aronson, *Financing State and Local Governments,* 3rd ed., (Washington, D.C.: The Brookings Institute, 1977).

---

[3]A complete theoretical analysis of tax-caused changes in product characteristics is developed by Yoram Barzel in a paper entitled "An Alternative Approach to the Analysis of Taxation *Journal of Political Economy* (December, 1976).

34

General
sales taxation

In the preceding chapter were discussed excise taxes that are imposed on the production, sale, or consumption of specific commodities or services. A more important revenue source for state governments may now be considered — that is, taxes levied uniformly, or approximately so, on the production, sale, or consumption of a wide range of commodities and services. These are *general* taxes, and the kind most commonly encountered in the United States is the *general sales tax*. As suggested in the last chapter, if particular excise taxes are imposed separately on a wide enough range of products, the results may approach those produced by explicitly general sales taxation.

For state governments, the general sales tax is the single most important revenue source. Normally, the tax is imposed as a percentage of the selling price. Use taxes are employed to supplement the sales tax in many jurisdictions as a means of ensuring that products purchased beyond jurisdictional boundaries are subject to taxation. Also, gross receipts taxes are employed in a few states in lieu of the general sales tax device.

Taxes may be imposed at the retail, wholesale, or manufacturer's level, and they may be levied on a multiple-stage basis or only at one stage in the production-distribution process. A multiple-stage tax, sometimes called a *turnover tax*, subjects the same good or service to a tax liability at each stage. For example, a turnover tax of 1 percent could be levied on each transfer of a good, so that by the time the good has passed through three stages of production and distribution before reaching the final consumer, the effective rate would amount to 3 percent. This sort of multiple-stage levy is criticized on the grounds that it provides an uneconomic and artificial incentive for vertical integration in production and distribution. Whereas in the absence of such a tax the widespread use of separate wholesaling firms might be economically feasible, this stage might be eliminated under such tax. The multiple-stage or *turnover tax* has not been widely employed in the United States, at any level, but it is an important revenue producer in Germany, Austria, and other European countries.

Some of the administrative advantages of the *turnover tax* may be retained, and its disadvantages eliminated, through the use of a *value added* tax, which levies charges upon processors at the separate stages only to the extent that value is added to the good. France has successfully used this type of tax in the postwar years. The *value added* tax has periodically commanded the attention of fiscal reformers in the United States but has never been adopted.

In the United States, the single-stage tax has been more widely employed by the separate states and localities. The characteristic form is the *retail sales tax*. The tax is placed on the act of selling goods (and sometimes services) at retail; this is the key transaction that creates a tax liability. The turnover of goods and services in the stages prior to the retail transaction is not subjected to tax. The tax is collected directly from retailing firms. The single-stage tax at the wholesale or the manufacturer's level is not widely used.

General commodity taxation is not employed, in any of its forms, by the federal government. The introduction of either a manufacturer's sales tax or a *value added* tax has been occasionally proposed, but the idea has never gained widespread political support. Somewhat implicitly, this important revenue source has been accepted by both the politicians and the public as being appropriately reserved for the states. If the desirability of maintaining separate revenue sources for the separate jurisdictions in the federal political system is accepted, the limitation of this source to state-local units seems desirable. As was suggested in the last chapter, the imposition of local sales taxes created difficult problems of administration. Local units use this revenue source to an extent, but problems of avoidance and evasion become serious. In the overall fiscal structure of the United

States as it now exists, the general sales tax, levied at retail, seems more appropriate as a *state*, rather than a federal or a local tax.

In 1978, 45 states and the District of Columbia employed general sales taxation (including gross receipts taxation) as a revenue source. Collections from this source made up almost $31 billion in 1977 or 30 percent of all state tax collections.

As suggested, the retail sales tax is imposed on a wide range of commodities, and the rate is usually a uniform percentage of the selling price. Rates in the several states range from 2 percent to the high of 7 percent in Connecticut (1978); the median rate is 4 percent. Each of the state taxes is supposedly "general" in the sense that no particular group of commodities is deliberately chosen for taxation. But in most states various commodities, and especially services, are exempted from inclusion in the general coverage. The extent of these exemptions varies widely among the separate states. Many states exempt food purchases, obviously a very important category which tends to remove a real element of "generality" from the institution. Other states exempt food purchases only in part. Services are rarely included fully in the tax base. Medicines, funerals, and a host of miscellaneous items are variously exempted. The exemptions seriously reduce the base of the tax in many states and hence reduce its revenue-producing potential. Despite the exemptions, however, the tax remains a very important element in state revenue structures.

ECONOMIC EFFECTS OF GENERAL SALES TAXATION

The most important distinction to be made between the analysis of a specific excise tax and that of a general sales tax lies in the method of approach. In the case of a specific excise tax, a partial equilibrium approach can lead to useful results. That is to say, the tax on one particular good can be examined in isolation. But by the very nature of "general" taxation, this partial or sectoral approach is unsatisfactory. General sales taxes, or general taxes of any kind, are applicable over many sectors of the economy. Hence, analysis must also be generally based; that is, it must incorporate the interdependencies over the whole economy. Failure to make this important distinction in method has led to serious errors in both popular and academic discussion of general sales taxation.

In order to emphasize the nature of this distinction, we may reveiw briefly the analysis of the specific excise tax in its simplest case. We assume fully competitive conditions and assume that the single product taxed is unimportant quantitatively and employs no specialized resources in its production. It was shown that the tax increases marginal costs; this in turn leads to a reduction in output in the taxed industry both in the short run and the long run. Resources shift out of the production of the taxed commodity, and the price of the commodity to consumers rises. This increase in relative price occurs regardless of the overall level of economic activity. The rate of increase in relative price will depend on the speed with which resources can shift out of the industry producing the product subjected to the tax into other, nontaxed industries. The increase in the price of the taxed commodity clearly harms those who consume relatively more of this commodity, and, to this extent, the consumer can be said to bear the burden of the tax.

This review of the analysis of a partial or specific tax on a single commodity is necessary in order to contrast it quite sharply with that of a general sales tax levied on the sale of many commodities. In the first place it should be noted that, insofar as any tax is *not truly general,* some effects similar to those described for the partial tax must take place. Since no "general" tax can be completely "general" in the economic sense (such a tax would have to be imposed on the use of leisure time, among other things), some shifting of resources out of taxed sectors into nontaxed sectors can be predicted to occur under almost any tax institution. But, and here is the important qualification, if the tax is broadly based, if it applies simultaneously to many commodities, much of the predictive analysis must be based on a general model of economic interaction rather than on the partial model sketched above.

Although almost all general sales taxes, so-called, embody certain specific exemptions and also omit large categories of consumption (notably services) from taxation through legislative and administrative neglect, it seems best to analyze such taxes *as if* they were, in fact, general. That is, it is appropriate to assume, for the analysis, that the tax applies to all commodities and services sold at retail, including things that the individual sells to himself, such as leisure, and also things that government purchases. This general tax model is now sharply different from the partial tax model for a quite simple reason. If the tax is uniformly imposed on the sale of all commodities and services, there can be no real shifting of resources from taxed employments to nontaxed employments. The shift in relative prices occasioned by the partial tax cannot occur under a truly general sales tax.

Will the general retail sales tax increase all prices, and does the final incidence rest with the consumer? This is a much debated question and competent scholars disagree on the answer, primarily because they define terms differently and employ somewhat different analytical models in reaching their conclusions. Here, as elsewhere, it is essential that the assumptions of the analysis be clearly and explicitly stated.

When the analysis of partial excise taxes was introduced, it was not necessary to make explicit any assumptions about monetary conditions in the economy. This was because the analysis was concerned with the shift in relative prices occasioned by the imposition of the tax; and these shifts occur regardless of the level of absolute prices. With the truly general tax, however, changes in relative prices cannot occur directly as a result of the tax. Therefore, any change in prices must take place in the whole level of prices, in the absolute price level. The analysis requires that the monetary setting be made clear at least in the model employed.

The first assumption that may be made is that the monetary authorities (the Federal Reserve Board) act in such a manner as to keep the absolute level of final product prices constant. In this setting, the introduction of a general sales tax cannot increase the level of prices, by definition. It follows that the tax must cause a net reduction in the prices of productive services or factors. The tax "wedge" must always be inserted between the final selling price of products and the net price received by firms. If monetary action prevents any increase in final product prices, the wedge caused by the tax must drive factor prices downward or else create unemployment for the owners of factors of production. In this model, therefore, the general sales tax tends to be shifted backward to factor owners or suppliers. Individuals, in their capacities as factor owners rather than in their capacities as consumers, bear the incidence or burden of the tax.

It is useful to trace the process of reaching these conclusions more carefully. As with the partial excise tax, the imposition of the general sales tax will increase marginal cost to the selling firm when initially imposed. The firm will, if it is acting to maximize profits, try to reduce output. This involves a reduction in the rate of input. Workers will be laid off, raw materials and equipment will not be purchased or hired at rates prevailing before the tax. But the result will be wholly different in this case from those traced for the partial tax. Workers who are laid off in one industry cannot now find employment in nontaxed industries. For, by definition of a general tax, there are no nontaxed employments. Alternative employment opportunities for resource owners do not exist. Unemployment will be the necessary result unless factor owners agree to accept lower prices for their resource services. Hence, insofar as factor markets are roughly competitive, productive service prices, and with these, factor incomes, will fall. In the long run, the supplies of the various productive factors may not be absolutely fixed, but these adjustments can best be ignored at this elementary stage of the analysis.

The point to be noted is that, in this model, the effects of a general sales tax are approximately equivalent to those of a proportional tax on all factor incomes. Consumers, as such, do not bear the burden of the tax.

These conclusions hold regardless of the assumptions made about factor markets or about the monetary setting, although the analysis becomes more complex. If the markets for productive factors are not competitive, factor prices may be rigid against downward pressures, and unemployment rather than price-wage reductions may occur. In this case, a disproportionate share of the tax tends to be borne by those who become unemployed. But these are factor owners, not consumers. Even here, consumers do not bear the tax.

Many variations may, of course, be made in the monetary assumptions, and it is here that the differences among the experts arise. We need not assume that the monetary authorities try to stabilize some index of final product prices. One approach is that of assuming that the monetary authorities are relatively passive, and that they will allow the money supply to expand sufficiently to finance the tax-induced price increases. In this model, final product prices do rise as a result of the tax. But it seems that this sort of price-level rise should be attributed directly to the increase in the supply of money, rather than to the tax, even if the latter is the motivating factor. The fact that the tax triggers the reaction does not alter the causal relationship between the increase in the money supply and the price level. If this is accepted, it can be seen that factor owners are still worse off than they would be without the tax, ignoring the expenditure side of the question. Differentially, the general sales tax remains similar to the proportional income tax.

From this analysis of a truly general sales tax, it is relatively easy to move to an analysis of the taxes that actually characterize modern fiscal systems. Insofar as exemptions and omissions narrow the base of the tax, there will be some shifting of resources from taxed into nontaxed employments and some shifting of the final burden forward to consumers. The proportion of forward and backward shifting will depend in every case on the degree of generality of the tax. If, for example, only one single state should levy a general sales tax, with all the other states in the national economy financing public services differently, the tax would tend to be shift forward almost fully in the long run. Although all products and services sold within the state might be subjected to the tax, these make up only a relatively small proportion of national output. On the other hand, if all of the states should simultaneously level general sales taxes, or if the federal government should do so, most of the burden would fall on owners of productive factors. In the current setting a sufficient number of states levy taxes that seem sufficiently general to ensure that at least some important share of the burden rests with factor owners. The popular image that general sales taxes are fully borne by consumers seems more erroneous than true, although consumers do, of course, bear some of the final burden.

Transfer income and tax incidence

Income transfers provide many individuals with income sources in addition to any direct factor earnings. Such income has become an increasingly important component of income for many households and its existence must be taken into account in attempting to assign tax incidence. The problem of assigning the incidence of a general sales tax provides a useful example of how transfers must be incorporated into any overall distribution of tax burden among households. Suppose, for example, that all income transfers were fixed in money terms. If an accommodative monetary policy were to allow a general sales tax to result in a general increase in product prices, the real value of transfer income would decline along with the decline in real factor earnings. A person who received income solely from transfers would bear a tax burden identical to that borne by someone receiving the same total income in the form of factor earnings. If, on the other hand, transfers were indexed to the price level or, alternatively, the monetary authority kept the price level stable, thus forcing a reduction in factor prices in order to accommodate the tax, transfer income would effectively escape any tax burden. Tax burden would then be effected by the relative allocation of household income between transfer and factor earnings.[1]

SECONDARY EFFECTS OF GENERAL SALES TAXATION

Just as with all fiscal action, the imposition of general sales taxation exerts secondary effects when the complete fiscal structure is examined. If the proceeds of the tax are employed to finance government purchases of goods and services, the overall pattern of resource use is modified. Some factor prices rise, others fall; some final product prices rise, other fall. Secondary effects stem from the combined taxing-spending operation, and there are almost certain to be net beneficiaries and net "taxpayers" in the process in each case.

The many models of secondary effects need not be elaborated in this textbook. But it is important to recognize that any complete analysis, especially of a reasonably general tax, must consider not only the primary or first-order effects but must also examine the secondary effects. There are three alternative assumptions under which these secondary effects may be traced out. The first, illustrated previously, assumes that the proceeds are to be used to finance supplemental public services. A second approach assumes that the proceeds of the tax to be analyzed are used to allow a corresponding reduction in another tax. A third possible approach assumes that the proceeds are not to be used. This third approach, involves the building up of government cash balances as a result of the tax collection. This, in turn, will cause deflation. This approach seems less satisfactory than the other two in that it mixes up what is essentially fiscal analysis with monetary analysis. It seems desirable to keep these analyses separate insofar as is possible.

ADVANTAGES OF GENERAL SALES TAXATION

The major advantage of general sales taxation lies in its potential revenue yield at what seem to be relatively low rates. Additional arguments in support of this tax appear when the desirability of separating revenue sources among levels of government is recog-

---

[1]This analysis is developed by Professor Edgar Browning in a paper entitled "The Burden of Taxation." *Journal of Political Economy* (August 1978).

nized. As the foregoing analysis has shown, the effects of the general sales tax are roughly equivalent to that of the proportional income tax. Even so, in a federal political system where income taxation is to a large extent reserved for the central government, the levy of general sales taxation by subordinate units is more acceptable. An advantage of a different sort lies in the relatively low cost of collection; rarely do the costs of administering this tax run more than 2 percent of total revenues collected.

A questionable advantage of this tax which is sometimes claimed is its ability to extend the real costs of government to individuals and groups of the population that would otherwise escape taxation altogether. Administrative costs of imposing income taxes on low-income families may be very great. Hence, even if not desired, income taxation usually exempts large numbers of low-income families through personal exemptions and deductions. Yet these families also participate in the decision-making processes of democratic governments, and it is argued that they should have some direct sense of the real costs of governmental activity. This argument would have much to recommend it were it not for the fact that sales taxation does not really cause individuals to become conscious of the costs of government as represented in the real tax burden. The tax imposes a "wedge" between factor prices and final product prices, but the individual factor owner or the individual consumer does not sense that his income is actually lower than it would otherwise be without the tax. In some respects, individuals are "conscious" of the tax in their roles as consumers in that the popularly accepted fallacy that consumers bear the full burden of all sales taxes is widespread. But even here, the consciousness is somewhat indirect and is of a wholly different nature from that involved in the payment of an income tax. It seems clear that indirect taxation, regardless of the form in which it is imposed, tends to foster a genuine "fiscal illusion" on the part of the taxpayers.

DISADVANTAGES OF GENERAL SALES TAXATION

The major disadvantage of sales taxation, specific or general, lies in the tax-consciousness aspects discussed previously. Individuals are not conscious of the real costs which the payment of the tax imposes on them individually. They cannot, therefore, correctly compare the net advantages yielded by the government services which are financed by the tax with the alternative private goods which could be consumed in the absence of the tax. To many students of public finance, this individual comparison is of little relevance since the decisions on both taxes and government spending are assumed to be made by the government as something apart from the individual citizens. However, as has been repeatedly emphasized, this book assumes that the problem is one of discussing fiscal institutions and public finance in a free democratic society. From this assumption it follows that, in the final analysis, individuals must, through their elected representatives and constitutionally sanctioned methods of legislation, make the choices concerning the relative magnitude of the various taxes and the public expenditures. In order to do this wisely, individuals and families must be placed in a position where they can make reasonably straightforward comparisons. Indirect taxation makes these decisions and comparisons especially difficult and, therefore, on these grounds alone, direct taxation is always to be preferred.

Having now discussed what seems to be the primary disadvantage of sales taxation (or of indirect taxation generally), there remains to be considered some of the alleged further disadvantages. One of the most popular and traditional of these objections to sales taxation is the claim that it is "regressive." As suggested earlier, this emotive word, like its opposite, "progressive," tends to cause much confusion in popular discussion. Several points need to be made. First of all, the general sales tax is proportional in rate, not regressive. The rate is a fixed percentage of the base, which is selling price. But this is not what the term "regressive" is held to mean in this case. Presumably, the argument suggests that the final burden in relation to income as a base is not proportional. The tax tends to be proportionately more onerous to lower income than to higher income families. This argument stems, of course, from the acceptance of the commonly held view, discussed previously, that all sales taxes, specific or general, are finally paid by consumers rather than by factor owners. Insofar as the tax is generally imposed, it will tend to fall on factor owners, and it will be proportional rather than regressive, even when estimated in terms of income base.

Even if the popular analysis is accepted, however, and it is concluded that general sales taxes are borne by consumers, the range of exemptions and omissions may be such that, in practice, the regressive features of the rate structure are largely, if not wholly, eliminated. However, even in those cases where the tax, as it works out, is regressive with respect to an imputed income base, there is no basis for the claim that such taxes are necessarily bad or undesirable, unless a specific value judgment is made to this effect. Again we must recall that any tax is only half of a fiscal operation — and it seems nonsensical to place value connotation on one half standing alone. A "regressive" tax may finance an even more "regressive" expenditure, or allow the reduction of an even more "regressive" tax. It is best to eliminate all reference to the advantages or disadvantages of individual taxes on the grounds of either regressiveness or progressiveness. Regression or progression can be discussed sensibly only in terms of an overall fiscal system, and redistribution as a fiscal goal is important largely at the central government level.

CONCLUSIONS

General sales taxation constitutes an important part of the overall fiscal structure of the United States. As the rapidly increasing financial needs of the states and the local governments multiply over the next quarter century, we can expect additional states to turn to this highly productive revenue source. The argument for keeping revenue sources separate among the levels of government suggests that the federal government should enter this field of taxation only as a last resort. However, as the national economy adjusts somewhat more permanently to the extremely high federal government expenditures which have characterized post-World War II years, some reduction in personal and corporation income taxes may be necessary to prevent serious erosion of these important tax bases. The general sales tax provides an available and attractive alternative to legislators who might be willing to impose indirectly tax burdens which the people would never accept if imposed directly. One thing appears reasonably certain: A federal sales tax, once imposed, would not be removed. This provides all the more reason for limiting these taxes to the states. Additional local governments will, without doubt, try to impose both general and specific sales taxes to meet rising revenue needs. These taxes can be only partially successful, and they will do their bit to add to the existing set of causes which are creating the modern sprawling of suburbia.

SUPPLEMENTARY READING

An exhaustive and comprehensive treatment of general sales taxation may be found in John F. Due, *Sales Taxation* (Urbana, Ill.: Univerity of Illinois Press, 1957).

For a summary of the views on the analysis of sales tax incidence, see John F. Due, "Sales Taxation and the Consumer," *American Economic Review*, vol. 53 (December 1963), pp. 1078–83.

For other contributions to the discussion, see R. A. Musgrave, *The Theory of Public Finance* (New York: McGraw-Hill Book Co., 1959), chaps. 15 and 16, and also Earl Rolph and George Break, *Public Finance* (New York: The Ronald Press Co., 1961), chap. 13.

For the most recent treatment, see Carl S. Shoup, *Public Finance* (Chicago: Aldine Publishing Co., 1969), chaps. 8 and 9. It is noted here that Shoup's treatise also provides useful discussion of many other traditional publc finance topics.

35

The taxation
of capital:
Comparative analysis

$\mathbf{R}$evenues collected from the taxation of property are exceeded only by those collected from individual income taxes, employment taxes and corporation income taxes in the overall fiscal system of the United States. Before discussing the characteristic of this important fiscal institution and analyzing its effects, we shall consider some of the conceptual issues raised by the taxation of capital values generally. Specifically, we shall compare capital taxation with income taxation. Following this we shall examine the ideological origin of modern property tax institutions. A factual discussion and analysis of property taxation in the United States will be contained in Chapter 36.

THE TAXATION OF CAPITAL AND INCOME:
A COMPARISON

Income, considered as a flow of real services over some specified time period, is the primary economic magnitude. Individuals consume, or use up, income. And all goods, physical goods, are valued, that is to say, command other goods and services in exchange, only because they have some capacity to yield income over time. Capital values are, therefore, derivative from income flows. The actual process of valuing any asset involves converting an anticipated income flow (a flow which must be stated in terms of some time dimension) into a capital sum, a sum which is without a time dimension although it must be placed uniquely in time; a capital value must be dated. Any income stream can be converted into a capital value, and any capital value can be converted into an income stream. The conversion process requires only the introduction of some appropriate rate of discount. Income expected in the next year is less valuable to the individual than income at present. Hence, next year's income must be "discounted" by some appropriate rate in order to arrive at some accurate present value. Normally, the forces of the market for assets tend to make the appropriate rate of discount for most assets equal to the "rate of interest," adjusted as necessary for different risks and differential liquidity features. The mechanics of capitalizing an income stream need not be considered in detail here. The important point to be noted is that, given a rate of discount, any real asset or claim can be expressed either as a capital sum, a present value, or an income flow over time. A bond yielding $100 annually, a consol having no maturity, with a discount rate of 5 percent, can be expressed as being worth $2,000. This dual manner of definition holds for any asset or claim and, conversely, it holds for any income stream.

This basic equivalence of an income stream and a capital value allows the first significant point in the comparison between income taxation and capital taxation to be made. There is no fundamental conceptual difference between these two methods of taxation if income and capital are defined similarly in the two cases. To levy a tax on the capital value of the bond at 1 percent, or $20 per year, is precisely equivalent to levying a tax on the income yield of the bond at 20 percent, or $20 per year. The ratio of the 1 percent to the 20 percent is equal to the rate of discount employed to convert the income flow into the capital sum. The individual owning the bond would be completely indifferent between these two taxes, and the economic effects of the two taxes would be identical.

The equivalence does not end here; the time sequence of the tax collection in each case need not be the same. For example, in our simple model, a once-and-for all capital levy of 50 percent on the value of the bond is identical with the levy of a 50 percent tax on the income produced by the bond over all future years. The fully rational bondowner would not be affected in his behavior by the substitution of one of these taxes for the other. Any capital tax can be converted into an income tax equivalent, and any income tax can be converted into a capital tax equivalent.

The conceptual equivalence between a tax on capital and a tax on income provides a useful starting point for a comparative analysis, because further steps in the analysis suggest important differences rather than similarities. As the income tax and the capital tax tend to be administered, the differences tend to overshadow the fundamental equivalence.

Recall the discussion of income taxation in Chapter 22. Two separate conceptions or definitions of income were noted, the *flow* conception and the *accretion* conception. In the former, income is viewed as a "flow" of real services over time, a physical flow which can, ideally, be measured quite independently of any person. Note here that it is this flow conception of income that has been used in our discussion of valuing capital assets. By contrast, the accretion conception defines income in terms of potential consumption opportunities open to the individual over time; income is measured by the goods and services actually consumed plus the accretion to individual net worth over time. As suggested, existing income tax institutions do not represent either of these conceptions faithfully. But, insofar as either conception must be given a place of dominance, the accretion conception seems to be somewhat more influential. Capital gains are taxed to some extent, and interest is allowed as a deduction. The taxation of capital, on the other hand, embodies the valuation of specific assets independent of the set of individual claims to these assets. That is to say, the taxation of capital is based almost exclusively on an acceptance of the flow conception of income. The two taxes, those on income and those on capital, are not, therefore, equivalent in practice. They become quite different in characteristics and effect, since they are based on opposing definitions of income itself.

These differences may perhaps best be demonstrated by examining briefly the way in which consistency could be introduced into a tax system using both income taxation and capital taxation. If the accretion conception of income were to be accepted for purposes of both taxes, the capital tax and the income tax would alike be *personal* taxes. Individuals would be subjected to tax, not on the basis of specific assets owned, but on their *net wealth*. Income taxes would be imposed on accretions to net wealth plus consumption, while capital taxes would be imposed on the aggregate net worth. Debts against property held in legal ownership would reduce the tax liability of the owner, and corporations would not be subjected to capital taxation at all. The value of all corporate property would be taxed through the intangible claims to property held by individual equity share-holders.

On the other hand, if the opposing flow conception of income were to be consistently followed in the organization of both taxes, neither tax would genuinely be a personal tax. Income would be subjected to taxation, not as received by any particular individual, but as it physically moves through the circular flow of the economy, as it is "produced," "distributed," "received," or "consumed." Assets producing this real flow of income would be taxed as real assets, not as owned by particular private persons. Corporations holding legal title to real property would be directly liable to pay the tax on real property, and individual holdings of intangible claims would be exempted from taxation. Any taxation of income at more than one point in the circular flow would be properly considered to be "double" taxation.

These two models of consistent income and capital taxation are helpful in indicating the hodgepodge that is actually represented in the U.S. fiscal structure. By and large, income taxation tends to be similar to that of the first model. The tax is a personal tax; capital gains are taxed, although at differentially favorable rates; and interest payments are allowed as deductions from taxable income. By contrast, capital (property) taxation in the United States more closely follows the second model. Property taxation is not personal taxation; the tax is imposed directly on the value of the assets. Failure to pay the tax creates a claim of the state against the asset, not against the owner. No deduction against taxable value is allowed for debt against the property.

Neither income taxation nor capital taxation is fully consistent in itself. As has been shown, capital gains are taxed at differentially favored rates, not full rates. The dividend credit in the personal income tax embodied some recognition that "double" taxation does occur, an institutional recognition of the validity of the flow conception of income. The property tax, similarly, does include the taxation of intangibles in some states, and many states attempt to classify property in terms of different individual uses. These measures represent attempts to make the tax more "personal," a denial of the complete acceptance of the flow conception of income.

Since the two taxes, those on income and those on capital, do have, to a large degree, different conceptual bases, several important differences may be expected. Only personal taxes can effectively discriminate among persons in terms of differences in the size of the tax base. That is to say, only with personal taxes can redistributive objectives be included in the organization of the rate structure. Because the income tax is a personal tax, it can be, as it is, a progressive tax. A nonpersonal tax cannot be progressive or regressive with anything approaching this same degree of distributive efficiency. The tax base is divorced from personal relationship; the tax must be proportional in the sense that the rate must bear a constant ratio to the base. Attempted discrimination in rates among persons would tend to be almost wholly arbitrary. Property or capital taxation tends, therefore, to be proportional in its nominal rate structure. The same rate applies to all units of property within a single classification. As will be seen when property tax administration is discussed in the next chapter, the classification of property and differential assessment can make the actual tax disproportional.

A second important difference between the tax on income and the tax on capital tends to make these two taxes complementary when the overall fiscal system is examined. Each tax tends to have built-in discrimination against or in favor of certain forms of income or capital, but these tend to be offsetting when both taxes are combined. When income taxation was discussed, we noted that the tax tends, in practice, to discriminate against income from labor and in favor of income from capital assets. The reason for this discrimination is that full allowance for the depreciation of capital assets is allowed as a deduction before net income is measured for tax liability. By contrast, the individual human being is not depreciated in tax accounting, although it is widely recognized that a certain share of labor income must, in all cases, be properly attributable to the "wearing-out" of the human asset. As shown, some countries do make a distinction in rates as between labor and nonlabor incomes, but this distinction is not made in the United States. Income taxation, therefore, tends to discriminate against labor incomes.

By comparison, property taxation or capital taxation tends to discriminate in favor of labor income and against income from assets. Legal institutions in Western countries do not allow the individual human being to convert expected earnings power into a capital sum and to market this power as a capital asset. Hence, the capitalization of income does not normally take into account the human asset, and the valuation of wealth does not include, normally, the capital values of human beings. This is perhaps the most important single category of capital assets existing at any moment of time, but these assets are never valued for tax purposes. Therefore, capital or property taxation tends to discriminate in favor of those individuals holding their real wealth in terms of their own personal earning power and against those individuals holding their real wealth in nonhuman forms. An example may prove helpful. Suppose that an individual, at age 20, inherits a sum of $10,000.00. Either one of two things may be done with this sum. It may be spent for a college education; or it may be invested in an income-yielding real asset. If the first alternative is chosen the investment will be personal, and presumably increase the capital value, the expectant earning power of the investor. As the income is earned over time, however, there will be no depreciation allowed on this capital value for tax purposes. The investor will, therefore, tend to pay a higher income tax over time, than with the second alternative. If, however, the second is chosen rather than the first opportunity, if the income-earning asset is purchased rather than the college education, it would be subjected each year to property taxation which the investor would altogether escape under the first alternative. The two taxes, existing in the same overall system, tend to be corrective of each other. Given the importance of the tax on real property in the American fiscal system, along with the high taxation of corporation incomes, it does not seem desirable to introduce any differential treatment of labor income under the income tax. Quite similarly, the extension of the property tax to include the estimated capital values of human beings seems unnecessary.

This comparison illustrates an important principle in public finance. Students have, in the past, been somewhat careless in condemning or praising particular features of the tax or the expenditure system in isolation from the overall or combined fiscal structure. It is difficult to appraise or to evaluate fiscal institutions in partial terms; criteria which show particular institutions to be desirable or undesirable are likely to be relevent only for the system considered as a whole. Particular institutions cannot be considered independently of the large system of which they form only a part.

IDEOLOGICAL ORIGINS OF PROPERTY TAXATION

The taxation of income is a relative newcomer in the group of tax institutions, and modern income taxes have their origin largely in late 19th- and early 20th-century ideas of distributive justice in allocating the burden of taxes among individuals. The taxation of capital or property has a much longer history, and the doctrinal history itself is both interesting and informative. Rarely do we have the opportunity to trace the impact of economic ideas so directly to political support for the subsequent development of existing institutions.

The taxation of property, or capital, suggests that the base of the tax must be real things, that is, real assets which assume physical location in space. "Land" has always been one important form of real assets, and in centuries past "land," as such, was far more important, relatively, than it is today. The origins of the taxation of land stem from medieval conceptions of land as being held in "common" ownership. The rights to private property in land have been suspect in almost every age, and land has been given mysterious qualities which set it apart from other real assets. Any complete history of the property tax would have to examine these important background ideas more carefully, for they were certainly influential in later thought. Here we shall be concerned only with ideas which were developed in modern times and which have been directly influential in the development of modern property tax institutions.

The physiocrats

In the middle of the 18th century a group of French court physicians, who have come to be known as the Physiocrats, developed the idea of the circular flow of income in the economy. As they tried to trace the movement of income from one sector of the economy to the other, they reached what appeared to them a startling conclusion. Agriculture was the only "productive" sector of the whole economy; all of the other activities were essentially "unproductive" or sterile and consisted in the mere transformation of goods into different forms and in the provision of services. Only in production on the land, in agriculture, was there produced a genuine "net product," a true surplus over and above the real costs of production. This net product or surplus was received by the owners of agricultural land as rents. On the basis of this model of the economy, the Physiocrats proposed that this net product, this surplus produced on agricultural land and received as rent by the landlords, be made the source of taxation. This was the only place in the economy which could, in fact, support taxation.

The Physiocrats were, of course, grossly in error insofar as their analysis was concerned. They were concentrating on the physical aspects of goods. They completely failed to see that the transformation of wheat into flour, of flour in Bordeaux to flour in Paris, of flour into bread, or of bread in the kitchen into bread on the dining table are all equally as productive of utility to the consumer as is the initial transformation of seed, labor, and land into wheat. They had none of the more modern notions about utility, and their economic analysis was very primitive. Nevertheless, the ideas are important in representing the origins of the idea that land is the suitable place for all taxation, since it is the only place where a net social surplus occurs. These ideas may still be found today in the common observation that the agricultural industry is, in some mysterious way, more basic or essential than other industries in the economy.

The Ricardian theory of rent

The work of the classical economists, notably Adam Smith and David Ricardo, was completed after the time of the Physiocrats, and it was influenced to a significant extent by their ideas. It was Ricardo who formalized the classical theory of rent, the implications of which are quite similar to those deriving from the Physiocratic theory of land use.

Ricardo was trying to explain the causes of value, and he sought to show that relative values of goods depended on the amount of labor involved in production. One of the difficulties in his way was the absence of any satisfactory explanation of the phenomenon of land rent. The return to capital could, conceptually, be explained away by calling this the reward to past labor, but there was no way that this idea could be applied to land. Ricardo surmounted this difficulty by explaining that all values of goods are really determined on marginal lands which earn no rents. As the population increases, it becomes necessary for food production to be extended to poorer and poorer grades of land. But since the amount of labor involved in production on the poor lands must exceed that on the rich lands, the price or value of the "wheat" must increase as the population increases and as cultivation is extended. Since the landlords owning the rich lands will not be required to pay more than the going wage for labor, there will accrue to them a "rent," which represents the return over and above the costs of production on the marginal lands, the latter being determined by the extent of the arable land and the rate of increase in the population. The rents on the superior lands would continue to rise as the population continued to increase.

Ricardo's analysis is considerably more sophisticated than that of the Physiocrats, but it reaches fundamentally equivalent conclusions. The rent of pure land, which Ricardo called "the original and indestructible powers of the soil," was, in a sense, a genuine surplus received by the landlords. There was no pain or disutility involved in securing this return, as was the case with labor or with the abstinence involved in saving and investing. Rent of land was not a real cost of production; it was the result of price and not a cause of it.

The Ricardian rent theory suffers from his failure to understand the ideas of marginal productivity or opportunity costs, ideas, and concepts that remained to be developed after his time. Marginal productivity theory can show, quite easily, that the rents received by the landlords in each case represent nothing more and nothing less than the marginal productivity of the land, the contribution of the land to the total production. In this respect, the theory shows that land is not different from any other productive resource; the traditional distinction was not based on any economic difference. The full rental returns of landlords represents a surplus only if land has only one possible use. Once land is recognized to have many uses, the rent of land becomes a cost similar to the payment for any productive service.

The single tax and Henry George

The modern neoclassical theory of rent was not developed until approximately the turn of the century. Prior to this time, the Ricardian ideas were very important in influencing discussion and in generating popular support for a policy of land taxation. This movement received its impetus in America through the efforts of Henry George and through the results of his book *Progress and Poverty*. George became the leader of a movement which supported the concentration and consolidation of all taxes into a *single tax* on land values. The proponents of the single tax accepted the Ricardian theory of differential rent without critical reflection. The gross returns to "pure land," apart from improvement to land, were considered to represent income shares that were surplus in the sense that no real efforts or sacrifice were involved in generating them. Onto this basic conception of rent was added the provocative idea, usually associated with Hobson, that the taxation of this social surplus could be accomplished without the economy being disturbed at all. The single tax was thus the most efficient of all taxes. The undesirable effects of ordinary taxation could be completely eliminated if only pure "land" were subjected to tax. The single tax became the perfect tax to its proponents. A third factor lent considerable support to the movement. Common observation of the rapidly growing urban areas in the United States revealed that the owners of land placed adjacent to the rapidly growing cities were in extremely favorable positions to reap large capital gains. Capital values of land in such areas were rising rapidly, as a result of no apparent effort on the part of the landowners. These three elements: Ricardian rent theory, Hobson's ideas of the efficiency of taxing social surpluses, and the empirical observation of increasing urban land values, gave substantial support to a policy of the taxation of real property, with a special emphasis on land. The single tax, as such, was never effectively supported. But the present importance of property taxation in the local government fiscal systems must be attributed, at least in part, to the strength of this movement. The separation of land values from the values of improvements to land is still supported by many modern writers, and differential classifications applying to these separate types of property are to be found in several fiscal systems.

The modern theory of economic rent

The modern approach to the theory of rent allows us to see both the strong and the weak points in the Ricardian rent theory and in its practical consequence, the single tax movement. Rent is commonly defined as the return to any resouce, whether this be land or any other form of capital. If the resources is permanently fixed in one employment, that is, if no alternative employment opportunity is available, all of the return may be defined as *economic rent*, as distinguished from *rent*, used without the adjective. This *economic rent* may be more precisely defined as the return to a given resource over and above what the resource could earn in its next most favorable employment. In one sense, therefore, the whole of *economic rent* is an unnecessary payment. It is unnecessary in the purely instrumental sense of not being required to get the resource into production. For example, suppose that a professional baseball player can earn $100,000 playing baseball, but no more than $10,000 in any alternative employment. Suppose further that he is motivated purely by pecuniary considerations. Nine tenths of his annual income, or $90,000, is economic rent; this part of his income serves no economic purpose, so to speak, since for any salary above $10,000 this individual would, presumably,play baseball. This example suggests the intuitive appeal of the tax on this "surplus."

The difficulty of imposing taxes on economic rents lies in the impossibility of distinguishing between those returns to resources which constitute true economic rents and those which constitute genuine opportunity costs of production. If an omniscient observer could be found to superimpose some "fiscal vacuum cleaner" over society that would take out only the pure economic rents, then taxation could proceed, perhaps, without undue economic effects. But the results would not be acceptable from the point of view of equity or justice. Some of the poorest of the social group secure most of their income for economic rent. A tax on such rent might well impose a disproportionately heavy tax burden on these individuals which would be generally regarded as inequitable.

The taxation of land presents an especially interesting problem from the point of view assigning final tax burden. To the extent that land is fixed in supply, its return constitutes a pure economic rent and a general tax on land might be expected to be neutral in its effect on resource allocation. However, it is generally accepted that "land," in any meaningful economic term can be "produced." The only grounds for particular distinction of land from other assets lies in the greater permanency of investment in land. This makes it seem probable that the returns to land include a greater element of what is called quasi-rent and, if short-run factors were the only relevant ones, the imposition of a differentially higher tax on pure land might exert less economic effect than a tax on other assets. When longer-run considerations are taken into account, on the other hand, there would seem to be little grounds for making any distinction.

Even if land were absolutely fixed in supply, over the long run, there exists a possibility of shifting some of the tax burden from land to other units of physical capital. Land and capital are highly complementary assets in terms of individual wealth accumulations. A tax on land lowers the return in that asset relative to other types of capital. If, in response, individuals seek to acquire greater stocks of capital assets, over the long run the stock of capital will increase relative to land. This will tend to lower the marginal product of capital and raise the marginal product of land (and, also labor) in the production process. Assuming that productive resources are paid their marginal products in a competitive economy, some of the burden of the tax on land is shifted, in the long run, to capital.[1]

The ideological bases for the taxation of property no longer exert major influence on the reforms proposed for modern tax institutions. Historically, these factors explain the taxation of land values in a differentially discriminatory fashion in some jurisdictions. In the modern era, immobile property, including land, tends to be subjected to higher effective rates of property taxation for much more practical reasons. Immobile property can be taxed more easily; the tax is far more difficult to evade, and less intergovernmental competition for tax sources can take place.

CONCLUSIONS

If income is defined consistently, income taxation and capital taxation are equivalent, and one may be converted into the other without difficulty. As these two taxing institutions exist, however, the conceptual underpinnings are different. Hence they become different taxes and exert different economic effects. The income tax is a personal tax; the tax on capital is not personal. But when considered together as parts of an overall fiscal system, the two taxes have offsetting faults. The income tax tends to discriminate against labor incomes; the capital tax in favor of labor incomes.

The modern property tax may be traced directly to the earlier ideas on the role of land in the economy. The Physiocratic idea that land was the only producer of a surplus and the Ricardian theory of land rents were influential in shaping public opinion and policy in the 19th century. The efforts of Henry George and his followers to introduce a system of single taxation were not wholly successful, although they were not without significant impact. The modern theory of economic rent suggests that the surplus return, embodied in the idea of economic rent, may be received by any resource. There is no par-

---

[1] This analysis is treated in detail in Martin Feldstein, "The Surprising Incidence of a Tax on Pure Rent: A New Answer to an Old Question," *Journal of Political Economy* (April, 1977).

ticular economic reason why land should have ever been subjected to differential taxation. The modern reason why immobile property is taxed more heavily is considerably more simple. The property tax is used largely by local governments. Land and immobile property generally cannot easily escape taxation, and local governments find that intergovernmental competition in property taxation, although severe, is less damaging than other forms of taxation.

36

The property tax

$\mathbf{P}$roperty taxation is the primary source of revenue for local units of government in the United States. More than 80 percent of all tax revenues at this level comes from this tax. Property is not subjected to federal government taxation, and state governments have in recent decades shown an increasing willingness to leave this important revenue source to localities.

More than $60 billion was collected by local governmental units under property taxation in fiscal 1977. Collections increased at an annual rate of more than 8 percent over the 1950s and 1960s, and increased threefold over the 20-year period between 1950 and 1970. Between 1971 and 1977, property tax revenue increased by 50 percent. In the United States in 1977, state-local property tax collections amounted to $46 per $1,000 of personal income. The per capita rate of tax was $289.

THE DEFINITION AND CLASSIFICATION OF PROPERTY

The general tax on property, as it is usually administered in the taxing jurisdiction of the United States, is a nonpersonal tax. The tax is imposed indirectly on the value of assets. Before we can discuss the problems that arise in the process of valuation, issues of definition and classification must be raised. What constitutes taxable property? What assets are to be included in the tax base? What assets are to be exempted? How are the different types of assets to be classified?

The *ad rem* or nonpersonal nature of property taxation suggests that certain restrictions should be placed on the conception of taxable property. This characteristic of the tax should, on any consistent application, exempt from the tax base all personal or individual assets which represent claims against the income from real assets but which do not embody legal title to the real assets themselves. Consistent application of the property tax should, therefore, exempt *intangible* assets from the tax base. Intangible property is defined to include such items as shares of stock in corporations, bonds, mortgages, notes receivable, and claims against the federal government in the form of money.

All physical or tangible assets, including both real property and personal property, should be included in the tax base if the conceptual bases of the tax are to be consistently applied. These tangible assets include, first of all, *real property,* which is technically defined to include land and permanent improvements to land such as buildings, fences, and irrigation systems. Real property is essentially immobile property, at least during any short period. Second, tangible *personal property* should be included in the base. This category covers such items as automobiles, furniture, jewelry, and furs, for individuals, and raw material and finished goods inventories, for firms.

Fully consistent application of the tax on capital would allow no exemptions of any real assets from the tax base because of personal or occupational characteristics of the property owners, and all assets would be subjected to a uniform rate on real value. As is normally the case, however, consistency has never been one of the virtues of institutions that emerge from democratic political process. Property taxation has never satisfactorily resolved the question of defining taxable property. As shown in the preceding chapter, land has always been assigned a unique place in the tax base, and the property tax arose out of early attempts to tax land and other specific types of property. As the tax base was broadened, the tax became more general, and the idea of a *general property tax* was widely accepted. This violated the implied exemption of intangible property implicit in the tax itself. General property taxes were extended to include not only real assets, valued in gross terms, but also claims to the income from such assets. In practice, however, it was clear from the outset that intangible property is extremely difficult to tax. When heavy tax rates have been imposed on intangible property, evasion has been widely prevalent. Governments soon found it necessary either to exempt intangible assets from taxation or to classify these assets separately and to subject them to a very low nominal rate of tax.

In 26 states no attempt it made to include intangibles in the property tax base, while in the remaining states, intangible personal property is taxed to varying degrees.

Whereas the complete exemption of intangible property, with the possible exception of money, seems consistent with the very nature of capital taxation, all items of tangible property should, conceptually, be included in the tax base. But attempts to include mobile personal property in the tax base at rates applicable to real property have also met with failure. The imposition of the property tax on mobile assets has been accompanied by widespread evasion and a rapid weakening of taxpayer morality, which could only be prevented through the incurrence of prohibitively high costs of administration and collection. The result of this experience has been the movement toward the separate classification of personal property for tax purposes. In some jurisdictions, personal property has been altogether exempted from the tax base; in others it has been taxed at effective rates that are only fractionally as high as the rate on real property.

Broadly speaking, therefore, the so-called general property tax has become largely a tax on one particular form of property: real estate— that is, land and permanent improvements to land. Even with the tax base restricted largely to this category of assets, specific exemptions have been introduced that have reduced the revenue capacity of this source. Several states have incorporated homestead exemption provisions through which the tax on owner-occupied residences is either eliminated or substantially reduced. All jurisdictions exempt property owned by certain religious and charitable organizations. And, for constitutional reasons, states and local units cannot impose the tax on real property held by the federal government. This last exemption is very important for certain jurisdictions. The federal government does, in many cases, make payments to the taxing units, in lieu of taxes, but no fully satisfactory arrangements have been worked out yet for this problem.

Within the broad category of real property, several states introduce additional subclassifications for the purpose of discriminating in tax treatment. These classifications may be on the basis of developed and undeveloped land, urban property and rural property, agricultural land, forest land, mining property, and many other possible subcategories.

In terms of taxation of real property, residential nonfarm real estate is the most important component, comprising almost 60 percent of the tax base. This is followed in importance by nonfarm commercial and industrial property which accounts for 24 percent of the tax base. Agricultural land provides only about 12 percent of assessed value in the real property tax base.

THE ASSESSMENT OF PROPERTY VALUE

Any tax on capital or property must be levied as a rated percentage of money value. Money value provides the only meaningful common denominator in terms of which widely heterogeneous physical assets may be compared and measured. A tax based on weight, size, or any other purely physical characteristic would be wholly arbitrary in impact. The use of money values of assets as the tax base requires that each asset be assigned some specific valuation for tax purposes. The process of determining the appropriate taxable value of assets, or property, presents some of the most difficult problems in the administration of the property tax. This process is called *assessment*, and the taxable value finally assigned to each asset is called *assessed value*.

There are several alternative approaches to the problem of assessment. It seems useful to examine each of these in general terms before going on to discuss some of the more practical problems faced by the tax assessor. To the economist, the value of any asset is determined by what that asset can command in exchange on the market. This approach suggests that the assessor should look initially at market prices for assets as representing appropriate values for purposes of determining tax liabilities. For assets falling within reasonably homogeneous groupings, and for which markets are reasonably perfect, assessment based on direct market values or prices is a very simple procedure. To take one of the more obvious examples, suppose that the task placed before the assessor is that of valuing shares of General Motors common stock. He would have to do no more than note from the financial page of his daily newspaper the market value of this stock on the relevant assessment date. But assessment problems rarely arise in connection with such readily marketable intangible assets, which are relatively unimportant in the total tax in any case. To some extent, direct market quotations can be applied in valuing certain items of personal property. In the case of automobiles, for example, the so-called Blue Book estimates for market prices may be the best guide for tax assessment purposes.

The most important items of real property in the tax base present more difficult problems of assessment. Separate items may be quite distinct, and market data on comparable assets may be absent, or at least far from perfect. A market approach may still be helpful. Let us take an example. Suppose that the problem is that of assigning a taxable value to a particular building on a particular street corner, the assessed value to include both the land itself and the improvements on the land. Records indicate to the assessor that the ownership of the property has not changed hands in a quarter century; there is no recent market price recorded for this property. The assessor may search for recent transfers of property which he considers to be roughly similar to the item to be assessed; and he will have to decide on the criteria by which he determines whether or not other items are "roughly similar." Data gathered from transfers of similar items of property can be very helpful, but they can never be wholly satisfactory, since the assessor must recognize that each particular item of property has its own peculiar characteristics.

A supplementary approach to the one suggested is indicated. The capital value of any asset is determined by discounting an anticipated or expected earnings stream by some appropriate rate of discount to arrive at a capital sum. If an available market for homogeneous assets exists, this capitalization process is done by the separate traders, and the appraiser need not undertake a separate capitalization. But if the market is highly imperfect, the assessor may find that the direct capitalization approach is helpful. It may be considerably easier to estimate the annual value of a piece of property than to estimate the capital value directly. By taking an estimated rental value for a year, adjusting this as necessary over a reasonable life for the asset and allowing for the accumulation of depreciation charges, the assessor may capitalize this value into a capital sum. This process provides, or should provide, a rough check on the market price data available. Again an example may be helpful. Suppose that the tax assessor estimates with some reasonable degree of accuracy that the rental value of a particular structure is $10,000 per year. This is a net rental over and above full charges estimated to cover maintenance and depreciation. Using, say, a 5 percent rate of discount, a capital value of $200,000 is essential for the structure. If the assessor then observes that property items which seem roughly similar have been recently transferred at prices not too far distant from this estimate, the task of finding a suitable evaluation will have been accomplished. On the other hand, if the capitalization estimate should be far off the mark in comparison with transfer values, this discrepancy should indicate that something further needs to be investigated.

In some cases, the capitalized values of current rentals will fall far short of the market value of the property. This is especially true with land units that are being held for purposes of appreciation in value. For example, an individual may own a very valuable block in a rapidly growing suburban shopping area, retaining this property as a vacant lot. The actual income received from the property is zero, and the capitalization process would indicate that the property has no capital value. Yet it will be evident to everyone that the property is very valuable. In this case the assessor must rely, as much as possible, on transfer prices on comparable pieces of property. Property held in this way for purposes of appreciation in market value should be assessed at the same percentage of actual market value as all other property. If too much reliance is placed on the income from property, such items will tend to be assessed relatively too low, and this low taxation will tend to encourage owners to hold property even longer for appreciation purposes. Property assessment for tax purposes should not be used directly as a means for encouraging or discouraging the development of real property. In many cases, rational investment criteria both from an individual and from the social point of view suggest that particular items of property be held in undeveloped stages for considerable periods of time. The tax assessment should not deliberately discriminate against such units of property with the purpose of accelerating development. But one of the costs of holding property undeveloped is the tax which is foregone. A neutral assessment procedure must, therefore, assess undeveloped property at approximately the same percentage of actual marketable value as developed property. A policy of assessing undeveloped real property at lower values, because of the absence of current income earnings, will tend to prejudice development in an uneconomic manner.

To this point we have discussed the assessment problem from the approach of the economist. An alternative approach taken might be that of the acountant. Property items tend to be carried on the balance sheets of firms (and of families if they keep balance sheets) in terms of original cost values. The assessor will have reasonably good access to data on original costs of each asset or on the costs of purchase by current owners. There may be a temptation to rely on this relatively simple means of assigning assessed valuations to property. In a period of overall economic stability, this method of assessment will not produce serious errors. It will fail to take into account the changing values of property which accompany changing land-use patterns within an area, but, aside from these, property values will tend to remain roughly stable over time. However, in a period of economic instability, either one of general depression or of general inflation, this approach to tax assessment is wholly unacceptable.

In a period of general and gradual growth in money incomes, whether this growth be generated by real factors or by inflation, the valuation of property at original cost to current owners (or some fraction thereof) will tend to cause older properties and long-occupied properties to be under-valued relative to newer and recently transferred properties. There is considerable evidence to indicate that this sort of distortion in assessments is quite common in most jurisdictions, especially in the postwar period when incomes (and property values) have increased rapidly. In such periods, proper assessment procedures must involve periodic reassessment of all properties within each jurisdiction. Unless this is done, the real rate of tax will tend to decline over time. As the data indicate, however, local communities have tended to increase assessed valuation rapidly in the postwar years, and the lag between the increase in real values and that in assessed valuations does not seem to present the problem for local tax administration that the fiscal experts once feared. Nevertheless, it remains true that unless local taxing jurisdictions are prepared to make the required periodic reassessments during periods of economic growth, real or monetary, financial crises may arise due to the declining real rate of tax.

ASSESSED VALUES AND REAL VALUES

The fundamental problem in assessing property for tax purposes is that of determining the relative values of separate assets. This relative evaluation can only be done in terms of "real" values; that is, the estimated equivalents to market values. When we consider the actual assessment procedure, however, we find that property is very rarely assessed at 100 percent of its "real" or market value. By tradition and convention, local governments tend to assess real property at varying percentages of value. In the mid-1970s, the national average ratio of assessed to real value was about 31 percent. This average covers, of course, a wide variety of different rates in the various states. For example, in 15 states the assessment ratio was less than 15 percent. Twelve states, on the other hand had assessment ratios in excess of 50 percent.

In the abstract, there seems to be no logical reason for this practice. The assessor must estimate the real value of property before a percentage of this value can be calculated; full value assessment would not make the assessor's task more difficult. Assessment at full value would increase the total amount of taxable property within the jurisdiction, and, in order to provide the same revenues, tax rates on assessed value could be lowered. The rational property owner should be indifferent between paying a tax of 1 percent on full value and a tax of 2 percent on 50 percent of full value.

This argument would hold true if local units of government employing the property tax were wholly independent of each other or of the state governments. This independence does not exist, and it is in the relationships between units that at least some of the explanation for the low ratios of assessed to real values are to be found. Local governments finance a sizable share of their own expenditures from funds received as transfers from the states. State transfers to the local governments for education, for roads, for health and welfare, and for similar services must be made on the basis of some formulas for apportioning funds among separate local units. These formulas, always subject to political pressures from conflicting interests in the separate local jurisdictions, have normally come to be based on certain simple, but definite, quantitative measures. The size of population in local jurisdictions is a popular criterion, and the total assessed valuation of property within the local unit has been a second very common measure determining local shares of both state-aid funds and direct state outlays in the units. By assessing property within its own borders at some percentage of full value, or at lower percentages of value than other local units, a single local government can increase its share of state-aid funds. In effect, the citizens of this unit can, in that way, shift a share of their taxation to citizens of other units.

This practice cannot be successfully undertaken by all local units simultaneously, and competition among local governmental units in reducing assessments has required that many states take action to impose certain restraints. Largely for this reason, state governments have set up various means of ensuring that assessment practices and procedures in the separate local units are standardized or equalized. The movement for state equalization followed the movement toward interunit competition; therefore, the low ratio of assessed values to real values remains characteristic of most property tax systems.

REVIEW AND APPEAL OF ASSESSMENTS

Under the income tax system in the United States, the primary reporting responsibility is placed on the individual taxpayer. He must report his own income accurately, and severe penalties are imposed for inaccuracies and omissions. The property tax is wholly different. Normally, the individual property owner is under no obligation to make a personal declaration concerning the value of his own assets. (One suggested reform in property taxation has embodied individual assessment as a central feature, coupled with some specified collective rights of purchase at some percentage of individually declared values.) The valuation, or assessment, is left to the tax assessor, as an administrative official of the taxing government. The assessor is assigned the task of placing a value on each unit of property, and the final tax must be paid as a designated percentage of this assessed value.

The individual property owner may not desire to accept the judgment of the tax assessor. To provide the property owner with an opportunity to have the assessment reviewed, a formal channel of appeal is to be found in the structure of most taxing jurisdictions. The property owner may appeal to a specially constituted board, and if successful in demonstrating that the property has been assessed at a value in excess of that placed on comparable property in the jurisdiction, may secure a reduction in tax liability. Tax assessment offers an example of an established institution in which individual appeals from administrative decisions have been substantially formalized through the process of special review.

THE SETTING OF TAX RATES

Property tax rates are determined by both the needs of the taxing governments for revenues and the assessed valuation of property. The rates may be imposed so as to cover all revenue needs, but normally they are broken down with separate shares of the combined rate attributed directly to the financing of the separate governmental functions. Rates are usually stated in terms of mills per $100 of assessed value or cents per $1,000 of assessed value. A basic rate will normally be levied for general expenditures, and this will be supplemented by special mill rates for schools, for roads, and other itemized expenditure categories. As we shall note at a later point, this procedure tends to bring the actual cost of the separate governmental programs more closely to the attention of the taxpayer than is the case with any other tax institution in the overall U.S. fiscal system.

A distinction must be made between the nominal rate of tax and the effective rate of tax based on real values. The nominal rate must be the same for all units of property within the same tax classification. In this sense, the tax must be proportional in rates within single-asset classes. Effective rates, on the other hand, may vary substantially even within property classifications due to differential ratios of assessed values to real values. As a result, the effective rate structure need not add up to proportional taxation. As suggested, tax classification, both formal and informal, makes the effective rate on real property much higher than on personal property. Assessment procedures tend to make effective rates on newly developed property higher than on old property. And there is evidence that effective rates are higher for property falling within lower price ranges than for property falling within higher price ranges. This discrimination is explained partially by the fact that market value data are more readily attainable for the more homogeneous lower priced assets, and by the fact that the owners of higher valued assets can afford to bring more pressure to bear on the assessor in an attempt to secure favorable evaluations. It seems also to be true that the property of business firms tends to be subjected to a higher effective rate of tax than is property owned by individual citizens. This discrimination seems especially to hold with respect to the property owned by large corporations. Local units of government have tended to place high effective rates of tax on assets owned by railroads, electric power companies, and similar utilities. Certain types of business property are, in turn, differentially favored in terms of effective rates. Local jurisdictions seeking to expand the industrial bases of the community have, in many cases, exempted the property of new firms from the tax base.

The property tax is employed largely by local governmental units. This fact makes any estimate of an *average* overall effective rate on all property very difficult and of questionable value. Not only do the separate units impose different effective rates because of assessment differences; they also classify property differently as among the separate states.

Property tax relief for the elderly

In the 1960s and early 1970s, considerable concern developed about the burden borne by local taxpayers. As a result of this concern, by 1975, 47 states and the District of Columbia had adopted some plans for local property tax relief. The targeted beneficiaries of most of these plans were elderly homeowners and in a few cases, elderly renters. Some states extended their relief programs to the poor and/or disabled and in five states the relief plans were generally available to all local property taxpayers.

The two most common forms of property tax relief were homestead exemptions and "circuit breakers." Homestead exemptions exempt some portion of assessed property from taxation. The so-called "circuit breaker," on the other hand, is designed to prevent tax "overloads" in the same way that an electrical circuit breaker prevents electrical overloads. Some maximum limit on property tax payments, usually calculated as a percentage of household income, is set by the state. Local property tax payments in excess of this amount are then rebated to the beneficiary either as a credit against state income tax liability or directly in cash. First adopted by the state of Wisconsin in 1964, the "circuit breaker" was in operation in 24 states by the end of 1974.

Locally financed property tax relief programs primarily take the form of exemptions from property tax of some percentage of the monetary amount of the assessed value of the property.

ECONOMIC EFFECTS OF PROPERTY TAXATION

The economic effects of property taxation depend to a large extent upon the generality of coverage. A general tax, levied equally on all real assets, would exert substantially different effects from a tax on classified types of assets, or one which is concentrated on particular types.

Effects of a general capital tax

The effects of a general capital tax have already been discussed to some extent in Chapter 35. A tax which includes all real assets in the tax base and which bears equally on all items may exert two primary effects. First of all, the tax will act to reduce the net productivity of investment generally. Insofar as this reduction in the marginal rate of return on capital causes individuals to save less income and to use up more income in consumption, the rate of economic growth is retarded and the burden of the tax is partially spread out or diffused among all the members of the social group. As was discussed in Chapter 29, however, economic theory allows either a positive or a negative relationship between the rate of interest and individual saving. Empirical evidence is mixed, making it impossible to ascertain the actual effect here.

A second primary effect may be that of generating an important shifting of investment. As the analysis in Chapter 34 showed, assets in the form of human earning power tend to be differentially favored by the property or capital tax. This implies that some shifting of initial investment from the production of real assets to the furthering of the human asset values might take place as a result of the tax. The investment in human beings, typified by educational expenditures, might be increased at the expense of investment in real capital. The degree to which investment decisions between these two broad alternatives represent effective substitutes at the margin and, in this way, affect individual behavior is highly speculative. Some shifting of savings between the two forms of investment can, no doubt, occur. But, on balance, the amount of shifting of investment funds between real capital formation and human capital formation that might be specifically caused by the tax on capital seems to be of minor significance.

If these two primary effects are held to be insignificant, a truly general tax on all real assets exerts little influence on individual behavior. This is the same as saying that the tax cannot readily be shifted. It must be borne by those individuals who *hold assets through time*. These individuals cannot modify their own behavior in any way to effectively shift the tax burden to other groups in the society.

Tax capitalization

It is necessary to determine quite clearly just who the damaged groups are in this case. In order to analyze this point carefully, we must introduce the idea of *tax capitalization*. A tax is said to be capitalized when its burden is concentrated in time on the current owner of property. The general property tax is often held to be capitalized, or substantially so. The analysis proceeds as follows. The imposition of the tax on real assets will reduce the net income from those assets through all subsequent time periods. Since the capital value of an asset is determined by discounting an expected net income stream, the tax will have the effect of reducing immediately upon its announcement the capital value of the assets. The current owners will be subjected to the full burden, and all future purchasers of the assets will escape taxation since they will pay no more than the reduced capital value. The tax will have become capitalized into the lower value. We shall return to this phenomenon of tax capitalization at a later point, but this brief introduction is sufficient to indicate its inapplicability to the case of general taxation of capital. While it is true that the capital value of an asset is determined by discounting an expected earnings stream and equally true that the tax will reduce all expected net earnings, *if the tax is truly general in impact* all earning assets will be similarly affected. The rate of interest, or rate of discount, is determined by the rate of yield on capital investment, the productivity of investment. Thus, the general tax not only reduces expected net earnings, but it also reduces the appropriate discount rate. If the tax is general, both earnings and the discount rate may be reduced proportionately. If this takes place, capital values remain unchanged. Current owners are not subjected to the full burden of the tax; instead they are subjected to the tax burden only as long as they hold the assets which now earn a similar net income. All holders of assets bear the incidence of the tax, whether they hold the assets during the current period when the tax is initially imposed or whether they purchase the assets later and hold them in future periods. There is no bunching of the tax burden in time, no tax capitalization, *if the tax is truly a general one.*

This is a major proviso, however, and it is difficult even to conceive of a tax which is truly general to the extent that no capitalization can occur. Consider, for example, the case in which the national government imposed a capital tax on all real assets in order to allow a corresponding reduction in the income tax. It seems evident that the offsetting reduction in the income tax would tend to prevent the effects postulated from happening. The income tax also reduces the net yield from capital and, insofar as this is reduced, the impact of the capital tax on the rate of yield is offset. The analysis becomes somewhat more complicated in other cases, but the important point to be noted here is that the property tax, as it exists, is not a general tax on capital. Hence, some tax capitalization can occur. In order to examine this process more clearly, we need to move to the other extreme and analyze the effects of a tax imposed on only one type of property.

Effects of a specific property tax

Let us suppose that the property tax is defined to include only one type of property in the tax base. To simplify our analysis, we assume that the tax is levied on urban residential property only, and that the tax is levied by only one local unit of government. All surrounding governmental units are assumed to raise revenues in other ways.

In this highly simplified model, the process of *tax capitalization* can be clearly traced. Immediately upon the imposition of the tax, the current owners of urban residential property in the taxing jurisdiction will be subjected to a capital loss. No prospective purchaser of property in that district will pay more for a unit of property than he could earn from a similar investment elsewhere in the community. Capital values of taxed property would immediately be reduced. The discount rate used in determining these capital values would not be affected, since this rate would be determined in the whole economy.

Insofar as the investment in urban residential property tends to be long term or quasi-permanent, the current owners at the time of the tax may be subjected to sizable capital losses. If, in fact, the property were genuinely indestructible, there would be a full capitalization of all future taxes onto the shoulders of current owners. They could not shift even a portion of the tax to future purchasers of property or future renters of residential units. In an economic sense, however, little property is genuinely indestructible. Therefore, as time passes, original owners may be able to shift a portion of the tax burden by failing to maintain the property. As the value of the property depreciates, and as old units are taken off the urban residential market, rents go up in the area, and the renters of residential units begin to bear a portion of the tax. Over a long time period, the tax will be shifted to all users of residential property in the area. But the capitalization process will have the result of concentrating a substantial portion of the tax burden on the owners of quasi-permanent property at the time of the original imposition.

The contrasting results follow from a reduction in a long-established tax. Since the demand for residential accommodations will not be changed, there will be no change in rentals. The windfall gain from the tax reduction will tend to be enjoyed by the owners of property at the time of the tax reduction, and these owners will continue to enjoy these gains until such time as new resources can be invested in real property in the community.

Effects of actual property taxes

The existing pattern of property taxation in the United States falls roughly between the two extremes of a general tax on capital and a specific property tax. The tax does not apply generally to all assets and there is much differential treatment. On the other hand, the tax is sufficiently general in application to affect the overall productivity of investment. The tax is levied by almost all local units of government, but at widely varying rates. This latter feature makes analysis of the actual economic effects of property taxation especially complex. To the extent that capital is mobile in the long run, it will tend to flow to the employment and, more important in this context, to the location where the rate of return net of tax is the highest. As a result, net rates of return will tend to be equalized across jurisdictional boundaries despite differences in tax rates. One effect of multiple local property taxes, then, is a lowering of the net return on investment on a nation-wide basis. The magnitude of this effect depends not only on the actual pattern of tax rates but also on such factors as production and demand conditions and the resource flows required to restore general equilibrium after imposition of the taxes.

A second consequence of local property taxation is likely to be changes in the relative prices of goods produced in the various local jurisdictions. With different tax rates, equalization of net returns across jurisdictional boundaries necessarily implies that gross rates of return, which measure the cost of capital as a productive input, will differ among jurisdictions. Suppose for example, the rate of return net of tax is equalized at 7 percent. Jurisdiction A is imposing a tax equivalent to 2 percent of annual capital income, jurisdiction B a tax of 4 percent. The cost of capital in the two jurisdictions will be 9 percent and 11 percent respectively. Because of these cost differences, the prices of goods produced in relatively high-tax jurisdictions will tend to be higher relative to goods produced in low-tax jurisdictions.[1]

---

[1]This analysis is developed by Peter Mieszkowski, "The Property Tax: A Profit or an Excise Tax," *Journal of Public Economics* (April 1972).

The preceding concentrated on what might be termed the general equilibrium effects of a system of local property taxes. It is also important, however, to examine the effects of the tax in a single taxing jurisdiction in terms of the consequences of that jurisdiction independently altering its own rate of tax. Because the tax rate set by any single jurisdiction will have negligible effects on the net rate of return to capital and the market interest rate, the local property tax can exert important capitalization effects at the local level. Suppose, for example, a tax reduction is being considered in a single local jurisdiction. The existing tax rate has been in existence for a sufficiently long period of time that all long-run adjustments to it have occurred. If the tax is now reduced, owners of taxed assets will enjoy an immediate windfall gain in the form of an increase in the market value of those assets. Over time some of this gain will be dissipated as new capital flows into the jurisdiction. This may take several years, however, and, in the meantime, consumers of products and services produced with the taxed assets will not enjoy any appreciable price reductions as a consequence of the tax. Renters, for example, will not experience any immediate reduction in rents nor will new homeowners, as opposed to current homeowners, gain from a lowering of housing prices until such a time as the actual stock of housing has been increased.

REAL PROPERTY TAXES AND COLLECTIVE DECISIONS

Real estate is taxed differentially under the property tax largely because it is the only base upon which municipal and local government taxation can be feasibly erected. Although investment and disinvestment in real estate can take place, the processes require time. Tax evasion is difficult and tax shifting is a long-run project. Property taxes on real estate have come, therefore, to be looked upon by fiscal theorists as more or less a necessary evil in the whole tax structure. On the basis of considerations of equity, the tax on real property has little to recommend it as it is actually administered in the United States. However, when the tax is viewed in the light of the tremendous difficulties of organizing collective action, it has certain merits that are absent in other tax institutions. First of all, like the income tax, it is a direct tax. The incidence of the tax, at least in the short run, is predictable in advance. Local property owners know full well that an increase in the tax will fall largely on their shoulders. Second, the tax, as it is administered, can be broken down and separate rates, mill rates, applied to each public service or function. Rarely do tax-payers get this sort of opportunity to weigh the relative costs of the separate public functions, one against the other. Finally, without the tax, the local unit of government, as an independently functioning agency, would be likely to disappear. And clearly for many of the more specific public functions, decisions can be more rationally made at the local government level than at any higher level in the political hierarchy. These points suggest that the tax on real property, while undesirable on equity grounds, finds considerable support in terms of other objectives which must be considered in any overall evaluation of a fiscal structure.

SUPPLEMENTARY READING

For the traditional work on the property tax, see J. P. Jensen, *Property Taxation in the United States* (Chicago: University of Chicago Press, 1931).

The modern standard work is Dick Netzer, *Economics of the Property Tax* (Washington, D.C.: The Brookings Institution, 1966).

Who Pays the Property Tax? by Henry J. Aaron provides a useful discussion of the controversy surrounding the assignment of property tax burden. (Washington, D.C.: The Brookings Institute, 1975).

part IX

Intergovernmental fiscal relations

37

Fiscal and economic aspects of federalism

T he United States fiscal system cannot be adequately discussed as a single, integrated unit; this should be evident from the organization of the preceding parts of this book. The division of fiscal authority between the federal or central government and the state governments, a division which is an essential feature of the political structure, has exerted and still exerts important influence in shaping the tax and expenditure patterns. The political system of the United States is that of *federalism*, characterized by a constitutionally protected division of sovereignty between the whole nation of citizens organized through the central government and the people organized through the separate state governments. Individual citizens are at once citizens of both the United States, as a national unit, and their own state of residence. Both of these governmental units possess the legal power to regulate and control their activities and impose restraints on their behavior.

It would, of course, be incorrect to imply that the division of power between the federal government and the state governments is permanently drawn along readily predictable lines. The political changes of the past half century along with the constitutional interpretations of these have sharply narrowed the independent authority of state governments and have correspondingly expanded the political responsibility of the central or federal government. Despite this acknowledged secular drift toward the centralization of political power, the polity remains *federal* in nature. The student of the whole fiscal organization makes a serious mistake if he or she ignores or neglects unduly this fact in evaluating and appraising the particular characteristics of the system.

INDEPENDENT FISCAL AUTHORITY

The independent political authority of the federal government and the states implies independent fiscal authority. The meaning of this independence may be made clear by contrasting a federal political system with both a federation of states and a genuinely unified government.

In a federation of independent states, as opposed to a federalism, the central governmental unit would possess no independent fiscal authority at all. This unit would have no power to levy taxes directly on the income or wealth of the individual citizen. Revenues would be collected from individuals by the independent states, and these states would then make contributions in support of the central government. The individual is responsible directly only to one unit of government. NATO is an example of a federation of nations organized for a single purpose. The central body has no real political independence; therefore, it possesses no fiscal authority.

By contrast, in a genuinely unitary state, the central government possesses the exclusive political and fiscal authority. The individual may be subjected to local governmental regulations and to local governmental taxes, but these units exist and perform their public functions only as "agents" of the central government. They cannot be said to possess genuine fiscal independence. It is the absence of ultimate fiscal authority in local governments that makes the relationship of local units to state governments wholly different from the state-federal relationship. In any unitary system some actual fiscal independence is granted to local units for reasons of efficiency in operation. Hence problems of intergovernmental coordination do exist. But the constitutional separation of fiscal authority between the federal or central government and the states in a true federalism serves to make the problems of fiscal adjustment more basic and complex.

THE ECONOMIC ASPECTS OF FEDERALISM

If political authority is to be divided among levels of government, the first problem is that of determining the appropriate public functions to be performed at each level. As suggested in the discussion of preceding parts of this book, the line of divison of function is not always clearly drawn. Broadly speaking, however, the federal government provides those public services that benefit the whole national population, while state-local units provide those services that are more divisible geographically. It is necessary to emphasize at this point that the existing division of responsibility between the federal and the state governments has *not* been drawn primarily for economic reasons. The reasonable efficiency that seems to characterize the division of responsibility attests, however, to the importance of economic considerations in shaping the fundamental institutions of the fiscal system. It will be useful here to consider some of the purely economic considerations in dividing political responsibility among the separate levels of government, although these considerations must be recognized as being of relatively minor importance in some cases.

Governments come into being, at least in an economic sense, in order to provide collective goods. These are defined as goods and services which yield certain indivisible benefits. That is to say, the availability of a collective good becomes equal to all citizens once the good is provided. The police officer on the corner protects the jewelry store as well as the hardware store; the Skipjack provides me with the deterrent protection offered by a nuclear-powered submarine as well as any other citizen in the United States. The benefits of such goods are indivisible in the sense that one person cannot receive such benefits without their being made available at the same time to others.

The two examples used in the preceding paragraph point toward an initial answer to the problem posed. National defense is quite clearly a responsibility for the federal government, the only unit which includes the whole national population. The protection afforded by the defense forces-in-being applies equally to the sun-drenched citizen of Florida and the sportsman of the Northwest. The externalities (the spillover of benefits) extend to the whole national population. Therefore, for collective goods and services like national defense, there is an economic reason for the central government to provide these. No doubt Texas could support a defense force of its own, as could the other states. But as a protection against external or foreign aggression, no single one of the separate states would provide sufficient investment in defense because of the spillover effects of individual state action.

By contrast the police officer yields protection to only a rather limited group of citizens. This remains true even if we recognize that a "police force" may be a more efficient method of organization than units of single officers. The benefits that the citizen of Rhode Island receives from the Boise, Idaho, police force are infinitesimally small. The spillover effects, the externalities, in this case extend only to the citizens of the local units of government. The implication is clear that the provision of police protection is a local government function. There is no reason at all for the federal government, at least no economic reason, to provide police protection.

These two examples suggest that the economic or efficient division of responsibility among the separate levels of government depends upon the geographic range of the spillover effects of collective action. Each collective good or service is "collective" to only a limited group. The extent of the group determines the "economic" size of the governmental unit which should perform the function.

This approach may be illustrated easily by a single diagram, Figure 37–1. The position of the individual citizen is shown at point A. For the great bulk of private goods and services, the actions of the individual do not externally affect the utility of any other individual or family. If an individual family at A purchases a television set, they pay the cost individually and receive the benefits individually (or privately within the family group). External costs or benefits are not imposed on other citizens; there are no spillover effects beyond the ordinary market mechanism. The whole set of private market transactions may, therefore, be conceived as taking place at point A, and this is shown by the large black dot in the figure.

Suppose now that the family considered desires a recreational facility, say, a park. The facility, once available, will be able to accommodate several families at once. Therefore the appropriate organization will be some collective-cooperative arrangement whereby, say 100 families join in the financing and the consumption of the facility. This arrangement may or may not be governmental; voluntary organization for such activities may arise, thus making governmental provision unnecessary. The important point is that the range of the activity extends beyond the single family. This sort of activity is illustrated by circle 2 on the figure. The circle includes more persons than the single individual (family) located at the black dot. The park facility is utilized jointly by 100 families.

For fire protection and control, the appropriate-sized group may be

FIGURE 37–1

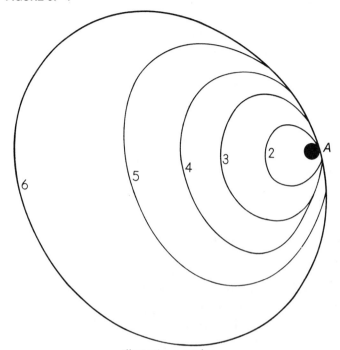

Illustrative examples:

A. Private goods and services.	4. Judicial system.
2. Local recreational facilities.	5. Education.
3. Fire protection.	6. National defense.

somewhat more inclusive that that for the park. This is shown conceptually by circle 3. We may, in this way, build up our set of circles or ellipses, drawing in one for each function or activity until we reach the largest of all, illustrated by national defense and, presumably, including all citizens of the national political community.

From this highly oversimplified view, the most efficient way of providing each of the services would be for the government unit (or the privately organized voluntary unit) to be organized to the size indicated as most efficient on some such diagram. However, several major qualifications must be introduced at this point, even if we continue to concentrate on the economic aspects of federalism alone.

In the first place, it should be noted that the external effects that are relevant to determining the appropriate-sized unit are those which are present on the demand or consumption side only. Take the public or community park. One hundred families in a particular suburban development can utilize this park jointly; for this group the park may be genuinely collective in nature. This fact alone suggests that some collective arrangement, public or private, should be formed to construct and maintain the facility. This interdependence in consumption does not imply that the most efficient means of providing the park services is for the local community to produce these services directly. This *production* decision should be considered quite independently, and the most efficient means of getting the required services should be chosen. The efficient production unit may happen to coincide with the range of collectivity in consumption. In this case, the local community will purchase the property, improve it, and maintain it as a park. On the other hand, the most efficient means of securing the local park facility may be for several communities to join in an agreement whereby common maintenance facilities and equipment are provided. The economies of scale in production may require that there be some extension beyond the range of consumption externalities. Finally, the most efficient means of getting the park services may be for the local sharing group to purchase or lease these directly from private firms specializing in such services and to negotiate maintenance contracts with such firms. The decision among these separate production alternatives should be based primarily on cost cor   'erations; the service should, in all cases, be provided physically in the manner that guarantees the lowest cost. In this respect the collective group, as a consumer of the joint service, is not in any way different from the individual consumer in the private economy.

A second important qualification of the model arises when it is recognized that the organization of decision itself is expensive. The larger the group, the more costly will be the making of collective decisions. Ten people can reach agreement easier than 100. The recognition of this fact suggests that the "optimal" sized governmental unit will not normally be so large as that suggested by the full range of the externalities. "Efficient" organization of a political structure must reflect the costs of decision making as well as the costs expected to arise from the presence of external effects in consumption.

A third major qualification to the simplified model may now be discussed. The approach suggested implies that the appropriate collective unit be of a different size for each collective service provided. The extension or range of the externalities in consumption need not, and probably would not, be the same for any two particular functions. But the very organizational costs of instituting collective action must be reckoned with. Only for the most important collective functions will wholly independent organization be justified on cost grounds. For the lesser public functions, the same collective unit may be required to provide several or all of the functions even though the unit may not coincide with the most "efficient" unit for organizing any one public service. For example, many of the public services must, because of the organizational cost involved, be performed by cities and counties in the United States. The range of externality in consumption extends in many cases beyond the limits of county or city boundaries. In other cases, the range of externality is much more limited than the whole area of the local unit. But the costs of organizing each activity separately would be greater than the promised added benefits from alternative organization. Some efforts have been made, and continue to be made, toward bringing actual governmental boundaries somewhat more into line with the extension of the externalities in consumption. For example, several major metropolitan areas have recently sought to combine local units for the performance of certain public functions.

A fourth important qualification to the simplified model presented in Figure 37–1 and the discussion surrounding it involves the recognition that the range of externality in consumption of collective goods is never precisely determinate. As Figure 37–1 is drawn, the lines clearly and distinctly separate those individuals within the circles from those without. In the park example, only 100 families are included within the collective group, all others are excluded. In the real world, however, collective goods and services are not consumed in this way. The great part of the benefits from the park may, in fact, be enjoyed by the 100 families in the suburb. But the fact that the park tends to keep children from roaming over other areas of the city and countryside ensures that there will be further benefits that "spillover" into other communities.

This problem can be most clearly discussed in terms of the collective aspects of educational services. Figure 37–2 may be used to illustrate the discussion. As suggested earlier, education does benefit certain individuals directly, those who are educated and their families. In other words, a significant part of the consumption of education is not "collective" at all. The benefits are concentrated at point *A*, just as is the case with any private good or service. It is clear, however, that all citizens in the local community also benefit greatly from the fact that the children of the community are provided with educational facilities. This community benefit makes educational services "collective" in the sense that we have used this term. The heavily shaded area enclosed by circle 2 indicates the extent of the local community. But it is also clear that significant boundaries of the single local community exist. The freedom of migration among separate communities means that each single community will be affected by the level of educational facilities made available in surrounding communities. The immigration of poorly educated workers from surrounding areas will not be generally desirable to any single community. Since we know that individuals who migrate tend to migrate for short distances, these effects are more pronounced in communities closest to the one under consideration. But it is also clear that some part of the "collective" benefits from educational services extend to the whole national population and beyond.

This fact raises the very important question as to just where the

FIGURE 37–2

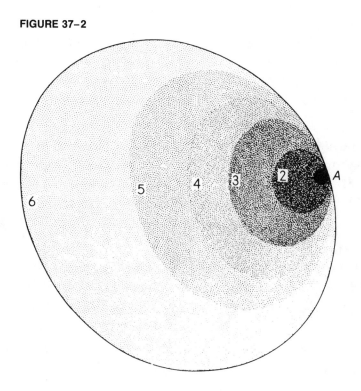

appropriate boundary line should be drawn. Every citizen in the nation has *some* interest in the educational services provided in every local community in the nation. But the interest of the citizen of Maryland in the educational services in Oregon may be quite slight. The problem is that of determining the point at which the externalities become insignificant enough to warrant drawing a line. And the location of this line will depend on the extent to which the external interest is inframarginal or marginal. The citizen in Maryland may have some interest in the education of Oregon children, but if Oregon ensures adequate educational services independently, the external interest becomes the inframarginal. In such cases, no action need be taken to secure the interest of those external to the limited jurisdiction. Only when external interests in the level of performance of a public service exist, and when this interest is exerted *marginally*, should some fiscal adjustment be considered. Only if the citizen in Maryland has some interest in seeing that Oregon children are educated *better than they are being educated* should some organizational change be examined. Even here, the added benefits from additional fiscal centralization must be sufficient to more than offset the added costs of decision making in larger units if organizational change is to be justified on economic grounds.

An interesting variation on this analysis of educational expenditure by local units in terms of the external effects has been introduced by Burton Weisbrod. The fact of migration among geographical areas ensures that educational outlays by one unit generate "spill-out" benefits to other units, and also that outlays by other units generate "spill-in" benefits. In other words, Maryland, or Baltimore, will recognize that in educating children who will later migrate to other localities, Baltimore taxpayers are, in effect, subsidizing other communities. Knowing this, Baltimore taxpayers, through their government, may be led to invest less in education than might otherwise be the case. On the other hand, Baltimore is subsidized by other communities to the extent that persons educated elsewhere move to Baltimore. Such "spill-in" benefits may not, however, serve to offset the effects of the "spill-out" benefits on the decisions of local authorities.[1]

The extent of national interest, that is, the interest of the whole population, in particular public services performed traditionally by

---

[1]See Burton Weisbrod, *External Benefits of Public Education* (Princeton: N.J.: Princeton University Press, 1964).

state-local units, looms as one of the most important problems in the current stage of federal-state relationships. To what extent is federal government participation in the provision of educational services justified? The answer to this question must depend, to a large extent, upon the appraisal of the significance of the spillover effects here discussed and upon the comparison of these effects with the costs of organizing activities differently. The major expansion of federal government activities in financing education at all levels that took place in the 1960s may be interpreted as embodying an increased political awareness of the importance of the spillover effects of educational services.

ECONOMIC ASPECTS AND POLITICAL REALITIES

The preceding section suggests that an economic approach may be used to determine the appropriate division of authority between the central government, the state governments, and the local governments in a federal political structure. It will be very useful to keep this approach in mind when we discuss particular aspects of the existing system. Broadly speaking, the economic considerations have been important in determining the division of functions that actually exists in the United States. But it would be a serious error to attempt to emphasize unduly the economic basis for the existing structure. The federal government has, to a large extent, always performed those public functions that have genuinely national aspects as contrasted with those functions which are primarily local in nature. But the federal government has also, on many occasions, taken over responsibility for certain activities which seem to be essentially local in nature. The clearest examples here are those federal activities having to do with regional development.

One reason for federal action in regional matters is the absence of any effective political unit of the appropriate size. States are, in many cases, not sufficiently inclusive to perform adequately certain regionally oriented activities, and interstate organizations have not been sufficiently flexible, or so it seems, to meet the needs. The New York Port Authority is the outstanding exception to this general statement.

State boundary lines are drawn arbitrarily from an economic point of view. These boundaries are historically determined, and the public services to be performed must be adjusted to conform to state boundaries rather than the reverse. Various attempts and proposals have been made to adjust state boundaries to conform more closely with economic structure. but state boundaries must be accepted as fact. These boundaries guarantee that states will be economic units when we consider the provision of public services.

The boundaries of local units are much more flexible. Considerable change takes place continually, roughly with a view toward keeping local collective units more closely aligned with economic realities. Significant improvements have been recently made toward enlarging metropolitan areas to take some account of the rapidly growing suburban developments. Further steps are urgently needed; but these need not be overwhelmingly difficult to achieve since local governmental boundaries are, after all, determined by the states.

POLITICAL DECENTRALIZATION AND INDIVIDUAL CHOICE

One important advantage of state-local governmental fiscal independence in a national economy should be especially stressed. The national or federal government encompasses the whole economy, and its activities impose restraints on the whole population. If a citizen happens to be in the minority as concerns a particular issue or set of issues, he can do little to make his situation more favorable. This applies to fiscal action as well as to other action of the federal government.

The same is not true of state or local governmental action. The individual who does not like the results of state or local political action may shift to another area and another locality within the country. The constitutional guarantees against restrictions on interstate commerce ensure that the individuals can always migrate rather freely within the national boundaries. This opportunity for migration is important in serving as a limit to the exploitation that separate states or local governments can impose on individuals. In many cases the alternative is not a real one, and in other cases the individual may migrate only at a high cost. But the possibility of shifting among the states and the local units serves as a very important check on irresponsible state and local action.

This is important in assessing state and local fiscal action, and it exerts both good and apparently bad effects. We have discussed the extent to which interstate competition has arisen in certain parts of the fiscal system. States find it difficult to impose very high taxes on either individual or corporate incomes for fear that citizens will migrate and resources will be shifted to other jurisdictions. Local governmental units find it necessary to rely primarily on the taxation of immobile real property for the same reasons. But the beneficial aspects of this possibility for divergence in state-local fiscal systems do not seem to have been nearly so widely recognized. The freedom of individual choice is greatly extended by this possibility of migration. Individuals and families will tend to be attracted to those localities that combine a tax and expenditure pattern which is the most suitable to their needs. More and more individuals and families are coming to recognize that the tax structure alone should not be considered; this must be considered along with the expenditure side in assessing the advantages and the disadvantages of any particular state or local community.

There exist high-tax, high-expenditure communities; medium-tax, medium-expenditure communities; and low-tax, low-expenditure communities. Individual families value public services differently; some of them place a high marginal value on particular public services; others value relatively low public services compared to privately supplied services. The first group will tend to migrate to the communities that provide the greatest amount of public services, and the families in this group will be quite willing to submit to the higher taxation required to ensure that these services are, in fact, provided. The second group will tend to migrate to the community that provides neither many public services nor taxes at very high rates.

To a limited extent, the freedom of migration among the separate states and local units in the nation allows individuals a choice among the different combinations of public services roughly analogous to the choice among private goods and services that they confront in the market. To this extent, the inherent compulsion that governmental activity involves is reduced, and the overall range of individual choice is widened. This consideration suggests, of course, that where possible, services should be provided by the states and local units rather than the federal government. Federal or national interest in a particular service should be demonstrably significant before federal action is taken.

INTERAREA DIFFERENCES IN FISCAL CAPACITY

If the national economy were divided into geographic areas of roughly equal economic potential, and if regional governmental units were drawn to correspond to these areas, many of the major fiscal problems of federalism would never arise. In this case, the division of function between federal and subordinate units could be drawn along reasonably acceptable lines, and the multiplicity of local units could ensure individuals considerable freedom of choice. But the existing subordinate units of the political structure, the states and the local units, do not enclose areas of equal economic potential. There is a significant difference in the fiscal capacities of the various units. This fact tends to create a whole set of new problems.

Certain states contain relatively more high-income receivers than other states. Total income and wealth are much greater in some areas than in others, and income and wealth of individuals and corporations provide the only final source for tax revenues. It follows that the "richer" states will find it much easier to finance a given level of public services than the "poorer" states. The "richer" state will have to levy a smaller proportionate tax burden on its citizens to finance a given level of public services than will the "poorer" state. Or, to say the same thing differently, in order to finance the same level of public services, the "poorer" state will, of necessity, have to levy a higher proportionate tax on its own citizens than the "richer" state.

There is a genuine fiscal differential against the poor states and local communities, and this differential will exert some influence on the locational decisions of both individual families and of business firms. Individual families who move into the poor states or communities can expect to find either higher taxes or a lower level of public services, or both. Individual families who move into the rich states or communities can expect to find a lower level of taxes and a higher level of public services. These general conclusions remain true in spite of the fact that particular differences in the fiscal system can, of course, always reverse the direction of effect for specific individual families or firms.

The disparity in fiscal capacity among the separate state and local units within the single national economy suggests the following questions: To what extent should the central or federal government take action to remove these fiscal differentials? To what extent should the federal government assume the task of "equalizing" the fiscal position of individuals in the separate states? If fiscal equalization is accepted as a federal function, should this be general or should it be directed toward specific services?

To a certain extent, the fiscal advantages to be secured by an individual family from living in a community characterized by a concentration of high incomes and wealth are genuine economic advantages. The availability of better schooling for children at a lower "price" in terms of taxes in the "richer" community is similar to the availability of better vacations at lower prices along the Florida beaches. Insofar as these real advantages are present, no attempt by the federal government to "equalize" fiscal opportunities and to remove the differential advantages of the richer areas is justified on purely economic grounds. Other things being equal, a more efficient overall allocation of economic resources is achieved by allowing families to move from poorer states to richer states in response to these fiscal differentials.

A portion of the net fiscal advantage or disadvantage from living in a certain area is, however, not genuinely economic. Even if all state-local fiscal systems were to be organized on a pure benefit basis, that is, if the tax-expenditure systems of state-local units should be purely neutral, there might still exist economic reasons why the central or federal government should try to equalize fiscal differentials as among the separate states. This is because of the existence of possible differentials in "fiscal surplus" as among the states, even if each state should organize its own system neutrally. State and local units do not, of course, organize their fiscal systems on an ideally neutral or benefit taxation basis. Considerations other than those of economic efficiency are relevant here as they are at the federal government level. To a certain extent, although less so than at the federal level, state-local fiscal systems are redistributive in effect. The fiscal process acts so as to transfer real income from high- to low-income receivers. Insofar as this takes place, additional differentials are introduced as between the high-income and the low-income states and localities. The high-income recipient who lives in a state or locality where other high-income recipients are concentrated will not be subjected to so great a reduction in income if he or she attempts, through the political mechanism, to bring the real income standards of the poor in the area up, as will the equally situated high-income recipient who lives in a state or locality where most of the people are poor. Similarly, the low-income receiver who happens to live in an area where there is a concentration of high-income receivers is differentially benefited by comparison with the low-income receiver who lives in the poverty-stricken area. This was well illustrated in the late 1970s by the wide divergences in the levels of welfare payments in the separate states.

For the several reasons outlined, the fiscal differentials among the separate state and local units may act to encourage an uneconomic or inefficient shifting or resources. Surely some part of the migration from southern rural communities to the large cities can be traced to the higher levels of welfare payments in the latter. And equally clearly, the shift of the affluent upper middle classes to the suburbs surrounding our major cities has been due to the increasingly burdensome taxes imposed by the latter. To the extent that fiscal differentials among states has encouraged or is encouraging an uneconomic allocation of resources over the national economy spatially considered, there is a positive argument for federal government action to equalize fiscal capacities so as to offset such differentials. Equity arguments can be added to those of efficiency in support of such equalizing transfers.

INTERSTATE DIFFERENCES IN PUBLIC SERVICE STANDARDS

Interarea or interstate differences in income and wealth, in taxable capacity, ensure that differentials will exist in overall or "average" fiscal treatment of individuals among the separate states. On the average, any given individual will tend to receive some net fiscal advantage from residence in the state with the higher fiscal capacity. As a rule, this advantage will take the form of both somewhat lower taxes and somewhat higher levels of standards in the provision of public services. But the need for intergovernmental fiscal adjustment has been focused much more directly on interstate differences in the provision of particular public services than upon overall differences in fiscal treatment of individual citizens. A general policy of fiscal equalization has never been seriously advanced; there have been numerous proposals for federal action to standardize the performance of particular services.

The argument for federal government action to remove interstate differences in the level of provision of specific public services must rest on different grounds from that for federal policy aimed at general equalization of fiscal treatment among the separate states. Insofar as the range of externality of the service, the extent of collectivity, does not extend beyond state boundaries, there can be no reason for federal government support regardless of the degree of disparity in performance among the separate states. Federal equalization measures in support of one specific public service must be based on the argument that the benefits from satisfactory performance spill over beyond state boundaries to the national economy as a whole. The equalization aspects themselves arise from the fact that the federal interest is more important at the margin of provision in the low-capacity states than in the high-capacity states.

CONCLUSIONS

The federal political structure exerts an important influence on the fiscal organization of the United States. The existence of dual fiscal authority in the central and the state governments should not be ignored. The division of fiscal responsibility among the levels of government can be discussed in economic terms, although economic considerations are only one among many in actually determining the division. When it is recognized that the extent of collectivity involved in the provision of a public service varies from one service to another, a purely economic criterion for determining the appropriate level of collective organization is suggested. To some extent, this criterion is helpful in explaining the existing division of responsibility, but political fact requires that traditionally organized collective units perform many functions for which, economically, they may not be "optimal" in any sense. The absence of any effective regional organizations for performing certain functions that involve externalities extending beyond state boundaries has led to federal action. State boundaries have, in many cases, little economic basis, although the existence of independent fiscal authority itself guarantees that states become separate economic entities for many purposes. Local units can more readily be adjusted to conform to the suggested or implied scale of operation, but, here too, the traditional local organizational structure may cause serious lags to be present between the recognition of the need for some reorganization and the final reorganization itself.

One of the most difficult problems in intergovernmental relations is introduced in connection with certain public services which, while primarily concentrated in benefit to the local jurisdiction, exert significant spillover or external effects on a much wider area. To the extent that some national interest in the provision of state-local services exists at the current margins of performance, some argument is provided for federal government action. But the decision as to when this national interest becomes important or significant enough to justify federal action is an extremely difficult one, and the added costs of centralizing decisions should not be overlooked. The provision of educational services by the state-local fiscal systems provides the most important current example.

The muliplicity of state and local units places certain limits on the fiscal organization of these units. The possibility of interstate and interarea migration of persons and resources tends to make the separate fiscal authorities steer clear of certain extreme institutional changes. The possible differences in state-local fiscal systems provide an important protection to the individual citizen. The possibility of migration provides the citizen with an effective protection against undue fiscal exploitation on the part of a state or local unit of government. This possibility also allows individuals to exert a considerable freedom of choice in moving to where the fiscal "mix" is most closely in conformity with their desires.

The most serious problems of intergovernmental coordination arise because the separate subordinate units of government differ substantially in fiscal capacity. Differences in incomes and wealth among the separate units ensure that the individual will be subjected to a fiscal disadvantage by residing in a low-income, low-wealth community. To a certain extent, this disadvantage is economic, and insofar as this is true, it provides no basis for action. But beyond this the overall national income could be increased by some federal action aimed at equalizing the fiscal treatment of individuals in the separate states. This approach toward general or overall equalization should be distinguished sharply from that aimed at equalizing the performance of specific services in the separate states or local units. This form of equalization must be based on the existence of the spillover of benefits previously discussed.

SUPPLEMENTARY READING

The student who is interested in exploring further some of the interesting problems raised by the existence of a federal political structure may consult the following papers: Charles M. Tiebout, "A Pure Theory of Local Expenditures," *Journal of Political Economy*, vol. 54 (October 1956), pp. 416–24; George Stigler, "Tenable Range of Functions of Local Government," *Federal Expenditure Policy for Economic Growth and Stability* (Washington, D.C.: Joint Economic Committee, 1957), pp. 213–19; Charles M. Tiebout, "An Economic Theory of Fiscal Decentralization," pp. 79–96; and Richard A.

Musgrave, "Approaches to a Fiscal Theory of Political Federalism," pp. 97–122, in National Bureau of Economic Research, *Public Finances: Needs, Sources, and Utilization* (New York, 1961).

For a modern discussion of the economics of federalism, see Albert Breton and Anthony Scott, *The Economic Constitution of Federal States*, (Toronto: The University of Toronto Press, 1978).

38

Federal-state fiscal coordination

Some of the more important fiscal and economic aspects of a multilevel political structure have been discussed in the preceding chapter. There remain to be considered the various institutional devices that may be introduced in an attempt to achieve the required fiscal coordination among the separate governmental units. Finally, from among the the many possible devices, those which have actually been employed in the United States must be more carefully examined.

SEPARATION OF TAX SOURCES

The real cost of providing collective goods and services lies in the sacrifice of private goods and services that could have been enjoyed alternatively. Income represents generalized command over private goods and services, and wealth is always a capitalized value of an expected income flow. Therefore, as suggested before in this book, all tax revenues must come, ultimately, from individual income, current or anticipated. The various tax institutions are distinguishable only in that they involve different distributions of the overall tax burden among individuals and in that they stimulate divergent psychological reactions and, because of this, exert important differences in behavioral responses.

If either efficiency or equity were the only relevant consideration to be taken into account in organizing the multilevel fiscal system, there would be a strong argument for levying all taxes at all levels directly on personal or individual incomes. If the fisc is conceived simply as the means through which the group of individual citizens may more efficiently purchase collective goods and services, the direct income tax would seem the best method of payment. This tax is the one most closely analogous to the "price" that is paid for goods and services in the market economy. The individual who purchases a book, for example, uses generalized purchasing power, money income, in making the purchase; the buyer does not use money that has already been earmarked for other specific purposes. Consistent application of the economic approach to collective activity would suggest that the income tax should provide the only revenue source, whatever the level of government.

Similar conclusions follow if we look exclusively at the equity considerations. If the fisc is considered to be organized solely for the purpose of redistributing real incomes among individuals, the introduction of positive and negative direct income taxes is suggested as the most desirable method.

Efficiency and equity considerations are not, of course, the only considerations. Those remaining may outweigh these two in importance in many cases. If the fiscal system is designed to accomplish both efficiency and equity objectives simultaneously, real problems arise when too much reliance is placed on the individual income tax as the primary revenue source. If both the federal government and the state-local units should collect most of their tax revenues from the personal income tax, and if the state-local units should attempt any redistribution of real income through the fiscal process, an incentive would be provided for individuals and resources to be shifted among the separate states in response to purely fiscal differentials, differentials which might not reflect genuine economic differences among states. This danger is recognized in practice; state governments do not attempt to raise more than a small part of total revenues through personal or corporate income taxes, and even when this tax source is used, the rates are kept rather low and only slightly progressive, if at all. Local governments are even more wary in their use of income taxation.

State-local governments collect slightly more than 17 percent of all tax revenues from personal income taxes, and about 5 percent from taxes on corporate income. These figures are sufficient to indicate that the income tax, either individual or corporate, is of limited productivity as a revenue source at the state-local level.

In a real sense, therefore, the fiscal system of the United States is organized fundamentally on the principle of separation of sources among the different levels of government. The federal government relies primarily on the tax on individual and corporate incomes. The major instrument in the whole fiscal system for accomplishing real income distribution among individuals is the federal tax on personal incomes. This tax, which can be made as progressive in rate as social attitudes permit, can serve redistributive purposes sufficiently to allow the remaining fiscal institutions to be less directly oriented toward redistributive objectives.

The state governments rely for revenues primarily on the taxation of commodities, levied on the production, sale, or consumption of a limited number of, or, substantially all, commodities and services. Revenues from sales taxes, and business license taxes make up more than 60 percent of state tax collections. These taxes, imposed directly on the business firms engaged in the act of producing or selling a commodity or service, must be borne by individuals, either in their capacity as consumers of taxed commodities or as resource suppliers to the firms manufacturing or processing these commodities. Commodity taxation has the major advantage of allowing the separate states to collect large revenues at low nominal rates and relatively low costs of administration and collection. Taxes on sales, precisely because they are indirect taxes, do not generate the same psychological reaction as do income taxes. They are to a certain extent paid "painlessly"; therefore, they do not exercise the same effects on the potential migration of men and materials as income taxes. The objections to state government reliance on sales taxation are the familiar ones. The taxes tend to be regressive when the actual tax burden is computed relative to an income base. But this objection is valid only if the objective of real income redistribution is admitted to be important at the state-local as well as at the federal government level. Even here, the combined effect of a state tax and expenditure system may, on balance, be redistributive even if the tax side, taken alone, is regressive. A second familiar objective is that commodity taxation involves an excess burden since it is levied on particular commodities. Individual choices are distorted, and this creates an unnecessary welfare issue. This objection is a valid one to any specific tax, taken alone, but its importance seems indeterminate.

Even more than the federal and state governments, local governments rely on a single tax source, in this case the property tax, which makes up 80 percent of local government tax revenues. As we have shown, property taxation, in an abstract sense, is equivalent to income taxation. But since real property tends to represent a relatively permanent form of capital investment, local units have found this tax productive as a revenue source. And one of the important reasons for continued reliance on this source is past experience. The removal of the tax would create many windfall gains to current property owners, and these gains would be transmitted to other groups in society only after a reasonably long period.

The separation of tax sources among the separate levels of government in the United States is not, of course, complete. The federal government does collect large amounts of revenue from specific excise taxes on the sales of particular commodities or services. Many of the states impose individual and corporate income taxes, and some of them still collect revenues from the property tax. A few local governments levy taxes on gross incomes, and many local units try to tax specific commodities or services. But despite these overlaps in the institutional arrangements, broadly considered, the U.S. fiscal system can be said to be characterized by a distinct separation of tax sources.

COMMON TAX SOURCES—SUPPLEMENTS, CREDITS, AND SHARES

Insofar as tax sources are not separated for the different levels of government, common sources must be employed. The degree of coordination between the taxes imposed on a common source by the separate units of government ranges from complete independence at the one extreme to effective unification of fiscal structures at the other. The tax sources themselves are rarely so sharply defined that two separate governmental units will actually impose levies on identical sources. For example, wholly independent action by the federal government and the states in taxing personal incomes would not likely result in precisely the same measure of income being employed in the several cases. In the United States, the taxation of personal and corporate income by the federal government and the state governments is perhaps the most important case where the separate units levy taxes on a roughly common source. In this particular case, the actual degree of coordination varies from state to state, but state income taxes are seldom, if ever, organized in complete isolation from the federal income tax. The coordination that is present is achieved, however, largely by the state fiscal systems being adjusted to the federal system. There is little explicit cooperation between the two levels of government in this respect.

States will normally define income for tax purposes in a manner roughly similar to that used by the federal government. Some states have allowed taxpayers to define income specifically as defined for federal tax purposes. In most cases, however, some differences will exist. Where similarity is present, this will assist the individual taxpayer in preparing his return for both units, and it will make the administration of a state income tax much simpler. Exemptions and deductions will also be allowed which are roughly similar to those allowed under the federal tax, although the quantitative size of these may differ widely.

Some coordination is implicitly achieved in commodity taxation. Federal authorities have deliberately refrained from entering the general sales taxation field despite persistent pressures to do so, especially in times of defense emergency. Federal taxes on particular commodities and services are admitted to be emergency levies despite their relatively long life as federal revenue sources. Conflict worthy of note here has arisen only in the case of highway user taxation.

Tax supplements

Deliberate coordination of separate governmental taxation of the same revenue source can take place through any one of several devices. Utilization of the same administrative structure for both levels of government with each unit levying separate rates of tax is one possibility. This device was adopted in 1972 with respect to collection of individual income taxes. The "Federal-State Tax Collection Act of 1972" authorized agreements between the various states and the federal government under which the federal Internal Revenue Service would collect and administer qualified state individual income taxes.

State individual income taxes collected by the federal government can be levied either directly on income or as a percentage of federal tax liability. Explicitly in the former case and implicitly in the latter, the definition of taxable income used for state income tax collections must conform closely to that used for purposes of the federal levy. In cases where the tax is levied directly on taxable income, federal taxable income must be adjusted for state taxation by subtracting from the federal total all interest on obligations of the United States, by adding the net state income tax deduction and by adding net tax exempt income. Similar adjustments are made in cases where the state tax is computed as a percent of federal tax liability.

Administratively, tax supplements have many advantages. There are some difficulties also, however, arising because the federal income tax is not a perfect tax. Given the existence of imperfections in the federal tax, the utilization of that same structure by the states will multiply the effects of the distortions generated by the imperfections in the federal tax. The state tax, if organized on a different basis, might be used to offset federal tax imperfections rather than to reinforce them.

Tax deductibility

The individual taxpayer, in computing taxable income for the purpose of determining federal tax liability, is allowed to deduct from adjusted gross income most payments of state-local taxes (the eligible state-local list was limited somewhat by the 1964 legislation which disallowed the deduction of some sumptuary taxes). The deductibility of state-local taxes for federal tax computation is one means of securing some coordination between the federal tax and the state-local fiscal system, especially in relation to the states' attempts to impose personal income taxes.

The federal government, through this deductibility, makes the fiscal task of the state governments somewhat simpler. The deduction allowance effectively shifts some portion of the state-local tax burden to the general federal taxpayer. For example, suppose that the state decides to levy an incremental tax of $100 on an individual who is paying a marginal rate of 40 percent under the federal income tax and who has not fully exhausted allowable deductions. The state collects the full $100, but the individual's taxable income is also reduced by $100 for federal tax purposes. The federal income tax is reduced by $40. Thus, the combined tax liability is changed only by $60, although the state government collects an additional $100. The federal government's loss of $40 in the process must be made up by some supplementary taxation of all federal taxpayers or some reduction in the rate of federal expenditure.

There seems to be little justification for the deductibility of state-local taxes as a coordination device. Since a substantial part of state-local tax payments are allowed, the net effect is simply that of providing some federal encouragement to an expansion of state-local expenditures. The real costs of state-local services to local citizens is reduced, but the real costs to the whole national population are unchanged. The deductibility feature could be employed by the federal government to encourage states to utilize particular forms of taxes. For example, if only state-local income tax payments were allowed as deductions, this would provide a strong incentive for subordinate units to shift toward more reliance on income taxation as a revenue source. In this way, after the 1964 disallowance of deductibility of tobacco and liquor taxes, states have a strong incentive to reduce the importance of such taxes in their own revenue structures. It seems doubtful whether this was an intended result of the federal action.

Tax credits

The tax credit is a device through which the central government may effectively coordinate from above the overall fiscal system. Tax credits may be used to encourage the subordinate units to utilize specific revenue sources. The device can be best explained by reference to the federal estate tax, the only important fiscal institution which has incorporated the crediting feature.

More than with most other state taxes, differentials among the separate states in the taxation of transfers at death will tend to encourage certain groups of individuals to shift out of those states imposing the heavier rates and into those states imposing the more favorable rates. Interstate competition for the retired wealthy population led to the introduction in the early 1920s of the federal estate tax with the credit feature included. A federal tax was levied on the value of all estates, but the payments of inheritance or estate taxes to states were allowed as credits against the federal tax liability. This feature effectively removed the differential advantage that a state might bestow on its wealthy residents, at least up to the point of the federal liability. If the state reduced its own tax below the size of the federal credit allowable, the individual would be liable for the federal tax payment anyway. This feature quickly led all states to impose inheritance and estate taxes that would at least fully exhaust the credit allowed against the federal tax. In the years since the introduction of this credit, both federal estate taxes and state taxes have been increased. The credit is not so important as it was at that time, although a few states still impose inheritance taxes only to the limit of the federal tax credit.

A similar plan has been followed to encourage states to adopt reasonably uniform unemployment insurance taxes. A basic federal tax of 3.28 percent is levied by the federal government; however, 2.7 percent of this is allowed as a credit if paid under a state tax.

As suggested earlier, proposals have been made that a crediting feature be extended to the income tax. Individuals would be taxed under the normal federal income tax, but insofar as they paid state income taxes, their federal tax liability would be reduced correspondingly. Such a feature would ensure that all states impose personal income taxes up to the limit of the federal credit allowed, and also that interstate differentials in income taxation would be reduced. But even to a greater extent than the tax supplement, this device involves what appears to be undue federal control over state independence of fiscal action. With the tax credit, not only would the federal government determine the type of state tax that would be allowed as a credit, but also it could effectively determine the extent of the state tax rates. The tax credit seems to be more appropriate to a politically unified system than to a genuine federal structure.

Tax sharing

Tax sharing is a coordination device that has never been employed to a large degree in federal-state relations in the United States but which is widely used in the relations between the state governments and the local units. The process of tax sharing involves the larger governmental unit administering and collecting the taxes and subsequently sharing the proceeds among the separate subordinate units on the basis of some prearranged formula. Tax sharing is founded on the recognition that the most efficient tax-collecting unit may be, in many cases, considerably larger than the most efficient public-spending unit.

If all taxes were to be based on personal incomes, as pure efficiency and equity considerations might suggest, there would be some point in trying to have these collected by the federal government with the proceeds shared in some manner with the states. The fiscal independence of the state could hardly be preserved under such an arrangement, however, and, even if this were not significant, the working out of a generally accepted sharing formula would be extremely difficult. Experience at the state-local level has shown that the major problem of tax sharing lies in the determination of the criteria upon which the revenues shall be allocated among the subordinate units.

If the process is of purely administrative origin, the appropriate formula would seem to be one that returns to the lower level units those revenues collected within those units. The tax would be collected by the higher level governmental unit only because of its superior efficiency in collection. But the determination of just what share of revenues is collected from individuals in specific localities is a difficult task, which is doubly complicated when other purposes are combined with this in the actual administration of the tax.

Normally, with state-local systems the tax is centrally collected, not purely for reasons of administrative efficiency but also because certain state aims are to be furthered in the sharing. Interarea equalization of fiscal capacity to finance certain specific services is a standard objective of sharing plans. Centrally collected revenues are shared on the basis of population, assessed value, school-age children, road mileage, geographic area, and many other criteria, depending on the specific tax to be shared.

FEDERAL GRANTS-IN-AID TO STATE AND LOCAL GOVERNMENTS

The whole problem of securing fiscal coordination in a multilevel political structure may be approached in two ways. The two preceding sections have discussed coordination devices that operate exclusively on the tax side of the fiscal account. A second approach is that of looking at the problem from the expenditure side. This approach recognizes that the governmental unit that collects taxes need not necessarily be the same unit that expends public funds. If the possibility of some intergovernmental transfer of funds is allowed, the problem of fiscal capacity can be effectively solved through a system of grants among separate governmental units.

Federal grants to state and local governments are a significant component of the federal budget. The sum of $83 billion was allocated to this general category in the 1980 budget. This represented 16 percent of total federal outlays. Similarly, federal aid is of substantial importance in the budgets of recipient units. Over 22 percent of total state-local expenditures during fiscal 1977 were financed from federal monies. Significant financial assistance to state and local governments from the federal government is a comparatively recent development in the intergovernmental relationships of the American federalism. In 1960, for example, only $7 billion of federal expenditures were allocated for this purpose.

There are two main categories of federal grants, unconditional or bloc grants and conditional grants-in-aid. In the fiscal 1980 budget, $8.7 billion of the $83 billion targeted for state and local grants was in unconditional or bloc grant form. The bulk of these funds was to be channeled through the federal revenue-sharing program which was instituted in 1972 and which marked the first significant venture by the federal government into this type of grant program. The more traditional conditional or categorical grants continued to characterize the bulk of federal aid to state and local governments in fiscal 1980.

Conditional grants-in-aid

A conditional grant-in-aid is specifically aimed at encouraging the states to expand the supply of selected public services. The receipt of funds is conditional on their being utilized in a designated fashion. Thus the states receive grants not for general purposes, but for use in highway construction, for vocational education, and so on. State receipt implies an acceptance of federal government direction of expenditure. The degree of fiscal independence retained by the lower level units in the federal hierarchy is substantially less than with bloc grants or shared taxes.

This fiscal independence of the recipient *units*, the states in most cases, is still further reduced if *matching provisions* are included in the conditional grants, as they are in the majority of instances in the United States. With matching provisions, the federal government not only specifies to the recipient states the manner in which the funds shall be used but, in addition, in order for the recipient unit to qualify to receive the grant-in-aid it must match the federal share in a specified proportion. This matching aspect leads states and local units to direct their own tax revenues toward those areas that will facilitate qualification for federal aid to the neglect of other public needs.

The conditional grant-in-aid, with or without matching provisions, can be looked upon as a means through which an interest in certain public service standards beyond the confines of the performing unit can be taken into account. Recall in Chapter 37 it was shown that the range of collective interest in many public functions (the example there was education) extends widely, but that this interest diminishes in magnitude as the area is expanded. Certain benefits from local government expenditure on schools, on highways, and on many other public services clearly extend beyond or spill over to citizens in other state units. For many of the state-local public functions, there is clearly some "national interest" in ensuring that the service levels are at least up to some commonly accepted "standard." It may seem desirable to try to represent this genuine national interest through grants-in-aid while at the same time allowing the state-local units to maintain the major responsibility for actually performing the public services. The conditional grant-in-aid is well suited to accomplish this dual purpose. It can, by attaching conditions to the receipt of the funds, ensure that state-local units will carry out public services up to desired service standards. At the same time, the actual administration of the public service may be kept at the state-local level.

Despite the advent of revenue sharing, conditional aid remains the most significant component of federal financial assistance to state and local units of government. Of the $83 billion allocated for federal aid generally in 1980, more than $70 billion was allocated to specific functions. In terms of the share of the total funds, the three most significant functional categories were education, training, employment and social services ($22.3 billion), health ($14.5 billion), and income security ($15.3 billion).

Unconditional grants—revenue-sharing

With passage of the State and Local Fiscal Assistance Act of 1972, the federal government embarked on a program of unconditional grants to state and local units of government for the first time in the history of the American federalism. The fiscal 1980 budget set aside $6.9 billion to be disbursed among the states and localities through this "revenue-sharing" program. As the term implies, unconditional grants involve only minimal restrictions on how recipient government units may spend the funds which they receive. The federal revenue sharing program exhibits this characteristic. Funds are allocated among the states on the basis of some rather complicated formulas which take into account such factors as per capita income, tax effort, and urban population. Within each state, one third of the state's share of total funds goes directly to the state government. The remaining two thirds is then allocated by formula among local units of government. All general purpose local units of government are qualified recipients of revenue sharing funds. Within very broad limits, recipient governments may spend their revenue sharing funds as they see fit.

Regardless of the formal base for tax (personal income, corporate income, real property and so on) all tax revenue must come ultimately from personal income or wealth. Examined in this context, it might well be asked what the revenue sharing program or any unconditional grant program might accomplish that could not similarly be accomplished by reducing federal taxes and returning funds directly to the taxpayers. Generally, there seem to be both redistributive and efficiency issues involved in an unconditional grant policy.

During the debate on revenue sharing, one of the arguments against simply returning funds to the states proportional to federal tax collections in each state was that such a plan would tend to return larger amounts per capita to wealthier states than to poor states. A net redistribution from wealthy states to poor states was an objective sought by many of the proponents of the program. The revenue-sharing formulas do take per capita income into account. Assuming two states to be identical with respect to other factors considered by the formulas, the state with the lower per capita income would receive the larger grant. At the same time, however, it is important to note that funds are being redistributed among the states and not directly among individuals. An alternative form of redistribution from rich to poor individuals would be to reduce federal income tax rates sufficiently to lower collections by the same amount as would be distributed via revenue sharing and simultaneously to alter the rate structure in the direction of increased progression, thus insuring a greater proportionate federal tax reduction for low income households.

With a direct federal personal income tax cut, state and local government spending would increase only if those units of government were to increase their own rates of taxation. It seems that one objective achieved by the revenue sharing program which might be more difficult to achieve via direct tax cuts is to insure that a greater portion of the federal revenue transferred to the states and localities is utilized to increase governmental spending and services rather than private consumption. Revenue sharing circumvents the need for state and local officials to increase taxes in order to expand services and discourages tax reductions at those levels through the tax effort component of the allocation formula.

Unconditional grants generally have the potential to improve efficiency in the provision of public services by state and local governments. There are two possible sources of such efficiency gains. The first is an efficiency gain from federal fiscal equalization. The second possible gain may occur if bloc grants overcome, at least to some extent, a tendency for suboptimal expenditures on state-local public services because fears of tax-base migration make the perceived costs of public services provided by these governments exceed the true social costs. Suppose that two communities are each providing the same public service at the same level and that the cost of providing the service is the same in each community. Suppose, also, that the number of citizens in each community is the same and that tax revenues are raised by a proportionate income tax. Citizens in community A are wealthy and those in community B are poor. Note that the tax price paid by each individual in this example is exactly the same. Assuming a unit price of $10 for the public service and ten citizens of each community, the individual tax price for the public service is $1 in each community. However, the tax rates are different in the two communities because of the different per capita incomes. Suppose that all residents in community A have incomes of $200 and that the incomes of individuals in community B are only $100. In community A, the income tax rate per unit of the public service purchased is 0.5 percent. In community B, the tax rate per unit is 1 percent. As a result of the differing tax *rates*, there is an obvious incentive for migration from community B to community A. The tax price for the service is lower for poor persons whose fellow citizens are wealthier than they.

Such fiscally induced migration may be inconsistent with economic efficiency if an individual's private product is lower in community A than in community B. Under these circumstances, an individual's decision to locate in community A rather than in B because of a differential tax advantage can generate an inefficient allocation of resources. Suppose, for example, that initially each community is spending $100 to provide ten units of the public service. Each individual's tax bill is $10. Private disposable income for the wealthy residents of community A is $190. In community B, private disposable income is $90.

Consider an example of an individual initially residing in B with a private gross income of $100. Suppose that if the individual moves to community A this private income would fall to $95. However, at a tax rate of 0.5 percent per unit of the public service the individual could move to community A, enjoy the same level of public service and also a higher level of private disposable income. That person's share of the costs of ten units of the public service would be 5 percent of $95 or $4.75 leaving a private disposable income of $90.25 rather than the $90 available in community B. (In fact, the increased number of people in community B and the large tax base would result in a tax rate lower than 5 percent being necessary to raise the required $100. This consideration makes the results above even stronger.)

Why is this migration inefficient? The source of the inefficiency can be easily seen if we simply add up the gains and losses. The individual has gained 25 cents in private disposable income. Public goods benefits have remained the same in both communities. However, $5 worth of private product has been lost to society as a whole. The value placed on the individual's services in community B was $100. In community A, such services were only valued at $95. A net loss of $4.75 has resulted from the individual's change of location. This loss is borne by the remaining residents in community B who now must pay higher individual tax prices for the same public service.

The above example may seem somewhat contrived to the student. Indeed, it is grossly simplified. However, it seems intuitively plausible that such a model is operative in many real-world situations. Not only are individual incomes likely to vary among different locations but also business income, which is also subject to taxation, is often very dependent on location.

Federal fiscal equalization can eliminate the incentives described above by distributing grants such that the same tax rate is required in each community to provide a given level of public service. In the above example, a grant of $50 to community B would necessitate only a 5 percent income tax rate to raise $100.

The redistributive aspects of revenue sharing have already been discussed in the context of possible equity gains. Support for such redistribution was discussed as it implied only a belief that the necessity of different tax rates to raise the same amount of revenue was unfair. The preceding discussion, however, has indicated the potential of improved efficiency in the sense of allowing increased consumption of both public and private services by all citizens. The degree of improvement in efficiency is clearly affected by the amount of equalization achieved. As the discussion earlier indicated, some redistribution is accomplished by the existing revenue-sharing program. However, complete equalization has obviously not been achieved and, in fact, the actual amount of equalization may be relatively insignificant. Arguments have been made that the federal government is more efficient in raising tax revenues than state or local governments, and thus there are net gains to be made from having the federal government raise at least some of the revenue to be ultimately spent by lower level governments. Tax-base migration is crucial to this argument. State and local governments are believed to feel severely constrained in the amount of tax revenue they can raise because of a fear that if tax rates become too high many businesses and individual taxpayers will find it desirable to move out of the jurisdiction. In a sense, this model is very similar to the preceding discussion. However, the implications are slightly different. In this model, public service expenditures tend to be lower than optimal because the costs of public services perceived by decision makers include possible loss of tax base to another jurisdiction. This component is not truly a social cost, however. One jursidiction's loss is another's gain. The resulting excess of perceived cost over social cost does, however, tend to generate suboptimal public expenditures.

If all funds spent by state and local governments were raised by the federal government, revenue sharing would effectively minimize tax-base migration problems. Although businesses and individuals can move out of a country as well as out of a city or state it is generally much more costly to do so. A partial revenue-sharing program does not prevent states or localities from competitively lowering their own tax rates in order to attract a large tax base. However, the present method of allocating revenue-sharing funds does punish states for this behavior as tax effort is a determinant of a state's share of the funds.

By mid-1979, when this text was being prepared, the future of the revenue sharing program was uncertain. Existing legislative authorization and appropriations for the program was scheduled to expire at the end of fiscal 1980. The 1980 budget made no recommendations regarding possible extension of the program and there was some sentiment in the Congress to stop the program. The "tax revolt" of 1978, during which several states placed restrictions on their own revenue sources, made many federal legislators question the desirability of continuing this form of aid, particularly in the face of considerable public pressure to restrain federal spending. At the same time, state and local officials could be expected to lobby vigorously for retention of the program.

CONCLUSIONS

There are numerous devices for securing a degree of fiscal coordination among the governmental units of a federalism. These include separation of tax sources, tax supplements, credits or tax sharing, and direct financial assistance from one unit of government to another. Most of these are used to some extent in the American federal system.

A clear separation of tax sources is the most simple means of securing coordination between the separate fiscal systems of governmental units in a multilevel political structure. When it is recognized, however, that all taxes must ultimately be drawn from income, this device may seem to offer much less than it promises. To a large extent the U.S. fiscal system is organized on a separation of sources principle. This is due, in part, to administrative necessity rather than rational design. The federal government relies heavily on the income tax, state governments on commodity taxation and local units on real property taxation. The separation is not complete, however, and may in fact, become less distinct in the future due to incentives provided by the federal revenue-sharing program for states to adopt and rely increasingly on income taxation. However, the principle of separation of sources will probably remain important enough to prevent any federal government attempt to impose general excise taxation.

The revenue-sharing legislation enacted in 1972 authorized, for the first time, a significant program of federal financial assistance to state and local governments via unconditional grants-in-aid. Conditional grants-in-aid have been in existence for a longer time and were projected to total approximately $74 billion during fiscal 1980.

SUPPLEMENTARY READING

The student who is interested in pursuing some of the issues raised in this chapter may read the careful survey by L. L. Ecker-Racz and I. M. Labovitz, "Practical Solutions to Finance Problems Created by Multi-Level Political Structure," in National Bureau of Economic Research, *Public Finances:*

Needs, Sources, and Utilization (New York, 1961).

For more general discussion of some of the fiscal problems of federalism and intergovernmental fiscal relations, see James A. Maxwell, *The Fiscal Impact of Federalism in the United States* (Cambridge, Mass.: Harvard University Press, 1946), and Kjeld Philip, *Intergovernmental Fiscal Relations* (Copenhagen: Institute of Economics and History, 1954). Also see Richard Wagner, *The Fiscal Organization of American Federalism* (Chicago: Markham Publishing Company, 1971).

For a particular and detailed examination of tax credits, see James A. Maxwell, *The Tax Credits and Intergovernmental Fiscal Relations* (Washington, D.C.: The Brookings Institution, 1962).

For a detailed listing of federal grant-in-aid programs, see *Special Analysis N: Budget of the United States Government for the Fiscal Year 1980.*

For a useful analytical discussion of revenue-sharing, see Charles J. Goetz, *What is Revenue-Sharing?* (Washington, D.C.: Urban Institute, 1972).

part X

Conclusion

39

Constitutional perspectives on fiscal reform

Т he purpose of this textbook in this fifth edition, as well as in earlier editions, is that of providing the student with a general introduction to "the public finances" of the United States at all levels of government. The set of institutions that we call the "fiscal system" is pervasive in its impact, compact in its operations, and essential to the viability of the American society. And, as any comparison between this edition and earlier editions will reveal, both the fiscal system and attitudes toward it are characterized by continuous change.

The late 1970s have been characterized by a resurgence of interest in the constitutional foundations of the fiscal structure, both at the level of popular discourse and scholarship. This new interest in constitutional foundations stems, in part, from an increasing awareness that the ordinary political institutions, through which taxing and spending decisions are made, have somehow "failed" in meeting the desires of the citizenry. There was expressed a widespread feeling that governmental processes had somehow "gotten out of hand" and that "the people" should regain control of government via constitutional means. This mood was embodied in the "anti-Washington" spirit of the 1976 and 1978 elections as well as in the various "tax revolt" attempts, only some of which were successful.

In later 1979, when this edition was written, there seemed to be little or no popular or political pressure for expanding the size and scope of the fiscal structure. Instead, pressures seemed concentrated on the side of constraints: through the balancing of the federal government budget, through tax reductions, through highly restrictive budget policies, and through the controlling of inflation. In part, these pressures stemmed from the relatively limited growth in disposable personal incomes of citizens during the whole decade of the 1970s. Citizens seemed to be demanding that at least some share of what little growth there was be returned for private rather than governmental disposition.

To an extent, these demands for constraint seemed to be doomed to frustration. Inflation showed no signs of being controlled, and the real tax increases implicit in inflation remained as an increasingly important feature of the federal revenue structure. Furthermore, so-called noncontrollable budget spending programs showed no signs of falling off, while, at the same time, demands for increased military spending emerged.

Fiscal prospects for the 1980s seemed to depend critically on the possible durability and successes of the "tax revolt" attitudes. Political leaders, regardless of party affiliation, recognized and acted on the "messages" from the citizenry in the late 1970s and budgets at all levels of government were smaller than they might have been in the absence of this set of attitudes. "Fiscal austerity" was pervasive, and especially by comparison with the "fiscal splurge" of the 1960s. If, however, the tax-revolt attitudes prove to be short-lived, the ever-present pressures for growth in taxing and spending will reassert themselves and the growth of government will return to the trend lines that seemed to be established in the late 1960s.

On the other hand, if the set of attitudes exemplified in the "tax revolt" movements should prove permanent and especially if this set should gain new adherents, the 1980s may be characterized by new constitutional initiatives that aim to constrain the fiscal proclivities of governments. By mid-1979, 30 states had enacted resolutions calling for constitutional change to require budget balance on the part of the federal government. Other proposals for constitutional tax and outlay limits had been introduced. What form any constitutional restriction might finally take cannot, of course, be predicted. Nor can the political-governmental reactions to possible constitutional fiscal constraints be known in advance. The shadow of California's Proposition 13 extends over the whole fiscal scene for the 1980s, but the length as well as the breadth of this shadow remains to be determined.

Index

*This book has been set in 10 and 9 point Aster,
leaded 3 points. Part numbers and titles are 24
point Aster. Chapter numbers are 30 point Aster
and Chapter titles are 20 point Aster. The size of
the type page is 27 by 45 picas.*